Guide to Housing Benefit and Council Tax Benefit 2000-2001

D1810296

by John Zebedee and Martin Ward

CHARTERED INSTITUTE OF HOUSING

Shelter

SHELTER

Shelter is Britain's largest homelessness charity, with a network of 59 housing aid centres and projects providing advocacy and assistance at a local level for people in housing need. The launch in December 1998 of Shelterline, Britain's first 24 hour free national housing advice line, increased the number of households we were able to help in 1999 to more than 118,000. Shelter's vision is that everyone should be able to live in a decent, secure and affordable home, within a strong community. The new Housing Green Paper offers an opportunity for the reform of housing benefit and rent policy, one of Shelter's key campaigning aims.

For further information about Shelter, please write to:

Shelter
88 Old Street
London
EC1V 9HU
or call 020 7505 4699.

Visit Shelter's website at www.shelter.org.uk (online ordering of Shelter publications now available).

CHARTERED INSTITUTE OF HOUSING

The Chartered Institute of Housing is the only professional body focusing on housing. Its purpose is to take a leading role in encouraging and promoting the provision and management of good quality affordable housing for all. The Institute merged with the Institute of Rent Officers and Rental Valuers in February 1999. There are currently 16,500 members in the UK, Hong Kong and throughout the world, working for local authorities, housing associations, educational establishments, voluntary bodies, private sector firms and rent officers.

For further information, please write to:

Chartered Institute of Housing
Octavia House
Westwood Way
Coventry
CV4 8JP.

Telephone: 024 7685 1700.
Fax: 024 7669 5110.

E-mail: customer.services@cih.org
Web site: www.cih.org

PUBLICATION DETAILS

Guide to Housing Benefit, Peter McGurk and Nick Raynsford, 1982-87 (1st to 9th editions); Martin Ward and John Zebedee, 1988-89 (10th to 12th editions).

Guide to Housing Benefit and Community Charge Benefit, Martin Ward and John Zebedee, 1990-92 (13th to 15th editions).

Guide to Housing Benefit and Council Tax Benefit, John Zebedee and Martin Ward, 1993-99 (16th to 22nd editions: 1st to 7th of this title).

Guide to Housing Benefit and Council Tax Benefit 2000-2001, John Zebedee and Martin Ward, 2000 (23rd edition: 8th of this title).

NOTE TO 23RD EDITION

This is the twenty-third edition in our series of guides. It is also the eighth edition of the title *Guide to Housing Benefit and Council Tax Benefit.*

This edition covers the rules about housing benefit and council tax benefit as they apply from 1st April 2000, using the information avaialble in late February 2000. A few minor amendments to the law may appear too late for inclusion in this Guide.

We welcome comments and criticisms on the contents of our guide and make every effort to ensure it is accurate. However, the only statement of the law is found in the relevant Acts and Regulations (paras. 1.27-29).

ISBN 1 870767 84 5

Production by Davies Communications (020 7482 8844)

Printed by WBC Limited, Bridgend (01656 668836)

ACKNOWLEDGMENTS

This Guide could not have been written without the help and encouragement of many people. Early editions were written by Nick Raynsford and Peter McGurk, and much is owed to them. This year, we are glad to acknowledge the contributions of Mary Connolly, Sam Lister, Rachael Littlewood, Spencer May, Jim McDonald, Lorraine O'Connell, Judith Paterson, Tristan Price, Jim Read, Janice Robinson, Pete Thorogood, Linda Davies and Peter Singer (editing, design, production and promotion) as well as staff from the Department of Social Security. Their help has been essential to the production of this Guide.

THE AUTHORS

John Zebedee is an independent benefits trainer and consultant.

Martin Ward is an independent benefits consultant and trainer (E-mail: mward@metronet.co.uk).

They have specialised in housing benefit since the introduction of the 1982-83 scheme and in council tax benefit since it was introduced in 1993.

JOHN ZEBEDEE and MARTIN WARD
February 2000

Contents

List of abbreviations

The principal abbreviations used in the guide are given below. For further information on marginal references, see paragraph 1.28 and overleaf.

AA	The Social Security Administration Act 1992
BA	Benefits Agency
CA	Court of Appeal
CBA	The Social Security Contributions and Benefits Act 1992
CTB	council tax benefit
CTBR	The Council Tax Benefit (General) Regulations 1992, SI No. 1814 (as amended)
DSS	Department of Social Security
ECR	European Court Reports
EP	extended payment
GM	The DSS Housing Benefit and Council Tax Benefit Guidance Manual, 1993, with several supplements to September 1997
HB	housing benefit
HBR	The Housing Benefit (General) Regulations 1987, SI No. 1971 (as amended)
HLR	Housing Law Reports (published by Sweet & Maxwell)
HRA	housing revenue account
IS	income support
JSA	jobseeker's allowance
JSA(Cont)	contribution-based jobseeker's allowance
JSA(IB)	income-based jobseeker's allowance
QBD	Queen's Bench Division
s	section(s)
sch	schedule
SI	statutory instrument
SO	subsidy order

How to use the marginal references

The following examples illustrate how to use the references found on the inside margins of this Guide (see also paragraph 1.28 and the abbreviations on the previous page).

The sections, regulations, paragraphs, etc. shown in marginal references have in many cases been amended by subsequent law. The sources mentioned in paragraph 1.26 set out the law as so amended.

AA s134(5), 139(4)   This means sections 134(5) and 139(4) of the Social Security Administration Act 1992 – in other words, paragraph (5) of section 134 and paragraph (4) of section 139 of that Act. *(These give the law about agency arrangements in HB and CTB: para. 1.9.)*

CBA s131(9)   This means section 131(9) of the Social Security Contributions and Benefits Act 1992 – in other words, paragraph (9) of section 131. *(This gives the law about the 'better buy' calculation in CTB: para. 9.18.)*

HBR 31(9)   These mean regulation 31(9) of the Housing Benefit
CTBR 22(9)   (General) Regulations 1987 and regulation 22(9) of the Council Tax Benefits (General) Regulations 1992 – in other words, paragraph (9) of each of those regulations. *(These give the law about assessing the income of self-employed childminders in HB and CTB: para. 15.25.)*

HBR sch 4 para 31   These mean paragraph 31 of schedule 4 to the Housing
CTBR sch 4 para 32   Benefit (General) Regulations 1987 and paragraph 32 of schedule 4 to the Council Tax Benefits (General) Regulations 1992. *(These give the law about Pensioners' Christmas Bonus in HB and CTB: para. 13.30)*

SI 1995 No. 1644   This means Statutory Instrument No. 1644 of 1995 (its full name may be found in Appendix 1). *(This gives the law about what counts as an 'exempt case' in HB: para. 11.53.)*

1 Overview

1.1 Welcome to the guide. This chapter:

◆ introduces the housing benefit (HB) and council tax benefit (CTB) schemes;

◆ sets out the purpose and structure of the guide;

◆ summarises the main features of the schemes;

◆ identifies the authorities responsible for their administration; and

◆ comments upon the legal and other sources of information.

Housing benefit and council tax benefit

1.2 HB and CTB are national welfare benefits. The purpose of the HB scheme is to help people on low incomes pay their rent. The CTB scheme provides assistance with the council tax

TWO FORMS OF CTB

1.3 CTB takes two forms. Main CTB helps people on low incomes pay their council tax. For a small number of people alternative maximum CTB (more commonly known as 'second adult rebate') is available. It is not based on the claimant's needs or resources but on the gross income of certain adults living in the claimant's household. Claimants eligible for both main CTB and second adult rebate are awarded whichever is the most valuable.

Purpose and structure of the guide

1.4 This guide describes the HB and CTB schemes administered throughout Great Britain (but not Northern Ireland) from April 2000. Where particular variations occur for Scotland or Wales these are identified in the main body of the text. The latest changes are identified throughout the guide.

1.5 The guide is of use to administrators, advisers, councillors and claimants. Its structure is as follows. Chapter 2 describes the importance of the schemes and places them in the context of the range of income-related benefits and tax credits. The council tax scheme, and the other methods of reducing the amount of council tax payable, are outlined in chapter 3. The rest of the guide (chapter 4 onwards) follows the logical order of events in the life of an HB/CTB claim. For an overview see tables 1.1-1.6. Chapter 5 identifies the specific rules that exclude certain 'persons from abroad' from entitlement. Chapter 10 describes second adult rebate in detail. Chapter 15 considers the rules relating to the assessment of a self-employed person's income for HB and CTB purposes. Chapter 20 examines the particular rules relating to claims from students and chapter 21 deals with subsidy issues for the 1999-2000 financial year.

1.6   Each chapter begins with a summary that identifies the main features of the subject under discussion. The factual details are then described with examples of key aspects contained in boxes. References to the relevant legislation are found in the margin. The guide also includes a comprehensive index.

TERMS USED IN THE GUIDE

1.7   A number of different public authorities are involved in the administration of HB/CTB. The term 'authority' is used in this guide to cover them all. The term 'housing benefit' is a generic one that covers the two types of payments which may be made under the scheme, otherwise described as rebates or allowances. It is used in this sense in the guide. Where, however, it is more appropriate, the specific term, i.e. rent rebate or rent allowance, is used. Also the term 'tenant' is used to describe any kind of rent-payer including, for example, licensees. The term 'CTB' is used to refer to both forms of CTB. One of these – 'alternative

---

Table 1.1 WHO CAN GET HB/CTB? (chapter 4)

◆ Anyone who has to pay rent on their home may get HB. This may be known as a rent rebate (council tenants) or rent allowance (private and housing association tenants).

◆ Anyone who has to pay council tax on their home may get CTB.

SPECIAL CASES

In some cases, additional rules apply to the following:

◆ Temporary absence from home (e.g. in hospital or prison).

◆ HB for two homes (e.g. because of fear of violence).

◆ People renting homes from close relatives and 'contrived' lettings.

◆ Certain persons from abroad (chapter 5).

◆ Students (chapter 20).

Table 1.2 MAKING A CLAIM FOR HB/CTB (chapter 7)

START

Person claims income support or income-based jobseeker's allowance and at the same time completes Benefits Agency's HB/CTB claim forms NHB 1	Person claims HB/CTB direct from the authority on the authority's own claim form(s)
Benefits Agency assesses income support/income-based jobseeker's allowance claim	
Benefits Agency forwards HB/CTB claim forms to authority	
Claimant provides any additional information requested by authority	Claimant provides any additional information requested by authority
Authority assesses entitlement to HB/CTB	Authority assesses entitlement to HB/CTB
Entitlement normally based on date of claim to Jobcentre or Benefits Agency local office or start of income support/ income based jobseeker's entitlement	Entitlement normally based on date of claim to authority

HB/CTB must be backdated for up to a year prior to a claim for a past period if the claimant has good cause for a late claim throughout that period.

Table 1.3 INFORMATION NEEDED FOR WORKING OUT HB/MAIN CTB

Membership of the household	The assessment takes into account the claimant and any partner and, in certain circumstances, children, young persons and non-dependants who are part of the household (chapter 6).
Eligible costs	The household's share of the eligible rent and/or eligible council tax is taken into account. This may be less than the actual rent and/or council tax due (chapter 11).
Non-dependant deductions	If there are non-dependants in the household, the claimant's HB/main CTB may be reduced (chapter 9).

◆ The following information is needed for claimants who are not in receipt of income support or income-based jobseeker's allowance:

Applicable amount	This reflects the 'needs' of the claimant and any partner, children or young persons. There are premiums for families, lone parents, people over 60/75/80, for people with disabilities or severe disabilities, and for carers (chapter 12).
Capital	The capital of the claimant and any partner is taken into account. Claimants with capital over £16,000 are not entitled to HB/main CTB. Some capital, including all capital of £3,000 or under, is disregarded (chapter 13). For claimants in residential care, nursing homes and certain other types of residential accommodation, the disregarded amount is £10,000. Capital taken into account is treated as generating 'tariff' income (table 13.2).
Net income	The net income of the claimant and any partner (and, in some cases, children or young persons) is taken into account. Certain income is disregarded (chapters 13 to 15).

◆ The different information needed for second adult rebate is described in chapter 10.

Table 1.4 WEEKLY AMOUNT OF HB/MAIN CTB (chapter 9)

PEOPLE ON INCOME SUPPORT/INCOME-BASED JOBSEEKER'S ALLOWANCE

They receive maximum benefit. This is:

◆ 100 per cent of the eligible rent (restricted in some circumstances) and/or eligible council tax (restricted to that of Band E for claimants with property in Bands F, G and H who claim for the first time on or after 1st April 1998, or who move home, or who have a break in entitlement to CTB of more than 12 weeks), minus in certain cases non-dependant deductions.

PEOPLE NOT ON INCOME SUPPORT/INCOME-BASED JOBSEEKER'S ALLOWANCE

If they have no income, or their net income is less than their applicable amount (or equal to it), they receive maximum benefit.

If their net income exceeds their applicable amount, they receive:

◆ Maximum benefit for rent, minus 65 per cent of that excess income.

◆ Maximum benefit for council tax, minus 20 per cent of that excess income.

OTHER MATTERS

◆ In HB cases check that the resultant amount is not below the minimum payable (50p).

◆ Different rules apply for working out second adult rebate (chapter 10).

◆ Entitlement is awarded for up to 60 weeks or (in some cases) until the claimant's circumstances change (chapter 17).

Table 1.5 NOTIFICATION, PAYMENT AND OVERPAYMENT (chapters 16 and 18)

◆ The authority should determine and notify HB/CTB within 14 days of receiving the information and evidence it reasonably needs from the claimant.

◆ In the case of rent paid by a tenant to a private landlord or housing association, the authority should pay HB to the claimant within 14 days, or, if necessary, make a 'payment on account'.

◆ In the case of rent paid by a council tenant, HB takes the form of a rebate which reduces the claimant's liability. This is also normally the case with CTB for the council tax.

◆ In certain cases, HB can be paid to the landlord.

◆ Overpaid HB/CTB may be recovered unless:

  • it was due to official error, and

  • the claimant, or the person to whom the payment was made, could not reasonably have realised that the overpayment occurred at the time of payment or receipt of any notification relating to that payment.

Table 1.6 APPEALS (chapter 19)

If the claimant or other person affected so requests, the authority must:

◆ provide a written statement of reasons;

◆ hold an internal review of the case;

◆ put the matter to a review board if the individual concerned remains dissatisfied. The review board's decision is normally binding but does not establish a precedent.

maximum council tax benefit' – in this guide, in common with DSS guidance and most local authority forms, is referred to as 'second adult rebate'. Where it is more appropriate, the specific term 'main CTB' or 'second adult rebate' is used.

Benefit and tax credit rates

1.8   In the case of all CTB claims and HB claims where rent is not on a weekly or multiple week basis the rates quoted are those which apply from 1st April 2000. For HB claims where the rent is paid weekly or on a multiple week basis the rates quoted are those which apply from Monday 3rd April 2000. Other benefit rates are increased during the week commencing 10th April 2000 but are taken account of for HB and CTB purposes from 1st or 3rd April 2000 as appropriate. Exceptions to this rule concern the uprated amounts of working families tax credit (WFTC) and disabled person's tax credit (DPTC) which apply only to awards starting on or after 11 April 2000. Awards of WFTC or DPTC that start before 11th April 2000 are not uprated. Student figures (Chapter 20) apply from September 1999. A summary of the benefit rates for 2000-2001 is printed at the back of the guide (appendix 5). The tax and national insurance (NI) rates quoted are those which apply from April 1999 to March 2000.

Administration

AA s 134, 139, 191   **1.9**   Different arrangements apply in England and Wales and in Scotland. In any individual authority HB/CTB may be administered by one or more departments, usually the housing or treasurer's/finance department or by an external contractor acting on behalf of the council.

ENGLAND AND WALES

1.10   Claimants in England should obtain HB, and CTB, from the local council in their area, i.e. the council of a district, London borough or the Common Council of the City of London. In Wales claimants should apply to the county or county borough council. In specific areas agency arrangements (para. 1.12) may exist or the ONE service may be in operation (para. 1.15).

SCOTLAND

1.11   Tenants of Scottish Homes receive rent rebates from their landlord. All other tenants, whether council, housing association or private should receive rent rebates or allowances from the local council, though agency arrangements (para. 1.12) may exist. Each authority administers CTB on the council tax collected by it.

AGENCY ARRANGEMENTS

1.12   Authorities may make arrangements by which: AA s 134(5), 139(4)

◆ one carries out the functions of the other; or

◆ functions are carried out jointly or by a joint committee.

For example, agency arrangements sometimes apply to local authority tenants living in property situated outside the landlord authority's boundaries. In such a case they may receive a rent rebate from their landlord authority as opposed to the authority in which they live if agency arrangements have been agreed.

'ONE' – THE SINGLE WORK FOCUSED GATEWAY TO BENEFITS

1.13   The Government has stated its intention to develop a new system for the administration of benefits. The idea is that there should be a single point of access and an interview with a job-finding focus for those who have the potential to work (DSS, *New ambitions for our country: a new contract for welfare*, CM 3805 and DfEE and DSS *A new contract for welfare: the gateway to work*, Cm 4102). The Welfare Reform and Pensions Act identifies HB and CTB as two of the benefits which may be accessed through the Single Gateway. The work-focused interview may be conducted by the Benefits Agency, the Employment Service, a private/voluntary sector contractor or by the authority.

1.14   For those claimants not required to seek work the Government's aim is that they should be able to claim benefits, child support and war pensions, give information and make enquiries concerning their social security business through a single point of contact. This could be the Benefits Agency or the authority. The Government also intends that claims for a range of benefits should be made on a single claim form. The Welfare Reform and Pensions Act enables authorities to obtain information on an individual's claim for benefits and advise them accordingly. It also enables authorities to answer queries from claimants about benefits they have claimed from other organisations such as the Benefits Agency.

1.15   The ONE service is being piloted in: Essex South East, Warwickshire, Clyde Coast and Renfrew, Lea Roding, Leeds, Suffolk, North Nottinghamshire, North Cheshire, Somerset, Buckinghamshire, Calderdale and Kirklees and South East Gwent. National implementation of the Single Gateway will depend on experience in the pilot areas.

CONTRACTING OUT ADMINISTRATION AND 'BEST VALUE'

1.16   Authorities can contract out the administration of HB and CTB to private companies and a number have done so. The Local Government Act 1999 replaces compulsory competitive tendering (CCT) in England and Wales with a duty of obtaining best value for the taxpayer from April 2000. A similar agenda operates in Scotland.

1.17   The best value initiative focuses on economy, efficiency, effectiveness and quality in local services. Authorities have to conduct performance reviews and publish annual local performance plans. The Government or, in Wales, the National Assembly, have devised performance indicators and national standards for local government activities including benefit administration. The indicators target the priorities of speed; accuracy; security of the benefit delivery; and also value for money and customer-focus.

1.18   In England as part of its plan to 'modernise' local authorities the Government has announced the Beacon Scheme (from April 1999) (DETR Press Release, 9 February 1999, *Beacon councils to lead the way*). This aims to:

♦   spread best practice (via the Local Government Improvement and Development Agency); and

♦   allow new freedoms and flexibilities to be tested.

The Government intention is that beacon status will be awarded for excellence in a number of different services including HB/CTB provision. Similar proposals have been put to the National Assembly in Wales.

1.19   Where an authority has contracted out benefit-related work this does not affect its administrative responsibility. The authority itself remains responsible for the functions and duties placed upon it by the relevant legislation. DSS circular HB/CTB (93)9 emphasised that authorities could not contract out certain functions. These include benefit decision-making, rent officer referrals and the exchange of information with the Benefits Agency. The contracting out of HB/CTB administration does not affect an individual's entitlement or his or her rights to a review or a review board hearing.

1.20   The Deregulation and Contracting Out Act 1994 permits contractors to communicate directly with the Benefits Agency but current arrangements result in the double handling of claims by the contractor and the authority and require authorities to maintain in-house teams to carry out the work. A provision in the Local Government Act creates wider powers to contract out functions. It could be used to enable authorities to contract out housing benefits and council tax benefit determination work.

Proper adjudication

1.21   The authority's primary aim is one of proper adjudication. It has to apply the rules of the HB/CTB schemes to the facts of the individual case with the aim of arriving at sound decisions (called determinations) regarding benefit entitlement. The necessary steps in the decision-making process are:

♦   the identification of the relevant facts in the case;

- proper consideration of the available evidence where the facts are in doubt or in dispute;
- establishing facts 'on the balance of probability' where necessary;
- correct interpretation of the law and its application to the facts of the case; and
- arriving at determinations that can be understood in terms of the relevant law and facts.

DISPUTED FACTS

1.22 The only facts which are relevant to the authority are those which have a bearing in relation to the application of the specific rules of the HB/CTB schemes. Where there is a disagreement about the facts between the authority and the claimant or other person affected, the authority must consider the available evidence to decide what the true position is. A factual dispute may also be the trigger for a request for an internal review and review board hearing (Chapter 19).

1.23 The requirement of proof means that a disputed fact must be established to the satisfaction of the authority and on 'appeal' the review board. This does not, however, mean that the fact must be established with absolute certainty. In civil cases, such as matters involving HB/CTB, the appropriate test is 'on the balance of probability'. In other words, if the greater weight of evidence supports for example the claimant's view of the disputed fact then the claimant has proved the matter on the balance of probability.

1.24 In the first instance the burden of proof is on the claimant to support his or her claim by supplying the authority with all the evidence it reasonably requires (para. 7.37). The Department of Social Security's Verification Framework seeks to set out the minimum standards for collecting evidence when a claim is made (para. 7.41). However, where the authority asserts a particular proposition, for example, that a recoverable overpayment has occurred, the authority must have evidence to support its assertion.

1.25 The burden of proof is only decisive, however, where:

- there is no evidence – consequently where the authority asserts a disputed fact it must have evidence to support that assertion; or
- the evidence is exactly balanced – in which case the party on whom the burden of proof lies should not succeed.

ISSUES OF LAW

1.26 The rules of the HB/CTB schemes are set out in legislation passed by the UK parliament. Issues of law involve the application and interpretation of that legislation. For example, the question as to whether or not the claimant's son counts as a non-dependant for HB/CTB purposes could only be answered by consideration of the definition of 'non-dependant' in the regulations as well as the relevant facts of the case. A dispute over the correct interpretation and application of the legislation may be the trigger for a request for an internal review and review board hearing (Chapter 19). While legal disputes do not fall with the Local Government Ombudsman's remit (para. 19.64) negligent reading of the benefit regulations by the authority may constitute maladministration (see for example Complaint 91/B/3223 against Newbury District Council, 26 August 1993).

THE ACTS

1.27 The outline rules relating to HB and CTB entitlement are contained in the Social Security Contributions and Benefits Act 1992 (as amended) and the outline rules on the administration of the schemes are contained in the Social Security Administration Act 1992 (as amended). The resulting repeals of earlier legislation and consequential amendments of related legislation are contained in the Social Security (Consequential Provisions) Act 1992. This Act also provides that the substitution of the consolidating Acts for the repealed enactments does not affect the continuity of the law.

DELEGATED LEGISLATION

1.28 The Acts enable the Secretary of State for Social Security, normally following consultation with the local authority associations, to formulate delegated legislation – 'regulations' and 'orders' – which contain and amend the details of the scheme (appendix 1).

1.29 The main rules of the HB scheme are contained in SI 1987 No. 1971, the Housing Benefit (General) Regulations as amended by subsequent regulations. The main rules of the CTB scheme are contained in SI 1992 No. 1814, the Council Tax Benefit (General) Regulations as amended. The DSS intention is that the CTB regulations should maintain common provisions with the HB regulations. The Acts and delegated legislation are binding upon authorities and review boards.

OBTAINING THE LEGISLATION

CBA s.123(3),(4)   **1.30** Members of the public have a right to see copies of the relevant legal material together with the details of any local scheme (para. 9.39) at an authority's principal office.

1.31 The many and frequent amendments to the relevant legislation and the government's failure to date to produce a consolidation of the HB and CTB regulations means that it can be quite difficult to keep track of the current rules of the schemes.

1.32 The current provisions relating to social security are set out in the loose leaf work entitled *The Law Relating to Social Security.* Volume 8 (Parts 1 and 2) contains relevant sections of the Acts and statutory instruments relating to HB/CTB. It is kept up to date with regular supplements. Many main public reference libraries hold this publication. It can be purchased from the Stationery Office by telephone (0870 600 5522) or on the internet at: www.tsonline.co.uk. The Child Poverty Action Group's *Housing Benefit and Council Tax Benefit Legislation* (ISBN 1901698084) also contains all the relevant law at the point of publication plus a useful commentary.

1.33   The Institute of Revenues, Rating and Valuation produce the *Benefit Legislation Database* CD-ROM. This contains the Acts and delegated legislation relating to HB/CTB. It may be obtained from IRRV, 41 Doughty Street, London, WC1N 2LF, by fax on 0171 831 2048 or by e-mail (enquiries@irrv.org.uk). Ferret Information Systems Ltd produce the CD-ROM *Social Security – Sources and Guidance*. This also contains the relevant law. It may be obtained from Ferret Information Systems Ltd, 4 Coopers Yard, Curran Road, Cardiff CF1 5DF by telephone: 01222 644660, fax: 01222 644661 or e-mail: sales@ferret.co.uk.

1.34   Copies of individual pieces of legislation, such as amending regulations, may be obtained from the Stationery Office (see para. 1.32) or viewed free of charge on-line at www.legislation.hmso.gov.uk.

REFERENCES

1.35   Where references are made in this guide to the Social Security Contributions and Benefits Act 1992 this is referred to as 'CBA' and references to the Social Security Administration Act 1992 are referred to as 'AA'. The number that follows in each instance is the section number of the relevant Act. The Housing Benefit (General) Regulations 1987 as amended are referred to as 'HBR'. The Council Tax Benefits (General) Regulations 1992 as amended are referred to as 'CTBR'. All other regulations and orders (appendix 1) are referred to by their statutory instrument number, e.g. SI 1997 No. 1984. Further guidance on the use of marginal references can be found on the page following the List of Abbreviations at the front of the Guide.

OTHER RELEVANT LEGISLATION

1.36   In addition to the Acts and regulations, other pieces of legislation circumscribe the manner in which authorities may administer the schemes. The Local Government Act 1972 or the Local Government (Scotland) Act 1973 contain most of the law relating to the powers and duties of local authorities and the way in which they must carry out their business. The Local Government Finance Act 1982 covers the auditing of, and public rights of access to, local authority accounts. It also places upon local authorities a duty to secure economy, efficiency and effectiveness in their administration of HB/CTB. The Sex Discrimination Act 1975 and Race Relations Act 1976 make it illegal to discriminate (either directly or indirectly) against someone, or victimise someone, on the grounds of their colour, race, nationality, sex or marital status. The Data Protection Act 1984 (to be replaced by the Data Protection Act 1998 when it comes into force) controls the use of, and access to, information about an individual held on a computerised system.

1.37   The Local Government Act 1992 gives the Audit Commission and the Accounts Commission in Scotland powers to require local authorities to publish indicators, i.e. information about the standard of service they provide. A number of the required indicators relate directly or indirectly to HB/CTB administration. The Audit Commission Act 1998 enables the Secretary of State to request the Commission to conduct or assist the Secretary of State in conducting studies designed to improve economy, efficiency, effectiveness and quality of performance in the discharge by authorities of functions relating to HB/CTB administration. From 1 April 2000 the Local Government Act 1999 places the new duty of best value upon authorities in England and Wales requiring them to make arrangements to secure continuous improvement in the way in which they carry out their functions.

STATUTORY INTERPRETATION AND CASE LAW

1.38   In the first instance, where there is no ambiguity, legislation should be taken to mean exactly what it says. The general rule is that the authority may not look beyond the relevant legislation itself to determine its meaning. However, certain forms of assistance are permissible, or must be considered, such as the precedents contained within case law on the meaning of a word or phrase. For example, where a matter in dispute goes from a review board to consideration in the High Court, or the Court of Session in Scotland, the interpretation that may be made by a judge in the course of deciding such a case will in particular instances be binding upon all authorities. Relevant cases are identified in appendix 2 and in the appropriate paragraphs of this guide.

1.39   Decisions in HB cases are often highly persuasive though not binding with regard to CTB and *vice versa.* Equally, many of the words and phrases which were brought forward into the HB/CTB schemes from the old supplementary benefit (SB) scheme, or other parts of social security law, have a body of case law attached. Again, as an aid to interpretation such decisions are of persuasive value though not binding upon authorities.

JUDGMENT

1.40   There are numerous occasions in the regulations where a determination, must be made on the basis of what is 'reasonable' or 'appropriate'. For example, where the claimant has left the home through fear of violence then in specific instances the authority must treat the claimant as occupying two dwelling and consequently potentially entitled to HB on both dwellings 'if it is reasonable' that housing benefit should be paid in respect of both dwellings. There is no single right or wrong answer. In such cases the authority must exercise judgment in the light of the facts of the individual case. For example, if the claimant had brought the threats of violence upon him or herself by engaging in criminal activities it might be considered inappropriate to use public funds to meet the cost of two homes.

DISCRETION

1.41   Where an authority has a choice under the regulations to do or not do something, e.g. to award or deny additional benefit to a claimant in exceptional circumstances, or who faces exceptional hardship as the result of the maximum rent calculation introduced in January 1996, this is a discretionary power. Such powers individualise the application of the regulations and make them flexible and adaptable to the circumstances of the claimant.

CONTROLS ON EXERCISE OF JUDGMENT OR DISCRETION

1.42   In exercising judgment or discretion, authorities are bound by the established principles of administrative law that the courts have steadily evolved. If they are not in accordance with these principles decisions may be open to legal challenge by way of judicial review (see *Judicial Review Handbook* by Michael Fordham, Hart Publishing, ISBN: 1841130788 or for Scotland see *Judicial Review in Scotland,* by T J Mullen and Tony Prosser, Wiley ISBN: 0471966142). For example an authority must consider its discretionary powers in individual cases. It must not fetter its discretion by applying predetermined rules rigidly without giving genuine consideration to the merits of the individual case. The authority cannot decide, for example, that it will never award additional benefit to claimants whose circumstances are exceptional.

1.43   A power must be exercised reasonably. An authority will be considered to have acted unreasonably if having regard to the nature of the subject matter:

◆ it takes into account matters which it ought not to consider; or

◆ refuses or neglects to consider matters which it ought to take into account.

An authority will also have acted unreasonably if it comes to a conclusion that no reasonable authority could have come to.

DSS GUIDANCE MANUAL

1.44   The Department of Social Security (DSS) is the central government department responsible for housing benefit and council tax benefit policy. It produces the Housing Benefit and Council Tax Benefit Guidance Manual (GM), ISBN: 011-761855-1. This manual advises authorities on how to interpret the regulations and on administrative arrangements. Interesting or contentious parts of the manual are identified in this guide.

DSS CIRCULARS

1.45   In addition to the GM, the DSS also issues regular circulars to authorities advising them of forthcoming changes and other important matters. Until April 1994 these were denoted by the initials HB/CTB, followed by the year and the number, e.g. HB/CTB (93)3. In April 1994 the DSS revised the contents and presentation of its circulars. There are now three types of circular distinguished by a prefix – A for adjudication and operations, S for statistics and subsidy and F for fraud. Each type has its own number series and starts from 1/94. Circulars issued since April 1994 are listed in appendix 3.

STATUS OF DSS ADVICE

1.46   While the Acts and regulations are binding upon authorities, the GM and DSS circulars are for information and guidance only and do not have the force of law (see Introduction to DSS GM). Authorities do, however, often cite DSS advice in support of their determinations, for example at review board hearings. The Courts sometimes rehearse the advice contained within the GM with approval whilst recognising that it is not an aid to legal interpretation (see for example R *v* Maidstone Borough Council *ex parte* Bunce, QBD, 23rd June 1994 and R *v* London Borough of Camden *ex parte* W, QBD, 21st May 1999, unreported).

OBTAINING DSS GUIDANCE

1.47   The Guidance Manual can be purchased from the Stationery Office (para. 1.26) and amended by way of supplements. (NB: when ordering this title the purchaser should also order the following supplements, ISBNs 0117620742; 0117621463; 0117623008; 0117624217; 011762442X; 01176255820). The DSS (A31/99) has stated its intention to have an updated version of the manual available by Easter 2000. Its aim is that the manual should be available in both its traditional format and on the DSS internet web site: www.dss.gov.uk. The current edition of the Guidance Manual with the existing updates is available on the Ferret Information Systems Ltd CD-ROM *Social Security – Sources and Guidance* (see para. 1.33). Authorities can choose to receive circulars by e-mail (DSS Circulars A9/98, A18/98 and A37/98 refer). The DSS has stated its intention that other organisations will be invited to receive circulars by e-mail once it is satisfied that the initial arrangements with authorities are causing no problems (A9/98 para. 2). DSS circulars are not available from the Stationery Office but it may be possible to obtain them from individual authorities. Some recent DSS circulars are available on the Ferret Information Systems Ltd CD-ROM.

2 Background

2.1 This chapter examines the context of the CTB and HB schemes. It considers:

◆ the importance of the HB/CTB schemes;

◆ the other income-related benefits, tax credits and the social fund;

◆ the principal changes since 1988.

Importance of the HB/CTB schemes

2.2 CTB helps people meet their council tax payments. In February 1999 5,200,000 people were in receipt of main CTB in Great Britain – 40,000 people were in receipt of second adult rebate. The number in receipt of main CTB was 3.1 per cent fewer than those in receipt of the benefit a year earlier. The number in receipt of second adult rebate 7.5 per cent less than a year earlier. Sixty-three per cent of CTB recipients in February 1999 were also in receipt of income support or income-based JSA. In May 1996:

◆ 49 per cent of CTB recipients were aged 60 or over;

◆ 14 per cent were under 60 with a disability premium; and

◆ 18 per cent were under 60 with a lone parent premium.

The average CTB entitlement in February 1999 was £8.20.

2.3 CTB follows the structure of the other main income-related benefits. Maximum CTB is 100 per cent of the claimant's net council tax liability after any restriction or reductions that may apply (chapter 3). CTB is withdrawn as the claimant's net income increases above his or her applicable amount. The taper for CTB is 20 per cent. Additionally, non-dependant deductions may be made from the claimant's CTB entitlement further reducing the amount of benefit awarded.

2.4 HB also follows the structure of the other main income-related benefits. In February 1999 4.37 million people were in receipt of HB in Great Britain, 2.59 million were council tenants, 0.92 million were private tenants and 0.86 million were housing association tenants. The number in receipt of HB was 3.6 per cent fewer than those in receipt of the benefit a year earlier. The biggest drop was in the number of private tenants entitled to HB, which was 7.4 per cent less than a year earlier. Sixty-four per cent of HB recipients were also in receipt of income support or income based JSA. In May 1996:

◆ 41 per cent of HB recipients were aged 60 or over;

◆ 14 per cent were under 60 with a disability premium; and

◆ 19 per cent were under 60 with a lone parent premium.

The average HB entitlement in February 1999 was £44.90. Council tenants received an average HB of £37.40 while private and housing association tenants received an average HB entitlement of £55.80.

2.5   Responsibility for running the CTB and HB schemes gives administering authorities a prime role in maintaining the incomes of the most disadvantaged groups. Effective administration of the schemes also reduces the scope for local authority council tax and rent arrears. Central government subsidy payments to meet the costs of each authority's benefit expenditure are a very significant portion of the authority's total revenue income.

The income-related benefits and the social fund

2.6   The main income-related (means tested) benefits and tax credits are:

◆ income support and income-based jobseeker's allowance;

◆ working families tax credit;

◆ disabled persons tax credit

◆ HB; and

◆ CTB.

Working families tax credit (para. 2.24) and the disabled persons tax credit (para. 2.29) replaced family credit and disability working allowance on 5th October 1999. In addition to the main income-related benefits and tax credits the social fund (para. 2.15) is available to help people with expenses which are difficult to meet from their regular income.

Income support/income-based jobseeker's allowance

2.7   Income support and income-based jobseeker's allowance both provide   CBA s.123 assistance for different groups of people whose income is below a minimum set by the UK Parliament and who are not in remunerative work. Income support is available to groups who are not required to look for work such as a people aged 60 or more, lone parent with a child under 16 living with them and people incapable of work. This is not an exhaustive list – certain other groups are also entitled to income support. Income-based jobseeker's allowance is available for unemployed claimants who are actively seeking and available for work. Someone who could claim income support but who nevertheless is available for and actively seeking work can choose to claim jobseeker's allowance.

INCOME SUPPORT

2.8   Income support replaced supplementary benefit in April 1988. It is administered by the Benefits Agency and provides a basic minimum income for people who:

◆ are normally not in remunerative work (defined as 16 hours plus per week or their partner works on average more than 24 hours per week),

◆ are not in full time education,

◆ have income is less than their state defined needs (applicable amount – para. 2.14 and chapter 12),

◆ aged 18 years or over (though certain claimants under 18, e.g. those not required to be available for work, are eligible with or without time limits – see CPAG's *Welfare Benefits Handbook 2000-2001* for more details),

◆ be resident in the UK; and

◆ do not have capital above £8,000 (or £16,000 where claimants are in residential care homes, nursing homes or other types of residential accommodation).

The amount of income support payable is the difference between the claimant's income and his or her applicable amount. Income support is disregarded in full in the assessment of HB/CTB and claimants in receipt of this form of the benefit are potentially eligible for maximum HB/CTB.

CLAIMING INCOME SUPPORT

2.9   Claims for income support may be made in several ways including visiting, telephoning or writing to the local Benefits Agency office and completing the supplied A1 or an SP1 claim form depending on the claimant's circumstances. The telephone number and address of the local office can be found in the Benefits Agency display advert in the business numbers section of the phone book. Claims for income support also provide an opportunity to claim HB/CTB (para. 7.18).

JOBSEEKER'S ALLOWANCE

2.10   From 7th October 1996 jobseeker's allowance replaced income support for the unemployed and unemployment benefit. There are two routes into jobseeker's allowance:

◆ contribution-based (as with the former unemployment benefit); and

◆ income-based (as with income support).

2.11 To get jobseeker's allowance the claimant must:

◆ be capable of, actively seeking and available for work, usually for at least 40 hours a week;

◆ have paid enough National Insurance contributions, or have income and savings below a certain level;

◆ be out of work, or working on average less than 16 hours a week (partners are able to work for, on average, up to 24 hours a week);

◆ normally be 18 years old or over and under pension age (but certain 16 and 17 year olds are entitled);

◆ have a Jobseeker's Agreement which is signed by the claimant and an Employment Service Adviser;

◆ not be in relevant education; and

◆ be in Great Britain.

2.12 Under the contribution-based jobseeker's allowance route, NI contributors obtain a personal rate of benefit for six months irrespective of their capital or partner's earnings. Under the income-based jobseeker's allowance route, income-related help is provided to unemployed people and dependants according to need, in a similar way to income support. Contribution-based jobseeker's allowance is taken fully into account as income in the assessment of HB/CTB. Income-based jobseeker's allowance is disregarded in full and claimants in receipt of this form of the benefit are potentially eligible for maximum HB and CTB.

CLAIMING JOBSEEKER'S ALLOWANCE

2.13 Jobseeker's allowance is normally administered through Jobcentres by Employment Service and Benefits Agency staff working together. Claims should be made at the Jobcentre on form JSA1. The claim form has been designed so that it may be used to claim both contribution-based jobseeker's allowance and income-based jobseeker's allowance. An Employment Service adviser:

◆ interviews the claimant; and

◆ decides whether the conditions of entitlement are satisfied; and if relevant

◆ applies benefit sanctions.

Benefits Agency staff assess and pay the benefit.

DIFFERENCES BETWEEN INCOME SUPPORT/INCOME-BASED JOBSEEKER'S ALLOWANCE AND HB/MAIN CTB

2.14   The income support/income-based jobseeker's allowance claimant's capital, income and applicable amount are worked out in much the same way as under the HB/main CTB schemes. There are, however, certain differences:

◆ the normal income support/income-based jobseeker's allowance capital cut-off is £8,000 compared with the HB/main CTB cut-off of £16,000;

◆ the personal allowance for most single claimants under 18 is £31.45 for income support/income-based jobseeker's allowance purposes and £41.35 for HB purposes;

◆ the protected family premium for lone parents is £15.90 in the assessment of income support/income-based jobseeker's allowance as opposed to £22.20 in the assessment of HB/main CTB;

◆ the income support/income-based jobseeker's allowance applicable amount may include additional housing costs, i.e. mortgage interest payments, interest on loans for repairs and improvements to the home, ground rent and related service charges, payments in a co-ownership scheme, rent payable on a crown tenancy, tent rentals and site fees; and

◆ the HB/main CTB earnings disregard for lone parents is £25 compared with the income support/income-based jobseeker's allowance £15 disregard.

The social fund

2.15   The social fund provides financial assistance by way of cash loans and grants. Payments are of two types: regulated and discretionary. Claims should be made on forms available from the Benefits Agency local office (the telephone number and address can be found in the Benefits Agency display advert in the business numbers section of the phone book).

REGULATED SOCIAL FUND PAYMENTS

2.16   Regulated payments to assist with the cost of maternity needs are available to people in receipt of income support, income-based jobseeker's allowance, working families' tax credit or disabled person's tax credit. HB/CTB recipients who require help with the cost of a new baby will normally be in receipt of one or other of these benefits. Payments for funeral needs are also available to recipients of the above benefits and HB or CTB claimants. Claimant savings over £500 (if the claimant and partner are under 60) or £1,000 (if the claimant or partner is 60 or over) are deducted pound for pound from any payment. Payments for funeral needs are recoverable from the estate of the deceased. Payments for maternity needs are not recoverable.

2.17   Regulated payments for fuel bills are also made automatically in periods of exceptionally severe weather to claimants who have been awarded income support/income-based jobseeker's allowance for at least one day during the period of cold weather and either their benefit includes a pensioner, disability, higher pensioner, severe disability or disabled child premium, or they have a child aged under five.

DISCRETIONARY SOCIAL FUND PAYMENTS

2.18   The second part of the social fund provides for other needs. It is divided into three elements:

◆ budgeting loans;

◆ crisis loans; and

◆ community care grants.

These loans and grants are discretionary; the amount of money available is cash limited.

BUDGETING LOANS

2.19   These are for 'one off' needs, e.g. essential household furniture and equipment, removal costs, redecoration, securing the home and rent in advance where the landlord is not a local housing authority. Deposits to secure accommodation are, however, excluded from assistance through the social fund. To obtain such an interest-free loan the claimant must be in receipt of income support or income-based jobseeker's allowance at the time the application is decided. The claimant and/or partner must have been in receipt of income support/income-based jobseeker's allowance throughout a 26 week period (any gap of up to 28 days is ignored) before the date the application is decided, and not involved in a trade dispute. Savings over £500, or £1,000 if the claimant or partner is 60 or over, are taken into account when assessing any loan.

CRISIS LOANS

2.20   These are paid to meet expenses in an emergency or as a consequence of a disaster. These interest-free loans are available if they are the only means by which serious damage or risk to the health or safety of the applicant or to a member of his or her family may be prevented. Circumstances where crisis loans may be payable include fire, flood and theft. They are also available for rent in advance payable to a non-local authority landlord if a community care grant is also being awarded to help the claimant or a member of the family re-establish themselves in the community (para. 2.22). Applicants need not be in receipt of a social security benefit to receive a crisis loan. They must, however, be without resources to meet the immediate need.

LOANS AND THEIR REPAYMENT

2.21   The minimum budgeting loan is £30. There is no minimum level for a crisis loan. In both cases the maximum amount of a loan is £1,000. The loans are interest-free and are repaid by way of deduction from benefit. Where the claimant is not on income support, deductions may be made from a wide range of other benefits (though not HB/CTB) or by some other method. The maximum repayment period is normally 78 weeks. The weekly repayment rate is normally 15 per cent of the income support applicable amount. Loans are not given to people who are too poor to repay them. Such claimants may have good grounds for a claim for additional HB/CTB if their circumstances are exceptional (para. 9.42).

COMMUNITY CARE GRANTS

2.22   These are generally used for removal expenses or essential household purchases such as cookers or beds. They are paid to:

◆ help the claimant or a member of his or her family re-establish themselves in the community following a stay in institutional care; or

◆ help the claimant remain in the community rather than enter such care; or

◆ help ensure that homeless people in hostels on a planned programme of resettlement do not end up back on the streets; or

◆ ease exceptional pressure; or

◆ allow the claimant or partner to care for a prisoner or young offender on home leave; or

◆ meet travel expenses within the UK to visit someone who is ill, attend a relative's funeral, ease a domestic crisis, etc.

2.23   The claimant must be in receipt of income support or income-based JSA; or due to leave institutional or residential care within six weeks of applying for the grant and expected to receive income support or income-based JSA. Savings over £500 (£1,000 if the claimant or partner is 60 or over) are taken into account when assessing any grant.

Working families' tax credit

2.24   Working families' tax credit (WFTC) supplements the low or moderate 16 hours plus per week earnings of a claimant with at least one dependent child/young person. WFTC replaced family credit from 5th October 1999. The Inland Revenue administers it. From April 2000 the employer is asked to pay WFTC with the claimant's earnings. Self-employed people continue to be paid direct by the Tax Credit Office.

2.25   Claimants with capital greater than £8,000 are not eligible. The claimant's household, capital and net income for WFTC assessment purposes are assessed in a similar manner to that for HB/main CTB. There are, however, no earnings disregards. Child benefit and HB/CTB and all maintenance payments are amongst the list of income types that are completely disregarded for WFTC purposes.

2.26   The amount of WFTC awarded is calculated on the basis of a maximum credit. This maximum credit is awarded where the claimant's assessable income is at or below an income threshold of £91.45. If the claimant's net income is above that level the maximum credit is reduced by 55 per cent of the difference between the claimant's assessable income and the threshold figure.

2.27   The maximum credit consists of:

◆ a basic tax credit of £53.15 (regardless of whether the claimant is a lone parent or has a partner);

◆ an extra 30-hour tax credit of £11.25 (when at least one earner works 30 hours plus per week);

◆ a tax credit for each child/young person according to age as follows:

- up to September following 16th birthday   £21.25
- till day before 19th birthday   £26.35

◆ a childcare tax credit worth up to 70 per cent of eligible childcare costs up to maximum cost of £100 per week for claimant's who pay for childcare for one child and £150 for claimant's who pay for child care for two or more children.

Example: Working families' tax credit calculation

A lone parent has a child of 9 and net assessable earnings of £200 per week from 35 hours work per week. She pays eligible childcare costs of £80 per week

Maximum tax credit:

Basic tax credit	£53.15
Child tax credit (age 9)	£21.25
30 hours credit	£11.25
Childcare tax credit (70% of £80)	£56.00
Maximum tax credit	£141.65
Less 55% of income in excess of £91.45	
(£200 – £91.45 = £108.55)	= £59.70
WFTC payable	= £81.95

CLAIMING WFTC

2.28   Applications are made by post on form WFTC1. This form is included in the WFTC application pack that can be obtained by phoning the Tax Credit Helpline 0845 609 5000 or Textphone 0845 606 6668 (lines are open from 7.30am – 6.30pm Monday to Friday). Application packs can also be obtained from Inland Revenue Enquiry Centres, Benefits Agency and Social Security offices and Employment Service Jobcentres.

Disabled persons tax credit

2.29   Disabled persons tax credit (DPTC) is similar to WFTC but is payable to those working 16 hours or more per week who have a physical or mental disability that puts them at a disadvantage in getting a job. Additionally, they must be, or within 182 days of the claim for DPTC, have been, getting a sickness or disability related benefit, invalid carriage or equivalent, or a disability or higher pensioner premium in the calculation of their IS, income-based jobseeker's allowance, HB or main CTB. A person is able to claim DPTC or WFTC but not both. Eligible claimants should find themselves better off than on WFTC. Unlike WFTC, DPTC is also available to single people and childless couples.

2.30   The claimant's household, capital and net income for DPTC are assessed in a similar manner to HB/main CTB. Claimants with capital greater than £16,000 are not eligible. As with WFTC, however, there are no earnings disregards and child benefit and HB/CTB are completely disregarded for DPTC purposes.

2.31   A person in receipt of DPTC is eligible for a disability premium or higher pensioner premium (para. 12.21). DPTC is taken into account in full as income for HB and CTB purposes.

CLAIMING DPTC

2.32   Applications are made by post on form DPTC1. This form is included in the DPTC application pack that can be obtained by phoning the Tax Credit Helpline 0845 605 5858 or textphone 0845 608 8844 (lines are open from 7.30am to 6.30pm Monday to Friday). The application pack may also be obtained from Inland Revenue Enquiry Centres, Benefits Agency and Social Security offices and Employment Service Jobcentres.

Impact of WFTC/DPTC on HB/main CTB

2.33   WFTC/DPTC (with the exception of that attributable to the 30-hour credit) is counted in full as income when assessing HB/main CTB. For every pound of WFTC/DPTC received there is a loss of 85p in HB/main CTB for claimants receiving help with both rent and council tax. The higher amounts awarded under the tax credit system will reduce the numbers entitled to HB/main CTB. The DSS estimate (A25/99) that the numbers of people entitled to receive both HB and main CTB should reduce by 100,000 as a result of being awarded WFTC/DPTC.

2.34   When an HB/CTB claim is received and WFTC/DPTC is not declared but the authority considers that there would be entitlement to one or other of these credits the DSS advise (A25/99) that the claimant should be prompted to make an application. If the claimant does not apply for the tax credit then the question of notional income may arise (para. 13.99)

Principal changes in HB and CTB

2.35   Table 2.1 provides a summary of the principal changes to HB and CTB since the commencement of the current schemes.

Table 2.1 SUMMARY OF PRINCIPAL CHANGES

1st April 1988	Introduction of new HB scheme. Capital limit £6,000.
30th May 1988	Capital limit increases to £8,000.
2nd/15th January 1989	The 1988 Housing Acts change the independent rented sector
1st April 1989	Abolition of domestic rates in Scotland. Introduction of community charge and community charge rebates in Scotland. Rent officer referral procedures begin. Standard deductions for meals introduced.
10th April 1989	Boarders on income support transfer to HB.
9th October 1989	Hostel residents on income support transfer to HB. Introduction of enhanced pensioner premium.
1st April 1990	Abolition of domestic rates in England and Wales. Introduction of community charge in England and Wales and CCB scheme throughout GB. Capital limit increases from £8,000 to £16,000. Rent officer referrals become a legal requirement. Boarders cease to count as non-dependants. Income from boarders now taken into account.
1st September 1990	Restriction on students' eligibility for HB.
1st October 1990	Introduction of carer premium.
14th January 1991	Most new residents in care and nursing homes excluded from HB entitlement.
1st April 1991	Official error overpayments now recoverable if claimant (etc) could have realised at date of notification that there was an overpayment.
1st/6th April 1992	Definition of remunerative work changed from 24 to 16 hours per week for HB/CCB and for income support and family credit. Changes consequent on the introduction of the disability living allowance and disability working allowance. Changes consequent upon commencement of the provisions of the Children Act 1989 (England and Wales only). New £15 disregard of maintenance payments.
1st July 1992	Social security primary legislation consolidated into Social Security Administration Act and Social Security Contributions and Benefits Act.

31st March 1993	End of community charge (poll tax).
1st April 1993	Introduction of council tax and CTB scheme throughout GB. Changes consequent upon introduction of new community care arrangements. Changes consequent upon introduction of new system of maintenance run by Child Support Agency. £15 carer's earnings disregard introduced. Introduction of anti-fraud subsidy incentives for authorities.
1st/4th April 1994	Certain 'persons from abroad' excluded from HB/CTB entitlement. Modification of the subsidy rules relating to disproportionate rent increases and modular improvement schemes. Rent officers required to identify rents which are exceptionally high in comparison with the levels of rents charged for other deregulated tenancies in the same rent registration area and make high rent determinations where appropriate. New subsidy control for exceptionally high private sector rents. New anti-fraud subsidy arrangements mean that authorities which fail to achieve certain savings will have subsidy reduced.
1st May 1994	General counselling and support service charges only eligible for HB payments where the landlord or landlord's employee spends majority of time providing other eligible services.
1st August 1994	'Habitual residence' test introduced into HB/CTB.
3rd October 1994	Introduction of maximum £40 childcare disregard in HB/CTB and in family credit and disability working allowance in respect of child under 11 where formal childcare provided. Revised definition of 'person affected' for HB/CTB and introduction of requirement that 'person affected' signs requests for further information, review and further review.
3rd January 1995	Deregulation and Contracting Out Act makes contracting out of HB/CTB administration easier by allowing contractor to exchange information with Benefits Agency.
1st/3rd April 1995	Restriction on period many claimants can be temporarily absent for HB purposes and introduction of same rule into CTB.
17th July 1995	New premium introduced into family credit and disability working allowance for those working 30-plus hours a week and resulting additional benefit disregarded for HB/CTB purposes.
2nd January 1996	New measures to restrict HB on above-average private sector rents. Rent officers' figures become binding on authorities in most cases.

	Protection for 'vulnerable' groups removed.
	Introduction of 'exceptional hardship' discretion.
5th February 1996	Restrictions on HB/CTB and IS entitlement for asylum seekers and sponsored immigrants.
1st April 1996	HB/CTB extended for an additional four weeks for certain claimants moving into permanent work after six months or more on income-related benefits.
	Subsidy incentives/penalties introduced to encourage authorities to speed the processing of new claims for HB/CTB from certain workers ('fast tracking').
	Increase in the lower capital limit from £3,000 to £10,000 for HB claimants in certain types of residential accommodation.
	The maximum child care disregard is uprated from £40 to £60.
7th October 1996	The maximum HB for certain single people under 25 in private sector tenancies is restricted to the single room rent (i.e. the general level of local rents for non-self-contained accommodation).
	New private sector claimants/landlords receive their HB in arrears. Authorities given discretion to make the first payment of HB payable to the landlord but sent to the tenant.
	Jobseeker's allowance (JSA) introduced to replace Unemployed Benefit and Income Support for unemployed people – consequential amendments to HB/CTB rules on claims and changes of circumstances.
15th October 1996	Retrospective payments of HB/CTB should be made to asylum seekers debarred from benefit after 5.2.96 up to the date refugee status is granted if claims are made in time.
1st/7th April 1997	New rate of family premium (Lone Parent Family Premium) replaces family premium and lone parent premium for lone parents.
	Changes to the trigger dates for the increases in dependants' allowances from the 11th and 16th birthday to the first Monday in September.
	Removal of the higher rate allowance for 18 year old dependants. First date on which higher meals deduction for 16 year old dependants is made moves to the first Monday in September following the 16th birthday.
	Introduction of two higher levels of non-dependent deduction in HB and CTB.
	Recovery of an overpayment from a private or housing association landlord reopens tenant's rent liability to that landlord and

	consequently landlord's ability to pursue rent arrears.
18th August 1997	Certain additional service charges for general counselling and support where claimant occupies supported accommodation are made eligible on a temporary basis.
6th October 1997	HB for certain private tenants restricted to the local reference rent (i.e, the general level of local rents for a suitable size of home). Single room rents cease to apply for people who qualify for a severe disability premium or who have one or more non-dependant(s).
3rd November 1997	New rules about payments to landlords, recovery of overpayments, and withholding and suspending HB/CTB.
1st/6th April 1998	Significant increase in maximum non-dependant deductions. Withdrawal of entitlement to Lone Parent Family Premium for new claimants. Restricting CTB so that new claimants with property in Bands F, G and H, and claimants who move or have a break in entitlement of more than 12 weeks, have their CTB restricted to that of Band E.
1st June 1998	Disregard for childcare costs increased from a maximum of £60 to £100 a week where there are two or more children in the family; and the maximum eligible age increased from 11 to 12.
9th November 1998	Increase to the under 11 year rate of child's HB/CTB personal allowance
25th January 1999	Introduction of more detailed rules that prescribe those people who are to be treated as not liable to make payments in respect of a dwelling and consequently not entitled to HB (Applies to new and repeat claims)
1st April 1999	Introduction in some authorities of the National Verification Framework, i.e. administration of HB/CTB according to DSS guidelines relating to required evidence and home visits designed to minimise fraud and error Restriction in council tax benefit subsidy where authority has made an 'excessive' increase in the council tax
June 1999	First pilots of 'ONE' – a single point of entry into the benefit system for people of working age
September 1999	Requirement to supply an NI number and evidence or information to corroborate claimant and any partner's identity as the owners of number becomes a qualifying condition for HB/CTB

October 1999	£4.70 a week increase to the under 11 year rate of child's HB/CTB personal allowance
	Changes to HB/main CTB consequent upon introduction of working families' tax credit and disabled persons tax credit
	Normal earnings disregard increased by the amount of the 30 hour credit in FC/DWA WFTC/DPTC for specific claimants.
	Maximum amount to be deducted from earnings in respect of relevant childcare charges increased
	Changes to HB/CTB extended payments as a result of the introduction of the lone parent's benefit run-on and the extension of the extended payments scheme to disabled people.
November 1999	Second pilots of 'ONE'
April 2000	Temporary eligibility of certain service charges for general counselling and support in 'supported accommodation' expected to come to an end
	Implementation of a time limited transitional HB scheme to provide support for specific charges for general counselling and support.
	Removal of entitlement to all non-contributory benefits including HB/CTB and welfare support from persons subject to immigration control including new asylum seekers
	Asylum support scheme administered by the National Asylum Support Service provides minimum assistance to destitute asylum seekers and dependants
	Transitional protection retains IS/HB/CTB entitlement for asylum seekers already in receipt of the benefit or eligible to claim at point of change
	A single rate of personal allowance covering children between birth and the September after their 16th birthday introduced.
	HB/CTB regulations relating to childcare amended to include a new category of 'Approved Providers'.
April 2001	Proposed abolition of review boards and start of right of appeal to tribunals administered by the Appeal Service
	Possible exclusion of the cost of rent rebates from local authority housing revenue accounts
April 2003	Proposed introduction of 'Supporting People' - an integrated funding framework for support services and the end of HB assistance with such costs

3 Council tax

3.1 This chapter:

◆ provides an overview of the council tax;

◆ indicates the dwellings exempt from the tax;

◆ identifies who must pay the tax; and

◆ describes other ways of reducing the tax in addition to the award of CTB.

Details of the council tax may be found in Martin Ward's *Council Tax Handbook* (Child Poverty Action Group).

Overview

3.2 On 1st April 1993 the council tax replaced the community charge as the means by which local people help meet the cost of local public services. The council tax is a tax on residential properties known as dwellings. Liability for the tax arises on a daily basis.

3.3 Dwellings include houses and flats, etc. whether lived in or not, as well as houseboats and mobile homes that are used for domestic purposes. Non-residential property is subject to non-domestic rates.

ADMINISTRATION OF THE TAX

3.4 There should only be one tax bill for each dwelling but a number of people may be responsible for paying it (para. 3.26). Local councils, known in England and Wales as billing authorities and in Scotland as local authorities, are responsible for the billing and collection of the tax. Scottish authorities are also responsible for collecting the council water charge.

VALUATION OF DWELLINGS

3.5 Existing and new dwellings are allocated to one of eight valuation bands on the valuation list according to their assumed market value as at 1st April 1991. The lower the valuation band the lower the tax.

3.6 General changes in house prices do not lead to a rebanding or give grounds for appeal. Where works to a dwelling have led to a material increase in its value, e.g. the building of an extension, this should lead to a revaluation and the possibility of a rebanding but only following sale or transfer of the property.

3.7 A revaluation, and possible rebanding, of the dwelling should take place immediately if there has been a material decrease in its value following:

◆ a partial demolition;

◆ a change in the physical state of the local area; or

◆ certain adaptations to make it suitable for a disabled person.

ROLE OF LISTING OFFICER/LOCAL ASSESSOR

3.8 In England and Wales the valuation of the dwelling, and the updating of the valuation list, is the responsibility of the listing officer at the local valuation office, an agency of the Inland Revenue. In Scotland it is the responsibility of the local assessor appointed by the council.

3.9 It is also the listing officer's, or local assessor's, responsibility to decide:

◆ whether or not a property is a 'dwelling'; and

◆ what proportion of a property with a mixed residential/non-residential use, such as a house where one room is used as a shop, should be designated as a 'dwelling'.

ACCESS TO INFORMATION ON BANDING

3.10 Members of the public may inspect the valuation list. In England and Wales it can be seen at either the local valuation office or the billing authority's main office. In Scotland it may be seen at the local authority's main office. The council tax bill also includes the individual dwelling's valuation band.

Exempt dwellings

3.11 Most dwellings on the valuation list are subject to the council tax. Some, however, are exempt from the tax either indefinitely or for a fixed period. Unoccupied dwellings, not covered by any of the exemptions, normally qualify for a 50 per cent discount but certain second homes in Wales may not qualify for such a discount (para. 3.36).

DWELLINGS EXEMPT WITHOUT A TIME LIMIT

3.12 The main categories of occupied dwelling exempt indefinitely from the tax are:

◆ halls of residence mainly occupied by students;

◆ dwellings where all the residents are students, including in England and Wales where that dwelling is only occupied during term time;

◆ armed forces accommodation;

♦ dwellings occupied only by persons under 18 years of age (from April 1993 in Scotland and from April 1995 in England and Wales); and

♦ dwellings where all occupants who would otherwise be liable for the council tax are severely mentally impaired (from April 1995) including (from April 1999) where the only other occupiers are students.

3.13   From 1st April 1997 in England and Wales, where an annex or similar self-contained part of a property is occupied by an elderly or disabled relative of the residents living in the rest of it, then it is exempt from the Council Tax. The valuation for 'granny annexes' in Scotland remains unchanged. In Scotland, certain dwellings used as trial flats by registered housing associations for pensioners and the disabled are exempt.

3.14   The main unoccupied dwellings exempt indefinitely from the council tax are those where the immediately former resident is:

♦ in prison or detention (except for non-payment of a fine or in England and Wales the council tax); or

♦ receiving personal care in hospital, a residential care home or nursing home or elsewhere; or

♦ living in someone else's home in order to provide them with care; or

♦ a student or certain student nurses studying elsewhere.

3.15   Other unoccupied dwellings exempt indefinitely include those:

♦ repossessed by a mortgage lender; or

♦ reserved for a minister of religion (of any faith) for the performance of his or her duties; or

♦ where occupation is prohibited by law.

3.16   In Scotland since the commencement of the scheme an unoccupied dwelling which is part of the same premises as another dwelling and difficult to let separately (such as an empty 'granny flat') or which was last occupied together with agricultural lands is exempt indefinitely. In England and Wales from April 1995 an unoccupied property which cannot be let separately due to planning controls is also exempt.

DWELLINGS EXEMPT FOR SIX MONTHS

3.17   The main dwelling types exempt from the council tax for up to six months are unoccupied dwellings that are:

♦ part of the estate of a deceased person following the date the grant of probate or letters of administration, or grant of confirmation to the estate was made; or

♦ substantially unfurnished new properties or

> **Example: Exemptions**
>
> Three full time students share a house. The house is exempt from the council tax. One has left his own property elsewhere to take up the course. That dwelling is also exempt while he is a student.

◆ substantially unfurnished properties which have undergone major repairs or structural alterations; or

◆ owned by, and used for the purposes of, a charity; or

◆ substantially unfurnished in any other circumstances.

OBTAINING AN EXEMPTION

3.18   The authority is expected to take reasonable steps to ascertain whether particular dwellings are exempt. It may have awarded an exemption on the basis of its existing records. If a dwelling is thought to be exempt, but an exemption not awarded, the owner may write to the authority making the case for an exemption. If the authority refuses to award it an appeal can be made (para. 3.47). There is no time limit on obtaining exemptions.

3.19   Once an exemption has been awarded the authority should write to the owner providing information on the exempt dwelling's valuation band and what the council tax would be if the dwelling were not exempt. The owner has an obligation to inform the authority if the exemption should be withdrawn. If this is not done a penalty may be applied (para. 3.42).

Who must pay the tax?

3.20   The council tax is normally payable by someone resident in the dwelling but in certain instances non-resident owners are liable instead.

RESIDENTS

3.21   A resident is someone aged 18 or over, solely or mainly resident in the dwelling. Where there is more than one resident the liable person is the one who comes first in the list in table 3.1.

3.22   Where there is more than one leaseholder, the liable leaseholder is the person with the inferior lease, that is, for the shortest period of time lasting over six months.

3.23   Normally a resident owner, a council tenant, a housing association tenant or a private tenant is the liable person. Where, however, the landlord lives with the tenant, the landlord and not the tenant is the liable person.

Table 3.1 HIERARCHY OF LIABLE RESIDENTS

◆ A resident owner.

◆ A resident long leaseholder (para. 3.22).

◆ A resident statutory, statutory assured or secure tenant.

◆ A resident sub-tenant.

◆ A resident licensee.

◆ Any other resident (including a squatter).

LIABLE NON-RESIDENT OWNERS

3.24 Where a dwelling is empty, or a second or holiday home, and no-one's sole or main residence, the non-resident 'owner' is liable for the council tax. The non-resident owner is also liable for the tax where the dwelling is:

◆ in multiple occupation, i.e. originally constructed or subsequently adapted for occupation by more than one household, or inhabited by a person who is not liable to pay rent or a licence fee in respect of the dwelling as a whole; or

◆ a residential care home, nursing home or certain hostels providing a high level of care; or

◆ occupied by religious communities; or

◆ occupied by a minister of religion (of any faith) and used for the performance of his/her duties; or

◆ not the owner's main residence, but the main residence of someone employed in domestic service; or

◆ in Scotland certain school boarding accommodation.

3.25 Since the 'owner' is liable in the above cases, residents who fall into one of the above categories are not liable for the council tax. In many instances, however, the cost of the tax may be passed on to them if the landlord follows the correct procedures. Non-resident owners are not eligible for CTB to help with the council tax (para. 4.89).

JOINT LIABILITY

3.26 People who have the same status (resident or non-resident) and the same legal interest in the dwelling as the liable person are jointly liable. For example, two resident owners, or two resident joint tenants where there is no resident

---

Examples: Liability

Two sisters jointly own and live in a property as their sole residence. Their brother also lives with them. Both sisters as joint owners are jointly liable for the council tax. The brother is not liable.

The younger sister allows her male friend to live with her as a partner. The two sisters and the male partner are now jointly and severally liable for the tax. The brother is not liable.

The older sister moves elsewhere on a permanent basis but retains her share in the property. The remaining sister and partner are jointly and severally liable for the council tax. Whilst the older sister has the same legal interest in the property as her younger sister she is no longer resident and therefore no longer liable for the tax. The brother is not liable.

---

landlord, are normally jointly liable for the tax. The partner of a liable person, whether or not they have the same legal interest in the dwelling, is also jointly liable so long as he or she is living with the liable person as a married or unmarried heterosexual couple. The definition of 'partner' for council tax purposes is similar to that which applies for HB/CTB purposes (para. 6.6).

JOINT LIABILITY AND SEVERE MENTAL IMPAIRMENT

3.27   The one exception to these rules on joint liability relates to a severely mentally impaired person (appendix 6). Such a person cannot be held jointly liable if there is someone else with the same status and legal interest in the property who is not severely mentally impaired. Prior to April 1995, a severely mentally impaired person was liable for the tax if he or she was the only liable person, or if all the jointly liable people were severely mentally impaired. Since April 1995 dwellings where all the occupants are severely mentally impaired are exempt. From April 1999 the dwelling would also be exempt if the only other occupiers are one or more students.

IDENTIFYING THE LIABLE PERSON

3.28   Many authorities use other records to identify the person liable for the tax on each property. In certain cases households may be sent a form requesting relevant information. Failure to complete and return the form within 21 days renders the individual concerned open to a penalty (para. 3.42). If liability is disputed an appeal may be made (para. 3.47). There is no time limit on the identification of the liable person.

IMPACT ON CTB

3.29   Where persons (other than a couple) are jointly liable the amount of council tax used for the purpose of working out a resident's CTB entitlement is based on the total liability divided by the number of jointly liable persons (including the members of a jointly liable couple) (para. 3.26). Changes in the number jointly liable affect their CTB entitlement and may result in under or overpayments of CTB. The authority may seek to recover all of the council tax from one or more of the jointly liable individuals even though that individual may be entitled to CTB on only a share of the liability. From April 1997 where a full-time student is jointly liable with a CTB claimant their presence in the dwelling is ignored in the calculation of CTB.

Reducing the council tax bill

3.30   In addition to CTB the council tax bill may be reduced as a result of:

◆   a disability reduction (para. 3.32); and/or

◆   the award of a discount (para. 3.35).

In addition to the above, transitional relief was available in England and Scotland in 1993-95 and in England alone in 1995-96. There is no general scheme of transitional relief in or after 1996-97. Transitional relief applied in Wales for 1998-99. Special transitional relief also applies currently in certain reorganised authorities.

Where both types of help are relevant they are applied in the order discussed above. In addition to these methods some authorities offer a discount for prompt payment of the tax or the adoption of certain payment methods (para. 3.41). Council tax liability may also be reduced or eliminated as a result of an appeal (para. 3.43).

RELATIONSHIP WITH CTB

3.31   Any discount related to lump-sum or non-cash payments is ignored in the calculation of CTB. Main CTB is calculated using the liable person's council tax after the deduction of any disability reduction, discount, or transitional relief. Second adult rebate is worked out using the council tax after the deduction of any disability reduction or transitional relief but ignoring any discounts which may apply. The retrospective award of any discount, reduction or relief, or the reduction or elimination of council tax liability following an appeal, may lead to a recoverable overpayment of CTB (para. 18.10).

Disability reduction scheme

3.32   The council tax bill may be reduced where the dwelling has certain features which meet the particular needs of a substantially and permanently disabled adult or child.

3.33   The reduction should be awarded where:

◆ the dwelling is the sole or main residence of at least one such person; and

◆ the home provides:

- an additional bathroom or kitchen for the use of the disabled person;

- a room, other than a bathroom, kitchen or toilet, used predominantly to meet the disabled person's special needs such as a downstairs room in a two storey house which has to be used as a bedroom by the disabled person; or

- sufficient floor space to enable the use of a wheelchair required by the disabled person within the dwelling.

In addition the authority must be satisfied that the facility in question is either essential, or of major importance, for the disabled person in view of the nature and extent of the disability.

OBTAINING A DISABILITY REDUCTION

3.34   To obtain the disability reduction the liable person should complete the authority's application form. The authority will normally request supporting evidence, such as a letter from a doctor, before awarding a reduction. If the reduction is awarded the tax bill is based on the next valuation band down. For example if the dwelling is in band E the council tax bill is based on that for a band D property. Prior to April 2000 someone with a property in band A - the lowest band - could not receive a disability reduction. From 1st April 2000 the council tax reductions for people with disabilities scheme is extended to dwellings in valuation band A. The reduction for dwellings in band A is 1/9th of band D, i.e. equivalent to that currently given to dwellings in bands B, C and D. Applications for a disability reduction must be renewed each year. If the authority refuses to award a disability reduction the liable person may appeal (para. 3.47). There is no time limit on obtaining a disability reduction.

Discounts

3.35   The council tax bill should be reduced by:

◆ 25 per cent where there is only one resident in the dwelling; or

◆ 50 per cent in England and Scotland where there are no residents in the dwelling.

The bill does not increase if there are more than two residents in the property.

3.36   In Wales, dwellings with no residents receive either a 50 per cent discount or, if they fall within a defined class that covers most second homes, a discount of 25 per cent or no discount at all. The individual Welsh authority decides what discount to give such a property.

DISREGARDED PEOPLE

3.37   When considering the number of people in the dwelling certain people including students, apprentices, Youth Training trainees and the severely mentally impaired are disregarded. Appendix 6 describes the categories of person who are disregarded. Someone may be disregarded for the purpose of awarding a discount but still liable to pay the tax.

OBTAINING A DISCOUNT

3.38   The authority is expected to take reasonable steps to ascertain whether any discount applies to a dwelling. It may have awarded one on the basis of previous information regarding the property or as the result of a canvass. If the bill does not contain a discount the liable person may write to the authority requesting one. The authority may require appropriate evidence in support of the request. If the authority refuses to award a discount the liable person may appeal (para. 3.47). There is no time limit on obtaining a discount.

3.39   Discounts are awarded on a daily basis. Liable persons have an obligation to inform the authority if a discount which has been applied should be withdrawn or reduced within 21 days. If they fail to do this they may be required to pay a penalty (para. 3.42).

Example: Discounts

There are three joint tenants in the dwelling all aged 18 or over. One is a Youth Training trainee under 25, the other a qualifying apprentice, only the third does not meet any of the descriptions of a disregarded person. The council tax bill should be reduced by 25 per cent. There is no resident landlord and the house is not in multiple occupation. The three joint tenants are jointly liable for the council tax.

Billing and payment

3.40   A liable person does not have to pay the council tax unless a demand bill has been issued to him or her by the billing or local authority. Where several people are jointly liable, the authority may send the bill in the joint names of all those liable or in the name of one liable person only. Where the authority cannot identify the liable person(s) by name they may address the bill to 'the council tax payer'.

3.41   Normally payment is in ten monthly instalments, though in certain authorities council tenants for example may pay council tax with their rent. Where liability to pay commences part way through the financial year, or a bill is issued late, the number of instalments is reduced. Authorities may offer a reduction in the council tax bill for lump-sum payments and payments by non-cash methods such as direct debit.

Penalties

3.42   A penalty of £50 may be imposed by authorities on people who fail to respond to a request for information relating to the liable person, or fail to notify the authority that the dwelling is no longer exempt, or that they are no longer eligible for a discount. A further £200 penalty can be imposed for each additional failure to provide requested information.

Council tax appeals

3.43   Any person aggrieved by an authority's decision on a transitional reduction may appeal to its review board. The procedure is as described in chapter 19 for HB/CTB appeals except that there is no time limit in which appeals against a decision on a transitional reduction need be made. Different routes must be taken for appeals relating to:

◆ the valuation of dwellings;

◆ tax liability and reductions;

◆ completion notices; and

◆ penalties.

In all cases payment of the council tax bill is still due even if an appeal has been made. A penalty does not have to be paid, however, until an appeal against it has been decided.

VALUATION APPEALS

3.44   If there is a disagreement over whether or not a property is a dwelling, or the banding of a property, a proposal can be made to the listing officer in England and Wales or the local assessor in Scotland for the valuation list to be altered. Such proposals can be made by:

◆ the liable person;

◆ the person who would be liable if the property were not exempt; or

◆ the owner of the dwelling.

3.45 Proposals on valuation matters can only be considered if made within six months of:

◆ someone first becoming liable for council tax on a dwelling but not where the same facts have previously been considered by an appeal body;

◆ the dwelling first appearing on the valuation list but not where the same facts have previously been considered by an appeal body;

◆ an appeal decision on a comparable dwelling which gives reasonable grounds for contending that the valuation band for the dwelling should be changed; or

◆ an alteration being made to the valuation list by the listing officer or assessor.

Proposals can be made at any time where:

◆ a property should be excluded from the valuation list;

◆ there has been a material reduction in the value of the dwelling; or

◆ a change has occurred in the mix between residential and non-residential use.

3.46 Where the listing officer or assessor disagrees with the proposed alteration, it must be sent, within a six-month period, to a valuation tribunal (VT) in England and Wales or a valuation appeal committee (VAC) in Scotland.

LIABILITY APPEALS

3.47 An aggrieved person may appeal in writing to the billing or local authority if it is thought that:

◆ the authority has identified the wrong person as liable for the tax;

◆ the dwelling should be exempt; or

◆ a discount or disability reduction should be awarded.

3.48 The authority has two months to consider the matter. In England and Wales, if it fails to respond within that period or the aggrieved person is dissatisfied with its decision, an appeal may be made to a VT. This must normally be done within two months of the authority notifying the aggrieved person of its decision; or within four months of the date the initial representation was made if the authority has not responded. In Scotland an appeal to the VAC must be made by writing to the authority within four months of the date the issue was first raised. The authority must pass the appeal on to the relevant VAC.

APPEALS AGAINST COMPLETION NOTICES

3.49   In England and Wales the authority, and in Scotland, the assessor, may issue a completion notice that states the date on which a newly erected or structurally altered property is considered to be a dwelling. In England and Wales, an appeal may be made directly to a VT but this must normally be done within four weeks of the notice being sent. In Scotland an appeal to the VAC. must be made by the aggrieved person writing to the assessor within 21 days of receipt of the completion notice. The assessor should pass the appeal to the VAC.

APPEALS AGAINST PENALTIES

3.50   These may be made normally within two months direct to a VT in England and Wales or via the local authority to a VAC in Scotland.

TIME LIMITS FOR APPEALS TO VT OR VAC

3.51   In England and Wales the President of the VT has power to allow an out-of-time appeal where the time limit has not been met for reasons outside the control of the aggrieved person. In Scotland there is no power to consider out-of-time appeals.

4 Who is entitled to benefit?

4.1 This chapter describes:

◆ who may be entitled to HB/CTB;

◆ the circumstance in which someone is or is not considered to be liable to make payments in respect of a dwelling for HB;

◆ the circumstance in which someone is considered to occupy a dwelling as a home for HB/CTB.

The rules excluding certain 'persons from abroad' from HB/CTB entitlement are described in chapter 5.

People who may be entitled to HB

CBA 130(1)(a) **4.2** A person may be entitled to HB if he or she is liable to make payments in respect of a dwelling in Great Britain which he or she occupies as a home. Certain people, even where they do make such payments, are not entitled to HB. Also HB is not payable on certain types of payments.

4.3 HB is available to many:

◆ public sector tenants who live in council or new town accommodation including tenants of Scottish Homes, and also people who are placed by housing authorities in 'bed and breakfast' establishments and hostels;

◆ private sector tenants, including boarders, who rent accommodation from a private landlord, housing association or co-op, as well as hostel dwellers.

People and types of payment excluded from the HB scheme

HOUSING COSTS MET THROUGH INCOME SUPPORT/INCOME-BASED JSA

BR 8(2)(a), 8(3) **4.4** Claimants whose accommodation costs are included in the calculation of their income support/income-based JSA are excluded from help via the HB scheme. But where a claimant not in receipt of income support/income-based JSA but in receipt of HB is awarded either benefit, his or her HB continues for the first four weeks after the date he or she becomes entitled to that benefit. The extra HB can be deducted from the appropriate benefit for that period.

PRIVATE AND VOLUNTARY REGISTERED RESIDENTIAL CARE AND NURSING HOMES

4.5   Prior to 1st April 1993 many residents in private and voluntary registered residential care and nursing homes had their home fees met through income support. Major changes occurred to these arrangements as a result of the government's community care policy. Individuals who need financial assistance from public funds to enter a residential care or nursing home must now contact their local authority social service or social work department. That department assesses the most suitable type of care and, only if appropriate, helps the individual choose or find a place in a home. The department should meet the home's fees but also assess how much the resident should contribute towards the cost on the basis of a means test.

4.6   People entering such homes can claim income support on the same basis as they could in their own homes. In addition, they also qualify for an income support residential allowance. This is to help towards the housing element of the home's fees. People entitled to an income support residential allowance are not entitled to HB.

4.7   Most residents of private or voluntary residential care or nursing homes   HBR 7(1)(k)
have been excluded from HB entitlement since 14th January 1991. Prior to that date residents not on income support, for example, those with capital over £8,000 (and therefore excluded from income support entitlement: para. 2.8) but under £16,000, could claim HB on the accommodation element of the home's fee.

4.8   Individuals in the following groups were still able to claim or receive HB on or after 14th January 1991:

◆ people living in registered homes paying rent to a close relative (para. 4.31) − and who therefore could not receive income support to cover their fees − so long as the close relative did not reside in the same dwelling (para. 4.33) and the arrangement was on a genuine commercial basis;

◆ people entitled to HB in the above accommodation on 29th October 1990;

◆ people in registered homes in remunerative work (para. 9.33);

◆ people whose entitlement to HB was subsequently determined to commence on or after 30th October 1990 but whose claim was posted or delivered to the local social security office on or before 29th October 1990;

◆ people in unregistered small residential homes in England and Wales if income support was not in payment.

4.9 Individuals in the first and third groups (in paragraph 4.8) who enter a home on or after 1st April 1993 are not entitled to HB. They may receive income support residential allowances. But if they were entitled to HB on 31st March 1993, or became so as a result of backdating, they retain that entitlement. It only lasts, however, while they remain in the same home. If they move, other than for a temporary period (para. 4.81), or cease to be entitled to HB for some reason, they lose their entitlement and become subject to the same rules as new residents. People who fall into the second or fourth group retain their HB eligibility while in any type of care home.

4.10 From 1st April 1993, the Registered Homes Act 1984 has been amended so that small homes are now required to seek registration with the local social service authority. This requirement includes accommodation provided under social service adult placement and supported lodgings schemes for less than four residents, but only if both board and personal care is provided. Small homes in Scotland were already subject to registration. Residents in all these homes have potential entitlement to the income support residential allowance. People entering into such homes on or after 1st April 1993 are excluded from HB entitlement. Residents of small homes which are not required to register, or which are refused registration, retain their eligibility for HB. Residents in previously unregistered small homes entitled to HB on 31st March 1993 retain that eligibility for as long as they remain in the same home. If they move, other than for a temporary period (para. 4.81) or cease to be entitled to HB for some reason, they lose this right and become subject to the same rules as new residents.

4.11 Residential accommodation managed or provided by a body constituted by Act of Parliament or incorporated by Royal Charter such as that provided by the Salvation Army does not have to be registered. New and existing residents in such accommodation retain their HB eligibility.

LOCAL AUTHORITY 'PART III' RESIDENTIAL ACCOMMODATION

HBR 8(2) **4.12** The local social service authority's powers to provide residential accommodation are contained within sections 21-24 and 26 of the National Assistance Act 1948 and in Scotland under section 59 of the Social Work (Scotland) Act 1968. Amendments made by the National Health Service and Community Care Act 1990 also enable social service authorities to place people in private and voluntary sector accommodation under those powers.

4.13 Residents of such 'Part III' accommodation are not entitled to HB unless the accommodation is neither owned nor managed by the social service authority, nor registered under the Registered Homes Act 1984 (as amended). The exception to this rule is where the accommodation is owned or managed by the social service authority but the resident does not pay an inclusive charge for the provision of both accommodation and cooked or prepared food. Even if board is not available claimants who were, or are treated as, occupying such accommodation on 31st March 1993 are excluded from HB entitlement. Residents not entitled to HB are potentially entitled to the 'Part III' rate of income support.

MEMBERS OF CERTAIN RELIGIOUS ORDERS

4.14   Members of a religious order are excluded from HB if they are maintained   HBR 7(1)(j)
fully by that order. Monks and nuns in enclosed orders are excluded under this provision. The DSS (GM para. A3.79) points out that members of religious communities (as opposed to religious orders) are often entitled to HB since they frequently do paid work or retain their own possessions.

MOST STUDENTS

4.15   Most, but not all, full-time students are excluded from HB entitlement as   HBR 48A, 50, ∢
they are treated as not liable to make payments in respect of their dwelling (para. 20.18). Students who are not excluded from HB entitlement under that provision are in any case not eligible if:

◆   they live in accommodation provided by the educational establishment they attend (paras. 20.22-24); or

◆   they are away from their term-time accommodation outside the period of study (para. 20.25).

OWNER-OCCUPIERS

4.16   Owner occupiers are not eligible for help via HB on their mortgage   HBR 2(1), 10(2
repayments. If they are in receipt of income support/income-based JSA, they may receive help with their mortgage interest payments from the Benefits Agency. Under the HB scheme the definition of 'owner' includes those who have the right to sell the freehold only with the consent of other joint owners. This definition invalidates the decision in *R v HB Review Board for Sedgemoor ex parte Weadon, The Times,* 6th May 1986. That decision had allowed such an owner where she had had 'exclusive use and occupation' of the property in return for additional weekly payments to the other joint owners, to receive a rent allowance.

LONG LEASEHOLDERS

4.17   Long leaseholders (those with a lease which, when granted, was for more   HBR 2(1), 10(2
than 21 years) are excluded from HB entitlement. But if they are in receipt of income support/income-based JSA they may also receive help with certain housing costs such as ground rent and service charges via the Benefits Agency. Equity sharers buying part of their home from a housing association or housing authority and renting the other part under a shared ownership scheme may receive

HB on the rental element. If they are in receipt of income support/income-based JSA they may also receive assistance towards their mortgage interest payments from the Benefits Agency.

PAYMENTS UNDER HIRE PURCHASE, CREDIT SALE OR CERTAIN CONDITIONAL SALE AGREEMENTS

10(1), 10(2)(d) **4.18** The following payments are not eligible for help under the HB scheme:

◆ a hire purchase agreement, for example, paid by individuals purchasing mobile homes;

◆ a credit sale agreement; or

◆ a conditional sale agreement.

Payments under a rental purchase scheme (i.e. where all or part of the purchase price is paid in more than one instalment and the purchase is deferred until a specified part of the purchase price has been paid) are eligible for a rent allowance. Conditional sale agreements are agreements for the sale of goods or land under which the purchase price is payable by instalments and the goods or land remain the seller's until the instalments are paid. Where such payments are attributable to land they are eligible for HB.

PAYMENTS UNDER A CO-OWNERSHIP SCHEME

R 2(1), 10(2)(b) **4.19** People in housing association co-ownership schemes who will be entitled, on ceasing to be a member of the association, to a sum related to the value of the building are excluded from HB entitlement (*R v Birmingham City Council HB Review Board ex parte Ellery and Weir*, 21 HLR 398), but co-operative tenants may get HB for their rent provided they have no more than a nominal equity share in the property.

CROWN TENANTS

R 2(1), 10(2)(e) **4.20** Crown tenants are excluded from HB entitlement. A crown tenant is normally a person renting his or her home from someone managing the property for the Crown or whose landlord is a government department. If the tenant receives income support/income-based JSA he or she may be entitled to an increase in IS/income-based JSA to cover housing costs. If not receiving IS/income-based JSA, crown tenants on low incomes may be entitled to rent rebates under voluntary schemes established by their landlords. Authorities often have a role in the administration of such schemes but the schemes themselves are quite separate from the HB scheme described in this guide (GM chapter A8). Government departments often use housing associations as managing agents to let properties and collect the rent. This does not alter the status of the tenants of such properties who remain excluded from HB entitlement (HB/CTB(93)27).

DSS circular A26/99 updates guidance and gives best practice advice for authorities dealing with claims from Crown tenants.

4.21   The following persons are not excluded from HB entitlement under the above rule:

◆ former tenants and licensees whose agreement to occupy a crown property has been terminated but who are liable to pay mesne or violent profits; and

◆ tenants or licensees of properties either managed by the Crown Estate Commissioners or belonging to the Duchies of Cornwall or Lancaster.

Liable to pay rent

CBA 130(1)(a)
HBR reg 10(1)

4.22   Normally to qualify for HB the claimant should be the person who is liable (has a legal obligation or duty) to pay rent for the home.

DOUBTS ABOUT LIABILITY

4.23 Normally liability is not in doubt. Table 4.1 identifies some of the circumstances in which liability may be an issue and the considerations the authority should bear in mind when determining the matter.

Table 4.1 LIABILITY – SOME CONSIDERATIONS

Circumstance	Considerations
There is no written agreement	The non-existence of a formal written agreement or the landlord's failure to comply with the duty to issue a rent book is not conclusive (rent liability can arise from a purely oral agreement (GM para. A3.06))
The claimant is not one of the parties to the written agreement	There are circumstances in which someone who is not legally liable may be treated as liable (para. 4.26)
The 'landlord' does not have the right to grant occupation	Unless acting as an agent for someone who does have such a right there can be no liability
The landlord is a friend/ relative of the claimant	The fact that the landlord is a friend/relative of the claimant does not mean that the claimant is not liable unless the landlord is a close relative residing with the claimant (para. 4.30)

The landlord would not seek to regain possession of the property or recover any arrears, if the claimant failed to make payments	A possible indicator of a contrivance (para. 4.37) – but is the landlord awaiting the outcome of a decision about benefit entitlement?
The claimant was the previous owner of the property	If the claimant has a preserved right to live in the dwelling for life (which could be either explicit or implied) s/he cannot be liable to pay for the dwelling (also see para. 4.52)
The claimant has granted the tenancy to him/herself	It is not possible in law to grant a tenancy to yourself but it is possible for a company to grant a lease to either its directors or shareholders (but see para. 4.49)
The claimant jointly purchased the property	If the property was purchased freehold the claimant cannot be eligible as he or she falls within the definition of 'owner' (para. 4.16). If the claimant is seeking HB for the share of the dwelling that he or she does not own (e.g. following a relationship breakdown) in most cases he or she will have a right to reside in the property (not just half of it) so the absent joint-purchaser is not in a position to grant a tenancy (also see para. 4.43).

4.24   The DSS has reminded authorities (HB/CTB A30/95 para. 12) that certain people, such as those with learning difficulties, may appear unable to enter into a liability but that someone formally appointed to act for them, such as a receiver appointed by the Court of Protection, can enter into a liability on that individual's behalf and that in such circumstances HB may be payable. The question of a child's or young person's liability to pay rent – particularly when assisted by a social services department – is examined in detail in HB/CTB A16/96.

4.25   In certain circumstances:

◆ a person who is not liable may be treated as liable;

◆ someone who is liable should be treated as not liable.

People who are not liable but who are treated as liable

4.26   People in the following categories may not be liable to pay rent but can be   HBR 6(1)(b)-(e), (2
treated as liable and thus potentially entitled to HB. There are no equivalent
provisions for CTB.

◆ The partner of the liable person;

◆ A former partner of the liable person who has to make the payments in order
  to continue to live in the home because the liable person is not doing so;

◆ Anyone who has to make the payments if he or she is to continue to live in the
  home because the liable person is not making the payments and the authority
  consider it reasonable to treat him or her as liable to make those payments;

◆ A person whose liability is waived by the landlord as reasonable
  compensation for repairs or redecoration work actually carried out by the
  tenant – but only up to a maximum of eight benefit weeks in respect of any
  one waiver;

◆ The partner of a full-time student excluded from HB entitlement (para 20.18);

◆ Someone who has actually met his or her liability before claiming;

◆ Where the rent is varied either during the benefit period or retrospectively,
  the claimant is treated as liable for the revised amount due.

Examples: Treated as liable to pay rent

A claimant has been deserted by her partner. Although she is not the
tenant the landlord will allow her to remain in the property if she
continues to pay the rent. She should be treated as liable if her former
partner is not paying the rent.

A claimant is the son of a council tenant. He takes over responsibility for
paying rent while his father is working abroad for two years. The son
should be treated as liable if it is reasonable to do so.

People who are liable but treated as not liable

4.27   The following paragraphs describe the circumstances in which the   HBR 7(1)
authority should treat someone as not liable to make payments in respect of a   SI 1998/No 3257
dwelling and therefore not entitled to HB. These rules were amended and extended
for all new and repeat claims made on or after 25th January 1999. Anyone who
was in receipt of HB before 25 January 1999 is not subject to the revised rules until
they make a repeat claim at the end of their current benefit period.

CLAIMANTS TREATED AS NOT LIABLE PRIOR TO 25TH JANUARY 1999

4.28   Where a claim for HB was made before 25th January 1999 the claimant should have been treated as not liable to make payments where:

◆ he or she 'resided with' (para. 4.33) a landlord who is a 'close relative' (para. 4.31); or

◆ he or she 'resided with' (para. 4.33) the landlord on a 'non-commercial basis' (para. 4.35); or

◆ he or she was jointly liable and at any time during the eight-week period prior to the creation of the joint liability was a non-dependant of one or more of the other joint occupiers of the dwelling unless the authority is satisfied that the joint liability was not created to take advantage of the HB scheme; or

◆ it appeared to the authority that the claimant's agreement to make payment in respect of the dwelling had been contrived to take advantage of the HB scheme (see para. 4.37) except someone who was, for any period within the eight weeks prior to the creation of the agreement liable to make payments in respect of the same dwelling.

CLAIMANTS TREATED AS NOT LIABLE ON OR AFTER 25TH JANUARY 1999

4.29   Where a new or repeat claim is made for HB on or after 25 January 1999 claimants are treated as not liable to make payments where they fall into any of the categories described in paras 4.30-4.53.

PEOPLE WHO RESIDE WITH CLOSE RELATIVES WHO ARE THEIR LANDLORDS

HBR 7(1)(b)   **4.30**   Where the claimant 'resides with' (para. 4.33) the person to whom he or she is liable to make payments and that person is a 'close relative' (para. 4.31) of the claimant, or of the claimant's partner, the claimant is not entitled to HB.

WHO COUNTS AS A CLOSE RELATIVE?

HBR 2(1)   **4.31**   A 'close relative' is:

◆ a parent, step-parent or parent-in-law; or

◆ brother or sister; or

◆ son, son-in-law, daughter, daughter-in-law, step-son, step-daughter; or

◆ the partner of any of the above.

4.32   Arguably the term 'brother' and 'sister' should be taken to include 'half-brothers' and 'half-sisters' (HB/CTB A27/97 para. 3 (following Commissioner's decision R(SB) 22/87)). 'Step-brothers' and 'step-sisters' are not treated as close relatives for HB purposes (HB/CTB A27/97 para. 4).

WHAT DOES 'RESIDES WITH' MEAN?

4.33   The term 'reside with' is a legal term. The claimant should only be   HBR 3(4)
considered to 'reside with' someone if they share rooms other than a bathroom,
lavatory, areas of common access such as halls and passageways, or rooms of
common use in sheltered accommodation. Consequently the claimant is not
excluded from HB simply because he or she rents accommodation from a close
relative, but because the claimant also resides with that close relative.

NON-COMMERCIAL AGREEMENTS

4.34   Prior to 25th January 1999 where the claimant 'resided with' (para. 4.33)   HBR 7(1)(a)
the person to whom he or she was liable to make payments and the agreement was
not on a commercial basis, the claimant was not entitled to HB. Since 25th
January 1999 where the agreement under which the claimant occupies the
dwelling is not on a commercial basis he or she should be treated as not liable to
make payments in respect of the dwelling. For this rule to apply it is no longer
necessary that the claimant 'resides with' the landlord.

4.35   What constitutes a 'commercial basis' is not defined in the regulations but   HBR 7(1A)
from 25th January 1999 the authority is required to have regard to whether the
agreement contains terms which are not enforceable at law in determining
whether or not it is a commercial one.

4.36   In *R v Sheffield Housing Benefit Review Board ex parte Smith and others,*
The Times, 28th December 1994, QBD, 8th December 1994 it was held that the
authority must not only consider the amount payable for the accommodation but
also the other terms of the agreement. The important factor is whether the
arrangements are at 'arm's length' or more akin to the arrangements that would
exist between close relatives who generally only make contributions to their keep
or household running costs (HB/CTB A30/95 para. 16). More specifically the DSS
advises that an arrangement that involves a former foster child remaining in his or
her foster accommodation and paying rent once the fostering allowance ceases, for
example, where the foster child reaches the age of 18, should not normally be
treated as a non-commercial arrangement (HB/CTB A 30/95 para. 17 iv).

CONTRIVED LIABILITIES

4.37   Where the authority is satisfied that the claimant's liability was created to   HBR 7(1)(l)
take advantage of the HB scheme, the claimant is not entitled to HB. Prior to the
15th January 1999, however, if the claimant was liable to make payments for the
same dwelling at any time within the eight weeks period prior to the creation of

the arrangement that was said to be contrived, he or she could not be excluded from HB entitlement under this provision.

4.38   DSS guidance on contrived liabilities can be found in circular HB/CTB A30/95 paras. 18-22 and A 15/97.

4.39   In *R v Solihull Metropolitan Borough Council Housing Benefit Review Board ex parte Simpson,* 26 HLR 370 QBD) the Court considered that whilst the ability to attract HB could never realistically be the sole purpose of a tenancy, equally, and importantly, anyone eligible for HB must, by definition, have entered into an agreement to pay a rent which he could not afford. The mere fact of having done so could not of itself, except perhaps in extreme cases, be evidence of an arrangement entered in order to take advantage of the scheme. A similar point was made in *R v Housing Benefit Review Board of the London Borough of Sutton ex. p. Keegan,* 27 HLR 92 QBD, 15th May 1992. The judge quashed the review board's decision not to award HB because 'it had attached a wholly disproportionate weight to the fact that the claimant could not meet her liability to pay rent'.

4.40   In the Sutton case the judge considered that before an agreement could be said to be 'contrived' the means, circumstances and intentions of the claimant and the landlord must be considered. In particular, consideration should be given to the consequences if HB is not to be paid. If it seems likely that the landlord will have to ask the claimant to leave the dwelling so that it can be re-let or sold this is evidence that the liability has not been created to take advantage of the scheme.

4.41   In the Solihull case it was held that 'an arrangement whereby persons, who would in any event be eligible for HB, were provided with accommodation by a parent or relation who was then to receive rent generated from HB was not of itself an arrangement created to take advantage of the HB scheme' (26 HLR 370). The DSS has advised authorities that mortgage rescue schemes developed by mortgage lenders to enable owner-occupiers in arrears with mortgage payments and facing repossession to convert the mortgage agreement into a tenancy for rent should not be regarded as contrived to take advantage of the scheme (HB/CTB(92)6).

4.42   *R v Manchester City Council ex parte Baragrove Properties,* 23 HLR 337 QBD, provides an example of the sort of extreme case envisaged in the Solihull judgment. In this case the authority was found to have acted correctly in interpreting the rule as permitting exclusion from HB entitlement cases where landlords were specifically charging higher rents to vulnerable tenants and where the authority could not use its powers to restrict the eligible rent (para. 11.62).

RENTING A FORMER JOINT HOME FROM AN EX-PARTNER

HBR 7(1)(c)   **4.43**   Where a married or unmarried couple separate and the one remaining in the home, or a new partner, makes payments to the one who has left in order to continue living in the dwelling then the person making the payments is treated as not liable.

RESPONSIBILITY FOR THE LANDLORD'S CHILD

4.44   A liable person should be treated as not liable where he or she is responsible, or a partner is responsible, for the landlord's child (i.e. someone under the age of 16). The DSS (A1/99, para. 15) emphasises that 'responsibility for a child' means more than 'cares for'. This is a difficult rule to interpret as it blurs certain established concepts so far as means-tested benefits are concerned. It would appear to apply where the 'landlord' is the biological mother or father of a child, or has adopted a child, but where the child is nevertheless considered to be part of the claimant's family for income support, income-based jobseeker's allowance or HB purposes. HBR 7(1)(d)

RENTING ACCOMMODATION FROM A TRUST OF WHICH THE LIABLE PERSON IS A TRUSTEE OR BENEFICIARY

4.45   A trust is an arrangement under which property is transferred to one or more people known as trustees. Trustees are required to look after the property or deal with it for the benefit of someone else 'the beneficiary' or alternatively for some other purpose such as that of a charity. HBR 7(1)(e)

4.46   A person should be treated as not liable to make payments where the payments are to a trustee of a trust of which one of the following is a trustee or a beneficiary:

◆   the liable person or partner; or

◆   the liable person's or partner's close relative (para. 4.31) if the close relative 'resides with' (para. 4.33) the liable person; or

◆   the liable person's, or partner's, former partner.

4.47   The exception to this rule is where the liable person satisfies the authority that the liability was not intended to take advantage of the HB scheme. In such cases the liable person should be treated as liable. HBR 7(1B)

RENTING ACCOMMODATION FROM A TRUST OF WHICH THE LIABLE PERSON'S CHILD IS A BENEFICIARY

4.48   A person should be treated as not liable to make payments where the payments are to a trustee of a trust of which the liable person's, or the liable person's partner's child is a beneficiary. HBR 7(1)(f)

RENTING ACCOMMODATION FROM A COMPANY OF WHICH THE LIABLE PERSON IS A DIRECTOR OR AN EMPLOYEE

HBR 7(1)(e)   **4.49**   A person should be treated as not liable to make payments where the payments are to a company of which one of the following is a director or an employee:

◆ the liable person or partner; or

◆ the liable person's or partner's close relative (para. 4.31) if the close relative 'resides with' (para. 4.33) the liable person; or

◆ the liable person's, or partner's, former partner.

The DSS advise (A46/99 para.13) that the reference to a 'company' here is to a registered company. Checks with Companies House will reveal whether or not a company is incorporated.

HBR 7(1B)   **4.50**   Again the exception to this rule is where the liable person satisfies the authority that the liability was not intended to take advantage of the HB scheme. In such cases the liable person should be treated as liable. Where someone is employed by a company and is liable to make rental payments to a landlord who is a director of the company this liability is not to the company but to the director and as such is not affected by this rule.

A PERSON WHO WAS PREVIOUSLY A NON-DEPENDANT OF SOMEONE WHO STILL RESIDES WITH THEM

HBR 7(1)(g)
HBR 7(1B)   **4.51**   If the liable person was at any time prior to the creation of the liability a non-dependant of someone who resided and continues to reside in the dwelling the liable person should be treated as not liable. The exception to this rule is where the liable person satisfies the authority that the liability was not intended to take advantage of the HB scheme.

A PERSON WHO PREVIOUSLY OWNED THE DWELLING

HBR 7(1)(h)   **4.52**   If the liable person, or a partner, previously owned the dwelling the liable person should be treated as not liable. The exception to this rule is where the liable person is able to satisfy the authority that he or she or a partner could not have continued to live in the dwelling without letting go of ownership. This could be for a variety of reasons. This would be the case, for example, where the liable person is able to provide evidence that a mortgage lender would have sought possession unless the liable person had agreed to the transfer of the property and the establishment of a rental agreement. The DSS has emphasised (A46/99) that inability to repay a lender money borrowed to purchase the property is only one of the possible reasons. It suggests that another example would be where a housing association agrees to take over ownership of the property and take on the ex-owner as a tenant. In each case the authority will need to obtain from the former owner an explanation of his or her reasons for giving up ownership of the property.

TIED ACCOMMODATION

4.53   A liable person should be treated as not liable if his or her, or a partner's, HBR 7(1)(i) occupation of the dwelling is a condition of employment by the landlord. The DSS emphasise (HB/CTB A1/99 para. 25) that this test should not be taken to mean 'as a result of the employment'. A retired employee, for example, may continue to live in previously tied accommodation but this would no longer be as a condition of employment by the landlord. The retired employee should consequently be treated as liable unless they fell under some other rule that requires them to be treated as not liable.

Occupation as a home

4.54   HB cannot usually be paid for accommodation that has not been occupied HBR 5(1) (moved into) by the claimant. HB is only payable where the dwelling is occupied as a home. Accommodation occupied only for a holiday or business purposes is not a home and therefore is not eligible. It is usually only payable on one home.

4.55   The following paragraphs describe:

◆ how the home normally occupied may be determined;

◆ circumstances in which the claimant may be considered to be occupying two homes at the same time and eligible for HB on both;

◆ circumstances in which the claimant may be treated as occupying the home before moving in;

◆ in what circumstances a claimant may be treated as occupying the home even though she or he is absent from it.

DOES THE CLAIMANT OCCUPY THE DWELLING?

4.56   Doubts about the claimant's occupation of the dwelling can often arise as a result of residency checks by an authority's visiting/fraud officers. If there is any doubt as to whether or not the claimant occupies the dwelling the authority should consider all of the relevant evidence before determining this matter.

DECIDING WHICH HOME IS 'NORMALLY OCCUPIED'

4.57   In considering which home the claimant normally occupies the authority HBR 5(2) must have regard to any other dwelling occupied by the claimant or family in, or outside, Great Britain (England, Scotland and Wales). The DSS advises authorities that this requirement is not intended to exclude from entitlement someone who has set up home in this country but whose family, no longer being part of his household, remain abroad. The purpose of taking account of homes outside GB is to avoid simultaneous payments under the HB schemes in Northern Ireland and Great Britain (GM para. A3.16).

EXCEPTIONS TO THE GENERAL RULE

HBR 5(3)-(4), (7A), (9) **4.58**   The exceptions to the rule that the dwelling normally occupied is the one that the claimant is treated as occupying, apply in certain circumstances where:

◆   the claimant is a single or lone parent student or trainee;

◆   the normal home has been vacated for essential repairs; or

◆   the claimant has left a property through fear of violence in the home or from a former member of the family and has no intention of returning to that property.

DECIDING WHICH HOME A STUDENT OR TRAINEE IS TREATED AS OCCUPYING

4.59   Following the general rule, the claimant should be treated as occupying the normal home (and no other) if he or she is:

◆   single or a lone parent; and

◆   an eligible student or on a government training course; and

◆   liable to make payments (including mortgage payments) in respect of two homes.

HBR 5(3)   **4.60**   If, however, such a claimant only pays for one of the homes, he or she should be treated as occupying the home that he or she pays for, whether or not it is the one in which he or she normally lives.

HBR 5(9)   **4.61**   The training courses referred to are those provided by, or under arrangements made with or approved by, a government department, any Secretary of State, Scottish Enterprise, or Highlands and Islands Enterprise. This definition includes training courses arranged by a local authority on behalf of one of these entities. The training course may be provided by the local authority itself or the local authority may contract with an external organisation to provide the course.

Example: Occupation as a home

The claimant normally lives with her parents but rents accommodation whilst on a government training course. In such circumstances she should be considered as normally occupying the rented accommodation during the period she is liable to pay housing costs.

DECIDING WHICH HOME THE CLAIMANT IS TREATED AS OCCUPYING WHERE THE NORMAL HOME HAS BEEN VACATED FOR ESSENTIAL REPAIRS

4.62   The claimant should be treated as occupying the home for which HBR 5(4) payments (including mortgage payments) must be made, where he or she has:

◆ had to leave the normal home whilst it is having essential repairs; and

◆ has to make payments on either that home or the temporary home, but not both.

If mortgage payments are being made in such circumstances there is no entitlement to HB.

THE NORMAL HOME WHERE THE CLAIMANT HAS LEFT A PROPERTY THROUGH FEAR OF VIOLENCE IN THE HOME OR FROM A FORMER MEMBER OF THE FAMILY

4.63   The claimant should be treated as occupying the formerly-occupied home HBR 5(7A) for a maximum period of four weeks if s/he:

◆ has left and remains absent from it through fear of violence

  • in the home, or

  • by a person who was formerly a member of the claimant's family, and

◆ has no intention to return to it, and

◆ has a liability to make payments in respect of that dwelling which is unavoidable.

4.64   Where this rule applies benefit can only be allowed for the previous home irrespective of whether the claimant also has a new rent liability (but see para. 4.65).

HB ON TWO HOMES

4.65   Normally HB is only payable in respect of a rental liability on one home. HBR 5(5) The following paragraphs set out the circumstances in which the claimant must be treated as occupying two dwellings as a home and thus potentially entitled to HB for both of them.

FEAR OF VIOLENCE

4.66   The authority must treat the claimant as occupying two dwellings for a HBR 5(5)(a) maximum period of 52 weeks where the claimant has left and remains absent from the former dwelling through fear of violence:

◆ in that dwelling; or

◆ by a former member of the claimant's family.

This duty only applies however if:

◆ it is reasonable that HB should be paid in respect of both the former dwelling and the present dwelling occupied as the home, and

◆ the claimant intends to return to occupy the former dwelling as a home.

4.67 It is estimated that there were about 6.6 million incidents of domestic physical assault in England and Wales in 1995 (Department of the Environment, Transport and the Regions, *Relationship breakdown: a guide for social landlords,* 1999). Actual violence need not have occurred, however, for the above conditions to be met. The claimant has only to be afraid of violence occurring. If the authority to not consider, however, that the fear of violence is one that is reasonably held or that the claimant brought it upon themselves, for example as a result of criminal activity, it may consider it unreasonable that HB should be paid in respect of both homes.

4.68 The feared violence in the home need not be related to a family or former family member. It could be related to anyone, e.g., a neighbour, so long as it is feared that violence could occur in the home. Where the fear is of violence outside the home it must be a former member of the claimant's family who poses the threat of violence. This would include not only an ex partner but also an adult child.

4.69 Authorities are advised to check regularly that the claimant intends to return to the previous home (A24/98. para. 10). If the claimant subsequently decides not to return HB on the former home should stop. The HB paid on the former home whilst the claimant had the intention to return will have been properly paid and should not be treated as an overpayment.

STUDENTS/TRAINEES

HBR 5(5)(b) **4.70** If the claimant, or partner, is a student eligible for HB (chapter 20) or is on a training course (para 4.61) and it is:

◆ unavoidable that the partners should occupy two separate dwellings; and

◆ reasonable that housing benefit should be paid in respect of both dwellings,

the authority should treat the claimant as occupying both dwellings as a home and potentially entitled to HB on both of them. There is no time limit on this rule.

LARGE FAMILIES

HBR 5(5)(c) **4.71** Where because of the size of the claimant's family they have been housed by a housing authority in two separate dwellings the claimant should be treated as occupying both dwellings as his home. The GM (para. 3.55.3) indicates that both homes should be local authority owned but there would appear to be nothing within the regulation that requires this. The rule would not apply however if the claimant found his or her own dwellings in the private sector.

UNAVOIDABLE OVERLAPPING LIABILITY

4.72   Where the claimant is liable to make payments in respect of two   HBR 5(5)(d)
dwellings, the authority must treat the claimant as occupying the two dwellings
as a home where he or she:

♦ has moved into the new dwelling; and

♦ could not reasonably have avoided liability in respect of both of them.

In such cases the authority should treat the claimant as occupying both dwellings
as a home for up to a maximum period of four benefit weeks and thus potentially
entitled to benefit on both of them.

4.73   The rule is extending the period that the claimant is treated as occupying
the old dwelling beyond that which would normally be the case and consequently
enabling HB to continue to be paid on the liability attributable to both the old and
new home for a limited period. There is no explicit requirement for a special or
specific claim to be made for the benefit attributable to this overlapping period.
An authority may, however, decide that the movement into the new home is a
change of circumstance that leads it to end the current benefit period and invite a
new claim (para. 17.9-10).

4.74   The GM (para. 3.55.4) indicates that the rule should only be used in
'exceptional circumstances' but there is no such test within the regulation. If the
conditions set out above are met then the authority must treat the claimant as
occupying the two dwellings as a home. The authority does, however, need
information and evidence that will enable it to identify an overlapping liability
and determine whether or not it could reasonably have been avoided.

4.75   This rule would apply for example where a claimant in housing need is
offered at short notice an appropriate new tenancy and is obliged to take up
liability for the new tenancy before the period of notice required by the landlord
of the old home has expired. HB is only payable on both properties during this
period, however, if the claimant has a liability for and has actually moved into the
new property whilst having a liability to make payments on the old home. If the
claimant is still in fact occupying and liable to make payments on the old home
then the fact that he or she has a liability on the new home and may have
transferred some items of furniture does not mean that he or she has met the test
of having 'moved into' the new home. In such instances HB is only payable on
the old home not the new home.

4.76   For this rule to operate both liabilities need to be eligible for HB.
Consequently the rule does not cover periods where the claimant is:

♦ moving into temporary accommodation with the intention or returning to
the former home including circumstances where essential works are being
carried out on the normal home;

◆ moving into owner-occupied property; or

◆ moving into residential care accommodation (para. 4.5-12).

DELAYS MOVING-IN DUE TO DISABILITY-RELATED ADAPTATIONS

HBR 5(5)(e)   **4.77**   A claimant who is liable to make payments in respect of two dwellings should be treated as occupying both dwellings as a home where he or she had to remain in the old home due to a reasonable delay in moving of up to four weeks caused by the requirement to make necessary adaptations to the new home to meet the disablement needs of the claimant or a member of the family (para. 4.79).

CALCULATION OF BENEFIT ON TWO HOMES

4.78   A question that is not explicitly address in either the regulations or DSS guidance is that of how benefit should be assessed in cases where the claimant is treated as occupying two dwellings as a home. The purpose of the above rules is to treat the claimant as occupying two dwellings as a home. Consequently it would appear that in these cases there is one benefit calculation based on the aggregated eligible rent of the two properties. Where the dwellings are in different areas authorities will need to establish agency arrangements (para. 1.12).

ENTITLEMENT PRIOR TO MOVING IN

HBR 5(6)   **4.79**   Normally a person is only treated as occupying the dwelling as a home and consequently entitled to HB from the date he or she moves in. The next paragraph sets out the circumstances in which the authority should treat a claimant as occupying the dwelling prior to moving-in. This determination can, however, only be made once the claimant has actually moved in to the dwelling. Claimants who meet the described conditions are treated as occupying the dwelling as a home and consequently potentially eligible for HB in respect of a maximum period of up to four week prior to actual occupation. Consequently if the claimant is liable to make payments for alternative accommodation during this period they are not able to receive housing benefit for the accommodation actually occupied during this period, i.e. this is not a rule that generally enables HB to be paid on two homes. The one exception is where the delay in moving is necessary to adapt the new home to meet the disablement needs of the claimant or a member of the family. This is also one of the conditions that enables HB to be paid on two homes (para. 4.77).

THE TESTS

4.80   The claimant should be treated as occupying the home for up to four weeks prior to moving-in if the following tests are satisfied:

(a) the claimant has moved into the new home; and

(b) was liable to make payments before moving in; and

(c) claims HB before moving in; and

(d) if the authority refused the initial claim (para. 7.76), a further claim is made or treated as made within 28 days of the date the claimant moved into the dwelling; and

(e) the delay in moving was reasonable; and

- the delay was necessary in order to adapt the building to the disablement needs of the claimant or a member of his or her family; or

- the move was delayed pending the outcome of an application for a social fund payment (para. 2.15) to meet a need related to moving into the dwelling, e.g. to meet the cost of removal or an item of household furniture or equipment; and a member of the claimant's family is aged less than six or the claimant satisfies the conditions for one of the age-related or disability-related premiums (chapter 12); or

- the claimant became liable to make the payments whilst an in-patient or in residential accommodation.

For the date such a claim is considered as made in such circumstances see paras. 7.76-77.

TEMPORARY ABSENCE AND HB/CTB ENTITLEMENT

4.81   The rules of entitlement to HB during periods of temporary absence were amended in April 1995. The same amended rules were introduced into the CTB scheme. Previously CTB had been payable for as long as the claimant was liable for the tax.

4.82   Claimants who are absent from their homes for a temporary period can only obtain HB/CTB for up to 13 weeks, or in particular circumstances (para. 4.85) 52 weeks, from the first day of absence. In *R v Penwith District Council Housing Benefit Review ex parte Burt,* 22 HLR 292, it was held that the absence must be continuous. Consequently if the claimant (with the exception of prisoners on temporary leave) returns to, and occupies the dwelling as a home, even for a short time, the allowable period of temporary absence starts again. The DSS suggests (GM para. A3.25) that a stay at home lasting, for example, only a few hours may not be acceptable but one that lasts at least 24 hours may be acceptable. Depending upon the facts of the case, however, the authority may decide that the claimant's normal home is elsewhere for HB purposes (para. 4.57). If another person occupying the dwelling starts paying rent in the absence of the claimant, the authority should consider treating that other person as liable and therefore eligible for HB (para. 4.26). In the case of the council tax the authority may, in specific instances, decide that an absent claimant is no longer solely or mainly resident in the dwelling and is therefore no longer liable for the tax (paras. 3.20-25).

4.83   To be entitled to HB/CTB during a period of absence:

◆ the claimant must intend to return to live in the dwelling within the 13-week or 52-week period;

◆ the part of the dwelling normally occupied by the claimant must not have been (sub-)let; and

◆ the period of absence must be unlikely to exceed 13 or 52 weeks as appropriate.

4.84   Once it becomes clear that the claimant is going to be away for more than 13 or 52 weeks, HB/CTB entitlement ends. The one exception to this rule concerns those claimants who may be absent for up to 52 weeks and retain entitlement. If their period of absence is unlikely to substantially exceed the 52-week period, and if there are exceptional circumstances, the authority must pay up to the end of the 52nd week of absence. DSS guidance (GM para. A3.31) suggests that the term 'substantially exceed' relates to periods of absence greater than 15 months. It is, however, for the individual authority to interpret the term. The circular illustrates the concept of exceptional circumstances with the examples of:

◆ someone prevented from returning home by an unanticipated event; and

◆ a discharge from hospital being delayed by a relapse.

Other circumstances may however be considered.

4.85   The categories of claimant who may be temporarily absent for up to 52 weeks and retain their HB/CTB entitlement are those:

◆ on remand including those in bail hostels;

◆ in hospital as patients;

◆ undergoing medical treatment or medically approved convalescence but not in 'residential care accommodation' etc (paras. 4.5-13);

◆ undertaking approved training courses (para. 4.61);

◆ providing medically approved care;

◆ providing care for a child whose parent or guardian is receiving medical treatment or medically approved care;

◆ receiving medically approved care but not in 'residential care accommodation' etc (paras. 4.5-13);

◆ certain students eligible for HB, e.g. those absent on residential study;

◆ in fear of violence who are not eligible for HB in the circumstances

Examples: Temporary absence

REMAND AND CONVICTION

A man has been receiving HB for a while. He is then arrested and detained on remand pending his trial.

◆ The authority should assume that he will be absent for no more than 52 weeks (para. 4.85). He therefore remains eligible for HB.

Fifteen weeks later he is tried, found guilty, and sentenced to a term of one year's imprisonment.

◆ Although he may well serve only six months in prison (after remission), and although the 15 weeks he has been on remand will count towards this, his *total* absence from home will now exceed 13 weeks (para. 4.82). So his eligibility for HB ceases, because the fact that he has been sentenced is a change in his circumstances (chapter 17). (But the HB he was awarded for his 15 weeks on remand was nonetheless correctly paid.)

TRYING OUT A RESIDENTIAL CARE HOME, AND THEN

DECIDING TO STAY THERE

A woman who owns her home has been on CTB for a while. She then goes into a residential care home for a six-week trial period to see if it suits her.

◆ She remains eligible for CTB (para. 4.87).

In the third week of her trial period, she decides she likes the care home. In the fourth week she tells her family and the managers of the home that this is the case. In the fifth week the managers make her an offer of permanent accommodation in the care home and she accepts this. She tells the authority straight away.

◆ Her eligibility for CTB ceases once it is clear that she will stay there permanently (para. 4.84), because this is a change in her circumstances (chapter 17). So she is not eligible for CTB from her sixth week in the care home onwards. (But the CTB she was awarded for her first five weeks there was nonetheless correctly paid.)

described in para. 4.66 because, for example, they are staying with close relatives and are not liable to pay rent on two homes but intend to return to occupy their original homes;

◆ receiving temporary care in residential care accommodation etc (paras. 4.5-13) but not those residing there on a trial basis (para. 4.87).

4.86   The term 'medically approved' means certified by a medical practitioner. HB/CTB A8/95 para. 18 advises that a medical practitioner could, for example, be a GP or nurse, and that the approval need not necessarily be in the form of a certificate.

4.87   If a claimant enters residential care accommodation etc (paras. 4.5-13) on a permanent basis he or she is no longer entitled to HB or CTB on the former home (but see chapter 3 for other forms of help with council tax). Where a claimant enters such accommodation with the intention of returning home he or she is entitled to benefit for up to 52 weeks (para. 4.85). Some people, however, go into residential care accommodation on a trial basis to see if it suits them. In these circumstances they should continue to receive HB/CTB for up to 13 weeks where:

◆ they intend to return to their former home if the residential care accommodation etc does not meet their needs; and

◆ the part of the dwelling normally occupied by them is not (sub-)let.

4.88   The 13-week period commences from the date the claimant enters the residential accommodation, provided that the total period of absence including, for example any period staying with a relative immediately before entering the residential care accommodation etc, does not exceed 52 weeks.

People who may be entitled to CTB

CBA 131(3)   **4.89**   To be entitled to main CTB, or second adult rebate, the claimant must be:

◆ liable to pay the council tax in respect of a dwelling; and

◆ a resident of that dwelling.

'Resident' has the same meaning as for council tax purposes (para. 3.21). Non-resident owners are not eligible nor are people under the age of 18 or tenants in houses in multiple occupation. The last two groups may however be entitled to increased HB if the landlord has increased their rents as a result of the introduction of the council tax.

4.90   The additional rules of entitlement relating to second adult rebate are described in chapter 10. As with HB, many full-time students are excluded from main CTB (para. 20.19). From April 1994 new claims from students also fall under the exclusions described in chapter 5. Eligible students may, however, be entitled to second adult rebate if the qualifying conditions for that form of CTB are satisfied (chapter 10).

4.91   There may be circumstances where couples are liable for the council tax at different addresses – for example, where one of the partners is working away for long periods from the couple's home. The DSS (HB/CCB(92)34) advises that where the couple are living at different addresses within the same authority only one of the partners must claim CTB for both – but where the two addresses are in different authorities separate claims must be made to each authority. The circular advises that CTB is calculated on the basis of the couple's income, capital and personal circumstances and divided between the partners.

HBR 7A
CTBR 3(3)

4.92   Unlike HB, there are no rules that enable those who are not liable for council tax to be treated as liable. However, there are rules relating to certain people, but not the CTB claimant, who fall within the categories described in para. 4.28, but where the intention has been to take advantage of the CTB scheme as well as, or instead of, the HB scheme. In such circumstances those individuals become the claimant's non-dependant for main CTB purposes (para. 6.21).

5 'Persons from abroad'

5.1 If the authority determines that the claimant is a 'person from abroad' he or she is not entitled to HB or CTB.

5.2 Significant changes have been made to the benefit entitlements of asylum seekers as a consequence of the provisions contained within the Immigration and Asylum Act 1999. The provisions of the Act as they impact upon HB/CTB are set out in paras 5.3-13. The HB/CTB rules in operation up to April 2000 for asylum seekers, and after that date for other claimants, are set out in the rest of the chapter. Transitional provisions made under the Immigration and Asylum Act ensure that those asylum seekers who were or could have been in receipt of HB/CTB prior to the April 2000 changes retain that entitlement after April 2000.

Implications of the Immigration and Asylum Act 1999

'PERSONS SUBJECT TO IMMIGRATION CONTROL' EXCLUDED FROM BENEFITS AND WELFARE ASSISTANCE

5.3 Section 115 of the Immigration and Asylum Act 1999, effective from April 2000, excludes persons 'subject to immigration control' from entitlement to a range of non-contributory benefits and tax credits including HB and CTB. Other sections of the Act remove the same persons from entitlement to most other major forms of welfare support such as assistance under section 21 of the National Assistance Act 1948 (duty of local authorities to provide accommodation) where their need arises solely because they are or are about to become destitute. Where the person concerned is an asylum seeker, or the dependant of an asylum seeker, alternative support may be available (para. 5.9).

WHO COUNTS AS 'A PERSON SUBJECT TO IMMIGRATION CONTROL'?

5.4 'A person subject to immigration control' means a person who is not a national of an EEA State (para. 5.27) and who:

◆ requires leave (permission) to enter or remain in the United Kingdom but does not have it (i.e. an illegal entrant or someone who has overstayed his or her leave); or

◆ has leave to enter or remain in the United Kingdom which is subject to a condition that he does not have recourse to public funds (such as a visitor or student); or

◆ has leave to enter or remain in the United Kingdom given as a result of a maintenance undertaking (i.e. a resident has formally agreed to sponsor him or her); or

◆ has had leave extended to allow an appeal against a decision to on the grounds that he or she is an asylum seeker;

◆ has leave to enter or remain in the United Kingdom only as a result of a pending appeal against

  • a decision to vary, or to refuse to vary, any limited leave to enter or remain in the United Kingdom; or

  • a requirement to leave the United Kingdom because he or she is an asylum seeker.

SIGNIFICANCE FOR HB/CTB

5.5   So far as the HB/CTB schemes are concerned most such persons 'subject to immigration control' had been previously excluded from entitlement to either benefit (para 5.53). The main groups to lose HB/CTB entitlement from April 2000 are the new asylum seekers who previously would have been determined exempt from the 'person from abroad rules' (para. 5.39).

PEOPLE RETAINING ENTITLEMENT TO BENEFIT

5.6   At the time of writing the relevant regulations are unavailable but the government has set out its proposals in a consultation document produced by the National Asylum Support Service – *Consultation Document on the Main Regulations under Part VI of the Immigration and Asylum Act 1999, November 1999*. It proposes that the following persons from abroad should retain their entitlement to income support, HB and CTB:

◆ people given limited leave to enter or remain in the UK without recourse to public funds who are temporarily without funds where there is a reasonable expectation that their funds will resume, (income support, HB and CTB are payable for a limited period – table 5.1, final bullet point);

◆ people admitted to the UK as a sponsored immigrant, resident in the UK for five years or more (para. 5.65);

◆ people admitted to the UK as a sponsored immigrant, resident in the UK for less than five years and whose sponsor has died (para. 5.65);

◆ ECSMA/Social Charter nationals (para. 5.61) who are lawfully present in the UK.

TRANSITIONAL PROTECTION FOR ASYLUM SEEKERS

5.7   The Government also proposes that there should be transitional protection for those asylum seekers who are in receipt of benefit, or who have an outstanding on-arrival asylum application (who have not received a negative decision on their asylum application) on introduction of the arrangements in April 2000. The transitional protection is expected to cover not only those receiving benefit but also those who may have been eligible to claim income support, HB or CTB at the point of change but had yet to make a claim.

5.8   The transitional protection:

◆ continues until there is a relevant change of circumstances, for example a negative decision on the asylum application;

◆ survives any break in entitlement to benefits;

◆ extends to an asylum seeker's dependants if they have to make a claim for benefit in their own right (for example if a couple separate).

THE ASYLUM SUPPORT SCHEME

5.9   A detailed description of the April 2000 support arrangements for asylum seekers and their dependants is beyond the scope of this Guide. Briefly, section 95 of the Immigration and Asylum Act enables the Home Secretary (through the National Asylum Support Service) to provide support to an asylum seeker and any dependants if he or she appears to be either:

◆ destitute; or

◆ likely to become destitute within a period of 14 days beginning with the date on which the application for support is made.

Destitution is defined as the lack of adequate accommodation or the means to obtain it, and/or the lack of resources to meet other essential living needs.

5.10   Under the support arrangements asylum seekers and dependants may be provided with:

◆ accommodation – on a 'no choice' basis – in clusters throughout the country; and

◆ support for day to day living costs – mainly by vouchers but with a small cash element.

AWARDS OF BENEFIT TO ASYLUM SEEKERS RECORDED AS REFUGEES OR GIVEN EXCEPTIONAL LEAVE

5.11   As was the case prior to April 2000, an asylum seeker who is:

◆ accorded refugee status (i.e. recorded by the Home Secretary as a refugee within the meaning of the Refugee Convention), or

◆ given exceptional leave,

is eligible for HB/CTB from the date the decision is recorded.

5.12   Where the National Asylum Support Service is providing support the support continues for a period of 14 days after the successful asylum seeker is notified of the decision.

RETROSPECTIVE AWARDS OF BENEFIT FOR REFUGEES

5.13   As was the case prior to April 2000 (para. 5.52) if an asylum seeker is recorded by the Home Secretary as a refugee and before that date he or she, or a dependant, was a person subject to immigration control and excluded from benefit entitlement then the refugee may apply for a backdated payment of income support, HB and CTB for the period of exclusion. In order to qualify for retrospective amounts of HB/CTB, the refugee needs to demonstrate an unmet rent and council tax liability during the period.

The tests

5.14   There are a number of tests that can result in the claimant being labelled a 'persons from abroad'. Some of these – 'the main tests' – are relatively common – the others are rare.

THE MAIN TESTS

5.15   The following are the main groups categorised as 'persons from abroad':

◆ those having limited leave to enter or remain in the UK where the leave is conditional on the claimant not resorting to public funds;

◆ those who have had limited leave but have stayed beyond the time permitted ('overstayers'); and

◆ those who are not habitually resident in the 'common travel area'.

5.16   There is a further test that was intended to remove HB/CTB entitlement from certain European Economic Area State (EEA) nationals. This was to have applied where they had been required by the Home Secretary to leave the UK. This test has, however, been rendered inoperable by the courts and is therefore not covered in this Guide (*Remelien v Secretary of State for Social Security and Another R v Same, ex p. Wolke,* House of Lords, November 27, 1997, *The Times,* 1st December 1997)

THE OTHER TESTS

5.17   The following are also 'persons from abroad':

◆ illegal entrants not given leave to remain by the Secretary of State;

◆ those subject to a deportation order which has not been deferred; and

◆ 'sponsored immigrants' for whom another person or persons have taken responsibility for their maintenance who have not been resident in the UK for five years.

Additionally an asylum-seeker who makes his or her claim whilst falling into certain of the above categories is also a 'person from abroad'.

PERSONS FROM ABROAD – A LEGAL TEST NOT A LITERAL DESCRIPTION

5.18   The term 'person from abroad' is a legal one that applies to those claimants who meet the terms of the tests contained in the regulations. It does not apply to all persons from abroad. Equally it can apply to British citizens where they fail the habitual residence test.

5.19   Many claimants, such as those in receipt of income support or on income-based JSA, are exempt from the 'person from abroad' rules. Additionally other claimants are not exempt but are not debarred from HB/CTB as a result of the tests.

DISCREPANCIES BETWEEN THE INCOME SUPPORT/INCOME-BASED JSA RULES AND THE HB/CTB RULES

5.20   To add more complexity the 'person from abroad' rules for income support and income-based JSA are not exactly the same as those for HB/CTB (HB/CTB A5/98). Certain claimants are not entitled to income support or income-based JSA because they are 'persons from abroad' but are not 'persons from abroad' for the purpose of HB/CTB. This is the case, for example, where the claimant is an asylum seeker who has received a negative decision on his or her asylum application but has been given temporary admission to enter the UK and is habitually resident here. It is also the case where the claimant is an illegal entrant who has been given subsequent temporary admission whether or not an application for asylum is also made.

5.21   For the authority to determine that a claimant is a 'person from abroad' for HB/CTB purposes it must be able to show more than that the claimant is not exempt from the tests. It must be able to show how the claimant meets the terms of one or more of the relevant tests.

THE TESTS ONLY APPLY TO THE CLAIMANT

5.22   For HB/CTB purposes the 'person from abroad' tests only apply to the claimant in person. They do not apply to the claimant's partner, regardless of the partner's nationality or immigration status. Where only one partner is excluded from entitlement, the other partner can claim benefit for both of them in the normal way. There is no provision to treat the partner who qualifies for benefit as a single person. Different rules apply in the assessment of IS/JSA(IB).

Table 5.1 PEOPLE EXEMPT FROM THE MAIN 'PERSON FROM ABROAD' TESTS

◆ Claimants who have lived in the Common Travel Area for more than five years – unless there is other evidence which clearly indicates the need for further enquiries about terms of entry, etc;

◆ Recipients of income support or income-based jobseeker's allowance;

◆ EEA nationals who are 'workers' for the purposes of Council Regulation (EEC) No. 1612/68 or (EEC) No. 1251/70;

◆ EEA nationals who have a right to reside in the UK under Council Directive No. 68/360/EEC or No. 73/148/EEC (e.g. the self-employed);

◆ Asylum seekers who satisfy certain conditions;

◆ Refugees;

◆ Claimants given exceptional leave to enter the UK;

◆ Claimants given exceptional leave to remain in the UK;

◆ Claimants who left the territory of Montserrat after 1st November 1995 because of the effect on that territory of volcanic eruption;

◆ Claimants given leave to enter or remain in the UK on the condition that one or more sponsors have given a formal, written undertaking under the 1971 Immigration Act to be responsible for maintaining and accommodating them during their stay, but where all such sponsors have subsequently died;

◆ Claimants subject to a deportation order under the 1971 Immigration Act but their removal from the UK has been deferred in writing by the Home Secretary;

◆ Claimants adjudged illegal entrants by the immigration authorities, who have not been given subsequent leave to enter or remain in the UK but who have nevertheless been allowed to remain with the written consent of the Home Secretary;

◆ Claimants with limited leave to remain in the UK (and thus normally ineligible for HB/CTB as 'persons from abroad) but whose funds from abroad have stopped temporarily. Subject to certain conditions, they cease to be excluded from HB/CTB for up to 42 days in any one period of leave.

5.23 The authority is advised to consider whether a claim should be invited from an ineligible claimant's partner (GM para. C13.71). Such claimants should also be told to seek advice regarding the effect of such a claim on immigration status. Certain non-U.K. nationals are admitted to the UK for a period of 12 months limited leave on the understanding that they will not have recourse to public funds. After 12 months foreign spouses can be granted settled status provided that the Home Office is satisfied that the relationship is continuing and that they are self-supporting. The Authority is not required to inform the Home Office when an ineligible claimant's partner claims benefit (GM C13.71).

DUAL NATIONALITY

5.24 Where a claimant has dual nationality, and would be able to satisfy the PFA tests on the basis of one of these nationalities only, the nationality which gives rise to benefit entitlement should be the one used for HB/CTB purposes.

People exempt from the main 'person from abroad' tests

5.25 Table 5.1 identifies the claimants exempt from the main 'person from abroad tests'. But some of these groups could still fall foul of some of the more unusual 'person from abroad' tests. For example, if an EEA worker is subject to a deportation order which has not been deferred then he or she would become a 'person from abroad' and consequently not entitled to HB/CTB. It should be noted however that persons subject to deportation orders are frequently held in custody pending removal from the UK, so the question of benefit entitlement will not arise. Most authorities ask on their claim form if the claimant has entered the Common Travel Area within the last five years. Only if the claimant indicates that this is the case will the authority go on to consider the 'person from abroad' rules (HB/CTB A7/94, para. 49). If the authority is to determine that someone who has entered the Common Travel Area within the last five years is exempt from the rules it will need to see evidence that supports such a determination. This will often require it to check passports as well as letters and forms from the Home Office and/or seek confirmation from the Home Office of the claimant's current status.

5.26 Most of the categories identified in table 5.1 are self-explanatory but some require clarification.

WHO COUNTS AS EEA WORKER?

5.27 The EEA states are: Austria, Belgium, Denmark, Finland, France, Germany, Greece, Iceland, Ireland, Italy, Liechtenstein, Luxembourg, Netherlands, Norway, Portugal Spain, and Sweden.

5.28   The definition of an EEA worker has become ambiguous due to a growing body of case law. To be classed as an 'EEA worker' a person must be currently, or in certain circumstances (see below) have been, engaged in remunerative work in the UK which is both:

◆ 'effective and genuine'; and

◆ not 'on such a small scale as to be purely marginal and ancillary'.

5.29   European case law has established that no-one should be denied EEA worker status simply because they are working part-time or because they are low paid and need to supplement their income with social security benefits. The DSS suggests that a number of factors should be considered before the authority decides whether any work done by the claimant is 'effective and genuine'. These include:

◆ the period of employment;

◆ the number of hours worked;

◆ the level of earnings; and

◆ whether the work is regular or erratic.

5.30   These factors are meant to be considered as a whole. The presence or absence of any one factor is not, by itself, conclusive.

5.31   The definition of an EEA worker does not include a UK citizen who is working in the UK. Such individuals do not need to exercise rights under European law in order to be able to work in their home state. However British citizens can obtain the status of EEA worker by living and working in another EEA country and then returning to the UK.

5.32   A former worker who retains EEA worker status is one who has worked in the UK in the past and who is:

◆ actively seeking to rejoin the workforce; or unemployed and undergoing retraining; or

◆ voluntarily unemployed in order to take up vocational training linked to a previous job; or

◆ retired after working in the UK for at least 12 months before pensionable age (60 for a woman, 65 for a man) and who has either resided continuously in the UK for more than three years or whose spouse is (or was at the time of marriage) a British national; or

◆ incapable of work through illness or injury sustained while working in the UK and who either:

  • is entitled to UK invalidity or disablement benefit, or

  • previously resided in the UK for two years or more, or

  • has a spouse who is (or was at the time of marriage) a British national; or

◆ seeking reinstatement or re-employment with the same employer after being temporarily laid off.

5.33 Self-employed people have a right to reside in the UK under specific EEC directives and are therefore also exempt.

WHO IS AN ASYLUM SEEKER?

5.34 An asylum seeker is someone normally subject to immigration control who seeks to enter or remain in the UK by applying for asylum as a refugee, or who otherwise indicates a fear of being required to return to his or her country of origin or habitual residence.

5.35 Asylum applications can be made:

◆ on arrival at the port when the person first enters the UK (port applicants), or

◆ later after the person has been allowed into the UK subject to immigration control (in-country applicants).

5.36 Applications are referred by Immigration Officers for determination by the Home Secretary. This now takes about 8 months on average. Applications may be subject to a process of appeal involving several stages via a special adjudicator, Immigration Appeal Tribunal and, ultimately, Judicial Review in the courts.

5.37 The final determination of an asylum application either:

◆ recognises the applicant's refugee status; or

◆ grants the applicant exceptional leave to enter/remain in the UK; or

◆ refuses the asylum application and expels the applicant.

5.38 For immigration purposes, an asylum application is not finally determined until all avenues of appeal are exhausted. No action is taken to require the applicant's departure from the UK in the meantime.

WHO COUNTS AS AN EXEMPT ASYLUM SEEKER FOR HB/CTB PURPOSES?

5.39 From 5th February 1996, the only people seeking asylum who are treated as having 'asylum seeker' status for benefit purposes and consequently exempt from the 'person from abroad' rules are:

◆ port applicants; or

◆ in-country applicants who are nationals of a country which is recognised by the Home Secretary as having undergone an 'upheaval'

EXEMPT PORT APPLICANTS

5.40   Port applicants are asylum seekers who:

◆ make an asylum application at the port when entering the UK (other than on re-entry during any one period of limited leave), and

◆ have entered the UK from outside the Common Travel Area, and

◆ whose application is recorded by the Home Office.

EXEMPT IN-COUNTRY APPLICANTS

5.41   In-country applicants are asylum seekers who make an asylum application:

◆ after entering the UK, whether legally or illegally, or

◆ at the port when entering the UK from another part of the Common Travel Area.

5.42   Additionally they must have come from a country which has subsequently undergone an 'upheaval' of a kind which has led the Home Secretary not to require anyone to return to that country for the time being.

5.43   The Home Secretary issues a list of countries recognised as having undergone an upheaval for use in determining benefit claims from in-country applicants. Each entry on the list remains valid for three months. As information about upheavals can be delayed in reaching the outside world new entries on the list will take effect from the date the events actually occurred rather than the later date when they became known. This means that additions to the list could have a retrospective effect for benefit purposes.

5.44   To be exempt from the 'person from abroad' rules, in-country applicants must:

◆ enter the UK before their home state is added to the 'upheaval list'; and

◆ make an asylum application, which is recorded by the Home Office, within three months of the date their home state is added to the 'upheaval list'.

5.45   In-country asylum applicants who entered the country on the basis of limited leave with no recourse to public funds or with limited leave and have overstayed that period of leave and who are not from a country on the upheaval list will be persons from abroad and not entitled to HB/CTB. Illegal entrants, subsequently given temporary admission, who make in-country applications for asylum are exempt from the 'person from abroad' rules.

END OF EXEMPT ASYLUM SEEKER STATUS

5.46   Exempt asylum seeker status ends on the date of the first negative Home Office decision refusing to grant refugee status or exceptional leave to enter or remain in the UK. This does not mean, however, that such individuals are not entitled to HB/CTB. It simply means that the authority must consider whether or not they meet the conditions contained within the 'persons from abroad' rules.

ASYLUM SEEKERS WHO CLAIMED HB/CTB PRIOR TO 5TH FEBRUARY 1996

5.47 Where HB/CTB was first claimed prior to 5th February 1996 and the claimant has renewed his or her claim without any break in entitlement he or she continues to be an exempt asylum seeker until the date of:

◆ the first negative Home Office decision refusing to grant refugee status or exceptional leave to enter or remain in the UK – if no decision had been made on the asylum application before 5th February 1996; or

◆ the next negative Home Office decision – if:

- a negative decision refusing to grant refugee status, or exceptional leave to enter or remain in the UK, had been made on the asylum application before 5th February 1996, and

- the claimant had a further right of appeal under the immigration rules which had been exercised before 5th February 1996, or which has been exercised within the specified 28 day time limit.

EFFECT OF THE COURT OF APPEAL JUDGMENT AND THE IMMIGRATION AND ASYLUM ACT 1996

5.48 The Court of Appeal in *R. v Secretary of State for Social Security ex p. Joint Council for the Welfare of Immigrants. R. v Secretary of State for Social Security ex parte B,* June 21st, 1996 (*The Times* 27th June 1996) ruled that the February 1996 changes (introduced by regulations to take away the exemption of certain asylum seekers who had not applied for asylum at the port of entry or had not exhausted their rights of appeal) required primary legislation. For a short period, the effect of this ruling was to return matters to the position prior to the introduction of the February 1996 regulations that had introduced the distinction between port of entry and in-country applicants for asylum. Once again, all asylum applicants regardless of whether they claimed on arrival or afterwards became eligible for income support and HB/CTB, and retained their exempt status when appealing against refusal of asylum.

5.49 The Immigration and Asylum Act 1996, given Royal Assent on 24th July 1996, restored the effect of the February 1996 regulations. It also provided that no claim made after Royal Assent could be backdated to cover an earlier period. Asylum seekers who gained exemption from the 'persons from abroad' rules as a consequence of the Court ruling lost that exemption when the new regulations came into force.

POTENTIAL HB/CTB ENTITLEMENT OF NON-EXEMPT ASYLUM SEEKERS

5.50   Asylum seekers who are not exempt, but who have been given temporary admission to the UK and meet the habitual residence test, are not 'persons from abroad' for HB/CTB purposes. A number of authorities have misunderstood the rules in the past and may have mistakenly rejected claims. If such claims are identified, the authority should review its previous determination on the grounds that it had made a mistake as to the law and pay arrears of benefit – subject to the usual 52 week limit. Certain people have been misadvised, or deterred from claiming earlier, and have grounds for claiming a backdated benefit on the basis that either of these events constitutes 'good cause' for failing to make a claim at an earlier date.

BENEFIT ENTITLEMENT FOLLOWING A SUCCESSFUL ASYLUM APPEAL

5.51   Where exempt asylum seeker status end, and where HB/CTB entitlement has also ended because of one or other of the 'persons from abroad' rules, but the claimant is subsequently successful in obtaining refugee status or exceptional leave to enter or remain in the UK on appeal; the claimant has a new HB/CTB entitlement from the date refugee status or exceptional leave to enter or remain in the UK is granted (subject to a valid claim being made).

THE REFUGEE'S POTENTIAL RIGHT TO RETROSPECTIVE HB/CTB

5.52   In those cases where refugee status (but not exceptional leave to remain) is subsequently granted to the claimant, there is a retrospective entitlement to HB/CTB from the date he or she was first excluded as the result of being a non-exempt asylum seeker. There is no limit on the time such claims can be backdated. Retrospective claims under these provisions must be made within 28 days from and including the date the claimant receives the notification that refugee status has been granted. Where the claimant has lived in more than one authority's area during the relevant period, the claim should be made to the authority in which the claimant currently occupies a dwelling as a home.

HBR 7B, sch 1A
CTBR 4D, sch 1A

The main immigration status tests

5.53   People classified as 'persons from abroad' and denied HB/CTB under the immigration status tests include:

◆   certain (mostly non-Western European) nationals who have been granted limited leave under the 1971 Immigration Act to enter or remain in the UK for a set period subject to the condition that they must not have 'recourse to public funds';

◆ certain (mostly non-Western European) nationals who have been granted limited leave to enter or remain in the UK for a fixed period only and who have remained beyond that period of leave (overstayers);

◆ persons who have been given leave to enter or remain in the UK on the condition that one or more sponsors have given a formal, written undertaking under the 1971 Immigration Act to be responsible for maintaining and accommodating them during their stay (unless they have been resident for 5 years or more or all their sponsors have subsequently died).

CLAIMANTS NOT SUBJECT TO THE IMMIGRATION STATUS TESTS

5.54   Certain claimants are not subject to any test of immigration status as a condition of receiving benefit. They are those who:

◆ fall into one of the groups exempt from all of the main 'persons from abroad' tests (table 5.1); or

◆ are a citizen of the United Kingdom, Channel Islands, Isle of Man, Republic of Ireland, Malta, Cyprus or Turkey; or

◆ have been allowed temporary admission to the UK but who have not yet been formally granted leave to remain in, or directed to leave, the UK because a decision is still pending on their immigration status (the exemption only applies until immigration status has been determined).

PERSONS WITH 'LIMITED LEAVE' TO ENTER OR REMAIN IN THE UK

5.55   'Limited leave' means that a person's stay in the UK is subject to a time limit. Having limited leave does not, by itself, bar any person from receiving HB/CTB. Claimants will only be ineligible as 'persons from abroad' where they have limited leave and:

◆ are also subject to the condition that they must not have 'recourse to public funds' during their stay; or

◆ have overstayed beyond the period of limited leave allowed.

5.56   Certain individuals, however, are allowed entry into the UK without being subject to 'limited leave'. These are persons:

◆ who are British Citizens; or

◆ who are nationals from certain European states; or

◆ who are nationals of any state who have been granted 'indefinite leave to remain in the UK'.

5.57   The term 'public funds', as used under the Immigration Rules, does not refer to all social security benefits or public services. It does, however, include:

◆ HB;

◆ CTB; and

◆ income support/jobseeker's allowance.

PERSONS WHO HAVE OVERSTAYED THEIR LIMITED LEAVE

5.58   Overstayers are persons who had limited leave to enter or remain in the UK but remained after the time limit for that leave had expired, including any extensions. Overstayers are classified as 'persons from abroad' and are not entitled to HB/CTB. This applies whether or not their period of limited leave was subject to the 'no recourse to public funds' restriction.

EXEMPT BRITISH AND EUROPEAN NATIONALS

5.59   Anyone with full British Citizenship is exempt from any test of immigration status. The following, however, are only exempt if they have also been granted 'indefinite leave to remain in the UK' or the 'right of readmission to the UK', or the 'right of abode in the UK':

◆ British Dependent Territories Citizens;

◆ British Overseas Citizens;

◆ British Protected Persons; or

◆ British Subjects.

5.60   European nationals able to enter and remain in the UK without being subject to 'limited leave' are those from member states which form part of:

◆ the Common Travel Area (CTA);

◆ the European Economic Area (EEA);

◆ the European Convention on Social and Medical Assistance (ECSMA); or

◆ the Council of Europe Social Charter (CESC);

5.61   The states which make up this group, in addition to the United Kingdom, are: Austria, Belgium, Channel Islands, Croatia, Cyprus, Czech Republic, Denmark, Estonia, Finland, France, Germany, Greece, Hungary, Iceland, Ireland, Isle of Man, Italy, Latvia, Liechtenstein, Lithuania, Luxembourg, Macedonia, Malta, Netherlands, Norway, Poland, Portugal, Romania, Slovakia, Slovenia, Spain, Sweden, Switzerland, Turkey and Ukraine.

SPONSORED IMMIGRANTS

5.62   Certain persons are allowed unlimited leave to enter and remain in the UK only on the strict condition that a friend or relative in this country sponsors them. This involves the sponsor providing a formal, written undertaking under the Immigration Act 1971 agreeing to maintain and accommodate the entrant while that person remains in the UK. Such mandatory sponsorship arrangements have been rare and should not be confused with the more common voluntary declarations of sponsorship which are often given to support applications to enter the UK but which are not themselves a formal condition of entry.

5.63 Prior to February 1996 there was no bar on entrants subject to a mandatory sponsorship arrangement claiming HB/CTB where they satisfied all the other relevant 'persons from abroad' rules. Such entrants are now excluded from HB/CTB in most cases where they make a new claim on or after 5th February 1996. Any cases involving only voluntary sponsorship undertakings remain unaffected, as before.

CLAIMS MADE BEFORE 5TH FEBRUARY 1996

5.64 Persons subject to a mandatory sponsorship arrangement remain entitled to HB/CTB where:

◆ they have claimed, and were entitled to, benefit before 5th February 1996 (including where a later claim was backdated to a date before 5th February under the 'good cause' provisions); and

◆ there has been no break in receipt or entitlement since 5th February 1996 (subsequent renewal claims made within 4 weeks of the end of the previous benefit period count as unbroken claims – otherwise there is no 'linking rule').

CLAIMS MADE ON OR AFTER 5TH FEBRUARY 1996

5.65 People subject to a mandatory sponsorship arrangement who are treated as 'persons from abroad', and not entitled to HB/CTB, are those who make a new claim on or after 5th February 1996, regardless of the date the sponsorship undertaking was made. This does not apply, however, where:

◆ any persons sponsoring the immigrant have all subsequently died; or

◆ the sponsored immigrant has been resident in the UK for a minimum of five years from either:

• the date of the sponsorship undertaking; or

• the date of entry to the UK;

The habitual residence test

5.66 If the claimant is not habitually resident in the Common Travel Area the authority should determine that he or she is a 'person from abroad' and not entitled to HB/CTB. The rule applies to all claimants who are not exempt from all of the 'persons from abroad' tests (table 5.1) irrespective of nationality.

THE MEANING OF 'HABITUAL RESIDENCE'

5.67 The term 'habitual residence' is not defined in the regulations. The DSS (HB/CTB A7/94 annex 3, para. 4) described the term as 'intended to convey a degree of permanence in the claimant's residence in the Common Travel Area'. The term 'habitual residence' arises in European legislation, in particular EEC Regulation 1408/71 dealing with social security for migrant workers and in family law.

'HABITUAL RESIDENCE' IN EUROPEAN SOCIAL SECURITY LAW

5.68   In *Angenjeux v. Hakenberg* [1973] ECR 935 the Court ruled that 'the place where one habitually resides must be understood in the case of a business representative... as the place in which he has established the permanent centre of his interests and to which he returns in the intervals between his tours'. In *Di Paolo v. Office National de l'Emploi* [1977] ECR 315 the Court ruled that where a person habitually resides also corresponds with where the habitual centre of his interests is situated. The Court also ruled that account should be taken of the length and continuity of residence before the person concerned moved, the length and purpose of his absence, the nature of the occupation found in the other member state and the intention of the person concerned as it appears from all the circumstances.

5.69   The judgment in the *Di Paolo* case emphasised that whenever a worker has stable employment in a member state there is a presumption that he resides there, even if he has left his family in another state.

5.70   The authority must establish the relevant facts on which it can make a determination as to whether or not someone is 'habitually resident'. Drawing on the relevant European case law, the DSS suggests (HB/CTB A7/94) that the authority, in deciding this question, should consider the following factors:

◆ length and continuity of residence;

◆ future intentions;

◆ employment prospects;

◆ reasons for coming to the UK; and

◆ centre of interest.

'HABITUAL RESIDENCE' IN FAMILY LAW

5.71   The prime authority on the ordinary and natural meaning of 'habitual residence' is the speech of Lord Brandon in *Re J (A Minor) (Abduction)* [1990] 2 AC 562. This was a case on the Convention on the Civil Aspects of International Child Abduction. Lord Brandon emphasised that: 'there is a significant difference between a person ceasing to be habitually resident in country A, and his subsequently becoming habitually resident in country B. A person may cease to be habitually resident in country A in a single day if he or she leaves it with a settled intention not to return to it but to take up long-term residence in country

B instead. Such a person cannot however, become habitually resident in country B in a single day. An appreciable period of time and a settled intention will be necessary to enable him or her to become so.'

PERSUASIVE COMMISSIONER'S DECISIONS

5.72 There are a number of Commissioner's decisions relating to the test of habitual residence within the income support scheme that must be considered persuasive for HB/CTB purposes. These decisions have adopted the key criteria of 'an appreciable period of time' and a 'settled intention'. The following key points arose from CIS 1067/1995:

◆ residence implies a more settled state than mere physical presence, thereby excluding short stay visitors;

◆ to be a resident the claimant must be seen to be making a home here;

◆ the home need not be his or her only home, nor need it be intended to be a permanent one, but it must be a genuine home for the time being;

◆ the length, continuity and general nature of a claimant's actual residence are more important than his or her intentions as to the future;

◆ a person may abandon habitual residence in a single day but this does not mean that he or she becomes a habitual resident of another country to which he or she intends to move;

◆ an appreciable period of time, as well as a settled intention, is necessary to enable the claimant to become habitually resident; and

◆ what counts as an 'appreciable period of time' must depend on the facts in each case – it must, however, be the kind of period which demonstrates a settled and stable pattern of living as a resident.

5.73 Commissioner's Decision CIS/2326/1995 agreed with the main points of CIS 1067/1995. It emphasised, however, that no particular periods should be mentioned as amounting to an appreciable period of time except in relation to actual cases that arise for decision. The Commissioner considered that the question in each individual case must be whether, in all the circumstances, including the settledness of the person's intentions as to residence, the residence has continued for a sufficient period for it to be said to be habitual.

LATEST DEVELOPMENTS

5.74 The House of Lords upheld the Commissioner decision in CIS 2326/1995. It found that an appreciable period of time of actual residence is needed to establish habitual residence for people coming to the UK for the first time (Nessa v CAO, [1999] 1 WLR 1937). Meanwhile the European Court of Justice in Case C-90/97 Swaddling v CAO (ECJ 25 February 1995) has ruled that a UK claimant who had returned to Britain after living and working in France for several years could not have his right to benefit made subject to any period of actual residence here after his return by the 'habitual residence' test.

5.75 The DSS has accepted that people returning to the UK from an EU member state and re-establishing their ties here should be treated as habitually resident immediately upon their return (see DSS Press Release 99/132, 14 June 1999). Authorities should do the same. Indeed the DSS has gone further than the principle established in the European Court case. Circular A12/99 (para. 5) advises authorities to extend the effect of the judgment to people of any nationality returning from any country overseas and re-establishing their ties in the UK, Republic of Ireland, Channel Islands or Isle of Man. In other words, they should be treat as habitually resident immediately on return. The DSS has also stated its intention to reduce the period when habitual residence enquiries are made from five years to two years (see DSS Press Release 99/132, 14 June 1999).

6   The claimant's household

6.1   This chapter describes:

◆ the different types of claimant, and different categories of people who may live in the claimant's household;

◆ the circumstances in which the claimant is considered to be responsible for a child or young person for HB and main CTB;

◆ the circumstances in which partners and children or young people are treated as members of the claimant's household; and

◆ other people who may reside with the claimant or live in the same dwelling.

6.2   Authorities need to identify and define the people who live with the claimant to work out HB/CTB entitlement since:

◆ only one member of what counts as the claimant's family for benefit purposes can claim HB/CTB;

◆ in the case of second adult rebate, partners and/or jointly liable persons can affect entitlement;

◆ in the case of HB/main CTB fixed deductions are made in certain cases for other people who live in the claimant's household who are classified as 'non-dependants';

◆ second adult rebate is worked out on the basis of the gross income of certain people who reside with the claimant known as 'second adults';

◆ the amount of HB/main CTB a non-income support/income-based JSA claimant receives is worked out with reference to the combined needs (in the form of the applicable amount) and the income and capital of the claimant's family;

◆ money from (sub-)tenants and boarders is taken into account in the case of a non-income support/income-based JSA claimant's income for HB/main CTB.

Household composition

6.3   The term 'household' is not defined in legislation. It should be given its normal everyday meaning, that is a domestic establishment containing the essentials of home life. People living in one dwelling (for example a house or flat) do not necessarily live together in the same household. The claimant's household may consist of:

♦ the claimant;

♦ the claimant's family;

♦ any other person who lives in the dwelling and who is classified as a 'non-dependant' for HB/main CTB.

In addition to the above, certain other people such as joint occupiers, (sub-)tenants, boarders and carers may live in the same dwelling as the claimant. Those 'non-dependants' and carers aged 18 or over who are not disregarded for the purpose of the council tax (appendix 6) count as 'second adults' for the purpose of second adult rebate.

CLAIMANT

6.4   The claimant may be: HBR 2(1)
                                                                          CTBR 2(1)

♦ single – i.e. a claimant who does not have a partner and is not responsible for a child/young person; or

♦ a lone parent – i.e. someone who does not have a partner but who is responsible for and is a member of the same household as a child/young person; or

♦ a member of a married or unmarried couple or polygamous marriage.

THE FAMILY

6.5   The claimant's family for benefit purposes consists of: CBA 137(1)

♦ the claimant's partner(s), if a member of the same household; and

♦ any children or young persons the claimant is responsible for and who are members of the household (not just sons and daughters).

PARTNER

6.6   A partner is included in all instances where he or she is married or   CBA 137(1)
polygamously married or, in the case of a couple, unmarried but living together   HBR 2(1)
                                                                          CTBR 2(1)
as husband and wife. The partner must be a member of the same household and, except in polygamous marriages, must be of the opposite sex to the claimant.

LIVING TOGETHER AS HUSBAND AND WIFE

6.7   A married couple are treated as one unit as long as they are members of the same household. Either but not both may claim benefit. The same rules apply to an unmarried couple who are 'living together as husband and wife'.

6.8   Neither the Act nor regulations define the phrase 'living together as husband and wife'. The administration of this particular rule can give rise to serious financial and relationship problems. For example, if a man who has a high income starts living with a woman with a low income and the authority determines that they are 'living together as husband and wife' the woman may lose the whole of her benefit entitlement under this rule though she receives no money from the man. The High Court decision in *Crake and Butterworth v the Supplementary Benefit Commission* (1982) established that the first test when a man and woman appear to be living together as husband and wife is that of the purpose of the parties in living together. The HB/CTB schemes recognise many different ways in which a man and woman could live together in the same household, e.g. joint occupiers, landlady/lodger, etc.

6.9   If the purpose of the parties is unclear, the question of whether a couple are living together as husband and wife can only be decided by looking at their relationship and living arrangements and asking whether they can reasonably be said to be that of a married couple. Whilst the phrase 'living together as husband and wife' existed in the former HB scheme, it attracted most attention with the former supplementary benefit scheme as the 'co-habitation rule'. A body of case law developed. This suggests that the following factors need to be considered before deciding that a couple are 'living together as husband and wife':

◆   whether or not they share the same household;

◆   the stability of the relationship;

◆   the financial arrangements;

◆   the presence or absence of a sexual relationship;

◆   shared responsibility for a child;

◆   public acknowledgment that they are a couple.

Whilst all these factors should be considered, none individually is conclusive.

POLYGAMOUS MARRIAGE

HBR 2(1)
CTBR 2(1)

6.10   A polygamous marriage is any marriage where there is more than one spouse. No marriage that takes place in the UK is valid if one of the partners is already married. Some other countries allow such marriages and these should be taken into account for HB/CTB purposes where they took place under the law of such a country.

PARTNER'S MEMBERSHIP OF THE SAME HOUSEHOLD

HBR 15(1),(2)
CTBR 7(1)

6.11   Any partner is normally treated as a member of the same household even when he or she is temporarily living away from the other members of the family. Temporary absence is not defined for the purpose of CTB but for the purpose of HB the partner is no longer counted as a member of the household where he or she is living away from the other members of the family and:

◆   does not intend to resume living with them; or

◆   the absence is likely to exceed 52 weeks, unless there are exceptional circumstances where the person has no control over the length of the absence such as hospitalisation and the absence is unlikely to be substantially more than 52 weeks.

CHILDREN AND YOUNG PERSONS

6.12   A child is defined as someone under the age of 16. A young person is someone aged 16 or over but under 19, not on income support or income-based JSA, nor in advanced education, who is treated as a child for child benefit purposes.

HBR 2(1), 13
CTBR 2(1), 5

6.13   To be treated as a child for child benefit the young person must receive 'relevant education', i.e. over 12 hours per week supervised study not above 'A' level, (G)NVQ level 3, OND, Scottish Higher Certificate or equivalent, at a recognised educational establishment or at some other place that the Secretary of State agrees to (the latter circumstance being confirmed by receipt of child benefit). Though child benefit is not payable for any week the young person is in full-time work, he or she is still treated as a child for child benefit purposes after leaving 'relevant education' up to and including the week of the appropriate terminal date or the first Monday before his or her 19th birthday whichever comes first. The terminal date is:

♦ the first Monday in January; or

♦ the first Monday after Easter Monday; or

♦ the first Monday in September. (From 1998, this is the terminal date for all 16-year-old school leavers: circular HB/CTB A45/97.)

6.14   Child benefit can be paid for an extended period beyond the terminal date where:

♦ the young person is registered for work/training under Youth Training (YT);

♦ the young person has not started YT;

♦ the young person has not reached the age of 18;

♦ the young person is not in remunerative work (paras. 9.33-36);

♦ child benefit was payable immediately before the extension period; and

♦ payment during the extension period has been requested in writing.

The child benefit extension period begins at the terminal date. If the terminal date is in September the extension period ends the week before the first Monday in January. For other terminal dates the extension period ends 12 weeks later.

6.15   Once the young person is no longer counted as a child for child benefit purposes he or she becomes a non-dependant for HB/main CTB purposes and HB and CTB claims should be re-assessed to exclude the young person's personal allowance and, where appropriate, the family premiums as well as any income the young person had. In the case of HB/main CTB no non-dependant deduction is made for anyone under 18 (table 9.2). Non-dependants, aged 18 or over, who are not disregarded for the purpose of council tax discounts (appendix 6) count as second adults for second adult rebate.

RESPONSIBILITY FOR A CHILD OR YOUNG PERSON

HBR 14(1), 2(a)
CTBR 6(1), (2)(a)

6.16 The claimant is considered responsible for any child or young person he or she normally lives with. This is usually straightforward but where the child or young person spends equal amounts of time in different households (e.g. where the parents have separated), or where there is doubt over which household he or she is living in, the child or young person is treated as normally living with the person who gets the child benefit. If no-one gets child benefit, the child or young person is considered the responsibility of:

HBR 14(2)(b)
CTBR 6(2)(b)

◆ the person who has claimed child benefit; or

◆ the person the authority considers has 'primary responsibility' if more than one person has made a claim for the child benefit or no claim has been made.

HBR 14(3)
CTBR 6(3)

A child or young person can only be the responsibility of one person in any one benefit week. If the claimant has a child or young person who lives with him or her and that child or young person in turn has a child, for example, the claimant's daughter and the daughter's baby, the authority must decide whether the daughter is dependant on the claimant or forms a family of her own. If the daughter receives income support (or income-based JSA) for herself and her baby she should not be considered part of the claimant's family.

CHILD/YOUNG PERSON'S MEMBERSHIP OF THE SAME HOUSEHOLD

HBR 15(1),(2)
CTBR 7(1)

6.17 Where the claimant is treated as responsible for a child or young person, that child or young person is counted as a member of the claimant's family even where he or she is temporarily living away from the other members of the family. Temporary absence is not defined for the purposes of CTB, but for the purposes of HB the child/young person is no longer counted as a member of the household where he or she is living away from the other members of the family and:

◆ does not intend to resume living with them; or

◆ the absence is likely to exceed 52 weeks, unless there are exceptional circumstances where the person has no control over the length of the absence such as hospitalisation and the absence is unlikely to be substantially more than 52 weeks.

6.18 The child/young person is also not counted where he or she is:

HBR 15(4)(a)
CTBR 7(3)(a)

◆ absent from the claimant's home and being looked after by, or in Scotland in the care of, a local authority;

BR 15(3)(a),(4)(b)
TBR 7(2)(a),(3)(b)

◆ placed with the claimant or partner by a local authority or voluntary organisation, or in Scotland boarded out with the claimant or partner; or

◆ placed for adoption or custodianship with the claimant or partner or elsewhere (though once adopted, he or she becomes a member of the household).

HBR 15(3)(c),(4)(c)
CTBR 7(2)(c),(3)(c)

6.19 A child or young person in local authority care who lives with the claimant under supervision must be treated as a member of the household. So must a child or young person in care who returns to live with the claimant for part or all of a benefit week if, given the nature and frequency of the visits, it is reasonable to do so.

HBR 15(5)
CTBR 7(4)

6.20 A child or young person who is absent in any other circumstance, e.g. attending boarding school, is treated as a member of the claimant's household.

Non-dependants

6.21 A non-dependant is someone who normally resides with the claimant such as an adult son or daughter, or other relative, or a person treated as not liable to make payments in respect of the dwelling for HB (para. 4.27) and related provisions for CTB (para. 4.92) but specifically excludes:

HBR 3(1),(2)
CTBR 2(1)

◆ members of the claimant's benefit family (para. 6.5);

◆ a child or young person who lives with the claimant but who is not a member of the claimant's household (paras. 6.17-20), e.g. foster children;

◆ the persons identified in paras. 6.23-26.

Non-dependants cannot claim HB/CTB for any payments they make for their keep. Such payments are disregarded from the claimant's income (table 13.4) – instead a fixed deduction is usually made from the claimant's HB/main CTB where a non-dependant is present (para. 9.21). If a claimant resides with his or her landlord neither the landlord nor a member of the landlord's family, e.g. a landlady's adult daughter, are treated as non-dependants of the claimant.

6.22 For HB purposes a person does not count as normally residing with the claimant if that person:

HBR 3(4)
sch 1 para 7

◆ only shares a bathroom, lavatory and/or communal area (e.g. halls, passageways and rooms in common use in sheltered accommodation); or

◆ is visiting the claimant and normally resides elsewhere.

Thus people in self-contained accommodation within the same building as the claimant, e.g. a granny annex, do not count as non-dependants even if they share a bathroom and lavatory with the claimant. There is no definition of 'residing with' in the CTB rules.

Other people who may live in the claimant's dwelling

BOARDERS

HBR sch 4 para 42
TBR sch 4 para 21

6.23   A boarder is someone who is liable to pay the claimant an accommodation charge which includes payment for at least some cooked or prepared meals made and consumed in that accommodation or associated premises. A person whose payment does not include an element for some cooked or prepared meals should be treated as a tenant or sub-tenant (para. 6.25). Income from a boarder is taken into account in the assessment of a non-income support/income-based JSA claimant's income in a different way from that of a tenant or sub-tenant (table 13.4). Boarders can claim HB but not CTB in their own right.

JOINT OCCUPIERS

HBR 3(2)(d)
CTBR 3(2)(d)

6.24   A joint occupier is someone other than the claimant's partner who is jointly and severally liable with the claimant to pay council tax in respect of the dwelling for CTB purposes; and/or is jointly liable with the claimant to make payments in order to occupy the dwelling for HB purposes, e.g. joint tenants. Joint occupiers may be eligible for the appropriate benefit in their own right. For the purpose of calculating benefit the total council tax and/or rent will be apportioned between them (paras. 11.4 and 11.111-11.114).

TENANTS AND SUB-TENANTS

HBR sch 4 para 20
CTBR sch 4
para 20

6.25   A tenant or sub-tenant is someone who is contractually liable to pay the claimant for the right to occupy part of the claimant's accommodation, but who is not:

◆ a member of the claimant's family;

◆ a non-dependant;

◆ a joint occupier;

◆ a boarder.

Where the payment includes something for meals the person should be treated as a boarder (para. 6.23). A formal tenancy or sub-tenancy does not have to exist for someone to be treated as a tenant or sub-tenant for HB/CTB purposes, nor does this treatment create or imply the existence of a legal tenancy or sub-tenancy. In this respect the HB/CTB regulations and the landlord/tenant provisions of the Housing and Rent Acts do not accord precisely. A tenant or sub-tenant is able to claim HB in his or her own right. However, where the authority thinks the tenancy or sub-tenancy is contrived, HB is not awarded and instead the tenant or sub-tenant is treated as a non-dependant. For the treatment of the claimant's income from a tenant or sub-tenant see table 13.4.

A CARER

6.26   A carer does not count as a non-dependant (or boarder) if he or she is looking after the claimant or partner and engaged by a charitable or voluntary organisation (not a public or local authority) which makes a charge for the service provided, even if the charge is paid by someone else.

HBR 3(2)
CTBR 3(2)

SECOND ADULTS

6.27   Non-dependants and carers, if they are aged 18 or over and are not disregarded for the purpose of council tax discounts (para. 3.37), count as second adults for the purpose of second adult rebate (chapter 10).

7 Making a claim

7.1 This chapter describes how to claim HB and CTB (including both main CTB and second adult rebate), and the various things that happen during the life of a claim. It covers:

◆ how and where to make a claim;

◆ what constitutes an effective claim;

◆ information and evidence;

◆ the life of a claim;

◆ the date of claim;

◆ the first day of entitlement;

◆ the duration of the benefit period;

◆ the last day of entitlement;

◆ renewal claims; and

◆ backdating.

This chapter does not cover the different rules for claiming HB/CTB 'extended payments' – which are in Chapter 17.

General rules

CLAIMING HB OR CTB OR BOTH

7.2 Although HB and CTB are legally distinct benefits, it is usually possible to make a combined claim for both. There are, however, categories of claimant who are eligible to claim only one of these benefits (e.g. CTB only in the case of a home owner) and authorities which administer only one benefit and not the other (paras. 1.10-11). Also, in theory, authorities may administer the two benefits separately and require independent claims for each. Furthermore it is perfectly possible for someone who is eligible for both benefits to claim only one if that is what he or she wishes.

CLAIMING MAIN CTB OR SECOND ADULT REBATE OR BOTH

7.3 CTB is a single benefit. As the DSS points out (GM para. B2.1), a claim for CTB is therefore a claim for both main CTB and second adult rebate. An authority receiving a claim for CTB has a duty to consider entitlement to both. Some claimants qualify for only one: for example, a claimant with no second adults can only qualify for main CTB. Also, some claimants may wish to be considered for second adult rebate only: for example a wealthy claimant with a second adult who has no income. In such cases, the claimant is making a claim for CTB which nonetheless covers both types.

COUPLES

7.4   In the case of a couple (or polygamous marriage) one partner makes the claim on behalf of both. They may choose between them which partner this is to be. If they cannot agree, the authority must choose. Some authorities ask both partners to sign their claim forms. It would usually be unreasonable for them to reject an otherwise complete claim form signed by only one.   HBR 71(1)
CTBR 61(1)

7.5   In some cases a couple may be better off if one partner rather than the other is the claimant. These are identified in this guide as they arise. In general, if the 'wrong' partner claims, the authority ought, as good practice, to return the claim form (having kept a photocopy) inviting the 'right' partner to sign it instead.

APPOINTEES

7.6   A claim may be made by a third party, known as an 'appointee', if the claimant is unable, for the time being, to act. In such cases, the appointee takes over all rights and responsibilities in relation to the HB/CTB claim. DSS guidance on appointees is in circular HB/CTB A16/97.   HBR 71(2)-(6)
CTBR 61(2)-(6)

7.7   The authority may accept a claim from:

◆ a receiver appointed by the Court of Protection;

◆ an attorney;

◆ in Scotland, a tutor, judicial factor, curator or other guardian; or

◆ a person appointed by the DSS to act on the claimant's behalf in connection with some other benefit.

7.8   In any other case, the authority may accept a written request from anyone over 18 to be an appointee, for example, a friend, a social worker or a solicitor.

7.9   Either the authority or the appointee can terminate the appointment by giving four weeks' written notice. It has become more common for landlords to request to act as appointees for their tenants. In these and all other cases it is appropriate for the authority to consider any potential conflict of interests before agreeing to the request.

How and where to make a claim

7.10   There are three ways of claiming HB/CTB, dealt with in turn in the following paragraphs:

- in parts of the country where the 'One' project is being piloted, certain claimants may make their HB/CTB claim via a gateway office;

- in any other case, people making a claim for income support or income-based jobseeker's allowance may make their HB/CTB claim at the same time via the Benefits Agency or Jobcentre;

- in all cases, people may make their HB/CTB claim direct to the local authority.

Claims via gateway offices ('One')

7.11   In certain parts of the country, a claim for HB and/or CTB may be made at a 'gateway office'. This is the legal term for what is also known as a 'One' office. 'ONE' is the new name for the Single Work-focused Gateway pilot. Its principal aims are to provide a single location for people who could be expected to work, at which they can get help with finding work and claim all relevant benefits on just one form.

GATEWAY OFFICES

HBR 2(1)
CTBR 2(1)

7.12   The Secretary of State nominates which offices are gateway offices. A gateway office may be located in a Benefits Agency or Jobcentre office or in an office designated by the local authority. In each case, the authority's HB/CTB claim form (or information attached to it) must give the details and state that this is an office at which HB/CTB may be claimed. Gateway offices may be staffed by Benefits Agency or Jobcentre employees or by staff or contractors of the local authority.

WHO MAY CLAIM HB/CTB AT A GATEWAY OFFICE

HBR 72(4)(d)
CTBR 62(4)(d)

7.13   A claimant may make a claim for HB/CTB at a gateway office if he or she:

- is aged 16 or more but under 60; and

- is not in remunerative work (para. 9.33).

7.14   This is in addition to any other office at which he or she may claim HB/CTB (para. 7.10); and at present no-one can be required to claim HB/CTB via a gateway office. Generally speaking, changes of circumstances may also be notified to a gateway office (chapter 17).

METHOD OF CLAIM

7.15   The details of the 'One' claim procedures differ nationally, but usually claimants are offered an extensive interview at the gateway office. There, they complete or are assisted to complete a lengthy claim form, providing information needed for the benefits relevant to their circumstances. A claim made to a gateway office does not – in its initial stages – have to be in writing (para. 7.36).

7.16   Further procedural arrangements vary nationally, but generally speaking:

◆   the gateway office forwards the above-mentioned claim form (or relevant parts of it, or relevant details) to the authority;

◆   the gateway office or the Benefits Agency notifies the authority of whether the claimant is entitled to IS or JSA(IB) and of other matters similar to those in paragraph 7.20;

◆   on receipt of a claim made via a gateway office, the authority may or may not need further information, evidence, etc. (para. 7.37), and may or may not have to refer the details to the rent officer (chapter 8).

Claims via the Benefits Agency or Jobcentre

7.17   Everyone who makes a claim for income support (IS) or income-based jobseeker's allowance – JSA(IB) – is invited to claim HB and CTB at the same time. Special rules apply in areas with 'gateway offices' (para. 7.11). The following paragraphs describe how this works in all other areas, and include information on the DSS's guidance on liaison between authorities and Benefits Agency and Jobcentre offices (GM paras. C7.01-30). The official forms (NHB1, etc.) are summarised in table 7.1 (and samples are given in GM chapter C7 annex A). The Jobcentre deals with claims for JSA(IB); the Benefits Agency (BA) deals with claims for IS and also with part of the administration of JSA(IB). In many areas, Jobcentre and BA staff are located in the same office.

METHOD OF CLAIM

7.18   With exceptions in areas with 'gateway offices' (para. 7.11), everyone claiming IS or JSA(IB) is given three forms:

HBR 2(1), 72(4)(a
CTBR 2(1), 62(4)(

◆   a claim form for IS or JSA(IB);

◆   a claim form for HB – form NHB1(HB); and

◆   a claim form for CTB – form NHB1(CTB).

7.19   The HB and CTB forms are known collectively as 'NHB1 forms'. An IS claimant is invited (in the covering notes) to complete all three forms and return them to the BA. A JSA(IB) claimant is invited to complete them and return them to the Jobcentre (which forwards them to the BA). Claimants who want only HB or only CTB need return only the relevant forms.

BENEFITS AGENCY PROCEDURE ON RECEIPT OF NHB1 FORMS

AA s. 127(1),
128(1)
HBR 72(4)(c)
SI 1988 No. 662
CTBR 62(4)(c), 92

7.20   The Benefits Agency keeps the NHB1 forms until the claimant's entitlement to IS or JSA(IB) is decided. The Benefits Agency then forwards them to the authority within two working days or as soon as reasonably practicable. They are sent with a decision form – form NHB(IS) or form NHB(JSA). These forms include:

◆ the name of the claimant and any partner;

◆ the address;

◆ national insurance numbers when known;

◆ whether HB, CTB or both have been claimed on the NHB1 forms;

◆ the date of the claim for IS or JSA(IB);

◆ whether the claimant is entitled to IS or JSA(IB);

◆ if the claimant is entitled to IS or JSA(IB), the date entitlement begins (and, if known, the date it ends); and

◆ in some cases, if the claimant is not entitled to IS or JSA(IB), the reason why not.

HBR 2(1), 72(3)
CTBR 2(1), 62(3)

7.21   To assist with these procedures, authorities are required to notify the Benefits Agency of the address to which it may send forms and correspondence about HB and CTB. This need not be the same as the authority's 'designated office(s)' (para. 7.31). If HB and CTB are administered by two separate departments of the same authority, it is up to the authority to distribute Benefits Agency forms and correspondence as appropriate.

AUTHORITY PROCEDURE ON RECEIPT OF NHB1 FORMS

7.22   On receipt of an NHB1 form, the authority may or may not need further information, evidence, etc. (para. 7.37), and may or may not have to refer details to the rent officer (chapter 8). In particular, in the case of private and housing association tenants' claims for HB, the authority is likely to need more information about rent. Sometimes the authority's normal application form is used for this.

7.23   If the claimant has been awarded IS or JSA(IB), information included on form NHB(IS) or NHB(JSA) (the decision forms) is binding on the authority in two respects:

◆ as proof of the claimant's entitlement to IS or JSA(IB) at the date shown;

◆ as proof that (at the date shown) the claimant therefore fulfils the income-related conditions for receiving maximum HB and/or maximum CTB (chapter 9).

7.24   The second point above was established in *R v Penwith District Council ex parte Menear,* QBD, (1991) 24 HLR 120, a case about HB. In that case the DSS had decided that a man and a woman were not a couple and that the woman was entitled to income support. The authority decided they were a couple and refused the woman maximum HB. The court held that the authority was not entitled to do this.

7.25   In other respects the authority must make its own determination about entitlement to HB/CTB. Since the Benefits Agency does not screen out ineligible HB/CTB claimants, authorities may receive forms from people not eligible for HB, such as owner-occupiers and non-householders, and from people not eligible for CTB, such as tenants in houses in multiple occupation. (Different considerations apply in the case of claims for HB/CTB 'extended payments': chapter 17.)

AUTHORITY FOLLOW-UP PROCEDURES

7.26   To avoid a breach of confidentiality, the authority should notify the Benefits Agency if the claimant is not entitled to HB/CTB at the outset of the claim, or later ceases entitlement. It should also notify the Benefits Agency of any change of circumstances likely to affect entitlement to income support. This should normally be done within five days.

AA s. 127(2),
128(2)
SI 1988 No. 662
CTBR 93

BENEFITS AGENCY FOLLOW-UP PROCEDURES

7.27   The Benefits Agency keeps a record of NHB1 forms forwarded to the authority. When the Benefits Agency hears of a change of circumstances likely to affect entitlement to HB or CTB, it sends details to the authority. It also notifies the authority if entitlement to IS or JSA(IB) ends. In both cases, the Benefits Agency uses form NHB(IS) or form NHB(JSA) (para. 7.8). The Benefits Agency computers keep records of up to eight NHB(IS) and/or NHB(JSA) notifications per case. These procedures do not remove the claimant's own duty to notify changes of circumstances to the authority.

AA s. 127(1),
128(1)
SI 1988 No. 662
CTBR 92

7.28   If a claimant on IS or JSA(IB) moves, the Benefits Agency sends him or her three NHB1A forms (as well as sending the authority a form NHB(IS) or NHB(JSA) notifying it of the move). These three forms are form HHB1A(IS) or NHB1A(JSA), NHB1A(HB) and NHB1A(CTB) – which are invitations to claim IS or JSA, HB and CTB respectively. NHB1A forms for HB and CTB are similar to NHB1 forms, but additionally give the date of the new tenancy (for HB purposes) and the date of the move (for CTB purposes). The claimant is invited to return all the forms to the Benefits Agency. The NHB1A forms for HB and CTB are then dealt with in the same way as NHB1 forms (paras. 7.20 onwards).

Claims direct to the authority

7.29   Anyone may claim HB or CTB or both direct from the authority. This is the only method available to claimants who are not also making a claim for income support or income-based jobseeker's allowance. A claim may be made on a form supplied by the authority or in some other format acceptable to the authority. The authority may or may not need further information or evidence and may or may not have to refer details to the rent officer (chapter 8).

APPLICATION FORMS

7.30   Authorities design their own application forms. Long forms may put people off claiming. One way of shortening them is by the use of 'trigger questions' (e.g. 'are you self-employed?') with additional information obtained using follow-up letters or forms (e.g. details of income from self-employment). The print should be reasonably large, the language clear and simple, and the design and layout comprehensible. Special forms may be used for various groups of claimants such as linguistic minority groups, students, council tenants, private tenants, those who are eligible only for CTB (e.g. home owners), and so on. Forms should include a question about whether the person has claimed income support or income-based jobseeker's allowance.

Table 7.1 HB/CTB FORMS FOR IS AND JSA(IB) CLAIMANTS

NHB1(HB)	HB claim form for IS and JSA(IB) claimants
NHB1(CTB)	CTB claim form for IS and JSA(IB) claimants
NHB1A(HB)	HB claim form for IS and JSA(IB) claimants moving home
NHB1A(CTB)	CTB claim form for IS and JSA(IB) claimants moving home
NHB(IS)*	Income support decision form for claims, changes and end of IS entitlement
NHB(JSA)*	Income-based jobseeker's allowance decision form for claims, changes and end of JSA(IB) entitlement
NHB 1EP	The special form for claiming HB/CTB 'extended payments' (chapter 17)

* It appears that different names are given to these forms in some areas.

THE AUTHORITY'S DESIGNATED OFFICE

7.31   The authority's application forms must give the address of its 'designated office(s)'. This is the place to which claims should be sent and changes of circumstances notified. Each authority must have at least one designated office. Designating two offices is possible when HB and CTB are dealt with at different addresses. Designating additional offices, such as the authority's homeless persons unit or a hostel, is often advantageous. The day a claim is received by these can then be the official 'date of claim' (para. 7.54). Forms must also give details of 'gateway offices' if appropriate (paras. 7.11-12).

HBR 2(1)
CTBR 2(1)

SPOTTING ENTITLEMENT TO IS AND JSA(IB)

7.32   If the authority considers the claimant may be entitled to income support or income-based jobseeker's allowance, it is good practice to advise him or her to claim it, and to do so promptly, since the IS or JSA(IB) claim will not be treated as having been made when HB or CTB were claimed. However, the authority has no power to require the claimant to do so.

Is the claim effective?

7.33   This section explains what constitutes an effective claim for HB/CTB – i.e. a claim which the authority must determine. The rules apply to claims made via a gateway office, a Benefits Agency office, a Jobcentre or an authority, whether fresh claims or renewal claims. There are two conditions for an effective HB/CTB claim:

◆ the first condition relates to the manner in which the claim is made;

◆ the second condition relates to the provision of information and evidence.

7.34   If both the conditions are fulfilled, the claim is effective from the day it is received. This may either be because both conditions are fulfilled at the outset; or because they are later fulfilled, as described below (paras. 7.36-39). (Different rules apply to claims for HB/CTB 'extended payments': chapter 17.)

MANNER OF CLAIM

7.35   Except as described in the next paragraph, the first condition for an effective claim is that it must be made in writing. Furthermore it must be:

AA s.1, 5, 6
HBR 72(1),(9)
CTBR 62(1),(9)

◆ on a form approved by the authority and completed in accordance with the instructions on the form; or

◆ in some other written form which the authority accepts as sufficient in the circumstances of a particular case or a class of cases.

Authorities' own application forms clearly fall in the first category. Authorities should also regard the Benefits Agency NHB1 and NHB1A forms as doing so. An example of the second category is a letter including a statement that the writer wishes to claim.

HBR 72(4)(d),(5), 72A
CTBR 62(4)(d),(5), 62A

7.36 The exception to the above rule applies only to claims which fulfil all three of the following conditions:

◆ they are fresh claims (i.e. not renewal claims); and

◆ they are made to a gateway office (para. 7.11); and

◆ they are made by a person who is 16 or over but under 60 and who is not in remunerative work (para. 9.33).

In these cases, a 'notification of intention to make a claim' is treated in the same way as a written claim, so long as an actual written claim is received within one calendar month of that notification. It is clear that such a notification can be oral: for example, the words 'I'm planning to claim housing benefit' spoken at a gateway office.

INFORMATION AND EVIDENCE: GENERAL

HBR AA s.1, 5, 6, 72(1), 73(1),(3), sch A1
CTBR 62(1), 63(1),(3), sch A1

7.37 The second condition for an effective claim is that the authority may require from the claimant 'certificates, documents, information and evidence' so long as these are 'reasonably required... in order to determine... entitlement'. The exception is that it may not require any information whatsoever about the following types of payment, whether they are made to a claimant, partner, child, young person, non-dependant or second adult. These payments are in any case always disregarded in the assessment of HB and CTB:

◆ payments from the Macfarlane Trusts, the Eileen Trust or the Fund, and in certain cases payments of money which originally derived from those sources (para. 13.40);

◆ payments of capital in kind from a charity or from the above sources;

◆ payments of income in kind from any source.

AA s 1
HBR 2A
CTBR 2A
SI 1999 No. 920

7.38 A further rule relating to National Insurance ('NI') numbers applies in all cases except for claims for HB made in respect of a hostel (as defined in para. 8.10). It is that (in order for a claim to be effective) the claimant must either provide his or her NI number and the NI number of his or her partner, along with information or evidence establishing these, or make an application for an NI number and give information or evidence to assist with this. DSS guidance on this is in circular HB/CTB A16/99 which also provides a form authorities can use to seek an NI number.

7.39 Though an authority may require the information, etc, by writing to the claimant for this, it may not require the claimant to attend an interview – though it may request this (*R v Liverpool City Council ex parte Johnson*, QBD, 31.10.94). An authority has no duty to determine a claim if a relevant document has been forged – even if the statements in the forged document are true (*R v Winston*, CA, 15.7.98; *Times Law Report*, 24.7.98). In the special case of refugees who were formerly asylum seekers (para 5.22), the authority may require information, evidence, etc, about any previous period for which they have become entitled to HB/CTB.

7.40   Apart from the points made earlier in this chapter and in relation to 'extended payments' (chapter 17), the law does not specify what type of proof the authority should require about any particular matter (though see below for DSS guidance under the 'Verification Framework'). It is clear, though, that the authority must not seek unnecessary proof. For example, a self-employed claimant should not be expected to have accounts prepared by someone else. Some information may require detailed proof, for example, if a claimant's capital is close to £16,000. In some cases, the authority may wish to check or confirm information with a third party. For example, authorities often ask claimants to get their landlord to confirm details of rent. If it is necessary for an authority to approach a third party direct, the DSS points out (GM para. C8.11) that 'such enquiries should normally be made only with the claimant's written agreement'. The only exception is that, in the circumstances described in paragraph 13.104 about notional income from a pension scheme, an authority may contact the pension provider direct.

INFORMATION AND EVIDENCE AND THE VERIFICATION FRAMEWORK

7.41   The DSS has introduced a 'Verification Framework' ('VF') for HB and CTB, suggesting in detail the types of evidence authorities may seek about the claimant's (and others') identity, residency, rent, household composition, income, capital, etc. This advice is not laid down in law. It is a set of instructions amounting to a voluntary code of practice for authorities. It was drawn up by the DSS after consultation with various bodies. Its objective is to prevent fraud.

7.42   Several but by no means all authorities have decided to adopt the VF. Those which adopt it in full can get additional subsidy from the DSS towards their set-up and on-going implementation costs. There is nothing to stop an authority from adopting only parts of the VF, if it considers this is reasonable. But only authorities which adopt it in full can get subsidy.

7.43   The legal test for what information and evidence authorities may require in order to determine a claim for HB or CTB is, in broad terms, that this must be 'reasonably required ... in order to determine ... entitlement' (para. 7.37). The DSS has taken the view that, with appropriate exceptions, the requirements of the VF meet this test. An authority which adopts the VF must inevitably have taken the same view. There may, however, be circumstances in which the requirements of the VF conflict with this legal test (for example, if an authority applies the requirements of the VF as a blanket rule in an inappropriate case: chapter 1).

7.44 For authorities which adopt the VF, the DSS has given instructions about the following main matters:

◆ what information should be verified before HB/CTB is awarded;

◆ what evidence is acceptable for this purpose;

◆ how claimants should be categorised into certain 'risk groups';

◆ how long benefit periods should be set at – for each such risk group; and

◆ what checks should be made during the life of a claim – for each such risk group.

7.45 The DSS's current instructions for authorities adopting the VF are in The Verification Framework, DSS, 11th November 1998 (issued with DSS circular HB/CTB F15/98). Since it was issued this has been amended and watered down by DSS circulars HB/CTB F20/98, F17/99, A37/99 and A48/99. The last-mentioned (issued in October 1999) is of importance for hostels: it states that the VF does not apply in the case of hostel claims for the first 13 weeks of a claim, and warns local authorities that over-zealous application of the VF can endanger hostels' work. Section 140B of the Social Security Administration Act 1992 (as amended by section 10 of the Social Security Administration (Fraud) Act 1997) provides (amongst other things) for the subsidy arrangements relevant to the Verification Framework.

REMEDYING DEFECTIVE CLAIMS

HBR 72(6)-(8),
73(1),(2), 76(2)
CTBR 62(6)-(8),
63(1),(2), 66(2)

7.46 Specific rules apply if a written claim does not comply with one or both of the conditions in paragraph 7.33:

(a) if it is not on an approved form (and the authority does not accept the form it is in as sufficient), the authority should send the claimant an approved form for completion;

(b) if it is on an approved form, but it is incomplete, the authority should return the form to the claimant for completion (and it is good practice to keep a photocopy of the returned form);

(c) if information or evidence is not given or included with the form, the authority must request the claimant to provide this. At the same time, it must also inform the claimant of the duty to notify relevant changes of circumstances which occur, and indicate what these are likely to be.

7.47 In all three cases, the authority must allow at least four weeks for the claimant to comply with the request, and should allow longer if reasonable to do so. For example, it is good practice to send a reminder, allowing a further period for the reply. If the claimant complies within four weeks (or longer if reasonable) the claim is effective from the original date. Furthermore, the three cases may apply one after the other (as illustrated in the example) or one of the cases may apply more than once (most commonly, a need for yet further information or evidence). Each time, the authority should allow the claimant four weeks to comply (or longer if reasonable).

7.48   In any of the above cases, the authority has no duty to determine a claim if the claimant takes so much longer than four weeks to comply that the delay becomes unreasonable. (This can arise when a claimant does not provide the information, evidence, etc. reasonably required by the authority – for example, under the Verification Framework.) It is generally accepted that, if the authority does not determine an HB/CTB claim for this reason, there is nothing about which the claimant can appeal using the HB/CTB appeals procedures (chapter 19) – since there has been no determination (para. 19.8). Instead, the claimant's options (not all of which would be appropriate in every case) are:

♦   to write to the authority asking it to reconsider anyway;

♦   to complain using the authority's complaints procedure;

♦   to invite the authority's Monitoring Officer to intervene;

♦   to complain to the Ombudsman;

♦   to seek judicial review.

Example: Remedying a defective claim

Claimant action	A claimant sends the authority a letter saying 'I wish to claim...'
Authority action	The letter does not contain sufficient details for the authority to assess the claim. The authority sends the claimant its ordinary application form for completion.
Claimant action	The claimant returns the form within four weeks, having omitted to answer some of the questions.
Authority action	The claim is now on an approved form, but is incomplete. The authority returns the form to the claimant for completion.
Claimant action	The claimant completes the form, and returns it after five weeks, with a note explaining he has been in hospital.
Authority action	The authority accepts that five weeks is reasonable, but needs evidence of income. The authority writes to the claimant requesting this.
Claimant action	The claimant returns the evidence within four weeks.
Authority action	The authority assesses the claim. The claim is effective from the date when the letter was received.

7.49   It is good practice for an authority receiving a claim which is not in writing (e.g. in person or over the telephone) to issue or send out an application form for completion. In this case the claim is not effective before the written application arrives. (Separate rules apply to claims made to gateway offices: para. 7.11.)

AMENDING A CLAIM

HBR 74(1)
CTBR 64(1)

7.50   A claimant may write amending a claim at any time before a determination is made on it. The amendment is treated as having been made from the outset of the claim. Once a determination is made, the equivalent of amending a claim is notifying a change of circumstances (para. 17.2).

WITHDRAWING A CLAIM

HBR 74(2), 76(2)
CTBR 64(2), 66(2)

7.51   A claimant may write withdrawing a claim at any time before a determination is made on it. The authority is then under no duty to determine the claim. Once a determination is made, there is no provision for withdrawing a claim.

The life of a claim

7.52   The remainder of this chapter describes the various things which happen during the life of a claim. The first few sections explain three things which must be determined at the beginning of a claim:

◆ the date of claim;

◆ the first day of entitlement; and

◆ the benefit period.

Table 7.2 summarises these and also indicates what can or will happen later on. Rules about the last day of entitlement and renewal claims are explained towards the end of this chapter. Changes of circumstances are dealt with in chapter 17.

BENEFIT WEEKS

HBR 2(1)
CTBR 2(1)

7.53   Many of the rules in this chapter refer to a 'benefit week'. For both HB and CTB, benefits weeks are defined as beginning on a Monday and ending on the following Sunday.

Date of claim

7.54   This section describes what counts as the 'date of claim' for HB and CTB. The general rule is given first, then the exceptions which may apply. Table 7.3 summarises the main rules. The 'date of claim' is an important concept: it affects the date on which entitlement to HB/CTB actually begins (which may be before, on, or after the date of claim, depending on the other circumstances of the case, as described later in this chapter).

Table 7.2 THE LIFE OF A CLAIM

THE THREE STEPS TO FOLLOW WHEN A CLAIM BEGINS

Step one: DATE OF CLAIM

The first step is to decide what is the 'date of claim'. Typically this is the day the HB/CTB application form is received by the authority. But there are many other rules. In particular, there are circumstances in which a claim must be backdated.

Step two: FIRST DAY OF ENTITLEMENT

The second step is to work out (from the date of claim) the day on which entitlement to HB/CTB begins – in other words, the first day for which HB/CTB is awarded. Typically this is the Monday following the date of claim. But there are exceptions to this.

Step three: BENEFIT PERIOD

The third step is to decide what the benefit period is to be – in other words, how long the award of HB/CTB will last. This is often 26 or 52 weeks.

WHAT HAPPENS NEXT

CHANGES OF CIRCUMSTANCES

Once the benefit period has begun the claimant's circumstances may change. Typically if a claimant qualifies for a different amount of HB/CTB because of a change, the new amount is awarded from the following Monday. But there are exceptions to this.

LAST DAY OF ENTITLEMENT

Entitlement to HB/CTB ends at the end of the benefit period, or earlier in the case of some changes of circumstances.

INVITING A RENEWAL CLAIM

When entitlement to HB/CTB ends, the authority must in most cases invite the claimant to make a renewal claim for a further period.

Table 7.3 DATE OF CLAIM FOR HB/CTB: SUMMARY

Rule	Date of claim *
General rule	The date the HB/CTB claim is received by the authority.
Claimants making a fresh claim for IS or JSA:	
◆ If IS or JSA(IB) is awarded; and a claim for HB/CTB is received by the Benefits Agency or Jobcentre or the authority within four weeks of the IS or JSA(IB) claim.	The first day of entitlement to IS or JSA(IB).
◆ If IS or JSA(IB) is awarded but the above time limit is not met.	The date the HB/CTB claim is received by the authority.
◆ If IS or JSA(IB) is not awarded.	The date the HB/CTB claim is received by the Benefits Agency or Jobcentre or the authority, whichever is earlier.
Claimants making a claim to a gateway office (but only if they meet the conditions in para. 7.36)	The above rules apply as though the gateway office was either the authority, the Benefits Agency or the Jobcentre – whichever would be most beneficial for the claimant.
Claimants on IS or JSA(IB) who become liable for rent or council tax for the first time:	
◆ If a claim for HB/CTB is received by the authority within four weeks of the start of their new liability for rent/council tax.	The first day of the new liability for rent/council tax. (For other rules about people moving home – whether they are on IS or JSA(IB) or not – see para. 7.63 onwards.)

* If more than one rule applies to a case, use the earliest of the various dates of claim. Further rules apply to renewal claims (as described later in this chapter).

GENERAL RULE

7.55   The general rule is that the date of claim is the day a claim is received at the authority's 'designated office' (para. 7.31). This includes cases where a claim is delivered on a day when the authority's offices are not open. So claims which are 'on the mat' after a weekend or a bank holiday should, if appropriate, be regarded as having been received on the Saturday, Sunday or bank holiday. The claimant may otherwise lose up to two weeks' HB/CTB (paras. 7.78-79).

HBR 72(5)(c)
CTBR 62(5)(d)

SUCCESSFUL IS AND JSA(IB) CLAIMANTS WHO CLAIM HB/CTB WITHIN FOUR WEEKS

7.56   This rule applies if:

HBR 72(5)(a)
CTBR 62(5)(a)

◆ a person claims income support (IS) or income-based jobseeker's allowance – JSA(IB); and

◆ as a result he or she is awarded IS or JSA(IB); and

◆ the person's or any partner's HB/CTB claim (whether or not on the NHB1 forms) is received by the authority or the Benefits Agency or the Jobcentre no more than four weeks after the IS or JSA(IB) claim was received by the Benefits Agency or Jobcentre.

7.57   In this case, the date of claim for HB/CTB is:

◆ the date of first entitlement to IS or JSA(IB). In the case of JSA(IB) this means the first 'waiting day' if the claimant has to wait for his or her JSA(IB) payments to begin. The relevant date for these purposes should be shown on form NHB(IS) or form NHB(JSA) (para. 7.18), though it is sometimes necessary to check that it is correct; or

◆ if earlier, the date the HB/CTB claim was received by the Benefits Agency or the Jobcentre (because of the rule described in para. 7.61). This would be relevant if the claimant's entitlement to IS or JSA(IB) was later than the date they received his or her claim for IS or JSA(IB); or

◆ if earlier, the date the HB/CTB claim was received by the authority (because of the general rule in para. 7.55).

This rule applies regardless of delays by the Benefits Agency or Jobcentre in providing the details to the authority.

7.58   The four weeks limit (para. 7.56) may not be extended. However it applies independently from the time limits allowed for the remedying of defective claims (e.g. if NHB1 forms are incomplete, or further information or evidence is required).

Examples: Date of claim

SUCCESSFUL INCOME SUPPORT CLAIMANT

A claimant applies for income support. The Benefits Agency receives her application on Wednesday 6th September 2000, and later assesses her as entitled to income support from that date.

The date of claim for HB/CTB is also Wednesday 6th September so long as the Benefits Agency or the authority receives a claim for HB/CTB (whether on the NHB1 forms or not) within four weeks of the date of claim for income support (i.e. on or before Wednesday 4th October 2000).

UNSUCCESSFUL JSA(IB) CLAIMANT

A claimant applies for income-based jobseeker's allowance and sends the NHB1 forms with it. The Jobcentre receives his application on Wednesday 6th September 2000, and the Benefits Agency later assesses him as not entitled to JSA(IB).

The date of claim for HB/CTB is Wednesday 6th September.

SUCCESSFUL IS AND JSA(IB) CLAIMANTS WHO CLAIM HB/CTB AFTER FOUR WEEKS

HBR 72(5)(c)
CTBR 62(5)(d)
7.59   If a person claims and is awarded IS or JSA(IB) but fails to claim HB/CTB within four weeks of making the IS or JSA(IB) claim, the date of claim for HB/CTB is the day the claim is received by the authority.

7.60   DSS advice on this has been clarified (GM paras. A2.18, B2.37 and C7.17). But it is still sometimes believed that if, for some reason, an HB/CTB claim is sent to the Benefits Agency or Jobcentre more than four weeks after a successful IS or JSA(IB) claim, the day the HB/CTB claim is received by the Benefits Agency or Jobcentre should be regarded as the date of claim for HB/CTB. Whilst this would be beneficial, it is unfortunately incorrect: as stated above, the day the HB/CTB claim is received by the authority is the date of claim for HB/CTB. However, in such cases there may be good cause for backdating the HB/CTB claim (para. 7.93).

UNSUCCESSFUL IS AND JSA(IB) CLAIMANTS, ETC

HBR 72(5)(b)
CTBR 62(5)(b)
7.61   If a person claims IS or JSA(IB) but is not awarded it, or claims JSA(Cont) regardless of whether he or she is awarded it, the date of claim for HB/CTB is the day the HB/CTB claim is received by the Benefits Agency or Jobcentre or the authority, whichever is earlier.

CLAIMS MADE TO A GATEWAY OFFICE

7.62   In cases in which a claim for HB/CTB may be made to a gateway office (para. 7.11), the rules mentioned earlier (paras. 7.54-61) apply as though the gateway office was either the authority's designated office or a Benefits Agency or Jobcentre office, whichever would be most beneficial in any particular claimant's case. This typically means that the date of claim in such cases is either the date the gateway office received a written claim for HB/CTB, or the date it received the claimant's notification of intention to claim HB/CTB, or the date the claimant is first entitled to income support or JSA(IB).   HBR 72(5), 72A CTBR 62(5), 62

Example: Date of claim

CLAIM MADE TO A GATEWAY OFFICE

A claimant visits a gateway office (under the 'One' project) on Wednesday 6th September 2000 to enquire about his entitlement to state benefits and to seek help with finding work. During his visit he says he intends to claim HB/CTB. He is invited back for a full interview a couple of weeks later. At that interview he is helped to complete an application form covering HB/CTB and other relevant benefits and in due course he is awarded income-based jobseeker's allowance from Wednesday 6th September.

The date of claim for HB/CTB is Wednesday 6th September (because he made his written application for HB/CTB within one month of notifying the gateway office of his intention to claim.

IS AND JSA(IB) CLAIMANTS MOVING HOME, ETC

7.63   This rule makes it easier for a person on IS or JSA(IB) to get HB/CTB from when he or she first becomes liable for rent and/or for council tax. (For related cases, see para. 7.66.) Specifically, the rule applies if: HBR 72(5)(bb) CTBR 62(5)(c)

◆ a person is receiving IS or JSA(IB); and

◆ he or she becomes liable for rent or council tax for the first time – whether at a new address or at a current address; and

◆ the person's or any partner's HB/CTB claim (whether or not on the NHB1 or NHB1A forms) is received by the Benefits Agency or Jobcentre or the authority no more than four weeks after the new liability begins.

In this case, the date of claim for HB is the first day of his or her new liability for rent; the date of claim for CTB is the first day of his or her new liability for council tax. Generally speaking this means that the person's HB/CTB will start straight away (paras. 7.79-80).

7.64   Examples of when this rule applies are when a claimant on IS or JSA(IB):

◆ moves to the first home on which he or she is liable for rent and/or for council tax (see also para. 7.66);

◆ inherits the tenancy of his or her home;

◆ becomes liable for council tax because of the death of someone in his or her home or some other change in circumstances;

◆ becomes liable for council tax on a dwelling which has been exempt.

7.65   So long as the claimant (or partner) is receiving IS or JSA(IB) immediately before the move, etc., the rule applies regardless of whether he or she continues to receive IS or JSA(IB) afterwards. The rule is also necessary for a further reason: when someone on IS or JSA(IB) moves, a fresh claim for that benefit is not required (GM para. C7.23).

FURTHER RULES ABOUT ALL CLAIMANTS MOVING HOME

7.66   The following additional points apply to all claimants who move home within the area of a particular authority – whether they are on IS or JSA(IB) or not:

◆ If the claimant was receiving HB in respect of the old address, a claim for the new address is dealt with under the rules about renewal claims (para. 7.86). So, as long as the claim for the new address is received by the authority within four weeks of the end of the benefit period for the old address, there will be no break in his or her entitlement to HB. Exactly the same applies in respect of CTB.

◆ Alternatively in such cases, the authority may treat the move as a change of circumstances, allowing his or her current benefit period to continue (chapter 17), in which case a new claim is not required – though, of course, the claimant will have to give the authority his or her new rent and/or council tax details. (In practice, only some authorities are prepared to take this approach, but it is subject to the ordinary appeal procedures: chapter 19.)

It is sometimes argued that the first point above (but not the second) could apply even if the move is from one authority area to another. The law is unclear on this, and it is a matter which has not been tested in the courts. Claimants should certainly not rely on this argument.

CTB CLAIMS IN ADVANCE OF LIABILITY

BR 62(10), 66(2)   **7.67**   A person may claim CTB up to eight weeks before he or she will become liable for council tax. The rule for dealing with this works as follows:

◆ The person claims CTB.

◆ The authority works out the date of claim in the ordinary way.

◆ He or she is not liable for council tax yet – so, although the claim may be processed, no award of CTB may be made for the time being – but it is anticipated that liability will begin at some point up to eight weeks after the date of claim.

◆ If liability does actually begin within that period, the authority must change the date of claim to the date liability begins.

◆ Because of the rule about when entitlement starts in such cases (para. 7.80), the person's CTB will start on that date.

If liability does not begin within the eight weeks mentioned, the claim is of no effect.

Examples: Date of claim

CLAIMANT ON IS OR JSA(IB) MOVING TO HER FIRST RENTED HOME

A claimant in receipt of income support or income-based jobseeker's allowance moves from her parents' home to her first rented home on Monday 4th September 2000, on which date she becomes liable for rent and council tax.

The date of claim for HB/CTB is also Monday 4th September so long as the Jobcentre or the Benefits Agency or the authority receives a claim for HB/CTB (whether on the NHB1 or NHB1A forms or not) within four weeks after her new liability for rent/council tax begins (i.e. on or before Monday 2nd October 1999).

CLAIMANT MOVING FROM ONE RENTED HOME TO ANOTHER

A claimant moves home to a new authority area on Monday 4th September 2000, on which date she becomes liable for rent and council tax.

The date of claim for HB/CTB is decided according to the general rule: it is whatever day the claimant's form reaches the new authority's offices. (Note that if the move was to the same authority area as the old address, the claimant would have four weeks to make her renewal claim: para. 7.66.)

7.68   One aim of this rule is that the person's council tax bill will, when it is issued, be able to show entitlement to CTB. Examples of when the rule applies are when a person:

◆ plans to move;

◆ expects that his or her home will cease to be exempt (e.g. if all the occupiers are students and one will soon cease to be a student);

◆ expects to become liable for council tax because the person currently liable will move out.

7.69   There is no specific rule in HB similar to the above. However in the case of HB, the following rule may be applied.

OTHER ADVANCE CLAIMS FOR HB/CTB

HBR 72(11)
CTBR 62(12)

7.70   If a claimant is not immediately entitled to HB/CTB, it may be clear that he or she will soon become entitled. The authority may treat the claim as an advance claim. The rule dealing with this works as follows:

◆   The person makes a claim.

◆   The authority works out the date of claim in the ordinary way.

◆   In the benefit week immediately following the date of claim, he or she does not qualify for HB/CTB.

◆   But the authority considers that he or she will qualify for HB/CTB with effect from a particular benefit week which is no later than the 13th benefit week after the date of claim.

◆   The authority may change the date of claim to a date in the benefit week immediately before that particular benefit week.

◆   Because of the general rule about when entitlement starts (para. 7.79-80), the person's HB/CTB will start in that particular benefit week.

7.71   Examples of when this rule might be used are if:

◆   someone in the family will soon have a birthday that will increase the claimant's applicable amount;

◆   it is known that the claimant's, a partner's, a non-dependant's or a second adult's income will soon go down;

◆   the claimant plans to move home soon to rented accommodation.

The last example applies in the case of HB only. In the case of CTB a different rule applies (para. 7.67).

CTB TRANSITIONAL RULES

1992 No. 1909

7.72   Several transitional rules applied from 1st April 1993 when council tax was introduced. Two of these can still arise, as follows.

7.73   A claimant is entitled to CTB from 1st April 1993 if:

◆   he or she was liable for council tax on 1st April 1993; and

◆   his or her first bill for a period including that date was issued at any time after that date; and

◆   the delay in issuing the bill was not due to the claimant's 'own act or omission'; and

◆   the claim is received at the authority's offices no more than eight weeks after he or she received that first bill.

This rule (sometimes called the '56-day rule') is not discretionary. It can arise if the authority has failed to issue a bill for a period including 1st April 1993; or issued a bill, but to the wrong person; and is now issuing one to the liable person for the first time. In such a case, the claimant is entitled to CTB for the whole of the period from 1st April 1993 until his or her claim is made, and then for a benefit period of up to 60 weeks (para. 7.82).

7.74   Also, any person who was in receipt of HB or community charge benefit on 31st March 1993 may be awarded CTB from 1st April 1993 without having to make a claim. Although most authorities applied this rule in 1993, cases can still arise where it was not applied. If so, the authority may, as a matter of discretion, apply it now even without a request from the claimant. Applying this rule does not constitute 'backdating' (para. 7.93).

DELAYS IN SETTING COUNCIL TAXES

7.75   Independent of the above rules, a further rule applies when any authority delays setting its council taxes until after 31st March in any year. In such cases, if a CTB claim is received within four weeks after the setting of the council taxes, the date of claim is set so that the claimant's entitlement begins on 1st April in that year (or the week in which the person's entitlement begins if this falls between 1st April and the date the claim is received). CTBR 62(11)

HB CLAIMS FOR RENT DUE BEFORE THE CLAIMANT MOVES IN

7.76   In certain cases, claimants can get HB (but not CTB) for a period of up to four weeks when they are liable for rent before moving in to their home (para. 4.67). But the HB due for that period cannot be awarded until the claimant has actually moved in. The rule for dealing with this can be illustrated as follows: HBR 5(7)

◆ The person makes a claim before moving in.

◆ The authority notes that it is one of the cases where claimants can get HB for a period before moving in.

◆ The date of claim for HB is worked out in the ordinary way. No award of HB is made for the time being.

◆ When the person actually moves in, HB is awarded based on the date of claim as already worked out (unless the person does not satisfy the conditions for getting HB before moving in until a later date, in which case that is the date of claim).

7.77   There is another way in which this rule can work:

◆ The person makes a claim before moving in.

◆ The authority refuses the claim for some reason.

◆ The person moves in and, no more than four weeks later, makes a further claim (or is treated as doing so under the backdating rules).

◆ The authority notes that it is one of the cases where claimants can get HB for a period before moving in.

◆ The date of claim for HB is worked out in the ordinary way but based on the first claim.

◆ HB is awarded based on the date of claim just worked out (unless the person does not satisfy the conditions for getting HB before moving in until a later date, in which case that is the date of claim).

First day of entitlement

GENERAL RULE

HBR 65(1)
CTBR 56(1)

7.78   The general rule is that:

◆ HB and CTB are awarded from the Monday following the 'date of claim' (as described earlier), even if the date of claim is a Monday.

Variations to the general rule are given below. Other variations apply for renewal claims (para. 7.86).

WHEN LIABILITY FOR RENT BEGINS

HBR 65(2)
69(4)(a),(5),(6)
70(2),(4)

7.79   If the date of claim is in the same benefit week as the claimant becomes liable for rent (or before then), HB is awarded from the benefit week in which the date of claim falls:

◆ if rent is expressed on a weekly basis (or in multiples of weeks), the full weekly amount of HB is awarded in that week (regardless of when liability began);

◆ if rent is expressed on a non-weekly basis (e.g. daily or calendar-monthly), entitlement for that week is assessed on a daily basis: divide the ordinary weekly entitlement by seven, then multiply the result by the number of days of liability.

This could arise if the claimant moves to a new home, or inherits a tenancy, or because of a rent-free period.

WHEN LIABILITY FOR COUNCIL TAX BEGINS

CTBR 56(2)

7.80   If the date of claim is in the same benefit week as the claimant or a partner becomes liable for council tax (or before then), CTB is awarded from the benefit week in which the date of claim falls:

◆ entitlement for that week is assessed on a daily basis: divide the ordinary weekly entitlement by seven, then multiply the result by the number of days of liability.

This could arise if, for example, the claimant moves into or within the area, or becomes liable because the previously liable person has died, or his or her dwelling ceases to be exempt because it was formerly occupied wholly by students.

Examples: First day of entitlement

GENERAL CASE

A man claims HB and CTB because his income has reduced. His date of claim is Thursday 20th July 2000. His rent is payable to his landlord each calendar month. He is liable for council tax.

HB and CTB are awarded from the benefit week commencing with the Monday following his date of claim. So Monday 24th July is the claimant's first day of entitlement. From that week onwards, he is entitled to his normal weekly amount of HB and CTB.

There would be no difference if his rent was due weekly or on any other basis.

CLAIMANT MOVING TO NEW HOME

A woman moves into her flat on Tuesday 1st August 2000. Her date of claim is Tuesday 1st August. Her rent is payable to her landlord each calendar month, and is due from 1st August. She is liable for council tax from 1st August.

HB and CTB are awarded from the benefit week commencing with the Monday in which her date of claim falls, i.e. Monday 31st July. But she is not liable for rent or council tax until the Tuesday, so Tuesday 1st August is her first day of entitlement. In that first week, entitlement to HB and CTB is six-sevenths of her normal amount (for the Tuesday to the Sunday).

If her rent was due weekly (or in multiples of weeks), there would be a difference in HB (only). Her first day of entitlement to HB would be Monday 31st July. From that week onwards she would be entitled to her normal weekly amount of HB. (But she would still only qualify for six-sevenths of the normal amount of CTB.)

Duration of benefit period

7.81   HB and CTB are awarded for a fixed period. This applies to claimants on IS and JSA(IB) and all other claimants. It is up to the authority to decide how many benefit weeks this is to be, taking into account any relevant circumstances

HBR 66(2)
CTBR 57(2)

which may affect the claimant's future entitlement – for example, if the authority knows that a claimant's income will change shortly. For authorities which have implemented the Verification Framework there is guidance about how long benefit periods should be.

HBR 66(1),(3)
CTBR 57(1),(3)

7.82   The maximum length of a benefit period is 60 benefit weeks, beginning with the first benefit week of entitlement or, if later, the benefit week in which the *authority* (not the Benefits Agency or Jobcentre) receives the claim. For example, if HB or CTB is backdated (para. 7.93), the first week to count towards these 60 weeks is the benefit week in which the claim is actually received by the authority. (For exceptions relating to extensions of the benefit period, see paras. 7.86 and 17.24.)

Examples: Duration of benefit period

In these examples, it is assumed that the authority concerned always sets its benefit periods at 60 benefit weeks (the maximum length).

CLAIMANT ON INCOME SUPPORT

A woman claims income support and is awarded it from Monday 2nd October 2000. She claims HB/CTB (on the NHB1 forms) via the Benefits Agency at the same time. The Benefits Agency accidentally delays forwarding the NHB1 forms and they do not reach the authority until Wednesday 8th November 2000. She has not recently moved into her home.

◆ Her date of claim for HB/CTB is Monday 2nd October.

◆ Her first day of entitlement to HB/CTB is Monday 9th October.

◆ The first week to count towards the 60-week benefit period is benefit week commencing Monday 6th November.

CLAIMANT WHOSE HB/CTB IS BACKDATED

A man's claim for HB/CTB is received by the authority on Wednesday 17th May 2000. He is not on IS or JSA(IB) and has not recently moved into his home. The authority agrees that he has proved good cause for failing to claim HB/CTB since Sunday 30th April 2000 (when he went into hospital). He qualifies for HB/CTB for both the backdated period and the current period.

◆ His date of claim for HB/CTB (because of the backdating rules is treated as being Sunday 30th April.

◆ His first day of entitlement to HB/CTB is Monday 1st May.

◆ The first week to count towards the 60-week benefit period is benefit week commencing Monday 15th May.

Last day of entitlement

7.83   An award of HB/CTB lasts until:

◆ the benefit period runs out; or

◆ the benefit period is brought to an early end.

BENEFIT PERIOD RUNS OUT

7.84   One way entitlement to HB/CTB can end is when the benefit period   HBR 67
originally set at the beginning of the claim reaches its end. In this case the last   CTBR 58
day of entitlement is the Sunday at the end of the final benefit week of the benefit
period. Except to the limited extent described in paragraph 7.91, there is no power
to continue awarding HB/CTB after this, unless a renewal claim is made.

BENEFIT PERIOD BROUGHT TO AN EARLY END

7.85   The other way entitlement to HB/CTB can end is when the benefit period   HBR 67
is brought to an early end. This can happen if there is a change in the claimant's   CTBR 58
circumstances. Chapter 17 gives all the rules about changes of circumstances,
about which changes can cause a benefit period to end early, and about how the
last day of entitlement is calculated in such cases.

Example: End of benefit period and renewal claim

A claimant aged over 80 is awarded HB and CTB from Monday 26th April
1999. Her benefit period is set at 60 benefit weeks, due to run out on
Sunday 18th June 2000. Throughout this time, she qualifies for a higher
pensioner premium.

On Monday 1st May 2000, the authority writes to the claimant inviting her
to make a renewal claim.

By Monday 2nd June 2000, the claimant has not submitted a renewal
claim.

The authority determines to extend her benefit period by four weeks, so
it is now due to run out on Sunday 16th July 2000. It also sends her a
reminder about submitting a renewal claim.

On Friday 11th August 2000, the authority receives a renewal claim from
this claimant (and she still qualifies for HB and CTB). This is within four
weeks of the end of her benefit period (Sunday 16th July 2000), so the
new benefit period for HB and CTB begins on Monday 17th July 2000.

Renewal claims

7.86   Whenever a benefit period runs out or is brought to an early end (including cases where this is because the claimant has moved within the authority's area), authorities should invite the claimant to make a claim for a further award of HB/CTB. In this guide, this is referred to as a 'renewal claim'. It is sometimes called a 'review' by authority benefit staff, a term which may be confusing, since the regulations use the term 'review' to refer to the HB/CTB appeal procedure. (In certain cases, the courts may prevent an authority from evicting its own tenant on the grounds of rent arrears, if the arrears result from the authority's failure to issue an HB renewal claim: *Saint v Barking and Dagenham LBC*, (1999), CA (unreported).)

HBR 72(14)
CTBR 62(15)

7.87   Authorities must invite a renewal claim:

◆ at some point during the eight weeks before a benefit period is due to run out (unless the benefit period was originally fixed as less than 16 weeks); and

◆ whenever a benefit period is brought to an early end because the claimant stops being entitled to IS or JSA(IB) or stops receiving payments of IS or JSA(IB).

And whenever benefit stops, even if the above rules do not apply, it is good practice to invite a renewal claim or (if appropriate) remind claimants that they may make a further claim as and when their circumstances change.

HBR 76(2)
CTBR 66(2)

7.88   It is also open to claimants to make a renewal claim at any time. However, if it is made more than 13 weeks before their benefit period runs out, the authority has no duty to act on it.

FIRST DAY OF ENTITLEMENT IN NEW BENEFIT PERIOD

HBR 72(12)-(14)
TBR 62(13)-(15)

7.89   In all cases, if a renewal claim is received by the authority (for the same or a different address within its area) within 13 weeks before the end of a claimant's benefit period, or within four weeks after it has ended, any new benefit period must run consecutively (so that there is no gap in entitlement). In other words, the first day of entitlement in the new claim must be the day after the last day of entitlement of the old claim. This rule applies equally to a renewal claim from the partner or former partner of a claimant.

7.90   The four weeks time limit mentioned above cannot be extended (though see chapter 17 in the case of a claimant who is awarded an 'extended payment'). If a renewal claim is received outside this time limit, the only way of avoiding the gap in entitlement is by backdating the renewal claim. It is therefore good practice for authorities to issue reminders well within the four weeks limit (though claimants should not rely on all authorities doing this).

EXTENSION OF OLD BENEFIT PERIOD

7.91   If no renewal claim has been received by the last week in the old benefit period, the authority may extend the old benefit period by up to four weeks (but no longer), i.e. award a further four weeks' HB or CTB or both. But this only applies if the claimant (or any partner): HBR 66(4)
CTBR 57(4)

♦ is on IS or JSA(IB); or

♦ fulfils the conditions for a disability premium, higher pensioner premium or severe disability premium (chapter 12).

7.92   This is designed to give the claimant a little more time to make a renewal claim, and to allow the authority to issue a reminder or make a home visit (GM para. A6.10). The four weeks mentioned here is independent from the four weeks allowed for submitting the renewal claim (para. 7.89) as illustrated in the following example.

Backdating

7.93   HB and CTB must be backdated for up to 52 weeks if the claimant requests this in writing, and 'had continuous good cause for [his or her] failure to make a claim'. It is possible for there to be 'good cause' for backdating HB but not CTB, or *vice versa*. Technically, it is the date of claim which is backdated. So HB/CTB can be backdated even if the claimant is not currently entitled to any HB/CTB. For example, a claimant whose capital has recently increased to over £16,000 could have his or her claim backdated for the period when it was less than £16,000. Benefit during any backdated period must be calculated according to the rules which applied at that time. Many authorities now include a question on their claim forms about whether the claimant wishes to make a claim for backdating. HBR 72(15)
CTBR 62(16)

'GOOD CAUSE'

7.94   Backdating is not discretionary. It is obligatory once the authority determines:

♦ that the claimant had good cause for failure to make the claim earlier; and

♦ that his or her good cause lasted throughout the period until the written request for backdating was actually made (whether for the same reason throughout, or for a combination of successive reasons).

7.95   The impact on the authority's financial position (e.g. under the subsidy rules: chapter 21) is irrelevant in deciding whether or not to backdate benefit. This is not affected by the *Brent and Connery* case.

7.96   However, the question remains of judging just what constitutes 'good cause'. It is clear that authorities should not have an immutable list of what does and does not constitute good cause, but should consider any relevant factor. Many authorities follow, in a general sense, the DSS's advice drawn from its social security 'Adjudication Officers' Guide' (reproduced in GM chapter A2, annex A). Whilst this includes an excellent summary of social security case law, often favourable to claimants, the guidance referred to itself states that the factors it covers 'are not an exhaustive list'. As yet there has been no case law on 'good cause' for backdating HB within the current HB scheme – nor on community charge benefit or CTB. Whilst case law on backdating other state benefits is not binding in HB and CTB, it may in many cases be persuasive.

7.97   Some examples of when claimants may have 'good cause' are listed below.

◆ If the claimant was waiting for a decision about another benefit.

◆ If the claimant did not immediately claim (or reclaim) HB/CTB after leaving hospital.

◆ If the claimant's partner made an unsuccessful earlier claim, and it is a case where it matters which member of a couple or polygamous marriage claims.

◆ If the claimant was ill and had no-one to make the claim on his or her behalf.

◆ If the claimant could not reasonably have been expected to know his or her rights, e.g. where there have been detailed changes in the law.

◆ If the claimant did not understand that he or she could claim perhaps because of age, inexperience, language difficulties, difficulty in understanding technical documents or some other reason.

◆ If the claimant was wrongly advised that he or she was not entitled to HB/CTB.

◆ If the claimant was unable to manage his or her affairs and did not have an 'appointee'.

7.98   Council tax and CTB contain many complicated rules. This can be a relevant factor in considering whether a claimant has 'good cause' for a late claim for CTB. Two of many possible examples are:

◆ If the claimant has become liable for council tax for a past period (not including 1st April 1993) because the authority, by its own error, has been attempting to bill a person who is not in fact liable.

◆ If the claimant qualifies for second adult rebate but has received inadequate information from the authority about this.

WHAT IS, AND IS NOT, 'BACKDATING'?

7.99   'Backdating' only arises when benefit is awarded for a past period for which the claimant has not already claimed HB/CTB. The following do not count as 'backdating' in this sense (and there is no subsidy penalty on authorities in these cases):

◆ awarding HB/CTB for a past period because other rules require it to be done;

◆ basing a claim on an application form which was (on the balance of probability) received by the authority or the Benefits Agency, Jobcentre or gateway office but was then mislaid;

◆ basing a claim on an application form which the authority originally (and wrongly) regarded as demonstrating that the claimant was not entitled to HB/CTB;

◆ basing a claim on an application which the authority originally treated as defective but which the authority no longer regards as such because the claimant has now provided relevant information, evidence, etc, within a timescale which the authority now accepts is reasonable;

◆ increasing entitlement retrospectively for someone who was awarded too little HB/CTB in a past period (chapter 17).

LIMIT ON BACKDATING

7.100   HB and CTB cannot be backdated more than 52 weeks before the date on which the authority received the claimant's written request for backdating (even if this is later than when the claimant made his or her claim for HB/CTB). This does not prevent a claimant from seeking compensation from the authority for earlier periods if the authority itself was at fault.   SI 1996 No 2432

7.101   If the special rule about asylum seekers who have become refugees applies to a claimant (para. 5.51), his or her date of claim as determined under that rule cannot be backdated.

8 Referrals to the rent officer

8.1 Authorities must refer details of many HB cases to the rent officer during the course of assessing a claim for HB (including some renewal claims) or following certain changes of circumstances. This chapter explains the rules and covers:

◆ which cases are referred to the rent officer and when they should be referred;

◆ making the referral (this includes details of the information the rent officer requires);

◆ the rent officer's determinations and how they are made;

◆ how errors and appeals are dealt with; and

◆ the rules about pre-tenancy determinations.

SI 2000 No. 1 This chapter gives the law and procedures as they apply from 3rd April 2000. The 1999-2000 edition of this Guide gives the rules applying before that.

8.2 Rent officer referrals can be required in many kinds of rent allowance cases (including claims from private tenants or licensees, hostel residents, people renting a houseboat or mobile home, people with a rental purchase agreement, and – in certain circumstances – housing association tenants). They are never required in rent rebate cases (claims from tenants of the authority administering HB). They relate only to HB: this chapter does not apply at all in relation to CTB.

8.3 Rent officers are employed by the Rent Service, an independent 'Next Steps' Executive Agency, which has various duties in addition to those relating to HB.

WHY ARE REFERRALS MADE TO THE RENT OFFICER?

8.4 As described in this chapter, the rent officer provides the authority with various figures in respect of the cases referred to him or her. These figures are used in different ways depending on whether the HB case in question is an 'exempt case' or not (as defined in para. 11.53).

◆ In 'exempt cases', the rent officer's figures are used to establish whether the authority will receive reduced HB subsidy on any part of the individual claimant's HB (chapter 21). In assessing the HB claim, the authority must make its own determination of eligible rent based on the HB regulations (paras. 11.53 onwards).

◆ In cases which are not 'exempt', the authority uses the rent officer's figures in calculating the claimant's 'maximum rent' (paras. 11.7 onwards): they are binding on the authority for this purpose. The claimant's eligible rent, used in assessing the HB claim, is frequently equal to this 'maximum rent' – but can also be higher or lower (paras. 11.6 onwards).

8.5   The rent officer does not distinguish (in making his or her determinations) between the above types of case: it is the authority that decides which cases are 'exempt'. This is an important duty for the authority, since it can make a substantial difference to the amount of HB a claimant qualifies for.

Which cases are referred and when?

8.6   With the exceptions given below, the authority must refer details of all HB   HBR 12A(1)
cases to the rent officer:

◆ whenever it receives a new HB claim (unless the time limit in para. 8.8 prevents this); and

◆ whenever it receives a renewal HB claim, even if there has been no change in circumstances (unless the time limit in para. 8.8 prevents this); and

◆ whenever it receives notification of a 'relevant change of circumstances' (as defined in para. 8.11) relating to an existing HB claim.

The authority's duties in making the referral are given in the next section (paras. 8.12-13).

GENERAL EXCEPTIONS

8.7   The authority must not make a referral to the rent officer in any of the   HBR 12(2)(b),
cases in table 8.1. Also, in the special case of refugees who were formerly asylum   sch A1, sch 1A
seekers (para. 5.51), it must not make a referral in respect of any previous periods
for which they have become entitled to HB.

Table 8.1 CASES WHICH ARE NEVER REFERRED TO THE RENT OFFICER

◆ Rent rebate cases (i.e. council tenants renting from the authority administering their HB: para. 1.5).

◆ Tenancies in England and Wales entered into before 15th January 1989 and tenancies in Scotland entered into before 2nd January 1989 (in other words, 'regulated tenancies': the dates just mentioned are those when the 1988 Housing Acts came into force).

◆ Any other 'regulated tenancies' which continue to fall within the Rent Act 1977 or the Rent (Agriculture) Act 1976 (these applied before the

1988 Housing Acts came into force). For example, a tenant whose tenancy began in 1988, but who was later transferred by the landlord to alternative accommodation, may still have a 'regulated tenancy'.

◆ Home Office bail hostels or probation hostels.

◆ Housing Action Trust lettings.

◆ Lettings of former local authority or new towns housing stock which has been transferred to a new owner (for example, a housing association) under the Housing Act 1985 (or equivalent new towns provisions) or the tenants choice provisions of the Housing Act 1988 – unless there has been a rent increase since the date of the transfer and the authority states in the referral that the accommodation is unreasonably large or the rent is unreasonably expensive.

◆ Lettings where the landlord is a registered housing association or other registered social landlord – unless the authority considers that the accommodation is unreasonably large or the rent is unreasonably expensive, in which case the authority must make a referral and must state in making the referral that the accommodation is unreasonably large or the rent is unreasonably expensive. In such cases, the authority should take into account all relevant factors: for example, in considering whether the accommodation is unreasonably large, the authority must not simply adopt the rent officer's size criteria (paras. 8.20).

TIME LIMITS ON FURTHER REFERRALS

HBR 12A(2)(b), sch 1A **8.8**   In any case which has previously been referred to the rent officer, no further referral must be made unless and until:

◆ the claimant has been on HB for 52 weeks or more, continuously, since the beginning of the benefit period (para. 7.81) to which the last referral related (whether one or more benefit periods ago); or

◆ the claimant's last benefit period was extended (as described in para. 17.24) and the extension lasted for 52 weeks or more; or

◆ 12 months have passed since the date of the rent officer's last determination; or

◆ there has been a relevant change of circumstances (para. 8.11) since the rent officer's last determination.

The last two apply regardless of changes of claimant, so long as the new claimant's letting is on the same terms as the previous claimant's or on terms which are substantially similar.

REPRESENTATIVE REFERRALS FOR HOSTEL CASES

8.9   For hostel cases (para. 8.10), no referral is required if a rent officer determination has been made for similar accommodation within the hostel during the previous 12 months, unless there is a 'relevant change of circumstances' (para. 8.11). For these purposes, accommodation must be treated as similar if it provides the same number of bed spaces. It may also be treated as similar in other appropriate cases. The earlier referral applies to any such similar accommodation within the hostel. `HBR 12A(2)(a),(7), sch 1A`

WHAT IS A 'HOSTEL'?

8.10   A 'hostel' is defined for these purposes as any building (other than a residential care home or nursing home: paras. 4.5-11) to which both the following apply: `HBR 2(1), 12A(8)`

◆ it provides domestic accommodation which is not self-contained together with meals or adequate facilities for preparing food; and

◆ it is:

- managed or run by a registered housing association or registered social landlord, or

- run on a non-commercial basis, and wholly or partly funded by a government department or agency or local authority, or

- managed by a registered charity or non-profit-making voluntary organisation which provides care, support or supervision with a view to assisting the rehabilitation of the residents or their resettlement into the community.

Table 8.2 'RELEVANT CHANGES OF CIRCUMSTANCES'

◆ Except in hostel cases (para. 8.10), there has been a change in the number of occupiers.

◆ Any child or young person in the household has reached the age of 10 or 16.

◆ There has been a change in the composition of the household (one example is when two people have ceased to be a couple).

◆ There has been a substantial change or improvement in the condition of the dwelling – regardless of whether there has been an associated change in the rent. (For example, central heating has been installed.)

- ◆ There has been a substantial change in the terms of the letting agreement (excluding a change in a term relating to rent alone) – regardless of whether there has been an associated change in the rent. (For example, the landlord has taken over the responsibility for internal decorations from the tenant or vice versa.)

- ◆ There has been a rent increase and:

  - the rent increase was made under a term of the letting agreement and that term is the same (or substantially the same) as at the previous referral to the rent officer; and

  - at the previous referral, the rent officer did not make any of the following determinations: a 'significantly high rent determination', a 'size-related rent determination' or an 'exceptionally high rent determination' (paras. 8.18-21).

- ◆ At the previous referral to the rent officer, the HB case was an 'exempt case' (para. 11.53), but the current HB case is not an 'exempt case'.

- ◆ At the previous referral to the rent officer, the claimant was not a 'young individual' (para. 11.8), but the claimant in the current case is a 'young individual'.

WHAT IS A 'RELEVANT CHANGE OF CIRCUMSTANCES'?

HBR sch 1A
SI 1997 No. 1984
SI 1997 No. 1995 **8.11**   Table 8.2 lists all the changes which count as a 'relevant change of circumstances' for the purposes of the rules described earlier. If there has been a 'relevant change of circumstances' since an HB case was last referred to the rent officer, a further referral must be made to the rent officer as a result of that change. If the authority does not become aware of such a change straightaway, a referral must be made when it does become aware of it.

Making the referral

TIME LIMITS AND METHOD OF REFERRAL

HBR 12A(3),(4) **8.12**   The referral must be made within three working days of the claim or change of circumstances giving rise to it, or as soon as practicable thereafter. Days when the authority's offices are closed for receiving or determining claims do not count as 'working days' for this purpose. The DSS recommends authorities use a standard form (HBR1). Authorities and rent officers may agree to communicate by electronic means (e.g. by fax) rather than in writing.

INFORMATION REQUIRED BY THE RENT OFFICER

8.13   Table 8.3 lists the information the authority should give when making a referral to the rent officer on or after 3rd April 2000. (Before then, the law and guidance was different.) The law specifically requires certain information to be included (this is indicated in the table) and also generally requires the authority to provide any other information required by the rent officer. This other information can sometimes vary from rent officer to rent officer: the table shows what information is normally required (see DSS circulars HB/CTB S3/97, A37/97, S4/98, A7/98, A36/98, A57/98, A15/99 and A47/99).

HBR 12A(1A),(1Z, (1B), (7A), 106 SI 1997 No. 198 SI 1997 No. 199

Table 8.3 INFORMATION REQUIRED BY THE RENT OFFICER

IDENTIFICATION AND GENERAL INFORMATION

◆   A case reference number.

◆   The claimant's name.

◆   The address of the property.

◆   The number of occupiers there.

◆   The age and sex of those occupiers and their relationship to the claimant (e.g. 'son', 'sub-tenant').

◆   The date the claimant commenced occupation (which may be approximate if necessary).

◆   Whether the landlord is a registered housing association or other registered social landlord.

◆   The details of the letting agreement, including the period of the letting.

◆   The type of accommodation (e.g. house, bedsit, room).

◆   In the case of a room, its location within the property (e.g. 'first floor, front').

◆   Details of all the rooms in the property, the ones the claimant has sole use of, and the ones the claimant has shared use of.

RENT, SERVICES, ETC.

In all cases (whether 'supported accommodation' or not)

◆ Whether the claimant is a 'young individual' (para. 11.8) *.

◆ If the rent includes a charge for any support charges (as defined in para. 11.89):

  • the fact that it does*;

  • the authority's valuation of the total value of such items which are eligible for HB (paras. 11.91-97)*; and

  • the authority's valuation of the total value of such items which are not eligible for HB (paras. 11.91-97)*.

◆ The gross actual rent on the property after deducting the authority's valuation of all the above items - whether eligible for HB or not*.

◆ Whether the rent includes any amount for water charges, fuel or meals (but no valuation of any of these is required) *.

◆ Details of all other eligible and ineligible services included in the rent, and details of any variable service charges.

◆ Whether central heating is provided.

◆ Whether a garage is provided.

◆ Whether the accommodation is furnished fully, partly or minimally, or is unfurnished.

◆ Who is responsible for internal decorations (landlord or claimant).

And in all the above cases:

◆ If the claimant is a joint occupier (para. 8.30) the figures for rent and services mentioned above should be those for the whole property.

◆ The figures for rent and services mentioned above should be given for the period for which rent is due. For example, if the claimant's rent is due calendar monthly, they should be given as calendar monthly figures.

* NOTE: Items marked with an asterisk are those specifically mentioned in the law (para. 8.13).

The rent officer's determinations

8.14   The rent officer may make one or more of the following determinations. More information on each is given in the next few paragraphs: SI 1997 No. 198
SI 1997 No. 199

◆ a significantly high rent determination;

◆ a size-related rent determination;

◆ an exceptionally high rent determination;

◆ a local reference rent determination;

◆ a single room rent determination;

◆ a claim-related rent determination;

◆ certain determinations relating to service charges.

8.15   The rent officer does not make any determinations if the referral is withdrawn by the authority.

8.16   The rent officer is not required to visit the dwelling but does so in many cases. He or she has no statutory right of access but, if the rent officer notifies the authority that he or she has been denied access to a dwelling, the authority may withhold HB (para. 16.41).

GENERAL RULES AND ASSUMPTIONS ABOUT DETERMINATIONS

8.17   In making the determinations described below (paras. 8.18-28), the rent officer: HBR 12A(6)
SI 1997 No. 198
SI 1997 No. 199

◆ must base these on the facts as they stood on the date on which the authority made the referral, unless the claimant had left the accommodation by that date, in which case they are based on the facts as they stood at the end of the claimant's letting;

◆ provides these for the same period (e.g. weekly, calendar monthly) as that for which the authority supplied the information to the rent officer (table 8.3);

◆ must 'assume that no one who would have been entitled to housing benefit had sought or is seeking the tenancy';

◆ must ignore all rents payable to housing associations, other registered social landlords and registered charities;

◆ must include the value of any meals provided to the claimant (except that, in the case of the exceptionally high rent determination, the rent officer may choose whether to include meals or not);

◆ must exclude the value of all other service charges which are ineligible for HB (chapter 11);

◆ must exclude the value of all the following support charges (as defined in para. 11.89) whether eligible or ineligible for HB.

SIGNIFICANTLY HIGH RENT DETERMINATIONS

1997 No. 1984
1997 No. 1995 **8.18**   The rent officer determines whether the referred rent for the dwelling is 'significantly higher than the rent which the landlord might reasonably have been expected to obtain'. If it is, he or she makes a significantly high rent determination: this is the amount 'the landlord might reasonably have been expected to obtain' for the dwelling, having regard to 'the level of rent under similar tenancies [or licences] of similar dwellings in the locality (or as similar as regards tenancy [or licence], dwelling and locality as reasonably practicable'. The general rules and assumptions apply (para. 8.17).

SIZE-RELATED RENT DETERMINATIONS

1997 No. 1984
1997 No. 1995 **8.19**   Except in the case of caravans, mobile homes and houseboats, the rent officer also determines whether the dwelling exceeds the size criteria given in paragraph 8.20 and table 8.4. If it does, he or she makes a size-related rent determination: this is the amount 'the landlord might reasonably have been expected to obtain' on a dwelling which:

◆ is in 'the same locality'; and

◆ is let under a similar tenancy under the same terms as the tenancy of the dwelling in question; and

◆ matches those size criteria; and

◆ is in a reasonable state of repair; and

◆ in other respects, matches the claimant's dwelling 'as closely as reasonably practicable'.

The general rules and assumptions apply (para. 8.17).

8.20   The size criteria (para. 8.19 and table 8.4) allow for every 'occupier' – which is defined for this purpose as 'a person (whether or not identified by name) who is stated [by the authority], in the application [to the rent officer] for the determination, to occupy the dwelling'. There is no further definition, but the term appears intended to have a degree of flexibility. Note that (as DSS circular HB/CTB A18/97 points out), the authority (not the rent officer) determines whether or not someone is an 'occupier'; and the term is not expressly limited to those whose circumstances are taken into account in the calculation of the claimant's entitlement to HB (though see below). It is clear that all the following should be included as 'occupiers' for this purpose:

◆ the claimant and members of his or her family (paras. 6.4-20); and

◆ everyone else who normally lives in the dwelling, such as non-dependants, (sub-)tenants, boarders, joint occupiers, certain carers (para. 6.26), foster children, and certain other children and young persons who do not count as a member of the family (para. 6.19).

In a recent case (*R v Swale Borough Council Housing Benefit Review Board ex p Marchant*, (1999)), the Court of Appeal held that a child who spends time in the homes of each of his or her parents (who live apart) counts as an 'occupier' only in the home of the parent who is 'responsible' for him or her (para. 6.16 – typically the one who receives child benefit). If this causes the other parent exceptional hardship, he or she could seek additional housing benefit (para. 11.21). This case does not apply in other difficult situations. One example is that of a grown-up child who lives away from home for part(s) of the year (perhaps as a student) but returns home from time to time (perhaps in the holidays). It is clear that he or she counts as an 'occupier' in weeks in which he or she is treated as a non-dependant. In other weeks (if any), it can be argued that he or she counts as an 'occupier' (since the definition of 'occupier' appears flexible and is unaffected in this situation by the Marchant case), but it is unlikely that all local authorities will agree with this. Matters such as this are open to appeal to the authority and its Review Board (chapter 19).

Table 8.4 THE RENT OFFICER'S SIZE CRITERIA

These are relevant for size-related rent determinations (para. 8.19), exceptionally high rent determinations (para. 8.21) and local reference rent determinations (para. 8.22). For who counts as an occupier for these purposes, see paragraph 8.20.

◆ One room is allowed as a bedroom for each of the following occupiers, each occupier coming only within the first category which applies to him or her:

  • a married or unmarried couple (paras. 6.4, 6.6);

  • a single person aged 16 or more;

  • two children of the same sex under the age of 16;

  • two children (of the same or opposite sexes) under the age of 10;

  • a child aged under the age of 16.

◆ One, two or three living rooms ('rooms suitable for living in') are allowed as follows:

  • one if there are one to three occupiers;

  • two if there are four to six occupiers;

  • three if there are seven or more occupiers.

◆ The size criteria relate to the total number of rooms allowed (under either of the above headings). It is irrelevant whether the claimant actually uses those rooms as bedrooms or living rooms.

> **Example: The rent officer's size criteria**
>
> A couple have two children aged 6 and 8. No-one else lives with them. Their dwelling has three bedrooms, one living room, a kitchen, a bathroom, a toilet and several uninhabitable cupboards.
>
> The rent officer's size criteria ignore the kitchen, bathroom and toilet. The criteria allow them four bedrooms/living rooms in all, as follows:
>
> ◆ one room as a bedroom for the couple;
>
> ◆ one room as a bedroom for the two children;
>
> ◆ two rooms as living rooms – because there are four occupiers.
>
> Their four rooms (three bedrooms and one living room) do not exceed the size criteria because bedrooms and living rooms are interchangeable for these purposes.

EXCEPTIONALLY HIGH RENT DETERMINATIONS

SI 1997 No. 1984
SI 1997 No. 1995

8.21   Except in the case of hostels (para. 8.10) or residential care homes or nursing homes (para. 4.5-11), the rent officer also determines whether either of the figures described above (paras. 8.18-20), or (if he or she has not made a determination in either of those cases) the referred rent for the dwelling, is 'exceptionally high'. If it is, he or she makes an exceptionally high rent determination: this is 'the highest rent, which is not an exceptionally high rent and which a landlord might reasonably have been expected to obtain' on a dwelling which:

◆ is in 'the same locality'; and

◆ matches the size criteria (table 8.4); and

◆ is in a reasonable state of repair.

The general rules and assumptions apply (para. 8.17).

LOCAL REFERENCE RENT DETERMINATIONS

SI 1997 No. 1984
SI 1997 No. 1995

8.22   Except in the case of hostels (para. 8.10) or residential care homes or nursing homes (para. 4.5-11), the rent officer also determines whether any of the figures described above (paras. 8.18-21), or (if he or she has not made a determination in any of those cases) the referred rent for the dwelling, is greater than the 'local reference rent' described below. If it is, he or she makes a local reference rent determination (in other words, notifies the authority of the local reference rent). If it is not, he or she notifies the authority that it is not.

8.23   In determining the 'local reference rent', the rent officer takes account of the range of rents 'which a landlord might reasonably have been expected to obtain' on dwellings which:

◆ are in the same locality; and

◆ match the size criteria (table 8.4); and

◆ in the case of one-room dwellings, are in the same category as the claimant's dwelling (categories (a) to (c) in table 8.5); and

◆ are let on an assured tenancy (or a similar tenancy or licence); and

◆ are in a reasonable state of repair.

The general rules and assumptions apply (para. 8.17).

8.24   The 'local reference rent' is then the figure which is half-way between:

◆ the lowest such rent which is not an 'exceptionally low rent'; and

◆ the highest such rent which is not an 'exceptionally high rent'.

SINGLE ROOM RENT DETERMINATIONS

8.25   Except in the case of hostels (para. 8.10) or residential care homes or nursing homes (para. 4.5-11), and only if the authority states in the referral that the claimant is a 'young individual' (para. 11.8), the rent officer also determines whether the claimant's rent is greater than the 'single room rent' described below. If it is, he or she makes a single room rent determination (in other words, notifies the authority of the single room rent). If it is not, he or she notifies the authority that it is not.   SI 1997 No. 1984
SI 1997 No. 1995

8.26   In determining the 'single room rent', the rent officer takes account of the range of rents 'which a landlord might reasonably have been expected to obtain' on dwellings which:

◆ provide exclusive use of one bedroom;

◆ provide no other bedroom or room suitable for living in;

◆ provide shared use of a toilet;

◆ provide shared use of a kitchen (and no exclusive use of facilities for cooking food);

◆ do not provide board and attendance;

◆ are in 'the same locality';

◆ are let on an assured tenancy (or a similar tenancy or licence);

◆ are in a reasonable state of repair.

The general rules and assumptions apply (para. 8.17).

8.27   The 'single room rent' is then the figure which is half-way between:

◆ the lowest such rent which is not an 'exceptionally low rent'; and

◆ the highest such rent which is not an 'exceptionally high rent'.

CLAIM-RELATED RENT DETERMINATIONS

SI 1997 No. 1984
SI 1997 No. 1995

8.28   In all cases, the rent officer must make a 'claim-related determination'. This is the only, lower or lowest of:

◆ the referred rent, adjusted (as regards service charges) in accordance with the general rules and assumptions (para. 8.17);

◆ the significantly high rent;

◆ the size-related rent;

◆ the exceptionally high rent.

SERVICE CHARGES DETERMINATIONS

SI 1997 No. 1984
SI 1997 No. 1995

8.29   Except in the case of a hostel (para. 8.10); the rent officer must determine the value of the ineligible service charges (apart from meals and support charges) he or she excluded in making the claim-related rent determination (unless the amount is negligible).

JOINT OCCUPIERS

SI 1997 No. 1984
SI 1997 No. 1995

8.30   In the case of accommodation occupied by joint occupiers (para. 11.4), the rent officer's determinations (apart from the single room rent determination) relate to the dwelling as a whole. The rent officer may suggest an apportionment but this is not binding on the authority.

NOTIFICATION AND TIME LIMITS

SI 1997 No. 1984
SI 1997 No. 1995

8.31   The rent officer has a duty to notify the authority of the following:

◆ the claim-related rent;

◆ the local reference rent (if there is one);

◆ the single room rent (if there is one);

◆ except in the case of a hostel (para. 8.10), the value of the ineligible service charges (apart from meals and support charges) he or she has excluded in making his or her claim-related rent determination;

◆ whether the claim-related rent includes an amount for ineligible meals (as can be the case if it is an exceptionally high rent determination).

8.32   The rent officer should notify the authority of the above determinations within five working days or, if the rent officer intends to inspect the dwelling, within 25 working days (or, in either case, as soon as reasonably practicable after that). The period begins on the day the rent officer receives the referral from the authority or (if he or she has requested this) on the day he or she receives further information needed from the authority.

INDICATIVE RENT LEVELS

8.33   Separate from the provisions described above, the rent officer provides each authority, on the first working day of each month, with 'indicative rent levels' for its area. The law allows the authority to take these into account in estimating payments on account (para. 16.16), and the subsidy rules encourage this. Indicative rent levels do not apply to caravans, mobile homes, houseboats or rental purchase agreements. (They also do not take account of the rent officer's size criteria: table 8.4.)   SI 1997 No. 1984
SI 1997 No. 1995

8.34   One 'indicative rent level' is provided for each category of dwelling shown in table 8.5. In determining the indicative rent level for each category, the rent officer takes account of the range of rents 'which a landlord might reasonably have been expected to obtain' on dwellings which:

◆   are in that category;

◆   are in the area of the authority (not 'the locality' of the dwelling);

◆   are let on an assured tenancy (or a similar tenancy or licence); and

◆   are in a reasonable state of repair;

◆   adjusted – as regards service charges only – in accordance with the general rules and assumptions (para. 8.17).

8.35   The 'indicative rent level' for each category is then:

◆   the lowest such rent which is not an 'exceptionally low rent'; plus

◆   one-quarter of the difference between that and the highest such rent which is not an 'exceptionally high rent'.

Table 8.5 THE RENT OFFICER'S CATEGORIES OF DWELLING

These are relevant for local reference rent determinations (para. 8.22) and indicative rent levels (para. 8.31).

(a) One-room dwellings where a 'substantial' part of the rent is 'fairly attributable' to 'board and attendance' included within the rent.

(b) Other one-room dwellings where the tenant shares a kitchen or toilet with someone who is not a member of his or her household (para. 6.3).

(c) Other one-room dwellings.

(d) Two-room dwellings.

(e) Three-room dwellings.

(f) Four-room dwellings.

(g) Five-room dwellings.

(h) Six-room dwellings.

Note: Definition of 'room'

For these purposes, a 'room' is defined as a 'bedroom or room suitable for living in':

◆ including a room the claimant shares with any member of his or her household, including a non-dependant (para. 6.21), or with a boarder or (sub-)tenant (paras. 6.23, 6.25);

◆ but (in the case of one-room dwellings: categories (a) to (c)) excluding a room he or she shares with anyone else.

Appeals and errors

APPEALS BY THE CLAIMANT

HBR 79(4A) **8.36** If any request for an internal review (para. 19.21) relates wholly or partly to any determination by the rent officer (and is within the appropriate time limit: paras. 19.21-24), the authority must, within seven days of receipt apply to the rent officer for a re-determination for the case in question. The authority must forward the claimant's representations at the same time. This must be done even if the internal review request is made by a later claimant at the same address. There are however limitations (in the next paragraph).

HBR 79(4B),(4C) **8.37** For any particular claimant and any particular dwelling, only one application to the rent officer may be made in respect of any particular determination (plus one in respect of any particular substitute determination: para. 8.44). This is the case regardless of whether the authority itself has previously chosen to make an application for a re-determination (para. 11.39).

8.38 However, a claimant who considers that a referral should or should not have been made in the first place (e.g. a claimant who disputes whether he or she falls within one of the exceptions described earlier in this chapter) has the right to use the ordinary HB appeals procedure (chapter 19) to challenge this. This is because the determination whether or not to refer a case to the rent officer is made by the authority.

APPEALS BY THE AUTHORITY

8.39   The authority may itself choose to apply to the rent officer for a re-   HBR 12B
determination. For any particular claimant and any particular dwelling, it may do
this only once in respect of any particular determination (plus once in respect of
any particular substitute determination: para. 8.44); unless a re-determination is
subsequently made as a result of an appeal by the claimant (para. 8.36), in which
case the authority may do this once more.

RENT OFFICER RE-DETERMINATIONS

8.40   In each of the cases described above (paras. 8.36-39), the rent officer must   SI 1997 No. 198
make a complete re-determination. Even if the application for a re-determination   SI 1997 No. 199
relates only to one figure, the rent officer has to reconsider all matters pertaining
to the case in question. All the assumptions, etc, applying to determinations (para.
8.14 onwards) apply equally to re-determinations. Re-determinations should be
made within 20 working days or as soon as practicable after that. The period
begins on the day the rent officer receives the application from the authority or (if
he or she has requested this) on the day he or she receives further information
needed from the authority.

8.41   The rent officer making the re-determination must seek and have regard
to the advice of one or two other rent officers. Usually at least one rent officer
from a different area will be involved and all the rent officers involved will have
at least five years' experience. Rent officers will usually, if so requested, give the
authority the reasons for their re-determination(s); and the authority should pass
these on to the claimant if so requested. The High Court has decided (*R v
Sandwell Metropolitan Council ex p Wilkinson*, QBD, 1998) that the rent officer
has no legal duty to give reasons for his or her determinations in relation to
'exempt cases' (para. 11.53) – since in such cases all determinations relating to
eligible rent are for the authority (not the rent officer) to make. This case
strengthens the argument (which most rent officers seem to accept) that in all
other cases (i.e. all cases in which the rent officer's determinations are binding on
the authority in its assessment of a claimant's maximum rent: paras. 11.6-7), the
rent officer must give reasons for his or her determinations if requested to do so,
failing which he or she may be subject to an application for judicial review in the
High Court (Court of Session in Scotland).

HOW THE RE-DETERMINATION AFFECTS HB

8.42   In broad terms, re-determinations affect HB in the same way as   HBR 79(5B)
determinations (para. 8.4). However, in cases which are not 'exempt' (i.e. in cases
in which the rent officer's figures are used to calculate the claimant's 'maximum
rent': para. 8.4 and chapter 11), the following further rules apply:

◆   If the effect of the re-determination is that the 'maximum rent' increases, this applies from the date of the rent officer's original determination. So the claimant is awarded any resulting arrears of HB (but this applies only to the claimant in question, not to a previous claimant at the same address).

◆   If the effect of the re-determination is that the 'maximum rent' reduces, this applies from the date of the rent officer's re-determination following the appeal: the reduction is not applied retrospectively. So it does not mean (unless the authority delays applying it) that the claimant has been overpaid HB.

DEALING WITH ERRORS

1997 No. 1984
1997 No. 1995

8.43   The rent officer has a duty to notify the authority, as soon as is practicable, upon discovering that he or she has made an error, other than one of professional judgment, in a determination or re-determination (including a substitute determination or substitute re-determination).

HBR 12C, 12D

8.44   In such cases the authority must apply to the rent officer for a substitute determination (or substitute re-determination). The authority must also do this if it discovers that it made an error in its application to the rent officer as regards the size of the dwelling, the number of occupiers, the composition of the household or the terms of the tenancy. In all such cases, the authority must state the nature of the error and withdraw any outstanding applications for rent officer determinations in that case.

HBR 79(5B)
1997 No. 1984
1997 No. 1995

8.45   All the assumptions, etc. applying to determinations (para. 8.17 onwards) also apply to substitute determinations/re-determinations. In broad terms, substitute determinations and substitute re-determinations affect HB in the same way as re-determinations (para. 8.42).

Pre-tenancy determinations

8.46   People can find out whether their HB would be likely to be restricted if they claimed HB, by asking for a 'pre-tenancy determination' ('PTD').

HOW TO GET A PRE-TENANCY DETERMINATION

HBR 12A(8)
1997 No. 1984
1997 No. 1995

8.47   Any 'prospective occupier' of any dwelling (other than a council letting) may apply to the authority requesting it to refer the rent to the rent officer. So may any current occupier of a dwelling who is contemplating entering a new agreement there (but see para. 8.50). Authorities have standard forms for people who require a PTD.

8.48   The main conditions for getting a PTD are that the person must:

◆   indicate on the form that he or she would be likely to claim HB if he or she took up the letting (or took up the new agreement);

♦ sign the form; and

♦ obtain a signature on the form from the landlord consenting to a referral. The landlord will be expected to provide the rent officer with necessary information and allow access to the dwelling.

THE AUTHORITY'S DUTIES

8.49   With two exceptions (para. 8.50), whenever an authority receives a request for a PTD, it must refer the details to the rent officer within two working days of the date of the request for the PTD. The rent officer's duties in such cases are described in paragraph 8.51.   HBR 12A(1)(c), (2A),(4)

8.50   First, if the request for the PTD is invalid (e.g. if the landlord has not consented), the authority must return it to the person along with a notification of why it is invalid. Secondly, if:

♦ the authority already has a rent officer determination which was made for the dwelling in question less than 12 months ago (whether a PTD or a determination made following a claim); and

♦ the circumstances for which that determination was made are the same as those indicated in the request for the PTD (i.e. there are no differences between them which constitute a 'relevant change of circumstances': para. 8.11),

the authority must, within four working days of the request for the PTD, supply details of that determination to the person along with a notification of why a current PTD referral cannot be made.

THE RENT OFFICER'S DUTIES

8.51   When the rent officer receives a referral requesting a PTD, he or she makes the same determinations as in any other case referred to him or her. The rent officer notifies the result to the authority within five working days.   SI 1997 No. 198
SI 1997 No. 199

CLAIMS FOR HB FOLLOWING A PRE-TENANCY DETERMINATION

8.52   With two exceptions (para. 8.53), when the authority receives an HB claim on a dwelling to which a PTD applies, the authority uses the PTD in the same way as if it had been a rent officer determination made following the claim (i.e. no additional referral is required).   HBR 10, 11, 12A

8.53   The PTD does not apply, and a referral must be made to the rent officer, if:

♦ the PTD was made more than 12 months ago; or

♦ the circumstances indicated in the claim for HB are different from those indicated in the request for the PTD (i.e. there are differences between them which constitute a 'relevant change of circumstances': para. 8.11).

CALCULATING 'MAXIMUM RENTS' FROM PRE-TENANCY DETERMINATIONS

HBR 11(6A),(6B) **8.54** With the exceptions described in the previous and following paragraphs, whenever the authority is required to calculate a 'maximum rent' in assessing a claimant's eligible rent (chapter 11), it uses the rent officer figures provided in the PTD.

8.55 If the claimant's actual rent at the date of his or her claim for HB is lower than the 'maximum rent' calculated from the rent officer figures provided in the PTD, similar points arise as in paragraph 11.12.

APPEALS

8.56 There is no right of appeal relating to a pre-tenancy determination until and unless it is used in connection with the determination of a claim for HB (in which case the ordinary rules about appeals about rent officer determinations apply: paras. 8.36 onwards).

9 Calculating HB and main CTB

9.1 This chapter explains how to calculate HB and 'main CTB'. Chapter 10 describes the other type of CTB known as 'second adult rebate'. This chapter covers:

◆ the information needed to calculate HB and main CTB;

◆ how to calculate HB and main CTB;

◆ non-dependant deductions;

◆ local schemes;

◆ additional benefit in exceptional circumstances; and

◆ how figures are converted to weekly amounts.

9.2 HB and main CTB are dealt with together because they are similar to each other (whereas the method of calculating second adult rebate is completely different). However, it is perfectly possible to be entitled to only one (chapter 4).

9.3 In general terms, claimants with no income or low income (including all claimants on income support or income-based jobseeker's allowance – paras. 2.7-14) qualify for maximum benefit – which may be reduced if there are non-dependants in their home. The more income claimants have, the less benefit they get, but there is no general upper limit. The level of income at which benefit entitlement runs out varies from claimant to claimant depending on a wide range of factors, as illustrated in appendix 4.

Information needed

9.4 The first piece of information the authority needs in calculating HB or main CTB is whether the claimant (or any partner) is on income support or JSA(IB). (In certain cases, a person can be treated as being on JSA(IB) for this purpose even though he or she is not being paid it: para. 9.10.)

9.5 If the claimant (or any partner) is on income support or JSA(IB) (or is treated as receiving JSA(IB)), the authority needs information about:

◆ the weekly eligible rent and/or council tax (chapter 11); and

◆ any non-dependants in the household (para. 9.21 onwards).

9.6 In all other cases, the authority needs the above information and also information about:

◆ the applicable amount (chapter 12); and

◆ income and capital (chapters 13 to 15).

The calculation

9.7   The next few paragraphs explain with examples how to calculate entitlement to HB and main CTB on a weekly basis. Table 9.1 summarises the rules. (Different rules apply to 'extended payments' of HB/CTB: para. 17.54.)

Although both benefits are always awarded for specific benefit weeks (para. 7.43), some of the CTB regulations are expressed on a daily basis. For example, the 'taper' mentioned in paragraph 9.14 is given as 2⁶⁄₇ per cent per day (exactly equal to 20 per cent per week). However, this is because of technicalities in the operation of the council tax itself. The 'weekly benefit' approach is adopted in this guide, with variations being described when they arise.

MAXIMUM BENEFIT

9.8   The starting point for all calculations of HB and main CTB is the claimant's 'maximum benefit'. On a weekly basis, this is:

◆ in calculating HB:

- the whole of the claimant's weekly eligible rent (para. 11.3),

- minus any non-dependant deductions which may apply;

◆ in calculating main CTB:

- the whole of the claimant's weekly eligible council tax (para. 11.108),

- minus any non-dependant deductions which may apply.

Note that 'maximum benefit' does not mean the same as 'maximum rent' (para. 11.7).

CBA s.130(1),(4), 131(1),(3),(4),(10 HBR 61 CTBR 51(1)

CLAIMANTS ON INCOME SUPPORT OR JSA(IB)

9.9   A claimant qualifies for maximum benefit whilst he or she (or any partner) is:

◆ on income support; or

◆ on JSA(IB); or

◆ treated as receiving JSA(IB) (as described in the next paragraph).

CBA s.130(1),(3) 131(5),(8) HBR sch 4 para ⸲ sch 5 para 5 CTBR sch 4 para sch 5 para 5

9.10   A claimant is treated as receiving JSA(IB) (and so qualifies for maximum benefit) whilst he or she (or any partner) is:

◆ entitled to JSA(IB) but not receiving it because of a sanction; or

◆ in the waiting days before his or her JSA(IB) starts – or would start apart from a sanction.

HBR 2(1), (3A) CTBR 2(1), (3A)

CLAIMANTS NOT ON INCOME SUPPORT OR JSA(IB)

9.11 In any case other than those described above, if the claimant's capital (valued as in chapters 13 to 15) is over £16,000, then he or she does not qualify for any HB or main CTB at all, and so the remainder of this chapter does not apply. Otherwise, the claimant's income (chapters 13 to 15) is compared with his or her applicable amount (chapter 12).

CBA s.130(1),(3), 131(5),(8)

9.12 If the claimant has no income; or has income which is less than, or equal to, his or her applicable amount; the claimant is entitled to maximum benefit. In other words, the claimant receives the same amount as if he or she was on income support or JSA(IB). (In some cases, the claimant may actually qualify for income support or JSA(IB), and should be advised of this.)

CBA s.130(1),(3), 131(5),(8)

9.13 If the claimant's income is more than his or her applicable amount, the difference between the two is known as 'excess income'. The claimant's maximum benefit is reduced by a percentage of this excess income, to give the amount of entitlement.

HBR 62
CTBR 53

9.14 The percentage used in calculating HB is different from that used in calculating main CTB. For weekly calculations, the percentages are as follows. They are also known as 'tapers':

◆ 65 per cent in calculating HB;

◆ 20 per cent in calculating main CTB.

9.15 The effect is that for each £1 of excess income a claimant has, his or her maximum benefit is reduced by 65p per week in HB, and by 20p per week in CTB.

MINIMUM BENEFIT AND ROUNDING

HBR 64

9.16 If the weekly amount of HB calculated as above is less than 50p, then it is not awarded. There is no equivalent rule in CTB, where there is no minimum award of benefit.

HBR 69(9)

9.17 In HB, the authority may round any amount involved in the calculation to the nearest penny, halfpennies being rounded upwards. In CTB, there is no similar rule: indeed the DSS recommends that entitlement should be calculated to six decimal places (GM para. B3.26). This is to avoid reconciliation errors at the end of the financial year. Notifications sent to claimants about their entitlement may be rounded to the nearest penny.

MAIN CTB AND THE 'BETTER BUY'

CBA s.131(9)

9.18 If the amount of a claimant's main CTB calculated as above is lower than his or her entitlement to second adult rebate, he or she will not get main CTB, but will get second adult rebate instead. This is because of the 'better buy' comparison, described in paragraphs 10.29 onwards. Examples are given at the end of chapter 10.

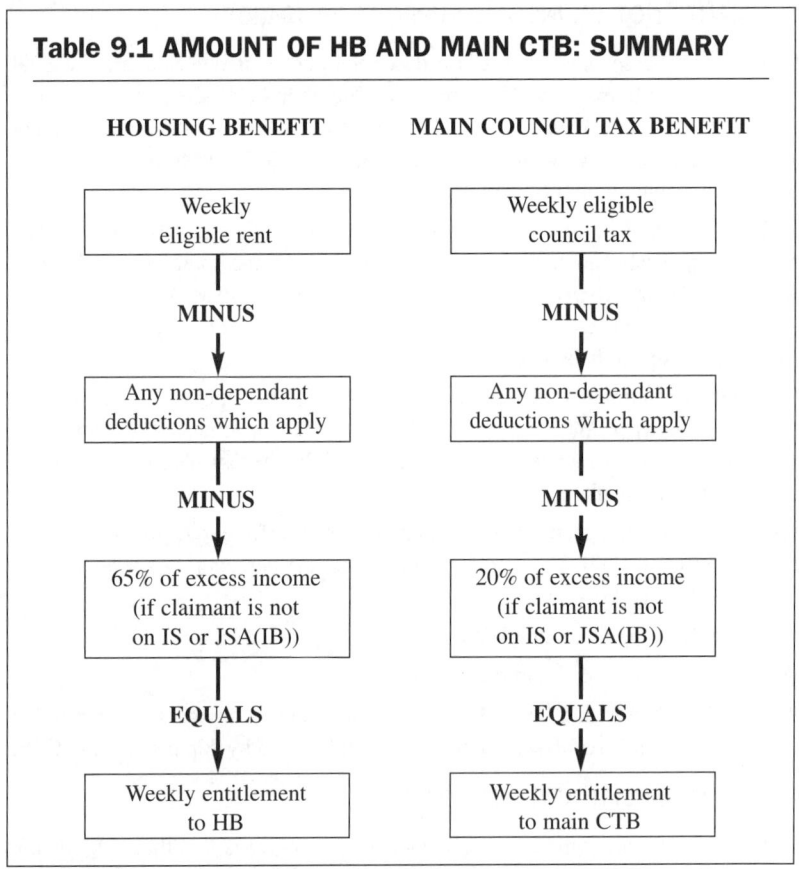

Table 9.1 AMOUNT OF HB AND MAIN CTB: SUMMARY

HOUSING BENEFIT   MAIN COUNCIL TAX BENEFIT

Weekly   Weekly eligible
eligible rent   council tax

MINUS   MINUS

Any non-dependant   Any non-dependant
deductions which apply   deductions which apply

MINUS   MINUS

65% of excess income   20% of excess income
(if claimant is not   (if claimant is not
on IS or JSA(IB))   on IS or JSA(IB))

EQUALS   EQUALS

Weekly entitlement   Weekly entitlement
to HB   to main CTB

HB AND RENT-FREE PERIODS

9.19   The following additional rules apply if a claimant has rent-free weeks or   HBR 70(1)
other rent-free periods. They do not apply in cases where a landlord has waived
the rent in return for works carried out by the tenant (para. 4.26).

9.20   No HB is awarded during rent-free periods (except in certain cases   HBR 70(2)
relating to extended payments: para. 17.66). HB is awarded only for periods in
which rent is due, during which periods the calculation factors (i.e. applicable
amount, income and any non-dependant deductions) are adjusted pro rata:

◆ If rent is expressed on a weekly basis: multiply the calculation factors by 52
or 53, then divide by the number of weeks when rent is due in that year.

◆ If rent is not expressed on a weekly basis: multiply the calculation factors
by 366 or 365, then divide by the number of days when rent is due in that
year.

Examples: Calculating HB and main CTB

SINGLE CLAIMANT ON INCOME SUPPORT OR JSA(IB)

A single claimant has no non-dependants: she lives alone. Her eligible rent is £55.00 per week. The council tax on her home would be £8.00 per week apart from the fact that she qualifies for a 25% council tax discount, which reduces her liability to £6.00 per week.

Claimants on income support or JSA(IB) get maximum benefit – which is based on their eligible rent and eligible council tax.

HB:	Eligible rent	
	equals weekly HB	£55.00
Main CTB:	Eligible council tax	
	equals weekly main CTB	£6.00

CLAIMANT NOT ON INCOME SUPPORT OR JSA(IB)

A couple have no non-dependants. They are not on income support or JSA(IB). Their joint weekly income exceeds their applicable amount by £20.00. Their eligible rent is £50.00 per week. Their eligible council tax liability is £7.56 per week.

Claimants with excess income get maximum benefit minus a percentage of their excess income.

HB:	Eligible rent	£50.00
	minus 65% of excess income (65% x £20.00)	£13.00
	equals weekly HB	£37.00
Main CTB:	Eligible council tax	£7.56
	minus 20% of excess income (20% x £20.00)	£4.00
	equals weekly main CTB	£3.56

Non-dependant deductions

HBR 61
CTBR 51(1)

9.21   HB and main CTB are normally reduced for each non-dependant living in the claimant's home. The next paragraphs explain when a deduction is or is not made, and the additional rules involved. In main CTB, the amounts of the deductions and some of the other rules are different from those applying in HB. The differences are mentioned whenever they arise.

9.22   Non-dependants are usually adult sons, daughters, other relatives or friends who live in the claimant's household on a non-commercial basis (paras. 6.21-22). Some claimants receive money from their non-dependants to pay for their keep. This may include a contribution towards rent, council tax, food or household expenses. This money is not treated as the claimants' income (table 13.3). Instead deductions are made from the claimant's HB and main CTB. However, these deductions are not related to what the non-dependant actually pays. They are fixed sums which apply even if the non-dependant pays the claimant nothing at all. The level of deductions (table 9.3) is high in some cases, and may cause claimants hardship. In exceptional circumstances it may be possible to obtain additional HB or CTB meeting part or all of the deduction (para. 9.42).

CASES IN WHICH NO DEDUCTION IS MADE

9.23   As described in paragraphs 9.24-26, there are three types of case in which no non-dependant deduction is made.

9.24   No deduction applies in respect of any of the following, because they are defined in the law as not being non-dependants (para. 6.21):

HBR 3(2)
CTBR 3(2)

◆ children aged under 16 and young persons aged 16 to 18 inclusive (whether or not they are counted as a member of the family for HB/CTB purposes);

◆ boarders, (sub-)tenants and joint occupiers;

◆ carers provided by a charity or voluntary organisation for whom the claimant or partner are charged;

◆ the claimant's landlord and members of the landlord's household (this applies only in HB: it is irrelevant in main CTB).

Table 9.2 NON-DEPENDANTS FOR WHOM NO DEDUCTION APPLIES: SUMMARY

◆ Non-dependants on income support or income-based jobseeker's allowance. However in HB (but not main CTB) there is a deduction if they are aged 25 or more.

◆ Non-dependants under 18.

◆ Non-dependants who are full-time students. However in HB (but not main CTB) there is a deduction in the summer vacation if they take up remunerative work.

◆ Non-dependants receiving a Work Based Training Allowance.

◆   Non-dependants in prison or otherwise detained.

◆   Non-dependants who have been in hospital for more than six weeks.

◆   Non-dependants who normally live elsewhere.

◆   Non-dependants who fall within any of the groups who are 'disregarded persons' for council tax discount purposes. However this applies in main CTB only. In HB there is a deduction (unless they fall within any of the earlier entries in this table).

Note:

Appendix 7 gives full information about all the above categories of people. It includes all the 'disregarded persons' mentioned above – such as (in various circumstances) education leavers, students, student nurses, apprentices, people who are severely mentally impaired, and carers.

HBR 2(1), 63(6)
CTBR 2(1), 52(6)

9.25   There are no non-dependant deductions in either HB or main CTB if the claimant or any partner:

◆   is registered blind or has ceased to be registered blind within the past 28 weeks because of regaining sight (para. 12.20); or

◆   receives the care component of disability living allowance payable at any rate (para. 12.22); or

◆   receives attendance allowance payable at any rate or constant attendance allowance (including the related benefits in para. 12.24).

In such cases, if the claimant has more than one non-dependant, no deduction applies for any of them. (Note that the second and third cases cease to apply when disability living allowance or attendance allowance themselves cease – for example, when the claimant or partner have been in hospital for four weeks.)

HBR 63(1),
(2),(7),(8)
CTBR 52(1),
(2),(7),(8)

9.26   No deduction applies in respect of any non-dependant who falls within certain groups. The main groups are summarised in table 9.2. As indicated there, there are some differences between the groups applying for HB purposes and those applying for main CTB purposes. Appendix 7 defines all the relevant categories of people and gives the detailed rules about whether a non-dependant deduction applies in HB and main CTB.

CASES IN WHICH A DEDUCTION IS MADE

HBR 63(1),(2)
CTBR 52(1),(2)

9.27   In cases other than those described above, a non-dependant deduction is made. The amount depends upon whether the non-dependant is in 'remunerative work' (para. 9.33) and, if so, on the level of his or her gross income. The amounts for HB and main CTB are different, and are listed in table 9.3. Additional rules for claimants who are joint occupiers and for non-dependant couples are in paragraphs 9.37-38.

NON-DEPENDANTS IN REMUNERATIVE WORK

9.28   For non-dependants in remunerative work, there are six possible levels of deduction in HB and four in main CTB (table 9.3), depending in either case on the level of the non-dependant's gross income (unless no deduction is appropriate at all: paras. 9.23-26).   HBR 63(1),(2) CTBR 52(1),(2)

9.29   It is the non-dependant's gross income, not net income, which is relevant. So long as the non-dependant is in remunerative work, the rule relates to his or her income from all sources. The only exception is that the following types of income are always disregarded: HBR 63(9) CTBR 52(9)

◆ disability living allowance (either or both components: para. 12.22);

◆ attendance allowance and constant attendance allowance (including the related benefits in para. 12.24);

◆ payments from the Macfarlane Trusts, the Eileen Trust, the Fund or the Independent Living Funds, including payments in kind from these sources and payments of money which originally derived from them (para. 13.40).

Table 9.3 SUMMARY OF WEEKLY NON-DEPENDANT DEDUCTIONS

	Deduction in HB	Deduction in main CTB
Non-dependants in remunerative work with gross income of:		
£259.00 per week or more	£47.75	£6.95
between £207.00 and £258.99 per week	£43.50	£5.80
between £157.00 and £206.99 per week	£38.20	£4.60
between £120.00 and £156.99 per week	£23.35	£4.60
between £81.00 and £119.99 per week	£17.00	£2.30
under £81.00 per week	£7.40	£2.30
Non-dependants not in remunerative work (regardless of income level)	£7.40	£2.30

Note:
'Remunerative work' is defined in paras. 9.33 onwards.

9.30   As regards any other source of income, there are no rules saying how the gross amount is to be assessed, though none of the disregards in chapter 14 applies. The DSS advises that for non-dependants with savings, the gross actual interest received should be included here (GM para. A5.18).

9.31   It is up to individual authorities to decide what level of evidence is required about the income of a non-dependant in remunerative work. If there is no evidence, the highest deduction is made (table 9.3). In such cases, if the evidence is later provided, and reveals that a lower deduction should have been made, this means that the claimant has been awarded too little benefit: the claimant must be awarded the arrears (but this is usually subject to a 52 weeks limit on retrospective increases: paras. 17.52-53).

NON-DEPENDANTS NOT IN REMUNERATIVE WORK

HBR 63(1)
CTBR 52(1)

9.32   For non-dependants not in remunerative work, the lowest level of deduction applies in both HB and main CTB (table 9.3) regardless of the amount – if any – of the non-dependant's income (unless no deduction is appropriate at all: paras. 9.23-26).

'REMUNERATIVE WORK'

`HBR 4(1)
CTBR 4(1)

9.33   Remunerative work is work:

◆ for which payment is made, or expected to be made; and

◆ which averages 16 hours or more per week.

HBR 4(2)-(4)
CTBR 4(2)-(4)

9.34   In calculating a weekly average of income, authorities should take into account any recognisable cycle. If there is no such cycle, they should take into account the expected hours of work per week and also (except where the non-dependant is just starting work) the average during the period immediately prior to the claim. This period should be five weeks unless some other period would result in a more accurate estimation in an individual case. Once it is established that a person is in remunerative work, he or she continues to count as being in remunerative work during any recognised, customary or other holiday, and also during any period of absence without good cause (but not during sick leave or maternity leave: para. 9.35).

A further rule applies to people employed in schools, other educational establishments, or anywhere else where their recognisable cycle of work is one year. Their average weekly hours are found by considering only the periods when they work (e.g. school term-times). The result applies both during those periods and during the periods when they do not work (e.g. school holidays). (Note however that changes in income – e.g. between term-time and holidays – are taken into account.)

9.35   A non-dependant is treated as not being in remunerative work in any of the following cases: HBR 2(1), 4(5), (6),(7) CTBR 2(1),4(5), (6),(7)

◆ in any benefit week during which he or she receives income support or income-based jobseeker's allowance for four days or more (regardless of his or her other circumstances);

◆ on any day on which she is on maternity leave, i.e. is absent from work because she is pregnant or has given birth, and has a right to return to work under her contract or under employment law;

Examples: Calculating HB and main CTB

CLAIMANT ON INCOME SUPPORT WITH WORKING NON-DEPENDANT

A lone parent is on income support. Her eligible rent is £65.00 per week. Her eligible council tax liability is £8.00 per week. Her 26-year-old son lives with her. He earns £260 per week gross for a 35-hour week.

Claimants on income support get maximum benefit, which in this case involves a non-dependant deduction. The son is in remunerative work with gross income of at least £259 per week, so the highest level of deduction applies in both HB and main CTB.

HB:	Eligible rent	£65.00
	minus non-dependant deduction, which in this case is	£47.75
	equals weekly HB	£17.25
Main CTB:	Eligible council tax	£8.00
	minus non-dependant deduction, which in this case is	£6.95
	equals weekly main CTB	£1.05

CLAIMANT ON INCOME SUPPORT WITH NON-DEPENDANT ON INCOME SUPPORT

The son in the previous example loses his job and starts receiving income support.

The calculation is as above, except that now there is no non-dependant deduction in main CTB and the lowest deduction applies in HB (table 9.2).

HB:	Eligible rent	£65.00
	minus non-dependant deduction, which in this case is	£7.40
	equals weekly HB	£57.60
Main CTB:	Eligible council tax	£8.00
	no non-dependant deduction applies	
	equals weekly main CTB	£8.00

◆ on any day on which he or she is absent from work because he or she is ill (whether or not receiving statutory sick pay and regardless of whether the employer is making up his or her wages). However, an absence due to illness which falls wholly within a benefit week (Monday to Sunday) will not be taken into account, because of the rules on changes of circumstances (para. 17.16);

◆ on any day for which he or she has been or will be paid a Sports Council sports award, so long as he or she is not expected to receive any other payment for that day.

9.36   The following are also not remunerative work:

◆ education (since this is not 'work');

◆ training (since this is not 'work') including attendance on government training schemes and on the 'intensive activity period' of the New Deal (para. 13.41)(but those paid by their employer do not count as trainees);

◆ voluntary or other work for which the person is paid expenses only (since it is not 'remunerative');

◆ periods of lay-off (since this is absence with good cause).

NON-DEPENDANT COUPLES

HBR 63(3),(4)
CTBR 52(3),(4)

9.37   In the case of a non-dependant couple (or a polygamous marriage), only one deduction applies, being the higher (or highest) of any that would have applied to the individuals if they were single claimants. In appropriate cases, there is no deduction (e.g. if they are both under 18). For the purpose of the various gross income limits in table 9.3, each non-dependant partner is treated as possessing the gross income of both of them.

NON-DEPENDANTS OF JOINT OCCUPIERS

HBR 63(5)
CTBR 52(35)

9.38   The following rules apply when a claimant is jointly liable for the rent or council tax on his or her home with one or more other persons who are not his or her partner, and there is also a non-dependant living there. They would arise, for example, if a brother and sister are joint occupiers and have a non-dependant living with them. The law is slightly unclear in some of these cases but, in informal terms, the key question is 'which of them does the non-dependant "belong" to?' Having decided that, the rules work as follows:

◆ If the non-dependant 'belongs' to only one of them, then the whole non-dependant deduction is made in any claim for benefit made by that one, and no deduction is made in any claim for benefit made by the others.

◆ If the non-dependant 'belongs' to more than one of them, the amount of the non-dependant deduction is shared between them. Any of them claiming benefit gets his or her resulting share of the non-dependant deduction. In main CTB, the share must be equal between the joint occupiers (but only between the ones who are jointly liable for the council tax on the home: paras. 11.111-114). In HB, the share need not be equal: the authority should take into account the number of joint occupiers concerned and the proportion of rent each pays (as in para. 11.4).

Local schemes

9.39   The HB and CTB schemes as described in this guide are those which authorities are required by law to operate. However, authorities may grant extra benefit under a 'local scheme' – that is, an improved version of the scheme. The only improvement authorities are permitted, however, is to disregard war disablement pensions and war widows' pensions, in whole or part, over and above the fixed disregard required by law (usually £10: para. 13.28). Some, but not all, authorities have decided to do this. The decision to run a local scheme is made by a resolution of the authority. The DSS advises that separate resolutions are required for HB and for CTB (GM para. B3.10). The question of whether or not an authority should run a local scheme is not open to the appeal procedure. Payments under local schemes are not eligible for subsidy (chapter 21).

AA s.134(8)-(10)
139 (6)-(8)
SI 1996 No. 677
SI 1996 No. 678

9.40   For technical reasons, part of the cost of a local scheme is subject to a 'permitted total' of 0.7 per cent of the authority's HB/CTB expenditure. This should have no effect on an authority's power to operate a local scheme (circular HB/CTB A31/95).

SI 1996 No. 678

9.41   The Act also gives the Secretary of State power to provide for local schemes to apply in other ways. This power has not been exercised.

Additional benefit in exceptional circumstances

9.42   If a claimant's circumstances are exceptional, the authority may increase the weekly amount of HB or CTB or both. A review board may also do this (paras. 19.50-51). This is a discretionary power (paras. 1.41). In the case of CTB, this applies whether the claimant is granted main CTB (as described above) or second adult rebate (chapter 10). The limitations on how authorities may exercise this discretion, which in some cases differ between HB and CTB, are described below. In both HB and CTB, however, claimants on income support or JSA(IB) who have no non-dependants cannot qualify.

AA s.134(11)
139(9)

ADDITIONAL HB

9.43   In the case of HB:

HBR 61(2)
SI 1996 No. 677

◆ the authority must be satisfied that the claimant's circumstances are exceptional;

◆ no increase may be awarded to a claimant who is not eligible for any HB, even if only because of the minimum benefit rule (para. 9.16);

◆ the increase must not take the total award of HB above 100 per cent of the eligible rent; and

◆ the authority has a budget limit of 0.1 per cent of the total value of HB it awards in the year. This is known as its 'permitted total'.

9.44 The effect is that, in relation to any particular benefit week, the increase must not exceed the amount of any eligible rent not covered by HB due to non-dependant deductions and (for claimants not on income support or JSA(IB)) the effect of the excess income 'taper' percentage.

The question of whether to increase a claimant's 'maximum rent' in cases of exceptional hardship (para. 11.21) is independent of the question of whether to award additional HB because of his or her exceptional circumstances.

ADDITIONAL CTB

TBR 51(5), 54(4)
SI 1996 No. 678

9.45 In the case of CTB:

◆ the authority must be satisfied that the claimant's circumstances are exceptional;

◆ no increase may be awarded to a claimant who is not eligible for CTB of either kind (main CTB or second adult rebate);

◆ the increase must not take the total award of CTB above 100 per cent of the claimant's eligible council tax liability if he or she is awarded main CTB – or 25 per cent if he or she is awarded second adult rebate;

◆ the authority has a budget limit of 0.1 per cent of the total value of CTB it awards in the year. This is known as its 'permitted total'.

9.46 The effect for a claimant awarded main CTB is that, in relation to any particular benefit week, the increase must not exceed the amount of any eligible council tax liability not covered by CTB due to non-dependant deductions and (for claimants not on income support or JSA(IB)) the effect of the excess income 'taper' percentage. The effect for a claimant awarded second adult rebate is that, for any particular benefit week, it can be increased to 25 per cent. (For a joint occupier, this means 25 per cent of the council tax for the dwelling, not 25 per cent of his or her 'share'.)

The increase cannot be used to compensate for the effect of CTB restrictions (chapter 11).

9.47 The question of whether to award additional CTB is considered before the 'better buy' (para. 10.29). So if a claimant qualifies (before any addition for exceptional circumstances) for more second adult rebate than main CTB, the authority can nonetheless increase his or her main CTB to a maximum of 100 per cent of his or her liability. The better buy is then main CTB.

THE TEST

9.48   This is a very wide discretion. The test is whether a claimant's circumstances are exceptional. If they are, the authority or review board may award additional benefit (but do not have to). There is no requirement for a claimant to request additional HB or CTB before it can be awarded: an authority may choose to do this simply on the facts before it (though this is in practice uncommon). Nor is there any restriction on what exceptional circumstances the authority can take into account. The examples in the DSS guidance ('loss of savings due to a burglary, or unforeseen need due to non-payment of wages': GM para. A5.58) are clearly not intended as exclusive. For example, a claimant's circumstances can be affected by those of his or her family, non-dependants (including 'second adults') and relatives living elsewhere. It is reasonable to take into account any exceptional circumstances about which information is available – for example, not only those relating to housing or housing need.

9.49   In deciding whether a claimant's circumstances are 'exceptional', the authority must focus on the particular facts of his or her individual circumstances: that these may be common to a group does not, by itself, mean that they are not exceptional (*R v Maidstone Borough Council ex parte Bunce,* QBD, (1994), *The Times,* 30.6.94). Otherwise, there is no definition of 'exceptional' in the Act or regulations. Dictionary definitions (e.g. 'that which does not follow the rule') beg a number of questions, to which there are no hard and fast answers. The term may be interpreted statistically – but how many cases can there be before something ceases to be an exception? And should the comparison be made only with other HB or CTB claimants in the authority's area, or on a wider basis? Alternatively, current circumstances may be compared with experience or expectations, regardless of the numbers involved.

HARDSHIP

9.50   In many cases, authorities are likely to take into account whether the claimant has suffered hardship, or would suffer hardship if not awarded additional benefit. However, hardship should not be regarded as the sole test of exceptional circumstances. In particular, a claimant with relatively high income may have exceptional circumstances which justify payment of additional HB or CTB or both.

OTHER SOURCES OF ASSISTANCE

9.51   It is open to authorities to take into account the availability of assistance from other sources. But it is also important for authorities to be aware of the limitations of the social fund (para. 2.15), and of the assistance available from social services.

RENT IN ADVANCE AND DEPOSITS

9.52   Social fund community care grants may be awarded for rent in advance, but usually only for claimants leaving care or who would otherwise have to enter care. They cannot be awarded for deposits. This may be a relevant factor in deciding whether to make an additional payment of HB to help with rent in advance or a deposit.

AMOUNTS

9.53   Subject to the limit in individual cases and to its budget limit, an authority chooses how much additional HB or CTB to award. Awards may be made for past periods of up to 52 weeks (para. 17.53) – as well as for the current period – and are subject to the appeal procedures (paras. 19.18-20).

THE IMPACT OF THE BUDGET LIMIT

SI 1996 No. 677
SI 1996 No. 678
9.54   Total expenditure by the authority on additional benefit is budget-limited on an annual basis to a 'permitted total' – which is 0.1 per cent of the total HB or CTB awarded (paras. 9.43, 9.45). The authority has no power to award any additional HB or CTB once this limit is reached in any particular year.

THE IMPACT OF SUBSIDY

9.55   The cost to the authority of exercising its discretion to award additional benefit is not eligible for subsidy (chapter 21). One result of the *Brent and Connery* case (para. 11.73) is that, in deciding whether or not to award additional benefit, authorities may take into account the implications for their own financial situation – e.g. the non-availability of government subsidy. This must not be regarded as the only consideration, however. The financial impact on the authority should be weighed against the exceptional circumstances of the claimant in each individual case.

Conversion to weekly amounts

9.56   The following paragraphs explain the rules that apply whenever figures involved in the calculation of HB and CTB (including second adult rebate) have to be converted to weekly amounts.

RENT AND SERVICE CHARGES

HBR 69(1),(2)
9.57   Whenever a weekly figure is needed for rent or for service charges, the following rules apply:

♦   for rent or service charges due in multiples of weeks, divide the rent by the number of weeks it covers;

◆ for rent or service charges due daily, multiply the daily amount by seven;

◆ for rent or service charges due calendar monthly (or at any other intervals which are not multiples of weeks), divide the rent by the number of days it covers to find the daily rent, then multiply the daily rent by seven. This means there are two possibilities for a calendar monthly tenant: 12 months' rent or service charges can be divided by 365 (or 366 in appropriate years) and then multiplied by seven, or a particular month's rent or service charges can be divided by 28, 29, 30 or 31 (as appropriate) and then multiplied by seven.

Further rules apply if the claimant has rent-free periods (para. 9.19).

COUNCIL TAX

9.58   Whenever a weekly figure is needed for council tax liability, the following   CTBR 51(1)(b)
rules apply:

◆ for annual figures, divide the council tax by 365 (or 366 in financial years ending in a leap year) to find the daily figure, and then multiply the daily figure by seven;

◆ for figures which do not relate to a whole year, divide the council tax by the number of days it covers to find the daily figure, and then multiply the daily figure by seven.

INCOME, ETC.

9.59   This applies to unearned income (chapter 13), income from employment   HBR 25(1)
(chapter 14), and the various disregards which apply in each of those cases (but   CTBR 17(1)
for self-employed income, see chapter 15). All such amounts are converted to a
weekly figure as follows:

◆ for an amount relating to a whole multiple of weeks, divide the amount by the number of weeks it covers;

◆ for an amount relating to a calendar month, multiply the amount by 12 to find the annual figure, then divide the annual figure by 52 or 53. In practice, authorities usually divide by 52 if there are 52 Mondays in the current financial year (as is the case in 2000-2001) or by 53 if there are 53, though the law does not specifically require this;

◆ for an amount relating to a year (this typically applies only to self-employed income), divide the amount by 365 (or 366 as appropriate) to find the daily figure, and then multiply the daily figure by seven;

◆ for an amount relating to any other period, divide the amount by the number of days it covers to find the daily figure, then multiply the daily figure by seven.

10 Second adult rebate

10.1 This chapter explains the type of CTB known as 'second adult rebate'. It covers:

◆ who is eligible for second adult rebate;

◆ the information needed to establish eligibility;

◆ how to calculate second adult rebate;

◆ the information needed to do the calculation; and

◆ the 'better buy' comparison.

10.2 In broad terms, second adult rebate is awarded when the claimant has a 'second adult' in his or her home who is on income support or income-based jobseeker's allowance or is on a low income. Although the level of the claimant's own income and capital (and that of the claimant's partner) is irrelevant, certain other circumstances of the claimant and other household members may prevent entitlement to second adult rebate. Also, because of the 'better buy' comparison (para. 10.29), second adult rebate is only awarded if the claimant does not qualify for the other type of CTB known as 'main CTB', or qualifies for more second adult rebate than main CTB. Chapter 9 gives details of how main CTB is calculated.

10.3 This guide, in common with DSS guidance and most Benefits Agency and local authority forms and other documentation, uses the informal term 'second adult rebate' for what is known in the law as 'alternative maximum council tax benefit'.

Eligibility for second adult rebate

CBA s.131(1),(3), (6),(7),(9) **10.4** Several pieces of information are needed to establish whether a claimant is eligible for second adult rebate and, if so, how much it is to be. These are summarised in the flow chart in table 10.1, and described in detail below.

PRESENCE OF SECOND ADULT

CBA s.131(6)(b), (7)(a),(11) CTBR 55(a),(c) **10.5** A claimant can only qualify for second adult rebate if there is at least one 'second adult' in his or her home. A person can only be a 'second adult' if he or she:

◆ is a non-dependant or a particular type of carer (paras. 10.6-7); and

◆ is not a 'disregarded person' (para. 10.8).

Table 10.1 SECOND ADULT REBATE FLOW CHART

PRESENCE OF SECOND ADULT
Is there at least one second adult in the claimant's home? (A second adult is usually a non-dependant who is not a 'disregarded person')

→ NO → Claimant is not eligible for second adult rebate – but may qualify for main CTB

↓ YES

PRESENCE OF BOARDERS OR (SUB-) TENANTS
Does the claimant receive rent from anyone in his or her home?

→ YES → Claimant is not eligible for second adult rebate – but may qualify for main CTB

↓ NO

PRESENCE OF PARTNER
Does claimant have a partner living with him or her?

→ YES → Are claimant or partner (or both) a 'disregarded person'?

↓ NO (from partner box)

(from disregarded person box) ↓ NO → Claimant is not eligible for second adult rebate – but may qualify for main CTB

YES →

PRESENCE OF JOINT OCCUPIERS
Apart from the claimant and any partner, is there anyone else jointly liable for the council tax on the dwelling (e.g. joint owners/tenants)?

→ YES → Taking into account the claimant, any partner and the other liable person(s), are all – or all but one – of them 'disregarded persons'?

↓ NO (from joint occupiers box)

↓ NO (from disregarded persons box) → Claimant is not eligible for second adult rebate – but may qualify for main CTB

YES →

CLAIMANT MAY QUALIFY FOR SECOND ADULT REBATE
Go to top of next page

Table 10.1 continued

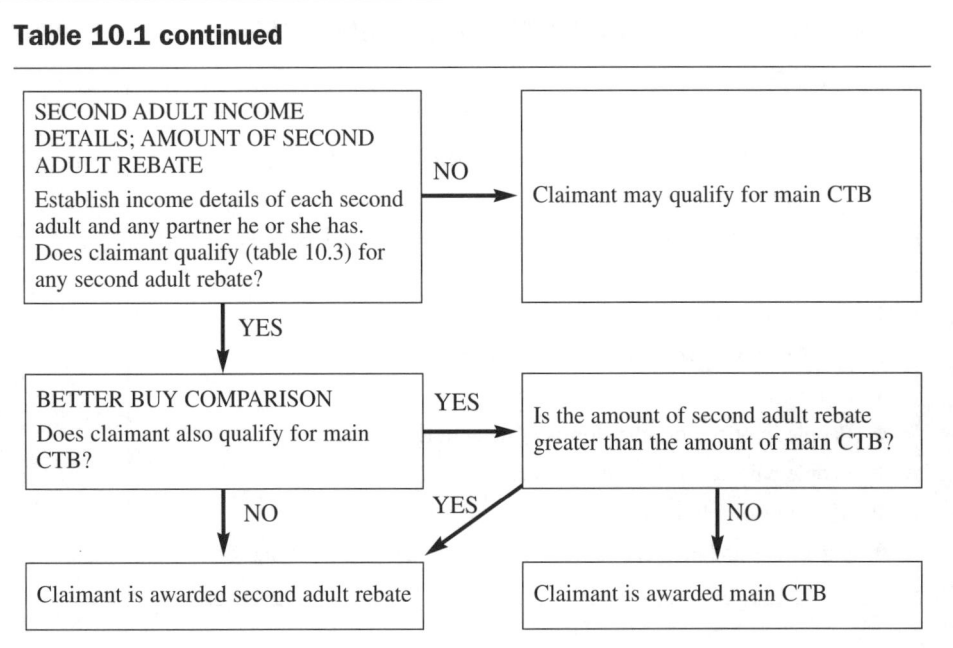

There may be two or more 'second adults' in the claimant's home: the claimant can still qualify for second adult rebate.

10.6   A non-dependant is by far the most common kind of second adult so long as he or she is not a 'disregarded person'. Typical non-dependants are adult sons, daughters, other relatives or friends who live in the claimant's household on a non-commercial basis (para. 6.21).

10.7   A person can also be a second adult if he or she is the type of carer who is defined in law as not being a non-dependant (para. 6.26) so long as he or she is not a 'disregarded person'. This kind of second adult is much less common – because many carers are 'disregarded persons'. (For the details, see categories 14 to 17 in appendix 7.)

10.8   A 'disregarded person' cannot be a second adult. This means a person who falls within any of the groups who are disregarded for council tax discount purposes (para. 3.37). The main groups are summarised in table 10.2. Appendix 7 defines all the relevant categories of people and gives the detailed rules about whether they are 'disregarded persons'.

Table 10.2 'DISREGARDED PERSONS': SIMPLIFIED SUMMARY

◆ People under 18, or aged 18 if child benefit is payable.

◆ Education leavers under 20.

◆ Various students, foreign language assistants and student nurses.

◆ Youth Training trainees under 25.

◆ Apprentices on NCVQ/SVEC courses.

◆ People who are severely mentally impaired.

◆ Carers.

◆ People in prison or other forms of detention.

◆ People who normally live elsewhere.

◆ Members of religious communities.

◆ Diplomats and members of international bodies or of visiting forces.

PRESENCE OF BOARDERS OR (SUB-)TENANTS

10.9   A claimant who receives rent from any resident in his or her home is not eligible for second adult rebate (even if all the other conditions are fulfilled). Typically, this means that home-owner claimants with boarders or tenants, and tenant claimants with boarders or sub-tenants, cannot get second adult rebate. CBA s.131
(6)(a),(11)
CTBR 2(1)

10.10   The exclusion from entitlement applies only if the person paying rent is 'resident' in the claimant's dwelling. A 'resident' means a person aged 18 or more

---

Example: A couple who have a tenant

A couple are liable for council tax on their home. The only people living with them are their adult son and a tenant. The tenant's letting agreement was signed by the woman in the couple, who takes all the responsibility for the letting and receives all the income from it.

They should ensure that the man is the claimant. No-one is liable to pay rent to him. So he may qualify for second adult rebate, so long as all the other conditions apply (and there are several in a case like this: table 10.1).

who has 'sole or main residence' there. Therefore, rent received from an under-18-year-old or a holiday maker does not prevent entitlement.

10.11 The exclusion appears in the Act of Parliament rather than the regulations. The Act does not, however, define 'rent'. The regulations give a definition of 'rent' for other purposes as being (in broad terms) a payment which could be met by HB, and this definition seems appropriate here.

10.12 The exclusion is worded in such a way that it applies only if someone is liable to pay rent to the claimant. It does not apply if someone is liable to pay rent to the claimant's partner (or any other resident).

CLAIMANT'S INCOME AND CAPITAL

10.13 None of the rules about eligibility for second adult rebate takes into account the amount of a claimant's (or partner's) income or capital in any way.

10.14 The £16,000 capital limit (which applies for HB and main CTB) does not apply when second adult rebate is being considered. Millionaires can get second adult rebate (so long as they fulfil the appropriate conditions).

CLAIMANT'S AND PARTNER'S OTHER CIRCUMSTANCES

CBA s.131(7)(b)   **10.15** If the conditions mentioned earlier are satisfied, the final condition about eligibility for second adult rebate depends on whether the claim is made by:

◆ a single claimant or a lone parent (with no joint occupiers);

◆ a couple (with no joint occupiers); or

◆ a claimant who has joint occupiers.

SINGLE CLAIMANTS AND LONE PARENTS

10.16 There is no further condition if the claimant is single or a lone parent. It does not matter whether he or she is or is not a 'disregarded person'. But if the claimant is jointly liable for council tax, see paragraph 10.18.

COUPLES

CTBR 55(b)   **10.17** There is a further condition if the claimant is in a couple. Couples are eligible for second adult rebate only if at least one partner is a 'disregarded person' (para. 10.8). It does not matter whether this is the claimant or the partner – and so long as one of them is a 'disregarded person' it does not matter whether the other one is or is not a 'disregarded person'. But if the couple are jointly liable for council tax with some other person, see paragraph 10.18. A polygamous marriage is eligible for second adult rebate if all – or all but one – of the partners are 'disregarded persons'.

JOINT OCCUPIERS

10.18   There is also a further condition if the claimant is jointly liable for the   CTBR 55(d)
council tax on his or her home with at least one other person (other than just his
or her partner if the claim is made by a couple). In such cases, information is
needed about all of these joint occupiers. Each one who makes a claim is eligible
for second adult rebate so long as either:

◆ all the joint occupiers are 'disregarded persons'; or

◆ all but one of the joint occupiers are 'disregarded persons'.

10.19   This rule typically applies to joint owners and joint tenants. For example,
if two sisters jointly own their home (and they have a second adult), each of them
is eligible for second adult rebate so long as at least one of them is a 'disregarded
person' (para. 10.8). Or if three single people jointly rent their home (and they
have a second adult), each of them is eligible for second adult rebate so long as
at least two of them are 'disregarded persons'.

10.20   In all such cases, each joint occupier who makes a claim qualifies for his   CTBR 54(2),(3)
or her share of the total amount of second adult rebate. This share must always be
equal between all the joint occupiers (para. 11.10), including any who are
students.

CALCULATING SECOND ADULT REBATE

10.21   Having established that the claimant is eligible for second adult rebate, the
authority needs the following information in order to calculate the amount on a
weekly basis:

◆ the claimant's weekly eligible council tax liability (para. 10.23); and

◆ details of the second adult's income or, if the claimant has more than one
    second adult, details of all the second adults' incomes (paras. 10.24 onwards).

10.22   As shown in table 10.3, the amount of second adult rebate may be 25 per   CTBR 2(3A), 54(1
cent, 15 per cent or 7½ per cent of the claimant's weekly eligible council tax –   sch 2 para 1(1)
depending on the income of the second adult(s). No matter how many second
adults a claimant has, the claimant can only get one amount of second adult
rebate.

10.23   The amount of a claimant's eligible council tax liability is described in
chapter 11. As described in that chapter, a claimant's eligible council tax can be
lower than his or her actual council tax liability if his or her dwelling is in
valuation band F, G or H (para. 11.117). Paragraph 9.58 explains how to convert
council tax figures to a weekly amount. Examples of the calculations follow. The
last example illustrates how a 25 per cent discount is dealt with in calculations
(see also para. 11.116). The example at the end of this chapter illustrates the
calculation of second adult rebate for joint occupiers.

Table 10.3 THE PERCENTAGE OF COUNCIL TAX MET BY SECOND ADULT REBATE

FOR CLAIMANTS WITH ONE SECOND ADULT

If the second adult is on income support or JSA(IB)*	25%

If the second adult is not on income support or JSA(IB) and his or her income** is:

£157.00 per week or more	nil
between £120.00 and £156.99 per week	7½%
under £120.00 per week	15%

FOR CLAIMANTS WITH TWO OR MORE SECOND ADULTS

If all the second adults are on income support or JSA(IB)*	25%

If at least one of the second adults is not on income support or JSA(IB) and the combined gross income of all the second adults*** is:

£157.00 per week or more	nil
between £120.00 and £156.99 per week	7½%
under £120.00 per week	15%

Notes

* For these purposes, a person is treated as receiving JSA(IB) (income-related jobseeker's allowance) if he or she is:
 ◆ entitled to JSA(IB) but not receiving it because of a sanction; or
 ◆ in the waiting days before his or her JSA(IB) starts – or would start apart from a sanction.

** If the second adult has a partner, the partner's income is added into the second adult's income.

*** For each second adult who has a partner, the partner's income is added into the combined income of the second adults. The income of any second adult who is on income support or JSA(IB) (or whose partner is) is disregarded.

ASSESSING SECOND ADULTS' GROSS INCOME

CTBR
sch 2 paras 2,3

10.24   To calculate the amount of second adult rebate (table 10.3), it is necessary to assess the gross income of any second adult who is not on income support or JSA(IB) (or treated as receiving JSA(IB): table 10.3). If the second adult has a partner, the partner's income is added in with the second adult's income (even if the partner is a 'disregarded person' and so could not be a second adult in his or her own right). If the gross income is £157.00 per week or more, the claimant does not qualify for second adult rebate.

Examples: Calculating second adult rebate

SINGLE CLAIMANT WITH SECOND ADULT ON JSA(IB)

A single claimant is the only person liable for council tax on his home. The only person living with him is his adult daughter, who is on JSA(IB). Neither the claimant nor his daughter is a 'disregarded person'. His eligible council tax liability is £8.00 per week.

Eligible for second adult rebate?

As a single claimant, he is eligible for second adult rebate because:

◆ he has a second adult living with him (his daughter); and

◆ he does not receive rent from a boarder or (sub-)tenant.

Amount of second adult rebate

His daughter is on JSA(IB) so the weekly amount is:

25% of weekly eligible council tax (25% x £8.00)   £2.00

COUPLE WITH TWO SECOND ADULTS

A couple are the only people liable for council tax on their home. The only people living with them are their two adult sons. One son is on JSA(IB). The other son is working and his gross pay is £117 per week. He also has savings which generate a weekly gross interest of £5 per week. One partner in the couple is a full-time mature university student. The other partner and the sons are not 'disregarded persons'. The couple's eligible council tax liability is £10.00 per week.

Eligible for second adult rebate?

As a couple, they are eligible for second adult rebate because:

◆ they have at least one second adult living with them. In fact they have two second adults (the sons); and

◆ they do not receive rent from a boarder or (sub-)tenant; and

◆ at least one of the couple is a 'disregarded person' (the student).

Amount of second adult rebate

If there is more than one second adult, their gross incomes are combined. But in this case the income of the son on JSA(IB) is disregarded. So only the other son's income counts. That son's gross weekly income is £117 (from the job) plus £5.00 (interest), which amounts to £122, so the weekly amount of second adult rebate is:

7½% of weekly eligible council tax (7½% x £10.00)   £0.75

DISCOUNT PLUS SECOND ADULT REBATE

A single woman is the only person liable for council tax on her home. The only other person living with her is her father, who is on income support. The woman is a student nurse, and is a 'disregarded person'. Her father is not a 'disregarded person'. The council tax for the dwelling (before any discount is granted) is £730 per year – which is £14 per week.

Discount

When calculating council tax discounts, 'disregarded persons' are ignored (appendix 7). So for discount purposes, this dwelling has one resident. The woman qualifies for a 25% discount which, on a weekly basis, is:

25% of the weekly amount for the dwelling (25% x £14.00)   £3.50

Eligible for second adult rebate?

As a single claimant her own circumstances are immaterial. She is eligible for second adult rebate because:

◆ she has a second adult living with her (her father); and

◆ she does not receive rent from a boarder or (sub-)tenant.

Amount of second adult rebate

Her father is on income support so she qualifies for second adult rebate of 25% of her weekly eligible council tax. This means 25% of liability for council tax before the discount is subtracted, which is:

25% of weekly eligible council tax (25% x £14.00)   £3.50

She qualifies for both the discount and the second adult rebate, the total of the two being £7.00 per week.

Better buy

It turns out in this particular case that, because of her own low income, the woman qualifies for main CTB of £4.00 per week. Since her main CTB is greater than her second adult rebate, she gets only her main CTB. The final result is that she qualifies for main CTB of £4.00 plus the discount of £3.50, so in total her council tax bill is reduced by £7.50 per week.

10.25 If a claimant has more than one second adult, it is necessary to combine the income of all of them, apart from any who are on income support or JSA(IB) (or treated as receiving JSA(IB): table 10.3) – adding in the income of the partner of each second adult. Once it is clear that the gross income of some of them has reached £157 per week, there is no need to go any further (because of course it is impossible that the gross income of all of them would be lower).

10.26 It is gross, not net, income which is relevant, and it is calculated in exactly the same way as a non-dependant's income is calculated for the purposes of main CTB, as outlined in paragraphs 9.29-30. However, the DSS points out (GM para.

B3.10) that the authority may adopt a 'local scheme' (para. 9.39) whereby a second adult's income from a war disablement pension or war widow's pension is wholly or partly disregarded. The authority is entitled to require the same level of evidence, proof, etc. as when it assesses a claimant's income (para. 7.37).

10.27 Providing details of second adults' income (and that of their partners) can pose several difficulties for claimants. They may not be able to obtain these details, or may not wish to ask. However, if the authority does not know how much the gross income is, it cannot award a second adult rebate.

ADDITIONAL BENEFIT IN EXCEPTIONAL CIRCUMSTANCES

10.28 If the circumstances of a claimant who qualifies for second adult rebate   CTBR 54(4)
are exceptional, the authority may award an additional amount of CTB. There are limits on how much this can be in various circumstances. These rules are explained in paragraphs 9.42-56.

The 'better buy'

10.29 A claimant cannot be awarded both main CTB and second adult rebate at   CBA s.131(9)
the same time. Deciding which one the claimant is actually awarded is often called a 'better buy' comparison. As indicated in table 10.1:

◆ a claimant who only qualifies for main CTB is awarded that;

◆ a claimant who only qualifies for second adult rebate is awarded that;

◆ a claimant who qualifies for both is awarded whichever of the two is higher or, if the two are the same, main CTB. This is decided entirely according to the amounts themselves and entirely by the authority. A claimant cannot choose to have the lower figure.

Some examples of the better buy calculation are given below.

JOINT OCCUPIERS AND THE BETTER BUY

10.30 If a dwelling has one or more joint occupiers and one or more of them   CBA s.131(9)
claims CTB, each joint occupier's entitlement to main CTB and second adult   CTBR 54(2),(3)
rebate is assessed separately, and the better buy comparison is done separately for each joint occupier. This can mean that one joint occupier is awarded main CTB, another second adult rebate. The second of the examples below illustrates this.

A RULE OF THUMB

10.31 If a claimant qualifies for a large amount of main CTB, it is unlikely that he or she will qualify for a larger amount of second adult rebate. As a rule of thumb, this is the case if the claimant's main CTB meets around 35 per cent or more of his or her council tax liability.

Example: Better buy

LONE PARENT WITH ONE NON-DEPENDANT/SECOND ADULT

A lone parent is the only person liable for the council tax on her home. She is not on income support and has excess income for main CTB purposes of £25.00. The only people living with her are her daughter of 15 and her son of 21. The son works 12 hours per week for a gross pay of £130 per week (and has no other income). Only the daughter (because of being under 18) is a 'disregarded person'. The lone parent's eligible council tax liability is £10.00 per week. Her circumstances means that she is eligible for second adult rebate (the son is her second adult) as well as main CTB (taking the son into account as a non-dependant).

Main CTB

Weekly eligible council tax	£10.00
minus non-dependant deduction for son (although the son's income is over £120 he is not in remunerative work, so the lowest deduction applies: table 9.3)	£2.30
minus 20% of excess income (20% x £25.00)	£5.00
equals weekly main CTB	£2.70

Second adult rebate

The level of the son's gross income means that the claimant qualifies for a 7½% second adult rebate:

weekly second adult rebate (7½% x £10.00)	£0.75

Better buy comparison

Her entitlement to main CTB is greater than her entitlement to second adult rebate, so she is awarded main CTB only.

Example: Better buy for joint occupiers

TWO JOINT HOME-OWNERS WITH ONE NON-DEPENDANT/SECOND ADULT

The only residents of a (d)well(ing) are three sisters, Elsie, Lacie and Tillie. Elsie and Lacie jointly own it, and are jointly liable for the council tax there. Tillie lives there rent-free. She is their non-dependant. The eligible council tax for the whole dwelling is £20.00 per week.

Elsie is a full-time university student (learning, as it happens, to draw) and is therefore a 'disregarded person'. She has capital of £20,000.

Lacie is working (as a treacle operative, in fact). She is not a 'disregarded person'. For main CTB purposes she has excess income of £30.00 (and capital under £3,000).

Tillie is on income support. She is not a 'disregarded person'. She is therefore a second adult.

Elsie's claim for CTB

Elsie is not eligible for main CTB – she has too much capital (and, in any case, most full-time students are not eligible for main CTB, though they are eligible for second adult rebate: chapter 20).

Elsie is eligible for second adult rebate (para. 10.18). Tillie is on income support, so the second adult rebate for the whole dwelling is 25 per cent of the council tax. Because there are two joint occupiers, Elsie qualifies for half of this,

which is (½ of 25% x £20.00)	£2.50

Lacie's claim for CTB

Lacie is eligible for main CTB. Because there are two joint occupiers, it is worked out on half the council tax for the dwelling. Because Tillie is on income support, there is no non-dependant deduction for her.

Lacie's entitlement to main CTB is:

weekly eligible council tax (½ x £20.00)	£10.00
minus 20% of excess income (20% x £30.00)	£6.00
which is	£4.00

Lacie's entitlement to second adult rebate is the same as Elsie's,

which is (½ of 25% x £20.00)	£2.50

Better buy comparisons

Elsie:	No better buy comparison is required.	
	She is awarded second adult rebate of	£2.50
Lacie:	A better buy comparison is required.	
	Her main CTB (£4.00) is greater than her second adult rebate (£2.50).	
	She is awarded main CTB of	£4.00
The total weekly CTB awarded on the dwelling is therefore		£6.50

11 Eligible rent and council tax

11.1 This chapter defines how 'eligible rent' and 'eligible council tax' are assessed. It covers:

◆ an overview of rent, 'eligible rent' and apportionment for joint occupiers;

◆ the general rules for assessing eligible rent;

◆ the variations to those rules for certain types of tenure (e.g. for council tenants, housing association tenants and several others) – including the variations for 'exempt accommodation';

◆ the further variations which apply in the case of certain older claims (e.g. for claims continuing from before 6th October 1997) – including the variations for 'exempt claimants';

◆ the special rules about HB restrictions for 'exempt cases' (i.e. 'exempt accommodation' and 'exempt claimants');

◆ the general rules about service charges in all the above cases;

◆ an overview of council tax and 'eligible council tax';

◆ how eligible council tax is assessed for main CTB purposes;

◆ how eligible council tax is assessed for second adult rebate purposes.

Paragraph 11.105 explains how the marginal references work in the HB parts of this chapter.

Overview of rent and eligible rent

WHAT IS 'RENT'?

HBR 8(1), 10(1) **11.2** The payments in table 11.1 count as 'rent' for all HB purposes, so long as the claimant is liable to make those payments on his or her normal home and does not live in certain types of dwelling (chapter 4). Certain payments which do not count as rent may be met by income support or JSA(IB) (appendix 6). In this chapter:

◆ the term 'actual rent' is used to mean the total of the payments listed in the table; and

◆ the terms 'dwelling' and 'accommodation' are used interchangeably (except in such combinations as 'exempt accommodation' and 'suitable alternative accommodation': these are described later).

Table 11.1 PAYMENTS COUNTED AS RENT FOR HB PURPOSES

◆ Rent in its ordinary sense, whether under a tenancy or licence, including board and lodgings payments and payments for 'use and occupation'.

◆ 'Mesne profits' in England and Wales or 'violent profits' in Scotland (paid after a tenancy or right to occupy is terminated).

◆ Houseboat mooring charges and berthing fees and caravan and mobile home site charges (even if owned by the claimant, and in addition to rental if not owned).

◆ Payments made by residents of charitable almshouses.

◆ Payments under rental purchase agreements.

◆ Payments for crofts and croft land in Scotland.

WHAT IS 'ELIGIBLE RENT'?

11.3   A claimant's 'eligible rent' is the figure used in calculating his or her   HBR 10(3)
entitlement to HB (para. 9.8). It is often less than his or her actual rent: the various ways in which it can be increased or reduced are described throughout this chapter. The rules about eligible rent have changed several times recently. This chapter gives the rules as they apply from 1st/3rd April 2000: table 11.2 summarises these rules.

Table 11.2 ELIGIBLE RENT: SUMMARY OF WHICH RULES APPLY

This table is much simplified. Full details are given throughout this chapter as they arise.

	Most private tenants	**Most council, housing association, and other tenants**
Most claimants who have been on HB since before 6th October 1997	See 'the general rules' (para. 11.5) and 'variations for older claims' (para. 11.42).	See 'variations for certain tenures' (para. 11.27) and 'variations for older claims' (para. 11.42).
Most other claimants	See 'the general rules' (para. 11.5).	See 'variations for certain tenures' (para. 11.27).

APPORTIONMENT FOR JOINT OCCUPIERS

HBR 10(5) **11.4** A joint occupier (or joint tenant) is one of two or more people who are jointly liable to pay rent on a dwelling, other than just a couple or polygamous marriage (para. 6.24). In such cases, many of the figures used in calculating eligible rent are apportioned between the joint occupiers. In doing this, the authority must:

◆ determine how much of the actual rent on the dwelling is fairly attributable to each of the joint occupiers, taking into account the number of people paying towards the rent, the proportion of rent paid by each, and any relevant other circumstances – such as the size and number of rooms each occupies, and whether there is any written or other agreement between them;

◆ apportion the actual rent accordingly;

◆ apportion any other figures it is required to apportion on the same basis (the following sections explain which figures this applies to: one example is ineligible service charges).

Eligible rent: the general rules

11.5 This section explains the general rules for assessing a claimant's eligible rent. It applies in all HB cases unless:

◆ the variations for certain tenures apply (paras. 11.27-41); or

◆ the variations for certain older claims apply (paras. 11.42-52).

ELIGIBLE RENT

HBR 10(3),(6A), 12A **11.6** The claimant's eligible rent is always the 'maximum rent' (para. 11.7) applying in his or her case, unless:

◆ the exceptions mentioned in paragraph 11.5 apply; or

◆ the claimant's rent details change during his or her benefit period (para. 11.11); or

◆ the claimant falls into either of the protected groups (para. 11.13); or

◆ the authority increases the maximum rent to prevent exceptional hardship (para. 11.21); or

◆ the authority reduces the eligible rent to below the maximum rent in certain cases (para. 11.25).

MAXIMUM RENT

HBR 2(1), 11 **11.7** In order to calculate the claimant's maximum rent, the authority needs the following figures. These are provided by the rent officer (chapter 8). In an individual case, he or she may have provided one, two or all three of them:

◆ the rent officer's claim-related rent determination;

◆ the rent officer's local reference rent determination;

◆ the rent officer's single room rent determination (only in the case of a 'young individual': para. 11.8).

The 'maximum rent' is the lowest of these figures (or the only one if he or she provides only one). But before deciding which is lowest, the figures must be adjusted in certain cases. Table 11.3 gives all the details of how to calculate maximum rent, and is followed by an example. (See also para. 11.81 as regards excessive service charges.)

Table 11.3: 'MAXIMUM RENT': ADJUSTING THE RENT OFFICER'S FIGURES

See paragraphs 11.5-7 for the cases to which this table applies and for further information. 'RO' means rent officer.

The following adjustments are made separately to each of the RO's figures.

1.   DEDUCT AN AMOUNT FOR MEALS

Deduct an amount for meals – but only if the claimant's actual rent includes meals. Use the amounts shown in table 11.8.

There are two exceptions:

◆ do not deduct anything for meals in the case of the single room rent;

◆ do not deduct anything for meals in the case of the claim-related rent if the RO said it does not include meals (which can occur only if the RO has used an exceptionally high rent determination as the claim-related rent: chapter 8).

2.   ADD AN AMOUNT FOR ELIGIBLE SUPPORT CHARGES

Add an amount for all eligible support charges. ('Support charges' are defined in para. 11.89. The paras. after that deal with which are eligible.) Use the authority's valuation for these.

3.   APPORTION FOR JOINT OCCUPIERS

If the claimant is a joint occupier, apportion the resulting figures (as described in para. 11.4). There is one exception: do not apportion the single room rent.

4.   MAXIMUM RENT

The claimant's 'maximum rent' is the lowest of the resulting figures – or if there is only one figure, it is that one (but also see para. 11.81 as regards excessive service charges). If necessary, convert the result to a weekly figure (para. 9.57).

Notes:

(1) No adjustments whatsoever are required for water charges, fuel charges or any other ineligible service charges.

(2) The figures used should be consistent all the way through the calculation: so if the actual rent is expressed calendar monthly, the RO's figures should be calendar monthly and any deductions should be calendar monthly. The final conversion to a weekly figure in step 4 is necessary as HB calculations are essentially weekly (chapter 7).

(3) This table does not apply to RO determinations made before 3rd April 2000 (see chapter 8): in those cases the former rules apply, as described in the 1999-2000 edition of this Guide.

Examples: Calculating maximum rent

EXAMPLE ONE: A STRAIGHTFORWARD CASE

A private tenant over the age of 25 makes a first claim for HB in May 2000. She falls within the general rules (paras. 11.5-7). Her actual rent is £100 per week including water charges and fuel charges. She is not a joint occupier. The rent officer has provided the following figures:

◆ a claim-related rent determination of £90 per week;

◆ a local reference rent determination of £70 per week;

◆ no single room rent determination (because the claimant is not a 'young individual')

Because none of the adjustments in table 11.3 apply in this case, her maximum rent is simply the lower of the above two figures, i.e. £70 per week.

EXAMPLE TWO: A JOINT OCCUPIER AGED UNDER 25

A private tenant under the age of 25 makes a first claim for HB in May 2000. He falls within the general rules (paras. 11.5-7). He is a joint occupier with two others: they share their rent equally. The actual rent for the whole property is £180 per week including water charges and fuel charges. The rent officer has provided the following figures:

♦ a claim-related rent determination of £150 per week;

♦ a local reference rent determination of £135 per week;

♦ a single room rent determination of £40 per week.

The only adjustment in table 11.3 which applies is the apportionment for joint occupiers:

♦ the adjusted claim-related rent is (£150 ÷ 3 =) £50 per week;

♦ the adjusted local reference rent is (£135 ÷ 3 =) £45 per week;

♦ the single room rent is not adjusted; it is £40 per week.

The claimant's maximum rent is the lowest of the resulting figures, i.e. £40 per week.

EXAMPLE THREE: SUPPORT CHARGES INCLUDED

A private tenant under the age of 25 makes a first claim for HB in May 2000. She falls within the general rules (paras. 11.5-7). Her actual rent is £115 per week including water charges, fuel charges, meals charges and eligible support charges (she has a community care assessment: paras. 11.95-96). She is not a joint occupier. The authority determines that the figure for meals is £18.65 per week (table 11.8), and has valued the eligible support charges as worth £20 per week. The rent officer has provided the following figures:

♦ a claim-related rent determination of £70 per week (including meals);

♦ no local reference rent determination;

♦ a single room rent determination of £40 per week.

The adjustments in table 11.3 apply as follows:

♦ the adjusted claim-related rent:

rent officer figure	£70.00
minus meals charge	– £18.65
plus support charges	+ £20.00
total	£71.35

♦ the adjusted single room rent:

rent officer figure	£40.00
(no adjustment for meals)	
plus support charges	+ £20.00
total	£60.00

The claimant's maximum rent is the lower of the resulting figures, i.e. £60 per week.

DEFINITION OF 'YOUNG INDIVIDUAL'

HBR 2(1),
11(3A),(3B) **11.8**   Every claimant who is a 'single claimant' (para. 6.4) and is under the age
of 25 is a 'young individual' (see also para. 11.10) unless he or she:

(a) rents his or her home from the authority itself;

(b) rents his or her home from a registered housing association or registered
social landlord;

(c) is under the age of 22 and was formerly in social services care under a court
order (under section 31(1)(a) of the Children Act 1989 in England and
Wales, or equivalent provisions in Scotland) which applied (or continued to
apply) after his or her 16th birthday;

(d) is under the age of 22 and was formerly provided with accommodation by
social services (under section 20 of the Children Act 1989 in England and
Wales, or equivalent provisions in Scotland) but is no longer in that
accommodation or remains in it but the accommodation is no longer
provided by social services;

(e) has one or more non-dependant(s);

(f) qualifies for a severe disability premium in the assessment of his or her HB
(para. 12.38), income support or JSA(IB);

(g) lives in a residential care home or nursing home (paras. 4.5-11);

(h) lives in certain types of hostel (as defined in para. 8.10).

11.9   As shown in table 11.3, the rules applying to young individuals take
account of the rent officer's 'single room rent determination'. It is the authority
(not the rent officer) which decides whether someone is a 'young individual' (see
also para. 11.10).

11.10   Technically, it is worth noting that the law works in a peculiar way in the
following cases:

◆   for claimants who fall in case (a) above, the law defines them as 'young
individuals' but then says that no referral may be made to the rent officer in
their case (chapter 8): this is the same as saying that they are not 'young
individuals';

◆   for claimants who fall in cases (e) or (f) above, the law defines them as
'young individuals' but then says that the authority must ignore any single
room rent determination made by the rent officer in their cases: this is the
same as saying that they are not 'young individuals';

◆   for claimants who fall in cases (g) or (h) above, the law defines them as
'young individuals' but then says that the rent officer may not make a single
room rent determination in their cases: this is the same as saying that they
are not 'young individuals' (except that it is the rent officer who determines

whether they live in the accommodation described in those cases, not the authority).

MAXIMUM RENT IF THE CLAIMANT'S RENT CHANGES

11.11 Once a claimant's maximum rent has been calculated (as in table 11.3) at the beginning of his or her benefit period (para. 7.81), it applies until the end of that benefit period unless the claimant's details have to be re-referred to the rent officer (paras. 8.6-11). In this case, a new maximum rent must be calculated as above and used for the remainder of his or her benefit period (whether it is higher or lower than the initial maximum rent). *HBR 11(6),(6A), (6B),(13)*

11.12 Following the amendments this year, the law is unclear about what happens if the claimant's actual rent reduces to below the maximum rent (an event which is, needless to say, almost unheard of). It seems likely that, over-riding all the above rules, the most a person's eligible rent can ever be is what he or she actually pays minus amounts for ineligible service charges as calculated by the authority (as in paras. 11.82 onwards). If this is not the effect of the law, it would seem reasonable for the authority to use its general power to restrict the eligible rent (11.25) to that figure.

MAXIMUM RENT: PROTECTED GROUPS

11.13 Two groups of claimants are protected against the effect of the rules about maximum rents. They are often called the 'protected groups', though this term is not used in the law. (These two protected groups – and the definitions in paras. 11.14-18 – also apply to certain other types of HB case, mentioned as they arise later in this chapter.)

THE PROTECTION FOR PEOPLE WHO COULD FORMERLY AFFORD THEIR ACCOMMODATION

11.14 A claimant falls within this protected group if: *HBR 11(9),(10)*

◆ he or she or any combination of the occupiers of his or her home (para. 11.19) could afford the financial commitments there when the liability to pay rent was entered into (no matter how long ago this was); and

◆ the claimant has not received HB for any period in the 52 weeks prior to his or her current claim. Receipt of CTB during those weeks is ignored.

11.15 In such a case, the protection lasts for the first 13 weeks of his or her entitlement to HB. During those weeks, his or her eligible rent is: *HBR 10(3), 11(9)*

◆ his or her actual rent (converted to a weekly amount if necessary: para. 9.57);

◆ minus amounts for water charges, fuel, meals and any other ineligible service charges (calculated by the authority as described in paras. 11.82 onwards);

◆ the above amounts being apportioned in the case of a joint occupier (para. 11.4).

11.16 This protection gives the claimant time to move, without the additional pressure of having insufficient HB. In the case of a couple, so long as the claimant has not received HB during the past 52 weeks, it is immaterial whether his or her partner has. In some cases it therefore makes a substantial difference which person in a couple makes the claim for HB (para. 7.5).

THE PROTECTION FOR PEOPLE WHO HAVE HAD A BEREAVEMENT

HBR 11(7),(8)   **11.17** A claimant falls within this protected group if:

◆ any of the occupiers of his or her home (para. 11.19) has died within the last 12 months (including occupiers who were temporarily absent); and

◆ the claimant has not moved home since the date of that death.

HBR 11(7)   **11.18** In such a case, the protection lasts until 12 months after that death. During that period it works as follows. If the claimant was on HB at the date of the death, his or her eligible rent must not be reduced to below whatever was his or her the eligible rent immediately before that date (it is, however, increased if any rule requires this). If the claimant was not on HB at the date of the death, his or her eligible rent is:

◆ his or her actual rent (converted to a weekly amount if necessary: para. 9.57);

◆ minus amounts for water charges, fuel, meals and any other ineligible service charges (calculated by the authority as described in paras. 11.82 onwards);

◆ the above amounts being apportioned in the case of a joint occupier (para. 11.4).

WHICH 'OCCUPIERS' ARE TAKEN INTO ACCOUNT?

HBR 11(11),(12)   **11.19** For the purposes of the above rules, the only 'occupiers' taken into account are:

◆ the claimant;

◆ any member of his or her family (partner, child, young person: paras. 6.5-20);

◆ any 'relative' (para. 11.20) of the claimant or partner (including non-dependants, boarders, tenants, sub-tenants and joint occupiers) who has no separate right to occupy the dwelling.

The claimant and members of the family should always count as 'occupiers' of the dwelling. Whether a relative (in the third item above) is an occupier is open to interpretation (since 'occupier' is not further defined for these purposes), but the term appears intended to have a degree of flexibility rather than being limited to those who permanently reside with the claimant. In practice, the *Swale and*

Marchant case is likely to affect how authorities interpret 'occupier' for these purposes (the case was about children whose parents live apart and may have further implications: para. 8.20). Nevertheless, there remains an argument that *Swale and Marchant* was about the definition of 'occupier' in a different context and, therefore, is not binding here. The question of who counts as an 'occupier' is for the authority to determine (not, for example, the rent officer) and is open to appeal (chapter 19).

WHO IS A 'RELATIVE'?

11.20 A 'relative' is defined for all HB purposes as: HBR 2(1)

◆ a parent, parent-in-law, daughter, son, daughter/son-in-law, step-daughter/ son, sister or brother; or

◆ a partner (married or unmarried: para. 6.6) of any of the above; or

◆ a grandparent, grandchild, aunt, uncle, niece or nephew.

INCREASING MAXIMUM RENT TO PREVENT EXCEPTIONAL HARDSHIP

11.21 The authority may, as a matter of discretion (para. 1.34), increase any   HBR 61(3),(4)
claimant's maximum rent (calculated as above) if it is satisfied that:

◆ the claimant would qualify for at least some HB (i.e. at least 50p per week: para. 9.16) without any increase in his or her maximum rent; and

◆ unless the maximum rent is increased, the claimant or any member of his or her family (para. 6.5) 'will suffer exceptional hardship'; and

◆ the limits in the next two paragraphs will not be exceeded.

11.22 The first limit (illustrated in the following example) is that the authority   HBR 61(3),(4)
may not increase any individual claimant's maximum rent beyond:

◆ his or her actual rent (converted to a weekly amount if necessary: para. 9.57);

◆ minus amounts for any water charges, fuel, meals or other ineligible service charges included in it (calculated by the authority as described in paras. 11.82 onwards);

◆ the above amounts being apportioned in the case of a joint occupier (para. 11.4).

The second limit is that the authority may increase maximum rents in its area only   SI 1997 No. 67
until it has reached its 'permitted total'. This is a fixed figure laid down by law   SI 1999 No. 64
for each authority. (The DSS pays authorities subsidy amounting to less than their permitted total. If this is not used on exceptional hardship increases it may be put towards other HB expenditure: chapter 21.)

11.23 Good advice on exceptional hardship additions may be found in DSS circular A35/99, which contains the following points (among others):

◆ it suggests that 'exceptional' means 'out of the ordinary' rather than 'very unusual';

◆ it points out that the mobility component of disability living allowance must be disregarded when considering whether someone will suffer 'exceptional hardship';

◆ it recommends that a home visit should be made when an authority is considering such matters;

◆ it points out that points-based scoring systems (for deciding what constitutes 'exceptional hardship' should be avoided;

◆ it recommends that authorities should determine whether or not to award an addition within 14 days of a request.

11.24 The discretion to award an increase to prevent exceptional hardship cannot be limited to particular categories of claimant. Each case must be considered on its merits. The conditions are stricter than those for awarding increases for 'exceptional circumstances' (para. 9.42). It is possible for a claimant to be awarded both of the increases just mentioned as follows (and as illustrated in the following example):

◆ the increase for 'exceptional hardship' (para. 11.21) applies to increase the claimant's maximum rent. This figure is then used to calculate entitlement to HB as described in chapter 9;

◆ the increase for 'exceptional circumstances' (para. 9.42) applies to increase the amount of a claimant's entitlement to HB after it has been calculated under the rules in chapter 9.

Example: Maximum rent: increases for 'exceptional hardship' and 'exceptional circumstances'

INFORMATION

A private tenant claims HB in July 2000. Her case is one to which table 11.3 applies. Her actual rent is £100 per week. Her letting agreement shows that this includes the following (and the authority agrees these figures are reasonable):

◆ £8 for ineligible fuel;

◆ £4 for ineligible cleaning.

She is over the age of 25. She is not a joint occupier. She does not fall into either of the 'protected groups'. She is on income support and has one non-dependant who is also over 25 and on income support. She pays for her council tax and water charges herself (i.e. these are not included in her rent).

The rent officer gives just a local reference rent determination of £80 per week.

'MAXIMUM RENT'

The claimant's maximum rent is simply the local
reference rent, which is   £80.00 pw

INITIAL CALCULATION OF HB ENTITLEMENT

Using the above as her eligible rent, her entitlement to HB (para. 9.8) is:

maximum rent	£80.00 pw
minus non-dependant deduction	– £7.40 pw
which is	£72.60 pw

INCREASE FOR EXCEPTIONAL HARDSHIP

The authority agrees to increase her maximum rent to £88 pw because of the exceptional hardship rule. This is the largest increase possible in her case (para. 11.22). So now her entitlement to HB is:

increased maximum rent	£88.00 pw
minus non-dependant deduction	– £7.40 pw
which is	£80.60 pw

INCREASE FOR EXCEPTIONAL CIRCUMSTANCES

The authority also agrees that she should be awarded an additional £7.40 HB pw because of the exceptional circumstances rule. This is the largest increase possible in her case (para. 9.42). So now her entitlement to HB is:

the figure calculated as above	£80.60 pw
plus the addition just mentioned	+ £7.40 pw
which is	£80.00 pw

REDUCING MAXIMUM RENT IN CERTAIN CASES

11.25   The authority has a general power to reduce any claimant's eligible rent   HBR 10(6B)
to below the 'maximum rent' calculated as above if:

◆ 'it appears to the authority that in the particular circumstances of the case
the eligible rent… is greater than it is reasonable to meet by way of housing
benefit.'

In such a case, the eligible rent is reduced to:

◆ 'such lesser sum as seems to that authority to be an appropriate rent in that particular case.'

11.26 In practice, reductions under this provision remain uncommon. They can be made only if the authority makes a proper judgment about the above matters (para. 1.33). This means (as the DSS pointed out in circular HB/CTB A7/96) that the authority 'should have evidence and an objective justification' before making a reduction.

Eligible rent: variations for certain tenures

11.27 This section explains how the above general rules (paras. 11.5-26) are varied in the case of:

◆ council tenants;

◆ housing association tenants (and similar registered social landlords);

◆ tenants of charities, voluntary organisations or non-metropolitan county councils;

◆ people in resettlement places;

◆ private tenants whose tenancy began before 15th January 1989 (England and Wales) or 2nd January 1989 (Scotland);

◆ claimants in 'exempt accommodation' (para. 11.37).

Yet further variations apply to certain older claims, as described in paragraphs 11.42-52.

COUNCIL TENANTS (RENT REBATES)

HBR 10(3),(6B), 12A

11.28 In the case of a claim for a rent rebate, the claimant's eligible rent is:

◆ his or her actual rent (converted to a weekly amount if necessary: para. 9.57);

◆ minus amounts for water charges, fuel, meals and any other ineligible service charges included within it. The authority calculates how much to deduct for these as described in paragraphs 11.82 onwards;

◆ the above amounts being apportioned in the case of a joint occupier (para. 11.4);

◆ but see also the next paragraph.

11.29 The figure calculated as above may be further reduced as described in paragraphs 11.25-26 (though this is in practice rare). The authority must not reduce the eligible rent for any other reason. (Different rules apply to a resettlement place: para. 11.35.)

HOUSING ASSOCIATION TENANTS

11.30 In the case of a claim from someone renting from a registered housing association (or from any other registered social landlord, or from a housing association which is a registered charity or non-profit-making voluntary organisation), there are two possibilities:

HBR 10(3)
SI 1997 No. 198

◆ if it is 'exempt accommodation' (as defined in para. 11.40), the claimant's eligible rent is calculated as in paragraphs 11.37-38;

◆ if it is not 'exempt accommodation' (for example, if it is 'general purpose' accommodation), the claimant's eligible rent is calculated as in the next paragraph.

11.31 In non-exempt housing association cases (para. 11.30), the claimant's eligible rent is:

◆ his or her actual rent (converted to a weekly amount if necessary: para. 9.57);

◆ minus amounts for water charges, fuel, meals and any other ineligible service charges included within it. The authority calculates how much to deduct for these as described in paragraphs 11.82 onwards;

◆ the above amounts being apportioned in the case of a joint occupier (para. 11.4);

◆ but see the next paragraph.

11.32 The figure calculated as above may be reduced if the authority considers that the claimant's accommodation is unreasonably large or rent unreasonably expensive. In such a case:

◆ the authority refers the claimant's details to the rent officer (table 8.1); and

◆ the claimant's eligible rent is then worked out according to the general rules relating to maximum rents (paras. 11.5-26) – in other words, in the same way as if the claimant was a private tenant.

The authority must not reduce the eligible rent if it does not refer the claimant's details to the rent officer.

11.33 Referring the rent to the rent officer can have serious financial consequences for the claimant, the housing association and even the council itself – for example, it can result in requests for increases for exceptional hardship (para. 11.21 and chapter 21). In some areas of the country such referrals are quite common; in others they remain rare.

TENANTS OF CHARITIES, VOLUNTARY ORGANISATIONS OR NON-METROPOLITAN COUNTY COUNCILS

11.34 In the case of a claim from someone renting from a registered charity or a non-profit-making voluntary organisation (other than a housing association:

HBR 10(3)
SI 1995/1644
SI 1997/1984

para. 11.30), or from a non-metropolitan county council (a typical example would be when a claimant rents from a county social services department), there are two possibilities:

◆ if it is 'exempt accommodation' (as defined in para. 11.40), the claimant's eligible rent is calculated as in paragraphs 11.37-38;

◆ if it is not 'exempt accommodation' (for example, if it is 'general purpose' accommodation), the claimant's eligible rent is worked out according to the general rules relating to maximum rents (paras. 11.5-26) – in other words, in the same way as if the claimant was a private tenant.

PEOPLE IN RESETTLEMENT PLACES

HBR 10(3)
SI 1995/1644
SI 1997/1984

11.35 In the case of a claim from someone in a resettlement place (para. 11.40), the claimant's eligible rent is calculated as in paragraphs 11.37-38.

TENANCIES BEGUN BEFORE 2ND/15TH JANUARY 1989, ETC.

HBR 10(3)
HBR Old 11(1),(1A)

11.36 In addition to all the rules described elsewhere in this chapter, if a claimant's rent has been fixed by a rent officer, rent tribunal or rent assessment committee (so that it is binding on the landlord), the claimant's eligible rent must not exceed that fixed figure. This rule is specified in HB law for exempt cases (paras. 11.37 and 11.48); for all other cases, it follows from the fact that a claimant cannot be liable for an amount of rent in excess of the fixed figure. This rule applies to:

◆ tenancies in England and Wales which were entered into before 15th January 1989;

◆ tenancies in Scotland which were entered into before 2nd January 1989;

◆ tenancies granted on or after those dates in which the landlord is required to preserve the tenant's rights (typically because the landlord has moved a tenant whose tenancy began before those dates);

◆ other tenancies granted on or after those dates, but only for one year from the date on which the fixed figure takes effect.

Tenancies in the fourth category fall within certain provisions of the Housing Act 1988 and the Housing (Scotland) Act 1988. Tenancies in the first three categories above all fall within the provisions of landlord and tenant law which applied before those Acts came into force (in the third category, under preserved rights).

PEOPLE IN EXEMPT ACCOMMODATION

HBR Old 10, 11

11.37 In the case of a claim from someone renting 'exempt accommodation' (as defined in para. 11.40), the claimant's eligible rent is:

◆ his or her actual rent (converted to a weekly amount if necessary: para. 9.57);

♦ minus an appropriate amount in certain cases when the rent is unreasonably high or the accommodation is unreasonably large (paras. 11.53-74);

♦ minus amounts for water charges, fuel, meals and any other ineligible service charges included within the claimant's actual rent. The authority calculates how much to deduct for these as described in paragraphs 11.82 onwards;

♦ the above amounts being apportioned in the case of a joint occupier (para. 11.4).

An example follows.

11.38 It is the authority which determines all the above matters, including the question of whether to restrict the eligible rent (the second item in the above list). Although in some cases the authority may refer the details to the rent officer (chapter 8), the rent officer's figures are never binding on the assessment of HB (para. 11.54).

11.39 Claimants who rent 'exempt accommodation' are one of the two kinds of claimants who count as 'exempt cases' (so called because they are exempt from the rules introduced on 2nd January 1996). The other kind of 'exempt case' is described in paragraphs 11.46-52.

WHAT IS 'EXEMPT ACCOMMODATION'?

11.40 'Exempt accommodation' is: SI 1995 No. 1644

♦ any accommodation 'provided by' a housing association, a registered charity, a non-profit-making voluntary organisation, a registered social landlord or a non-metropolitan country council, where (in each case) 'that body or a person acting on its behalf also provides the claimant with care, support or supervision' (the wording has changed this year to emphasise, among other things, that it is the claimant who is considered, not occupants generally); or

♦ any resettlement place provided by a local authority or non-profit-making voluntary organisation which has received a grant under section 30 of the Jobseekers Act 1995.

11.41 For the purposes of the first type of exempt accommodation, there is no definition of 'care', 'support' or 'supervision': these terms take their ordinary English meanings and are open to appeal (chapter 19). Also, what it means for a accommodation to be 'provided by' the body concerned is open to debate, though it is not restricted to cases where the claimant pays rent to that body. (For example, if a registered charity makes arrangements with a private landlord to use accommodation owned by him for its clients, and the landlord collects the rent but the charity retains the right to say who will live in the accommodation, it may be argued that the accommodation is 'provided by' the charity.)

Example: Eligible rent in exempt accommodation

INFORMATION

A tenant of a registered housing association makes a first claim for HB in June 1999. She is not a joint occupier. Her housing association provides her with support, so she counts as living in exempt accommodation (para. 11.40). Her actual rent is £70 pw including water charges, fuel and support. The authority determines that the water charges are £2.65 pw and the fuel charges are £12.35 pw; that the support is eligible for HB (paras. 11.90-91); and that her accommodation is not unreasonably large and her rent is not unreasonably expensive (paras. 11.52 onwards).

CALCULATION OF ELIGIBLE RENT

Her actual rent is	£70 pw
The deductions for ineligible service charges (water and fuel) are	£15 pw
So her eligible rent is	£55 pw

Eligible rent: further variations for older claims

11.42   This section explains how all the earlier rules in this chapter (both the general rules in paras. 11.5-26 and the variations for certain tenures in paras. 11.27-41) are further varied in the case of certain older claims. It covers:

◆ the rules for claims continuing from before 6th October 1997;

◆ the (former) rules for claims continuing from before 7th October 1996;

◆ the rules for claims continuing from before 2nd January 1996 and certain other exempt cases.

CLAIMS CONTINUING FROM BEFORE 6TH OCTOBER 1997

HBR 11(4),(5)
SI 1997 No. 852
SI 1997 No. 1975
SI 1999 No. 2734

11.43   The variations described in the next paragraph apply to any HB claim in which the claimant:

◆ was 'entitled to and in receipt of' HB on Sunday 5th October 1997; and

◆ has remained 'entitled to and in receipt of' HB continuously since that date (disregarding breaks of up to 52 weeks in the case of a 'welfare to work beneficiary': table 13.3; but in any other case with no breaks whatsoever): this includes renewal claims so long as they run continuously or are backdated to run continuously (disregarding breaks as just mentioned); and

◆ has not moved to occupy a new dwelling as his or her home since that date (regardless of the reason for the move); and

◆ has not, in any new benefit period beginning after that date, ceased to qualify for a '50 per cent top-up' (as described in table 11.4); and

◆ was not entitled to HB on Monday 1st January 1996; and

◆ is not an 'exempt claimant' (as defined in paras. 11.48-52).

Table 11.4: 'MAXIMUM RENT' FOR CLAIMS CONTINUING FROM BEFORE 6TH OCTOBER 1997

See paragraphs 11.43-44 for the cases to which this table applies and for further information.

To calculate the 'maximum rent' in these cases, work through the following steps

1.   ADJUST THE RENT OFFICER'S FIGURES

Adjust all the rent officer's figures exactly as shown in table 11.3. In the following, all references to rent officer figures are to those figures as so adjusted.

2.   THE '50% TOP-UP'

◆ If there is no local reference rent, the claimant does not qualify for a '50% top-up' (his or her maximum rent is simply calculated as in table 11.3).

◆ If the local reference rent is greater than (or equal to) the claim-related rent, the claimant does not qualify for a '50%' top-up' (his or her maximum rent is simply calculated as in table 11.3).

◆ If the local reference rent is less than the claim-related rent, the '50% top-up' is half of the difference between them.

3.   MAXIMUM RENT

◆ The 'maximum rent' is the local reference rent plus the '50% top-up'.

◆ But if the single room rent determination is lower, then that is the 'maximum rent' instead (i.e. the claimant does not qualify for a '50% top-up' after all).

(The notes to table 11.3. apply equally here.)

> ## Example: Calculating 'maximum rent' for claims continuing from before 6th October 1997
>
> A private tenant over the age of 25 makes a renewal claim for HB in May 2000. She was on HB on 5th October 1997. She has not moved since then and her case is one to which table 11.4 applies. Her actual rent is £100 per week including water charges and fuel charges. She is not a joint occupier. The rent officer has provided the following figures:
>
> ◆ a claim-related rent determination of £90 per week;
>
> ◆ a local reference rent determination of £70 per week;
>
> ◆ no single room rent determination (because she is not a 'young individual).
>
> Because the adjustments in step 1 of table 11.4 do not apply, her '50% top-up' is half the difference between the above two figures, i.e. £10 per week. Her maximum rent is the local reference rent plus this 50% top-up, totalling £80 per week.

11.44 All the earlier rules about eligible rent (paras. 11.5-41) apply in these cases, except that whenever a 'maximum rent' applies (paras. 11.6-7) it is calculated as shown in table 11.4 (not as in table 11.3). As shown in table 11.4, the claimant qualifies for a '50 per cent top-up' which sometimes (not always) means that his or her 'maximum rent' is higher. An example follows the table.

CLAIMS CONTINUING FROM BEFORE 7TH OCTOBER 1996

SI 1996 No. 965   **11.45** The rules about 'young individuals' and the rent officer's 'single room rent determination' (paras. 11.8-9) were introduced on 7th October 1996. However, for any claimant who was 'entitled to and in receipt of' HB on 6th October 1996, those new rules did not apply until he or she moved home or made a renewal claim (whichever first occurred). It is now too late for this transitional provision to apply in any current HB case (because by now every such claimant must have made at least one renewal claim).

CLAIMS CONTINUING FROM BEFORE 2ND JANUARY 1996 AND OTHER 'EXEMPT CLAIMANTS'

HBR Old 10, 11
SI 1996 No. 1644   **11.46** In broad terms, all claimants who have been on HB since before 2nd January 1996 (and some claimants who have more recently taken over an HB claim from someone who has been on HB since before then) count as 'exempt claimants' (the full details are in paras. 11.48-52). For an 'exempt claimant' (regardless of what kind of accommodation he or she lives in), the claimant's

eligible rent is worked out in exactly the same way as it is for claimants in 'exempt accommodation': the rules are given in paragraphs 11.37-38.

11.47 'Exempt claimants' are one of the two kinds of claimants who count as 'exempt cases' (so called because they are exempt from the rules introduced on 2nd January 1996). The other kind of 'exempt case' is described in paragraphs 11.37-38.

WHO IS AN 'EXEMPT CLAIMANT'?

11.48   A claimant is an 'exempt claimant' if he or she: SI 1995 No. 1644

◆   was 'entitled to' HB on Monday 1st January 1996 (including cases where this is because HB was backdated to include this date); and

◆   has remained 'entitled to and in receipt of' HB continuously since that date (disregarding breaks in HB entitlement/receipt of up to 52 weeks in the case of a 'welfare to work beneficiary': table 13.3; or in any case disregarding breaks of four weeks or less): this includes renewal claims so long as they run continuously or are backdated to run continuously (disregarding breaks as just mentioned); and

◆   has not moved to occupy a new dwelling as his or her home since that date, or has moved only because a fire, flood, explosion or natural catastrophe made his or her former home uninhabitable.

11.49   A claimant is also an 'exempt claimant' if he or she has become entitled to HB on or after 2nd January 1996 in any of the ways in which exemption is transferred from one person to another (paras. 11.51-52).

11.50   Also, in the special case of a refugee who was formerly an asylum seeker   HBR sch. A1
(para. 5.34), the refugee is an 'exempt claimant' in respect of any previous period for which he or she has become entitled to HB.

TRANSFERRING EXEMPTION: DEATH, DEPARTURE AND DETENTION

11.51   The following are the three ways in which exemption is transferred from   SI 1995 No. 1644
one claimant ('A') to another claimant ('B') who continues to occupy the dwelling (see also para. 11.52). 'Partner' and 'member of the household' have their specific HB meanings (paras. 6.3 onwards):

◆   A dies; and B was (until then) his or her partner or any other member of the household;

◆   A leaves the dwelling; and B was (until then) his or her partner;

◆   A is 'detained in custody pending sentence upon conviction or under a sentence imposed by a court' (and is not entitled to HB under the rules about absences from home: chapter 4); and B is (or was until then) his or her partner.

11.52 Additionally, in all three cases:

♦ A must be in receipt of HB on the date of his or her death, departure or detention (or be a 'welfare to work beneficiary' (table 13.3) at that date who was in receipt of HB no more than 52 weeks previously);

♦ B must occupy the dwelling as a home on that date (or be treated as occupying it: chapter 4);

♦ B's claim for HB must be made within four weeks of that date (or backdated to fall within those four weeks: para. 7.86);

♦ B's claim is then treated as having been made on that date;

♦ B then continues to be exempt for as long as he or she:

• remains 'entitled to and in receipt of HB' continuously (disregarding breaks in HB entitlement/receipt of up to 52 weeks in the case of a 'welfare to work beneficiary': table 13.3; or in any case disregarding breaks of four weeks or less): this includes renewal claims so long as they run continuously or are backdated to run continuously (disregarding breaks as just mentioned), and

• does not move to occupy a new dwelling as his or her home, or moves only because a fire, flood, explosion or natural catastrophe makes his or her home uninhabitable;

♦ B's exemption is then transferred to any other claimant in the same way as described above (paras. 11.51-52). There is no limit to the number of transfers of exemption so long as the above conditions are complied with in each case.

Examples: Exempt claimants and transferring exemption

(1) Mrs Sawable is a part-time magician's assistant who is in receipt of HB on 1st January 1996. Her husband and adult daughter reside with her. So she is an 'exempt claimant' from 2nd January.

(2) Her HB claim becomes due for renewal on various dates in 1996, 1997 and 1998. She renews it on time in each case, so there is no break in her entitlement to HB.
So she continues to be an exempt claimant.

(3) Mrs Sawable dies in May 1999, due to an accident at work. Mr Sawable makes a claim for HB within four weeks of her death.
So, because of the rules about 'transferred exemption', he is an exempt claimant.

(4) Mr Sawable is convicted and sentenced to three years' imprisonment in July 1999. His daughter (who has continued to live there

> throughout the above) agrees with the landlord to take over the
> tenancy and makes a claim for HB within four weeks of his conviction.
> So, because of the rules about 'transferred exemption', she is an
> exempt claimant.
>
> (5) The daughter (who was previously on JSA(IB)) gets a job in January
> 2000. She does not make a renewal claim for HB until May 2000
> (and it is not backdated).
> So, because there has been a break in her entitlement to HB of
> more than four weeks, she is not an 'exempt claimant' for the
> purposes of her renewal claim.

HB restrictions for 'exempt cases'

OVERVIEW

11.53 This section applies only to 'exempt cases' (i.e. cases where the claimant *SI 1995 No. 1644* rents 'exempt accommodation': para. 11.40, and cases where the claimant is an 'exempt claimant': paras. 11.48-52). In exempt cases, the claimant's eligible rent may be lower than his or her actual rent either because of ineligible service charges (paras. 11.75 onwards), or because the authority restricts it (para. 11.54), or both. In broad terms, 'exempt cases' can include claims from private tenants (for whom eligible rent restrictions are in practice common), council tenants (for whom restrictions are very uncommon), housing association tenants (for whom restrictions are becoming more common in some parts of the country), and various other tenants.

11.54 The rules about eligible rent restrictions in exempt cases are summarised *HBR Old 11, 12* in table 11.5. In applying them, authorities: *SI 1997 No. 852*

◆ must not take a blanket approach (GM para. A4.99): each step must be considered in the individual circumstances of each case and each step is open to appeal;

◆ must not restrict a claimant's eligible rent just because of the subsidy rules (chapter 21). The requirements of the HB regulations (described below) are the only test that is relevant in deciding whether or not benefit should be restricted.

Table 11.5 HB RESTRICTIONS FOR EXEMPT CASES:

A SIMPLIFIED SUMMARY

STEP ONE: IS THE RENT UNREASONABLE? (paras. 11.55-61)

The claimant's HB can be restricted only if, compared with suitable alternative accommodation:

◆ the rent is unreasonably high; or

◆ the dwelling is unreasonably large; or

◆ a rent increase is unreasonable.

STEP TWO: IS THE CLAIMANT IN A PROTECTED GROUP? (paras. 11.62-69)

Protections against HB restrictions can apply for claimants:

◆ who could afford their accommodation when their letting began; or

◆ who have had a death in their home; or

◆ who have children or young persons, or are aged 60 or more, or are sick or disabled.

STEP THREE: SHOULD THE ELIGIBLE RENT BE RESTRICTED? (paras. 11.70-74)

◆ If the rent is unreasonable (step one) and none of the protections applies (step two), the authority must decide how much (if at all) the claimant's eligible rent should be reduced.

WHAT COUNTS AS 'UNREASONABLE'?

HBR Old 11(2)   **11.55**   In exempt cases, the authority must consider whether (taking into account the points in paras. 11.58 onwards):

◆ the claimant's rent is unreasonably high; or

◆ the claimant's accommodation is unreasonably large for the needs of all the occupiers (para. 11.56).

If it is, the authority must consider whether the claimant falls within the protected groups (paras. 11.62-69) and what (if any) is an appropriate reduction in the claimant's eligible rent (paras. 11.65 and 11.70).

11.56   For the above purposes of deciding whether a claimant's accommodation is unreasonably large for all the 'occupiers', the question of who counts as an *occupier*

is open to interpretation (since 'occupier' is not further defined for these purposes), but it is certainly not limited to the groups listed in paragraph 11.19. The term appears intended to have a degree of flexibility rather than being limited to those who permanently reside with the claimant. In practice, the *Swale and Marchant* case is likely to affect how authorities interpret 'occupier' for these purposes (the case was about children whose parents live apart and may have further implications: para. 8.20). Nevertheless, there remains an argument that Swale and Marchant was about the definition of 'occupier' in a different context and, therefore, is not binding here. The question of who counts as an 'occupier' is for the authority to determine (not, for example, the rent officer) and is open to appeal (chapter 19).

11.57 In exempt cases, a subsidiary rule applies once a claimant's benefit period (para. 7.81) has begun. It arises if the authority considers that (taking into account the points in paras. 11.58 onwards) a rent increase is:

◆ unreasonably high; or

◆ unreasonably soon after another increase during the previous year.

If it is, the authority must consider whether the claimant falls within the protected groups (paras. 11.62-69) and what (if any) is an appropriate reduction in the claimant's new eligible rent (para. 11.72). An authority must not regard a rent increase as unreasonable if it is made to include support charges (para. 11.89) which are from this year eligible for HB.

HBR Old 12(1)
SI 1999 No. 273

MAKING THE COMPARISON

11.58 In all the above cases, authorities:

◆ must make a comparison (as regards the rent, size or rent increase, as appropriate) with suitable alternative accommodation (para. 11.61);

◆ may additionally take account of figures provided by the rent officer (if the case was referred to the rent officer: chapter 8) – and the DSS advises that they 'ought' to do this (GM para. A4.99), bearing in mind that the rent officer's function is different;

◆ must not, at this stage, take into account the impact of the subsidy rules on their own finances (para. 11.74).

HBR Old 11(2), 12(1)

11.59 Making a comparison with suitable alternative accommodation is essentially a matter of *making a valuation* of what would be suitable alternative accommodation for the claimant by working through the following questions:

(a) what is the rent (including all eligible and ineligible services) for the claimant's dwelling?

(b) what type of alternative accommodation is suitable for the claimant? and, in order to determine this, what services are requisite in order to regard the alternative accommodation as suitable and what other factors need to be taken into account (para. 11.61)?;

(c) what rent (including all eligible and ineligible services) would be payable for such accommodation?

(d) is the rent in (a) unreasonably high by comparison with the rent in (c)?

11.60   Questions (a) to (d) above are based on the judgment in *R v East Yorkshire Borough of Beverley Housing Benefits Review Board ex p Hare*, (1995), QBD, *The Times* 28.2.95. As regards question (d) above, 'unreasonably high' means more than just 'higher': *Malcolm v the Review Board for Tweeddale District*, Court of Session, August 1991.

WHAT IS SUITABLE ALTERNATIVE ACCOMMODATION?

HBR Old
11(6)(a),(7),(8)

11.61   In deciding what alternative accommodation would be suitable for the claimant (question (b) in para. 11.60), authorities:

◆ must take account of the nature of the alternative accommodation and the exclusive and shared facilities provided, having regard to the age and state of health of all the occupiers (as defined in paras. 11.19-20). 'For example, a disabled or elderly person might have special needs and require more expensive or larger accommodation than would otherwise be the case' (GM para. A4.112);

◆ must only take into account alternative accommodation with security of tenure which is reasonably equivalent to what the claimant currently has;

◆ 'must have a sufficiency of information to ensure that like is being compared with like... Unless that can be done, no safe assessment can be made of the reasonableness of the rent in question or the proper level of value': *Malcolm v the Review Board for Tweeddale District*, Court of Session, August 1991 (transcript, pages 10,11);

◆ may take account of alternative accommodation outside the authority's own area if there is no comparable accommodation within it. But if this is necessary, it is unreasonable to 'make comparisons with other parts of the country where accommodation costs differ widely from those which apply locally' (GM para. A4.114).

PROTECTED GROUPS

HBR Old 11(3)-(5),
12(2),(3)

11.62   Three groups of claimants are protected against the effect of the above rules about HB restrictions. The first two groups, and the rules applying to them, are the same as those described in paragraphs 11.14-20; the details of the third group, and the rules applying to it, are described below.

THE PROTECTION FOR CERTAIN VULNERABLE PEOPLE

11.63 A claimant falls within this protected group if any of the occupiers of his   HBR Old
or her home (as described in paras. 11.19-20) is: 11(3),(6)(b)

◆ aged 60 or more; or

◆ responsible for a child or young person in the household (paras. 6.12-20); or

◆ incapable of work for social security purposes.

11.64 The last category applies to any occupier who satisfies either of the tests
relevant for incapacity benefit (the 'own occupation test' or the 'all work test')
immediately he or she does so (i.e. there is no 'waiting period'). It includes
people who have not claimed or are not entitled to incapacity benefit (including
those receiving statutory sick pay from their employer), and people who have
been disqualified from incapacity benefit (but are incapable of work).

11.65 In such a case, the authority must not reduce the claimant's eligible rent
unless:

◆ there is suitable alternative accommodation available (para. 11.66); and

◆ it is reasonable to expect the claimant to move (para. 11.68).

VULNERABLE PEOPLE: AVAILABILITY

11.66 What counts as suitable alternative accommodation was described in   HBR Old 11(3)
paragraph 11.61. The key point here is that it must be *available*. For example,
accommodation the claimant has recently left, or an offer of accommodation the
claimant has refused, may be available – but only whilst it actually remains
available to the claimant, and not after it has been let to someone else. The DSS
advises that 'it is not necessary for an authority to be able to identify specific
properties' but emphasises that 'authorities should regard accommodation as not
available if, in practice, there is little or no possibility of the claimant being able
to obtain it, for example because it could only be obtained on payment of a large
deposit which the claimant does not possess' (GM para. A4.121).

11.67 This question of 'availability' arose in *R v HB Review Board of East
Devon Council ex p Gibson* (1993) 25 HLR 487 CA, in which the claimant was
a vulnerable person because he had dependent children. The judge said: 'It has
been repeatedly said that it is not part of the local authority's function and no part
of the Review Board's function to identify specific property available for [an HB]
recipient's occupation... I unreservedly accept that. Neither the local authority
nor the Review Board is an accommodation agency; neither of them can be
expected to assume what would be an appropriate role... It is... quite sufficient
if an active market rent is shown to exist in houses in an appropriate place at the
appropriate level of rent to which the [eligible] rent is restricted. There must,
however, be evidence at least of that in a case falling within [the protected group

of vulnerable people]; otherwise the recipient, if he had to move, would have nowhere to go. It is, however, sufficient, as I wish to stress, to point to a range of properties, or a bloc of property, which is available without specific identification of particular dwelling houses' (transcript pages 7-9). However, this judgment leaves unanswered the question of how an authority is to identify 'a range of properties, or a bloc of property which is available' and ensure that it meets the criteria of suitability and reasonableness.

VULNERABLE PEOPLE: REASONABLENESS

HBR 11(6)(b)   **11.68**   In deciding whether it is reasonable to expect the claimant to move, authorities must take into account:

◆ the claimant's prospects of retaining employment; and

◆ the effect on the education of a child or young person who would have to change school (this means any child or young person mentioned in para. 11.19).

11.69   This question of 'reasonableness' arose in *R v Sefton Metropolitan Borough Council ex p Cunningham,* (1991) 23 HLR 534 QBD, in which the claimant had a daughter aged eight. The judge emphasised the authority's duty to take individual circumstances into account when considering 'suitability', 'availability' and 'reasonableness'; and said: 'The Review Board acted on the basis of inadequate evidence from the local authority, which went merely to the generality of the availability of alternative accommodation and not in any sense to its suitability for the [claimant's] needs... There is no evidence that the Board considered such matters [as the effect of a move on the child's education] at all... [which] are just the sort of matters which ought to be investigated (transcript pages 9, 12, 13).

HOW MUCH TO REDUCE AN UNREASONABLE RENT?

HBR Old 11(2)   **11.70**   This question arises if the rent is unreasonably high or the accommodation unreasonably large by comparison with suitable alternative accommodation, and only if the forms of protection described above do not apply. In such cases, the authority must consider whether to restrict the claimant's eligible rent by working through the following questions:

(a) is it appropriate to make a reduction in the claimant's eligible rent? and if it is

(b) what is the appropriate amount for the reduction? and

(c) how was that appropriate amount arrived at?

11.71   Questions (a) and (b) above are based on the judgment in *Mehanne v Housing Benefit Review Board of the City of Westminster,* (1999), CA, *The Times* 5.3.99, which confirmed that all reasonably relevant factors must be taken into account and weighed against factors relating to the cost of suitable alternative accommodation (para. 11.61). Questions (b) and (c) above are based on the judgment in *R v East Yorkshire Borough of Beverley Housing Benefits Review Board ex p Hare,* (1995), QBD, *The Times* 28.2.95. As regards question (b), the authority must not reduce the claimant's eligible rent below the cost of comparable alternative accommodation: *R v Brent London Borough Council ex p Connery,* (1989) 22 HLR 40 QBD. As regards all the above questions, authorities must consider what is appropriate in the individual circumstances of each case. There are cases in which no reduction is appropriate. There are also cases in which no reduction is appropriate for the time being but may become appropriate later on. In practice in such cases, some authorities still tend to restrict claimants' eligible rents to what the rent officer has recommended (in cases which have been referred to the rent officer: chapter 8). However, the rent officer's figures do not take into account personal circumstances at all, whereas the question of what is 'appropriate' places a duty on authorities to do so.

HOW MUCH OF A RENT INCREASE TO DISALLOW?

11.72 This question arises if a rent increase occurring during a benefit period is unreasonably high by comparison with rent increases for suitable alternative accommodation, or is unreasonably soon after a previous increase which occurred in the last year; and only if the forms of protection described above do not apply. The question is whether, and to what extent, to disallow the rent increase. In considering this, authorities must not disallow so much that the resultant eligible rent is below the cost of comparable alternative accommodation.

HBR Old 12(1)
SI 1999 No. 2734

THE IMPACT OF SUBSIDY

11.73 In *R v Brent London Borough Council ex p Connery,* (1989) 22 HLR 40 QBD, it was held that: 'An authority was entitled, except when acting in those cases where an absolute duty was to be fulfilled, to take into account the implications for its own financial situation [e.g. subsidy] when exercising its discretion' (*The Times* Law Report, 25.10.89, reproduced in GM ch. A4, annex A).

11.74 As described earlier, there are three main questions to be considered in applying the rules about HB restrictions;

◆ whether the rent, size or rent increase is unreasonable;

◆ whether people fall within the protected groups; and

◆ whether to reduce the eligible rent or disallow a rent increase and, if so, by how much.

The first two are questions of fact. Subsidy considerations cannot therefore play a part in answering them. The DSS's opinion is that the authority may take subsidy into account in answering the third question, though not as the only consideration (GM para. A4.115).

Services and related charges

OVERVIEW

HBR 10, 11, sch. 1 **11.75** This section deals with service charges (and certain related charges) which may be included in a claimant's actual rent. It applies to all HB claims and explains which charges are eligible for HB and which are not.

◆ If a charge is 'eligible for HB', this means that it is in principle a charge which can be included in a claimant's eligible rent. With certain exceptions (mentioned below as they arise), it does not need to be valued; and no deduction is made for it at any stage in deciding the amount of a claimant's eligible rent unless the charge for it is excessive (para. 11.81).

◆ If a charge is 'ineligible for HB', this means that it is in principle a charge which cannot be included in a claimant's eligible rent. With certain exceptions, it needs to be valued and deducted at some point in deciding the amount of a claimant's eligible rent (para. 11.76).

11.76 This section also explains how ineligible charges are valued by the *authority;* chapter 8 describes how they are valued by the rent officer. Details of who does the valuation, and at what stage on the calculation an amount is deducted, are given at the relevant places throughout the earlier sections of this chapter (paras. 11.5-52).

ELIGIBILITY: GENERAL RULES

HBR 10(1),(3),(7) **11.77** Many rent-payers pay for services either in with their rent (in which case it is immaterial whether they are mentioned in their letting agreement) or separately. The law defines 'services' as 'services performed or facilities... provided for, or rights made available to, the occupier...' Charges for these are eligible for HB, so long as they:

◆ have to be paid as a condition of occupying the dwelling as a home; and

◆ are not listed in the regulations as ineligible (as described in the following paragraphs); and

◆ are not excessive in relation to the service provided (para. 11.81).

The first of these conditions need not have applied from the date the letting agreement began. A service charge is eligible for HB (subject to the other conditions) whenever the claimant agreed to pay it, if the only alternative would have been to lose his or her home.

11.78 Details of which service charges are eligible for HB (subject to the above points) follow, and are summarised in table 11.6. Good advice on services is given by the DSS (GM paras. A4.57-95). Councils, housing associations and many other landlords provide details of service charges to their tenants (and in many cases, tenants have a right to this information: for good information on this, see *Housing Rights Guide* by Geoffrey Randall, published by Shelter). It is in their interests as well as their tenants' to bear in mind the detailed rules when deciding what services to provide and how much to charge for them.

11.79 Sometimes services are provided free to a claimant. The DSS points out in relation to hostel residents (thought the point is relevant to all claims) that 'Authorities should... ensure that they ascertain which services are included within the hostel charge. Authorities should not attempt to deduct the value of ineligible items funded from other sources' (GM para. A4.69).

DEDUCTIONS FOR INELIGIBLE SERVICE CHARGES

11.80 For charges which are ineligible for HB (except when they are valued by the rent officer): HBR 10(3), sch. 1 para. 2

◆ if the amount can be identified from the letting agreement or in some other way, the authority deducts the amount so identified (unless this is unrealistically low);

◆ if this identified amount is unrealistically low for the service provided, or if the amount cannot be identified, the authority must decide what amount is fairly attributable to the value of the ineligible service and deduct that.

Different rules can apply for water charges, fuel and meals (paras. 11.82-87).

DEDUCTIONS FOR EXCESSIVE ELIGIBLE SERVICE CHARGES

11.81 No amount is deducted for any charge which is eligible for HB – unless the charge is excessive for the service provided, taking account of the cost of comparable services. In that case, the authority must decide how much would be reasonable for that service and deduct the excess. HBR 10(6AB), sch. 1 para. 3

Table 11.6: SERVICE CHARGES SUMMARY

Further details apply in many of the following cases. See paragraphs 11.82 onwards.

Type of service charge	Is it a 'support charge'?	Eligible for HB in 'supported accommodation?'	Eligible for HB elsewhere?
Water charges	NO	NO	NO
Provision of a heating system	NO	YES	YES
Fuel communal areas	NO	YES	YES

Other fuel	NO	NO	NO
Meals	NO	NO	NO
Furniture/household equipment	NO	YES	YES
Communal window cleaning	NO	YES	YES
Other exterior window cleaning which no-one can do	NO	YES	YES
Other interior window cleaning which no-one can do	YES	YES *	NO
Other window cleaning	YES	NO	NO
Communal cleaning	NO	YES	YES
Other cleaning which no-one can do	YES	YES *	NO
Other cleaning	YES	NO	NO
Emergency alarm systems in certain accommodation	YES	YES *	NO
Emergency alarm systems otherwise	YES	NO	NO
General counselling and support which meets the conditions in paragraph 11.93	YES	YES *	NO
General counselling and support otherwise	YES	NO	NO
Personal counselling and support	YES	NO	NO
Medical/nursing/personal care	YES	NO	NO
Day-to-day living expenses	NO	NO	NO
Most communal services relating to the provision of adequate accommodation	NO	YES	YES

*These are 'support charges' which are eligible only in 'supported accommodation'.

WATER CHARGES

11.82 Water charges (including any sewerage or environmental charges) are not   HBR 2(1), 10(3)
eligible for HB. The amount of the deduction is valued by the authority as
follows:

◆ if the water charge varies according to consumption, either the actual
   amount or an estimate;

◆ otherwise, if the claimant's accommodation is a self-contained unit, the
   actual amount of the water charge;

◆ otherwise, a proportion of the water charge for the self-contained unit. The
   proportion should equal the floor area of the claimant's accommodation
   divided by the floor area of the self-contained unit (but in practice,
   authorities sometimes use different, simpler methods);

No deduction is made at any stage if the claimant pays water charges direct to the
water company.

FUEL ETC.

11.83 Charges for fuel (such as gas, electricity, etc. and also any standing   HBR 10(3)
charges or other supply costs) are not eligible for HB. But there are two   sch. 1 paras. 4,
exceptions:

◆ a charge for the provision of a heating system is eligible for HB, but only if
   it is separate from the fuel charge;

◆ a fuel charge for communal areas is eligible for HB, but only if is it separate
   from the fuel charge for the claimant's own accommodation. Communal
   areas are areas of common access (e.g. halls, stairways, passageways) and,
   in sheltered accommodation only, they also include common rooms (e.g. a
   dining room or lounge).

The amount of the deduction is valued by the authority depending on whether the
amount of the fuel charge is known to the authority, as described below. No
deduction is made at any stage if the claimant pays fuel charges direct to the fuel
company.

11.84 In certain cases the amount of a fuel charge may be identified from the
claimant's letting agreement or rent book in some other way: the regulations
assume this is always the case for council tenants. In such cases, the amount of
the deduction is the actual amount of the fuel charge. However, if this is
unrealistically low or includes an element for communal areas which cannot
readily be separated out, the fuel charge is treated as unidentifiable (para. 11.85).

11.85 If the amount of a fuel charge is not readily identifiable (para. 11.84), the
amount of the deduction is found by reference to standard amounts depending on
what the fuel is for, as shown in table 11.7. As shown there, the standard amounts

are lower for claimants who occupy one room only. There is no definition of what counts as 'one room only'. The DSS advises that this includes cases where a claimant has shared used of only one room; and that communal areas should be disregarded (GM para. A4.90).

Table 11.7 STANDARD WEEKLY FUEL DEDUCTIONS

Amounts are added together if fuel is provided for more than one of the purposes shown.

IF THE CLAIMANT AND ANY FAMILY OCCUPY MORE THAN ONE ROOM

Fuel for heating	£9.25
Fuel for hot water	£1.15
Fuel for lighting	£0.80
Fuel for cooking	£1.15
Fuel for any other purpose	NIL
Fuel for all the above	£12.35

IF THE CLAIMANT AND ANY FAMILY OCCUPY ONE ROOM ONLY

Fuel for heating	£5.60
Fuel for hot water:	
if fuel for heating is also provided	NIL
if fuel for heating is not also provided	£1.15
Fuel for lighting:	
if fuel for heating is also provided	NIL
if fuel for heating is not also provided	£0.80
Fuel for cooking	£1.15
Fuel for any other purpose	NIL
Fuel for all the above: £5.60 for heating + £1.15 for cooking (+ NIL for hot water and lighting)	£6.75

11.86 If the authority has deducted a standard amount for fuel, it must invite the claimant to provide evidence on which the 'actual or approximate' amount of the actual charge may be estimated; and, if reasonable evidence is provided, the authority must estimate the fuel charge and deduct the estimated amount. This is an important rule which is sometimes overlooked (or is buried in the mass of information sent to the claimant in the notification of his or her claim). The evidence need not be from the landlord and need only be of the approximate amount: for example, the claimant might provide evidence of what it would normally cost to provide fuel for the kind of accommodation he or she occupies.

MEALS (INCLUDING FOOD)

11.87   Charges for meals are not eligible for HB. For these purposes, 'meals' includes the preparation of meals (e.g. where meals are prepared somewhere else and then delivered) and also the provision of unprepared food (e.g. cereal, bread still in its wrappings). The amount of the deduction is always valued by the authority by reference to standard amounts depending on what meals are provided, as shown in table 11.8. Those amounts cannot be varied; the actual amount the landlord charges for meals is never used. As shown in the table, one deduction applies for each person whose meals are paid for in the claimant's rent (whether this is the claimant, a member of the family or some other person such as a non-dependant). No deduction applies for anyone whose meals are not included (for example, a baby). When appropriate, deductions are calculated separately for each person (for example fewer meals may be provided for someone who goes out to work than for someone who does not).

HBR sch. 1 para 1(a),1A

Table 11.8 STANDARD WEEKLY MEALS DEDUCTIONS

A separate amount is assessed and deducted for each person whose meals are provided.

IF AT LEAST THREE MEALS ARE PROVIDED EVERY DAY

For the claimant, and each other person from the first Monday in September following his or her 16th birthday	£18.65
For each other person	£9.40

IF BREAKFAST ONLY IS PROVIDED

For the claimant, and each other person of any age	£2.25

ALL OTHER CASES

For the claimant, and each other person from the first Monday in September following his or her 16th birthday	£12.40
For each other person	£6.25

FURNITURE AND HOUSEHOLD EQUIPMENT

HBR 10(3),
sch. 1 para. 1(b)

11.88 Charges for the use of these are eligible for HB; unless there is an intention that they will become part of the claimant's personal property, in which case they are ineligible.

SUPPORT CHARGES - DEFINITION AND OVERVIEW

HBR 12A(1ZA)

11.89 The following count as 'support charges':

◆ cleaning and window cleaning – excluding any charge for cleaning or window cleaning of communal areas and for cleaning the outsides of other windows which no-one in the household can do;

◆ emergency alarm systems;

◆ counselling and support;

◆ medical, nursing and personal care.

The following paragraphs detail which are eligible and which are ineligible for HB. Some are eligible for HB only in 'supported accommodation' (para. 11.95 and table 11.6).

11.90 The current rules (in paras. 11.91-97) apply from 3rd April 2000 in the case of rents payable weekly or in multiples of weeks and 1st April 2000 in other cases. The DSS sometimes refers to the current rules as the 'transitional scheme'. The previous rules were called the 'interim scheme' (introduced on 18th August 1997), and were quite different. For example, there were rules about when the accommodation had existed from, about how much time was spent on different things, and about the provision of 'adequate accommodation' - all swept away unmourned: their details are in the 1999-2000 edition of this Guide. Further changes are planned from April 2003, when the DSS plans to take financial help with counselling and support out of HB altogether and for help to be administered jointly by housing services, social services and probation services - in a system to be know as 'Supporting People'.

CLEANING AND WINDOW CLEANING

BR 10(3), sch. 1
para. 1(a)(iv),
sch. 1B para. 3

11.91 New rules apply this year, as follows. Charges for these are eligible for HB in the following three cases:

◆ cleaning/window cleaning of communal areas;

◆ exterior window cleaning elsewhere if no-one in the claimant's household is able to do it;

◆ in 'supported accommodation' (para. 11.95) only, other cleaning/window cleaning which no-one in the claimant's household is able to do.

Otherwise they are ineligible for HB. The first two items in the list are not 'support charges', only the third item is.

EMERGENCY ALARM SYSTEMS

11.92 New rules apply this year, as follows. Charges for these are eligible for HB only in 'supported accommodation' (para. 11.95) which (in addition to the definition referred to) is designed or adapted for elderly, sick or disabled persons, or particularly suitable for them as regards size, heating systems and other major features or facilities. Otherwise they are ineligible.

HBR 10(3),
sch. 1 para. 1(c
sch. 1B para. 4

GENERAL COUNSELLING AND SUPPORT

11.93 New rules apply this year, as follows. Charges for these are eligible for HB only if all the following criteria are met:

HBR 10(3),
sch. 1 para. 1(♦
sch. 1B para. 2

◆ it is 'supported accommodation' (para. 11.95); and

◆ the charges are for time spent on 'general counselling' (compare para. 11.97) or 'other support services'; and

◆ the services are provided by the landlord personally or by a person on the landlord's behalf; and

◆ the services fall within the list in the following paragraph.

Otherwise they are ineligible for HB.

11.94 The services which are eligible for HB if the above criteria are met are general counselling and support which:

◆ assists the claimant with maintaining the dwelling's security;

◆ assists the claimant with maintaining the dwelling's safety (including arranging for checking the claimant's own appliances if they could be a safety hazard);

◆ is directed at assisting the claimant with complying with the terms of his or her letting agreement relating to nuisance, rent liability, maintenance of the interior and/or the period of the letting – including in each case assisting the claimant with contacts with individuals or professional or other bodies with an interest in ensuring the claimant's welfare;

◆ is for any other general counselling and support provided by a resident or on-call warden – but in this case only in accommodation which:

• it is the practice of the landlord to let to people in need of general counselling and support, and

• is one of a group of dwellings, and

• the warden is wholly or mainly devoted to that group of dwellings.

THE DEFINITION OF SUPPORTED ACCOMMODATION

HBR 2(1),
sch. 1 para. 7

11.95 For the purposes of the above rules (paras. 11.89-94), 'supported accommodation' means accommodation which is:

◆ provided by a housing authority, a registered housing association, a registered charity, a non-profit-making voluntary organisation, a non-metropolitan county council in England, or a registered social landlord (or, in Scotland a 'recognised body' under section 1(7) of the Law Reform (Miscellaneous Provisions) Act 1990) - so long as (in each of the cases just listed) the landlord, or someone on the landlord's behalf, also provides the claimant with care, support or supervision; or

◆ a resettlement place; or

◆ any accommodation occupied by a person for whom the social services (in Scotland, social work) department has made a community care assessment (CCA) stating that the person needs services which are eligible for HB only in supported accommodation (paras. 11.91-93 and also table 11.6), and that the landlord is capable of providing these services or of arranging for them to be provided.

HBR 68(1),(8),
sch. 1 para. 7

11.96 If the social services (or social work) department makes a retrospective CCA, it also has full effect retrospectively for HB purposes, with the following two time limits. Support charges become eligible retrospectively for HB:

◆ only if, and to the extent that, they were provided to the claimant continuously up to the date the CCA was made; and

◆ only back to 1st or 3rd April 2000 (para. 11.90) at the earliest.

Note that the above is not 'backdating' (para. 7.86) and there is no further time limit. It may have the effect of increasing someone's entitlement; or it may have the effect that someone thought not to qualify for HB now qualifies, in which case (subject to the above time limits) the HB claim they made must be reconsidered.

SPECIAL COUNSELLING AND SUPPORT;
AND MEDICAL, NURSING AND PERSONAL CARE

HBR 10(3),
1 para. 1(d)-(f)

11.97 Charges for the following are ineligible for HB:

◆ counselling (and support) which is of a specific nature (i.e. is not 'general' as described in paras. 11.90-91);

◆ 'medical expenses (including the cost of treatment or counselling relating to mental disorder, mental handicap, physical disablement or past or present alcohol or drug dependence)'; or

◆ 'the provision of nursing care or personal care (including assistance at meal-times or with personal appearance or hygiene)'.

OTHER DAY-TO-DAY LIVING EXPENSES, ETC.

11.98　Charges for the following are ineligible for HB:

HBR 10(3),
sch. 1 para. 1(g)

◆ laundering (e.g. washing sheets, etc, for the claimant);

◆ transport;

◆ sports facilities;

◆ TV and radio rental and licence and (in most cases) satellite service charges;

◆ any other leisure items or day-to-day living expenses; or

◆ any other services which 'are not related to the provision of adequate accommodation'.

OTHER COMMUNAL SERVICES, ETC.

11.99　Charges for the following are eligible for HB:

HBR 10(3),
sch. 1 para. 1(a

◆ children's play areas;

◆ TV and radio relay;

◆ other services which are related to the provision of adequate accommodation.

11.100 The DSS advises (GM paras. A4.71, A4.85) that the last item includes:

◆ portering and refuse removal;

◆ lifts, communal telephones and entry phones; and

◆ communal laundry facilities (e.g. a laundry room).

OTHER OVERHEADS INCLUDING MANAGEMENT COSTS AND COUNCIL TAX

11.101 Whether the landlord's normal overheads (such as maintenance, insurance and repair costs) count as 'services' or simply as part of the claimant's rent is an arguable point. But in either case they are eligible for HB. In particular, any part of the rent towards the landlord's liability for council tax (e.g. if the claimant has a resident landlord or lives in a house made up of bedsits) is included as part of the rent on the home.

INCREASES TO COVER ARREARS OF RENT

11.102 If a claimant's rent has been increased in order to recover arrears of rent or other charges, that part of the rent is ineligible for HB. This rule applies only if an individual claimant's rent is increased to cover his or her own arrears on a current or former home. It does not apply when landlords increase rents on all their properties as a result of arrears generally.

HBR 8(2A)

GARAGES, GARDENS, ETC.

HBR 2(4)(a) **11.103** The rent on a garage or garden (or any other buildings or land included in the claimant's letting agreement) is eligible for HB, but only if:

◆ they are used for occupying the dwelling as a home; and

◆ the claimant acquired them at the same time as the dwelling; and

◆ the claimant has no option but to rent them at the same time.

Otherwise, they eligible for HB only if the claimant has made or is making reasonable efforts to end liability for them.

BUSINESS PREMISES

HBR 10(4) **11.104** Rent on any part of a property which is used for business, commercial or other non-residential purposes is not eligible for HB. For example, if a claimant rents both a shop and the flat above it, only the rent relating to the flat is eligible for HB. If the rent on the business premises is not specified separately from the rent on the home, it is necessary for the authority to decide how much relates to each. For self-employed claimants who work from home, see paragraph 15.22.

Note on marginal references in this chapter

SI 1995 No. 1644
SI 1996 No. 965 **11.105** In all the above sections of this chapter, marginal references to:

◆ 'HBR 10' and 'HBR 11' are to regulations 10 and 11 of the Housing Benefit (General) Regulations 1987 No. 1971 as they currently apply (para. 1.29);

◆ 'HBR Old 10', 'HBR Old 11' and 'HBR Old 12' are to regulations 10 to 12 of those regulations as they stood immediately before 2nd January 1996 (i.e. ignoring the amendments made on and after that day).

In the preceding section on services and related charges, references to 'HBR 10' and 'HBR 11' should be regarded as including references to 'HBR Old 10' and 'HBR Old 11'.

Overview of council tax and eligible council tax

11.106 The remainder of this chapter applies only in CTB cases. It covers:

◆ 'eligible council tax' for the purposes of main CTB;

◆ 'eligible council tax' for the purposes of second adult rebate; and

◆ CTB restrictions.

COUNCIL TAX

11.107 The amount of council tax due on a dwelling (unless the dwelling is exempt) depends first on the valuation band in which that dwelling is placed.

There are eight bands: band A (the lowest) to band H (the highest). It also depends on whether the claimant qualifies for a disability reduction, a council tax discount, a council tax transitional reduction and/or CTB. Chapter 3 gives further details of these and of the council tax scheme in general.

WHAT IS 'ELIGIBLE COUNCIL TAX'?

11.108 A claimant's 'eligible council tax' is the figure used in calculating his or her entitlement to main CTB (para. 9.8) and/or second adult rebate (para. 10.23). The eligible council tax figure used in calculating main CTB can differ from that used in calculating second adult rebate; and in each of those cases it can be lower than the claimant's actual liability for council tax: the details are given in the remainder of this chapter.

Eligible council tax for main CTB purposes

GENERAL RULES

11.109 For the purposes of calculating main CTB (para. 9.8), a claimant's weekly eligible council tax is calculated as follows: <small>CTBR 51(1),(2)</small>

◆ start with the council tax due on his or her home. The means the amount due after deductions have been made for any disability reduction, transitional reduction, or council tax discount granted to the claimant (but no deduction is made for any entitlement to second adult rebate);

◆ then, for certain claimants whose dwelling is in band F, G or H, multiply the result by the fraction referred to in the following paragraph;

◆ then apportion the result if the claimant is a joint occupier (paras. 11.111-114) and convert it to a weekly figure (as described in para. 9.58).

See also paragraph 11.115 about other items which can affect a council tax bill.

CTB RESTRICTIONS

11.110 Except as described below, a claimant's eligible council tax is restricted if his or her dwelling falls in valuation band F, G or H. This is done by multiplying it by the fraction shown in table 11.9. The effect of the fractions is that claimants with dwellings in bands F, G or H are awarded CTB as though their dwelling was in band E: in other words they get less CTB. Unlike the rules about HB restrictions, the authority has no discretion to award an addition compensating for these restrictions.   <small>CTBR 2(1), 51(2A),(2B) SI 1997 No. 184?</small>

The restrictions do not apply to any claimant ('**A**') if:

◆ **A** was entitled to CTB on 31st March 1998; or

◆ **A** resided on 31st March 1998 with a partner ('**B**') who was entitled to CTB on that day and continuously thereafter for the same dwelling, and either:

- **A**'s entitlement to CTB for that dwelling begins no more than 12 weeks after the date on which **B**'s entitlement ceased (regardless of why **B**'s entitlement ceased and regardless of whether **A** and **B** are now partners), or

- **A**'s claim for CTB is made no more than 12 weeks after the date on which **B** died or ceased to reside in the dwelling – but in this case only if **B** was on that date a 'welfare to work beneficiary' (table 13.3).

However, in the above cases, the restrictions start to apply if:

◆ **A** moves to a new dwelling; or

◆ there is a break in **A**'s entitlement to CTB of more than 4 weeks (52 weeks if **A** is a 'welfare to work beneficiary': table 13.3).

Table 11.9 COUNCIL TAX RESTRICTIONS: FRACTIONS USED

	FRACTION *
Claimants who do not qualify for a disability reduction	
◆ Dwellings in valuation band F	11/13ths
◆ Dwellings in valuation band G	11/15ths
◆ Dwellings in valuation band H	11/18ths
Claimants who qualify for a disability reduction **	
◆ Dwellings in valuation band F	N/A **
◆ Dwellings in valuation band G	11/13ths
◆ Dwellings in valuation band H	11/15ths

Notes

* Rounded to the nearest 1 per cent, 11/13ths is 85 per cent, 11/15ths is 73 per cent, and 11/18ths is 61 per cent (but the authority must not round the figures in this way).

** For claimants who qualify for a disability reduction (para. 3.32), these fractions apply after the disability reduction has been deducted. There is no restriction in such cases for dwellings in band F.

Example: Council tax restrictions

CALCULATIONS IN MAIN CTB

In a particular council's area, the annual council tax for dwellings in band E is £550 for the year, for dwellings in band F is £650 for the year, and for dwellings in band G is £750 per year. A claimant moves into a dwelling in the area which is valued as falling in band G. She claims CTB and qualifies for main CTB (but not for second adult rebate). She also qualifies for a disability reduction (para. 3.32). She does not qualify for a discount or for a transitional reduction. She is not a joint occupier.

Her eligible council tax for main CTB purposes is calculated as follows:

◆ annual council tax for a dwelling in band G   £750.00

◆ minus disability reduction   − £100.00

◆ which equals   £650.00

◆ her annual eligible council tax for main CTB purposes
  is found by multiplying the last figure by the fraction
  11/13ths (table 11.9): £650 x 11/13 =   £550.00

◆ to convert this to a weekly figure, divide by 366 and
  multiply by 7: £550.00 ÷ 365 x 7 (to the nearest 1p) =   £10.55

If she is on income support or income-based jobseeker's allowance and has no non-dependants, her annual entitlement to main CTB (£550.00) is £100.00 less than her annual liability for council tax (£650.00).

THE RULES FOR A 'WELFARE TO WORK BENEFICIARY'

On 31st March 1998, Mr and Mrs Twoshoes resided in a house and Mr Twoshoes was getting CTB there. He continued to get CTB there until July 2000, when he became a 'welfare to work beneficiary' (and his CTB stopped as a result). In late November 2000, Mr Twoshoes (still at that time a 'welfare to work beneficiary') died. Mrs Twoshoes claims CTB for the same house in early January 2001.

The CTB restrictions did not apply to Mr Twoshoes' CTB throughout his entitlement to CTB. They also do not apply to Mrs Twoshoes' CTB from when she claims. This is because she meets the criteria in paragraph 11.106: in particular, her claim is made within 12 weeks of Mr Twoshoes' death, and at the date of his death he was a 'welfare to work beneficiary'.

APPORTIONMENT FOR JOINT OCCUPIERS

CTBR 51(3),(4)   **11.111** A joint occupier (also known as a joint tenant or joint owner) is one of two or more people who are jointly liable to pay the council tax on a dwelling, other than just a couple or polygamous marriage (para. 6.24). In such cases, the figures used in calculating eligible council tax are apportioned between the joint occupiers for main CTB purposes.

11.112 This apportionment is found by dividing the total council tax liability (para. 11.109) by the number of people who are jointly liable, ignoring any person who is both:

♦ a student as defined under CTB law (para. 20.3); and

♦ ineligible for main CTB (i.e. does not fall within one of the eligible groups for students listed in table 20.1).

For example, if three single friends jointly rent a house and are jointly liable for council tax there, but (only) one of them is a student who is ineligible for main CTB, each of the other two is eligible for CTB on one-half of the council tax liability.

11.113 If amongst several jointly liable people some are a couple or polygamous marriage, the law is unclear. The DSS advises (GM para. B2.14) that if there are three jointly liable people, two of whom are a couple, then the couple are eligible for main CTB on two-thirds of the council tax liability and the other person on one-third.

11.114 It is also worth noting here that, in certain cases, people who are severely mentally impaired are not jointly liable for council tax (para. 3.27) so the apportionment ignores them.

OTHER ITEMS AFFECTING A COUNCIL TAX BILL

CTBR 51(2)   **11.115** The following additional rules apply to main CTB and also to second adult rebate:

♦ in the case of an authority which offers discounts against its council taxes for people who pay in a lump sum or by a method other than cash (e.g. direct debit), CTB is calculated on liability before those discounts are subtracted;

♦ when lower council taxes are set as a result of council tax 'capping' procedures, these apply from the beginning of the financial year, and CTB is worked out (throughout the financial year) on the lower amount;

♦ if a council tax bill is increased to recover an earlier overpayment of CTB or of community charge benefit, CTB is calculated before those amounts are added;

♦ if a penalty is added to a council tax bill, CTB is calculated as if that penalty was not included.

Eligible council tax for second adult rebate purposes

GENERAL RULES

11.116 Except as described in the following paragraph, for the purposes of calculating second adult rebate (para. 10.23), a claimant's weekly eligible council tax is calculated as follows:

CTBR 54(1),
sch. 2 para. 1(2

◆ start with the council tax due on his or her home. The means the amount due *after* deductions have been made for any disability reduction or transitional reduction has been granted to the claimant, but *before* any council tax discount is deducted (and no deduction is made for any entitlement to main CTB);

◆ then, for certain claimants whose dwelling is in band F, G or H, multiply the result by the fraction referred to in table 11.9;

◆ then convert the result to a weekly figure (as described in para. 9.58) – but do not at this stage apportion it if the claimant is a joint occupier (para. 6.25).

See also paragraph 11.115 about other items which can affect a council tax bill.

CTB RESTRICTIONS

11.117 The rules about CTB restrictions are the same for second adult rebate as they are for main CTB (para. 11.110).

CTBR sch. 2 pa
1(3),(4)
SI 1997 No. 18

Example: Council tax restrictions in second adult rebate

In a particular council's area, the annual council tax for dwellings in band G is £750 per year. A claimant moves into a dwelling in the area which is valued as falling in band G. He claims CTB and qualifies for second adult rebate (but not for main CTB). He also qualifies for a 25% council tax discount (para. 3.35). He does not qualify for a disability reduction or for a transitional reduction. He is not a joint occupier.

His eligible council tax for second adult rebate purposes is calculated as follows:

◆ annual council tax for a dwelling in band G   £750.00

◆ although he qualifies for a discount, it is ignored here

◆ his annual eligible council tax for second adult rebate purposes is found by multiplying the above figure by the fraction 11/15ths (table 11.9): £750 x 11/15 =   £550.00

◆ to convert this to a weekly figure, divide by 366 and multiply by 7: £550.00 ÷ 365 x 7 (to the nearest 1p) =   £10.55

It turns out that the above claimant has one second adult who is on income support or income-based jobseeker's allowance. So his annual entitlement to second adult rebate is 25% of £550.00 (table 10.3) – which is £137.50; and his resulting annual liability for council tax is then calculated as follows:

◆ annual council tax for a dwelling in band G   £750.00

◆ minus his annual council tax discount:
   25% of £750.00   – £187.50

◆ minus his annual second adult rebate:
   25% (table 10.3) of £550 (as above)   – £137.50

◆ so his resultant liability (after both the above have been
   granted) is   £425.00

NOTE ON COUNCIL TAX DISCOUNTS

CTBR 54(1),
sch. 2 para. 1(2)
11.118 For second adult rebate purposes, as indicated in paragraph 11.116, a claimant's eligible council tax is calculated as though he or she did not qualify for any council tax discount. This is mainly for mathematical reasons: as illustrated in the following example, a claimant who qualifies for a discount does not lose it (and see also para. 10.23).

NOTE ON JOINT OCCUPIERS

CTBR 52(2),(3)
11.119 As indicated in paragraph 11.116, second adult rebate is always calculated on council tax liability for the whole dwelling. If there are joint occupiers (para. 6.25), the amount of second adult rebate is apportioned between them after the calculation is otherwise complete (as described in para. 10.20).

`Example: Entitlement to CTB and liability for council tax

(1) INFORMATION

In a particular council's area, the annual council tax for dwellings in band D is £450 per year. A claimant in the area resides in a dwelling valued as falling in band D. He is single and qualifies for a council tax disability reduction (para. 3.32). He is also a 'disregarded person' for the purposes of calculating council tax discounts (para.3.37 and appendix 7) (but is not a student or severely mentally impaired). The only other person in his home is his adult daughter (who is his non-dependant for main CTB purposes: chapter 9, and also counts as a 'second adult' for second adult rebate purposes: chapter 10). For these reasons, he qualifies for a 25% council tax discount. It is also the case that both the claimant and his daughter are on income support or income-based job-seeker's allowance.

(2) ANNUAL LIABILITY FOR COUNCIL TAX IF HE DID NOT CLAIM CTB

If he did not claim CTB his annual liability for council tax would be:

- ◆ annual council tax for a dwelling in band D   £450.00
- ◆ minus disability reduction: this would be   − £50.00
- ◆ which leaves   £400.00
- ◆ minus discount (25% of £400.00)   £100.00
- ◆ so his annual liability would be   £300.00

(3) ELIGIBLE COUNCIL TAX FOR MAIN CTB PURPOSES

His annual eligible council tax for main CTB purposes is the amount of his liability after both the disability reduction and the discount have been deducted; which is   £300.00

Converted to a weekly amount this is (to the nearest 1p)   £5.75

(4) ELIGIBLE COUNCIL TAX FOR SECOND ADULT REBATE PURPOSES

His annual eligible council tax for second adult rebate purposes is the amount of his liability after the disability reduction has been deducted but before the discount has been deducted; which is   £400.00

Converted to a weekly amount this is (to the nearest 1p)   £7.67

(5) CALCULATION OF MAIN CTB

◆ Weekly amount of eligible council tax for main CTB purposes
(see (3) above)   £5.75

◆ Minus non-dependant deduction (nil in this case)   – £0.00

◆ So his weekly entitlement to main CTB is   £5.75

(6) CALCULATION OF SECOND ADULT REBATE

◆ Weekly amount of eligible council tax for second adult rebate
purposes (see (4) above)   £7.67

◆ Multiplied by 25%, equals (to the nearest 1p)   £1.92

◆ So his weekly entitlement to second adult rebate is   £1.92

(7) THE 'BETTER BUY' AND HIS ENTITLEMENT TO CTB

Because of the 'better buy' (para. 10.29), he is granted weekly
main CTB of   £5.75

(8) ANNUAL LIABILITY FOR COUNCIL TAX AFTER CTB HAS BEEN AWARDED

On an annual basis this is:

◆ The figure shown at the end of (2) above   £300.00

◆ Minus the annual equivalent of his entitlement to CTB: £5.75
per week as in (7) above, converted to an annual figure is – £300.00

◆ So his annual liability for council tax (after the disability
reduction, the discount and CTB have all been granted) is   NIL

12 Applicable amounts

12.1 An applicable amount is the figure used in calculating HB and main CTB to reflect the basic living needs of the claimant and family. People on income support or income-based jobseeker's allowance have already had their applicable amount worked out for the purpose of assessing entitlement to those benefits. This chapter does not apply to them. This chapter covers:

◆ personal allowances;

◆ general rules about premiums;

◆ the detailed rules for each premium in turn; and

◆ further rules and special cases.

CBA s.135
HBR 16
CTBR 8 **12.2** A claimant's applicable amount is the same for both HB and main CTB purposes. It is the total of any personal allowances and premiums which apply in his or her case.

Personal allowances

HBR 16(a),(b),
sch 2 paras 1,2
CTBR 8(a),(b)
sch 1 paras 1,2 **12.3** Personal allowances are awarded for the claimant and any other family members (para. 6.5). There are different amounts for single claimants, lone parents and couples. Additions are made for children and young persons (sometimes known as dependants' allowances). The amounts, which vary with age, are given in table 12.1.

ADDITIONS FOR CHILDREN AND YOUNG PERSONS

HBR sch 2 para 2
CTBR sch 1 para 2 **12.4** The two possible levels of addition for children and young persons (para. 6.12) are listed in table 12.1. The claimant qualifies for one addition for each child or young person:

◆ the lower addition (£26.60) applies from the Monday following the day on which the child is born;

◆ the higher addition (£31.75) applies from the first Monday in September following his or her 16th birthday.

Table 12.1 WEEKLY APPLICABLE AMOUNTS

PERSONAL ALLOWANCES

Single claimant	aged under 25	£41.35
	aged 25 or over	£52.20
Lone parent	aged under 18 (HB only)	£41.35
	aged 18 or over	£52.20
Couple	both aged under 18 (HB only)	£62.35
	at least one aged 18 or over	£81.95
Child/young person addition	lower rate	£26.60
(see para.12.4)	higher rate	£31.75

PREMIUMS

A claimant is awarded any of the following which apply:

Family premium	basic rate	£14.25
	protected lone parent rate	£22.20
Disabled child premium	each child/young person	£22.25
Severe disability premium	single rate	£40.20
	double rate	£80.40
Carer premium	claimant or partner or each	£14.15

Plus the highest of any of the following which apply:

Pensioner premium	single parent or lone parent	£26.25
	couple	£40.00
Enhanced pensioner premium	single claimant or lone parent	£28.65
	couple	£43.40
Higher pensioner premium	single claimant or lone parent	£33.85
	couple	£49.10
Disability premium	single claimant or lone parent	£22.25
	couple	£31.75

Examples: Applicable amounts

Except for the lone parent in the fourth example, none of the following qualifies for any of the premiums for disability or for carers.

SINGLE CLAIMANT

A single claimant is aged 23.

Personal allowance:	
single claimant aged under 25	£41.35
No premiums apply	
Applicable amount	£41.35

COUPLE, TWO CHILDREN

A couple have children aged 9 and 13.

Personal allowances:	
couple at least one over 18	£81.95
child aged 9 (lower addition)	£26.60
child aged 13 (lower addition)	£26.60
Premium: family premium (basic rate)	£14.25
Applicable amount	£149.40

PENSIONER COUPLE

A couple are aged 58 and 65.

Personal allowance:	
couple at least one over 18	£81.95
Premium: pensioner premium (couple rate)	£40.00
Applicable amount	£121.95

DISABLED LONE PARENT

A lone parent aged 31 fulfils the conditions for a disability premium. She has a baby a few months old.

Personal allowances:	
lone parent aged over 18	£52.20
child (lower addition)	£26.60
Premiums:	
family premium (basic rate)*	£14.25
disability premium	£22.25
Applicable amount	£115.30

*   *She cannot get the protected lone parent rate of the family premium because she qualifies for a disability premium (para. 12.8).*

Premiums

12.5   Many claimants – but not all – qualify for one or more premiums. Table 12.1 lists the premiums available and gives their amounts. A premium is awarded if its conditions of entitlement are satisfied. Some of the conditions are straightforward, some more complicated and less well known. Claimants may therefore miss entitlement unless authority staff are fully trained and claim forms are carefully designed. The next few sections give the conditions for each premium.

HBR 16(c),(d)
sch 2 paras 3-6,1
CTBR 8(c),(d)
sch 1 paras 3-6,1

Some, but not all, premiums can be awarded at the same time as each other. The limits to the possible combinations are shown in table 12.1 and illustrated in the examples following it.

Family premium

12.6   The condition for this premium is that there is at least one child or young person in the claimant's family - whether the claimant is in a couple or is a lone parent. The terms 'child', 'young person', 'family', 'couple' and 'lone parent' are used in the specific senses defined for HB and CTB (paras. 6.5-20). In particular, a child or young person need not be the natural child of the claimant but could, for example, be a grandchild living as part of the claimant's family.

HBR 16(c),
sch 2 para 3
CTBR 8(c),
sch 1 para 3

12.7   There are two rates of this premium:

◆ lone parents who satisfy the conditions in paragraph 12.8 get the protected lone parent rate (which is higher than the basic rate);

◆ other lone parents get the basic rate;

◆ couples (with at least one child or young person) get the basic rate.

12.8   A lone parent qualifies for the protected lone parent rate of the family premium if, and for as long as, all the following conditions apply:

◆ on 5th April 1998, he or she was entitled to HB or CTB and satisfied the conditions for the lone parent rate of the family premium or would have done so but for the fact that 5th April 1998 fell within a rent-free period;

◆ he or she has remained entitled to HB or CTB continuously since that date (ignoring breaks due only to rent-free periods);

◆ he or she has not ceased to be a lone parent at any time since that date;

◆ he or she has not become entitled to income support or to income-based jobseeker's allowance, or ceased to be entitled to both those benefits, at any time since that date; and

◆ he or she has not become entitled to a pensioner premium, enhanced pensioner premium, higher pensioner premium or disability premium at any time since that date.

As soon as any of the last four conditions ceases to apply, the person ceases permanently to qualify for the protected lone parent rate (but may still qualify for the basic rate: paras. 12.6-7).

Premiums relating to age

12.9   The conditions for these three premiums are only about age – not whether the person gets a pension or has retired from work. Single claimants and lone parents always get the single rate of the premium. Couples always get the couple rate (i.e. even if only one fulfils the age condition).

PENSIONER PREMIUM

HBR sch 2 para 9
CTBR sch 1 para 9

12.10   The condition for this premium is that the claimant (or in the case of a couple, the older partner) is aged between 60 and 74 inclusive.

ENHANCED PENSIONER PREMIUM

HBR sch 2 para 9A
CTBR sch 1 para 10

12.11   The condition for this premium is that the claimant (or in the case of a couple, the older partner) is aged between 75 and 79 inclusive.

HIGHER PENSIONER PREMIUM AWARDED BECAUSE OF AGE

HBR sch 2 para 10
CTBR sch 1 para 11

12.12   To get a higher pensioner premium this way, the condition is that the claimant (or in the case of a couple, the older partner) is aged 80 or more. For the two other ways of getting this premium see paragraphs 12.16-17.

Overview of other premiums

12.13   The rules about five more premiums remain to be described:
◆   disabled child premium;
◆   disability premium;
◆   higher pensioner premium;
◆   carer premium; and
◆   severe disability premium.

The first three have several similarities: in general terms they are for when someone in the family is disabled or long-term sick; and couples who qualify for the disability or higher pensioner premium always get the couple rate. The last two differ from them in many ways: the carer premium is for certain people who care for a disabled person, the severe disability premium is for certain people who need such care; and for both premiums the rates for couples can vary. Receipt of various state benefits affects all five premiums, and general points about this are given in paragraphs 12.43-45. Because the conditions for these premiums are strict, the needs of some disabled people and carers are not reflected in the assessment of their applicable amount. In some of these cases, the authorities may agree to award additional HB or CTB because of their exceptional circumstances (para. 9.42).

Disabled child premium

12.14 The condition for this premium is that a child or young person in the family:

◆ is registered or certified blind; or

◆ has ceased to be registered or certified blind within the past 28 weeks because of regaining sight; or

◆ receives disability living allowance (either or both components).

HBR sch 2
para 14
CTBR sch 1
para 15

A disabled child premium is awarded for each child or young person to whom this applies (i.e. in appropriate cases, there can be more than one disabled child premium per family). Background information is given below about being registered or certified blind (para. 12.20) and about disability living allowance (para. 12.22).

Disability premium

12.15 There are two conditions for this premium. They are that the claimant (or in the case of a couple, at least one partner):

◆ is aged under 60; and

◆ is disabled or long-term sick in one or more of the ways described in paragraphs 12.19-31.

HBR sch 2 para
CTBR sch 1
para 12

For couples, at least one partner must satisfy both conditions. If either partner is aged 60 or more, see the next two paragraphs.

Higher pensioner premium

AWARDED BECAUSE OF DISABILITY, ETC

12.16 There are two conditions for getting a higher pensioner premium this way. They are that the claimant (or in the case of a couple, at least one partner):

◆ is aged 60 or more; and

◆ is disabled or long-term sick in one or more of the ways described in paragraphs 12.19-29.

HBR sch 2 para
CTBR sch 1
para 11

For couples at least one partner must satisfy each condition, *but it need not be the same partner who satisfies both.* For the two other ways of getting this premium, see paragraphs 12.12 and 12.17.

THE 'AUTOMATIC TRANSFER RULE'

BR sch 2 para 10
CTBR sch 1
para 11

12.17 This way of getting a higher pensioner premium arises when a claimant (or in the case of a couple, either partner) reaches the age of 60; and only if the claimant:

◆ is in receipt of HB or CTB at the time of that birthday, or there is a break in his or her receipt of both of no more than eight weeks (52 weeks in the case of a 'welfare to work beneficiary': table 13.3) including that birthday; and

◆ qualifies for a disability premium (in respect of either partner in the couple) at the time of that birthday, or at any time in the eight weeks (52 weeks in the case of a 'welfare to work beneficiary': table 13.3) before that birthday.

In these cases, the claimant automatically qualifies for a higher pensioner premium for as long as he or she remains on HB or CTB with no breaks in entitlement to both of more than eight weeks (52 weeks in the case of a 'welfare to work beneficiary': table 13.3). This is the case even if the claimant qualified for a disability premium in respect of his or her partner (see the second condition above) and that partner subsequently dies.

Examples: Disability premium and higher pensioner premium

COUPLE QUALIFYING FOR DISABILITY PREMIUM

A couple who own their own home are claiming CTB. The man is aged 55 and receives disability working allowance. The woman is aged 59.

Receipt of disability working allowance is one of the ways of satisfying the disability condition (para. 12.21). The couple, since both are under 60, qualify for a disability premium (at the couple rate).

QUALIFYING AUTOMATICALLY FOR HIGHER PENSIONER PREMIUM

The woman in the above example reaches 60. There is no change in their circumstances and they continue to qualify for CTB.

Because their CTB includes a disability premium at the time she reaches 60, they now automatically qualify for a higher pensioner premium (at the couple rate) – even if the man later ceases to receive disability working allowance for any reason.

12.18 No further conditions have to be met. The rule applies regardless of improvements in anyone's health, etc. so no evidence of disability or long-term sickness is needed to show that the higher pensioner premium applies, once the rule has started to take effect. The rule continues even if the person moves from one authority area to another (though in practice there is the danger that it may be missed in such cases). Before 1st April 1993, the rule applied in the same way except that every mention of CTB was then a reference to community charge benefit. Transferring from community charge benefit to CTB does not count as a break in entitlement.

Disabled or long-term sick

12.19 The following paragraphs apply for the purposes of qualifying for:

◆ a disability premium (para. 12.15); or

◆ a higher pensioner premium when it is awarded because of disability, etc. (para. 12.16).

In both cases, the first condition for qualifying is about age, the second is that the claimant or any partner is disabled or long-term sick. All the different groups of people who satisfy the second condition are given in paras. 12.20-32 (and see also paras. 12.43-45).

PEOPLE WHO ARE REGISTERED OR CERTIFIED BLIND

12.20 For the purposes of qualifying for a disability premium or higher pensioner premium, the claimant or any partner counts as disabled or long-term sick if he or she: [HBR sch 2 para 12(1),(2) CTBR sch 1 para 13(1),(2)]

◆ is registered or certified blind; or

◆ has ceased to be registered or certified blind within the past 28 weeks because of regaining sight.

People who are blind or (in some cases) partially sighted can apply in England and Wales to be registered blind with the social services department, or in Scotland to be certified blind with the social work department.

PEOPLE RECEIVING DISABILITY LIVING ALLOWANCE OR DISABILITY WORKING ALLOWANCE

12.21 For the purposes of qualifying for a disability premium or higher pensioner premium, the claimant or any partner counts as disabled or long-term sick if he or she receives: [HBR 2(1), sch 2 para 12(1) CTBR 2(1), sch 1 para 13(1)]

◆ disability living allowance (either or both components); or

◆ disabled person's tax credit.

12.22 *Disability living allowance* has two components, and people may qualify for one or both of these (the current amounts are given in appendix 6):

◆ The *care component* is for people whose disability arose before the age of 65; and for such people there is no lower or upper age limit. It can be paid at one of three rates. The highest and middle rates are (broadly speaking) for people who need attention, supervision, etc. by day or by night and for some people who are terminally ill. The lowest rate is for certain people with less severe disabilities.

◆ The *mobility component* is not available for children under five. A claim must usually be made before the claimant's 65th birthday; and for such people there is no upper age limit. It can be paid at one of two rates. The higher rate is (broadly speaking) for people who have difficulty walking, etc. The lower rate is for certain people with less severe mobility difficulties.

12.23 *Disabled person's tax credit (DPTC)* is a state benefit administered by the Inland Revenue and employers. It replaced disability working allowance in October 1999. It is for certain people with disabilities who work an average of 16 hours or more per week and whose disability makes it more difficult for them to compete for jobs.

PEOPLE RECEIVING OTHER BENEFITS FOR ATTENDANCE

HBR 2(1), sch 2
para 12(1)
CTBR 2(1), sch 1
para 13(1)
12.24 For the purposes of qualifying for a disability premium or higher pensioner premium, the claimant or any partner counts as disabled or long-term sick if he or she receives:

◆ attendance allowance; or

◆ constant attendance allowance; or

◆ 'old cases' attendance payments; or

◆ severe disablement occupational allowance; or

◆ exceptionally severe disablement allowance; or

◆ any other increase for attendance paid with war disablement benefit.

12.25 All are references to state benefits, the first two being the most common:

◆ *Attendance allowance* is only for people whose disability arose on or after their 65th birthday; and there is no upper age limit. It is (broadly speaking) for those who need attention, supervision, etc. by day or night or both, and for some people who are terminally ill.

◆ *Constant attendance allowance* is an addition paid with industrial disablement benefit or war disablement benefit.

◆ *'Old cases' attendance payments* are for industrial injuries from before 5th July 1948.

◆ *Severe disablement occupational allowance* is almost always only paid to people who receive constant attendance allowance with their industrial or war disablement benefit.

◆ *Exceptionally severe disablement allowance* is almost always only paid to people who receive constant attendance allowance with their war disablement benefit.

PEOPLE RECEIVING OTHER BENEFITS FOR MOBILITY

12.26 For the purposes of qualifying for a disability premium or higher pensioner premium, the claimant or any partner counts as disabled or long-term sick if he or she:

HBR sch 2
para 12(1)
CTBR sch 1
para 13(1)

◆ receives mobility supplement; or

◆ has part or all of his or her disability living allowance paid to the Motability fund; or

◆ has an invalid vehicle supplied by the NHS; or

◆ receives DSS payments for car running costs.

12.27 The last two are not available for new applicants.

◆ *Mobility supplement* is an addition paid with war disablement benefit.

◆ If part or all of someone's disability allowance is paid to the *Motability fund,* this is used towards the cost of providing him or her with a rented vehicle.

PEOPLE WHO ARE INCAPABLE OF WORK: THE MAIN RULE

12.28 For the purposes of qualifying for a disability premium or higher pensioner premium, the claimant or any partner counts as disabled or long-term sick if he or she:

HBR sch 2
para 12(1),(4),(7)
CTBR sch 1
para 13(1),(4),(6A)
SI 1995 No. 626

◆ receives incapacity benefit payable at the long-term rate, or is terminally ill and receives it at the short-term higher rate; or

◆ receives severe disablement allowance; or

◆ transferred from incapacity benefit (or the former invalidity benefit) to retirement pension whilst he or she was on HB or CTB, and has since remained on HB or CTB with no breaks in entitlement to both of more than eight weeks.

People who are disqualified from incapacity benefit do not satisfy the rule. Before 1st April 1993, the third rule applied in the same way to community charge benefit. Transferring from community charge benefit to CTB does not count as a break in entitlement.

12.29   The following is a broad summary of the state benefits mentioned above.

◆ *Incapacity benefit* is for people who are incapable of work and who have paid a certain amount of national insurance contributions:

  • The *long-term rate* is for people who have been incapable of work for 52 weeks or more.

  • The *short-term higher rate* is for people who have been incapable of work for 28 weeks or more. The amount for terminally ill people is greater than the amount for others, and is at least as great as the long-term rate.

  • The *short-term lower rate* is for people who have been incapable of work for less than 28 weeks and do not get statutory sick pay.

◆ *Severe disablement allowance* is for some disabled people who have been incapable of work for 28 weeks or more but have not paid enough national insurance contributions to get the above benefits.

PEOPLE WHO ARE INCAPABLE OF WORK: THE '28/52-WEEK RULE'

HBR sch 2
para 12(1),(3),(6)
CTBR sch 1
para 13(1),(3),(6)
SI 1995 No. 626
12.30   Additionally, for the purposes of qualifying for a disability premium (but not a higher pensioner premium), the claimant counts as disabled or long-term sick if he or she:

◆ is incapable of work; and

◆ has been incapable of work for a 'waiting period' (calculated as described in para. 12.32) of:

  • 28 weeks if he or she is terminally ill, or

  • 52 weeks in any other case.

After the waiting period is completed, there are further 'linking rules' (para. 12.32).

This way of qualifying for a disability premium 'fills the gap' for people who are incapable of work but do not get incapacity benefit or severe disablement benefit. For couples, it must be the claimant – not his or her partner – who fulfils this rule. It can therefore be important which partner makes the claim (para. 7.5).

12.31   'Incapable of work' means the same here as it does for incapacity benefit purposes. Broadly, during the first 28 weeks the person must satisfy an 'own occupation test', and thereafter (or from the outset if he or she has no normal occupation) an 'all work test'. Broadly, a person is 'terminally ill' if his or her death can be expected within six months. DSS circular A42/98 encloses a form which authorities may use to obtain information from the Benefits Agency relevant to whether someone is 'incapable of work'.

THE 'WAITING PERIOD' AND THE 'LINKING RULES'

12.32 In the following, a 'gap' means a period during which the person is not incapable of work or is disqualified from incapacity benefit. The waiting period (para. 12.30) need not be continuous. Any number of periods are added together so long as the gap between each is eight weeks or less.

Once a person has completed the waiting period, there are linking rules as follows:

◆ the claimant does not qualify for a disability premium during a gap;

◆ after a gap of eight weeks or less, the person qualifies for a disability premium straight away;

◆ after a gap of more than eight weeks, the person does not qualify for a disability premium until he or she has completed a fresh waiting period.

Breaks in entitlement to HB or CTB during the waiting period or after it have no effect on this rule.

Carer premium

12.33 The condition for this premium is that the claimant (or in the case of a couple, either the claimant or partner or both of them):

HBR sch 2 para 14ZA CTBR sch 1 para 16

◆ receives invalid care allowance; or

◆ ceased to receive invalid care allowance within the past eight weeks; or

◆ has claimed invalid care allowance and continues to qualify for it (or qualified for it within the past eight weeks), but is not awarded it because of the rules on overlapping social security benefits (para. 12.45).

12.34 *Invalid care allowance* is a state benefit. It is paid to the carer of a disabled person – who may live at the same or a different address. The carer must be aged at least 16 and neither gainfully employed nor in full-time education; the disabled person must be receiving the highest or middle rate of the care component of disability living allowance (para. 12.22) or one of the other state benefits for attendance listed in paragraph 12.24.

12.35 If the disabled person stops receiving any of those benefits, the carer stops qualifying for a carer premium.

12.36 A single claimant or lone parent who fulfils the condition gets one carer premium. A couple get one or two carer premiums – one if only one of them fulfils the condition, two if both fulfil the condition.

12.37 One of the problems here is that when a carer claims invalid care allowance, although he or she may thereby gain a carer premium, the disabled person may lose a severe disability premium (though not retrospectively: para. 12.38). Both parties should seek advice before a claim for invalid care allowance is made.

Severe disability premium

HBR 2(1), sch 2 para 13 CTBR 2(1), sch 1 para 14

12.38 There are three conditions for this premium:

◆ the person must be receiving the highest or middle rate of the care component of disability living allowance (para. 12.22) or one of the other state benefits for attendance listed in paragraph 12.24; and

◆ the person must have no non-dependants (with the exceptions mentioned below); and

◆ no-one must be receiving invalid care allowance (para. 12.34) to care for the person (though it does not count if someone ceased to receive invalid care allowance only because the person has been in hospital for four weeks or more). A backdated award of invalid care allowance is ignored for this purpose as regards any period before the award was made: in other words the backdated part does not cause an overpayment.

12.39 A single claimant or lone parent who fulfils all three conditions gets the single rate of severe disability premium.

12.40 In the case of a couple, a severe disability premium is awarded as follows:

◆ if both partners fulfil all three conditions, they get the double rate;

◆ if both partners fulfil the first two conditions but only one fulfils the third condition, they get the single rate;

◆ if the claimant fulfils all three conditions, and his or her partner is registered or certified blind or ceased to be within the past 28 weeks (para. 12.20), they get the single rate. In this case, if the 'wrong' partner makes the claim, they should be advised to 'swap the claimant role';

◆ if they have been getting the double rate, but one partner then ceases to fulfil the first condition because of having been in hospital for four weeks, they get the single rate from that point.

12.41 For the purposes of the above rule, the following non-dependants do not count (i.e. do not prevent the award of a severe disability premium):

◆ non-dependants under 18;

◆ non-dependants themselves receiving the highest or middle rate of the care component of disability living allowance (para. 12.22) or one of the other state benefits for attendance listed in paragraph 12.24;

◆ non-dependants who are registered or certified blind or who ceased to be within the past 28 weeks (para. 12.20).

12.42 It should also be borne in mind that a number of categories of people are excluded from the definition of a non-dependant (para. 6.21).

Example: Severe disability premium

A husband and wife are both under 60 and both receive the middle rate of the care component of disability living allowance. Neither of them is or has recently been registered or certified blind. Their daughter of 17 is in full-time employment and lives with them. Their son lives elsewhere and receives invalid care allowance for caring for the husband. No-one receives invalid care allowance for the wife.

Disability premium: Because of receiving disability living allowance, they are awarded the couple rate of disability premium.

Severe disability premium:

◆ Both receive the appropriate type of disability living allowance.

◆ Although their daughter Is a non-dependant, she Is under 18.

◆ Someone receives invalid care allowance for caring for only one of them.

So they are awarded the single rate of severe disability premium (for the second reason in para. 12.40).

General rules

BEING 'IN RECEIPT' OF A BENEFIT

12.43 Receipt of a state benefit forms part of the condition for many of the premiums. A person is 'in receipt' of a benefit only if it is paid in respect of himself or herself, and only during the period for which it is awarded.

HBR
sch 2 para 14B
CTBR
sch 1 para 18

DSS CONCESSIONARY PAYMENTS

12.44 For the purpose of entitlement to any premium, a DSS concessionary payment compensating for non-payment of any state benefit is treated as if it were that benefit.

HBR
sch 2 para 14A
CTBR
sch 1 para 17

OVERLAPPING SOCIAL SECURITY BENEFITS

12.45 If any benefit is not paid to the claimant because of the rules about overlapping social security benefits, it is nonetheless treated as received for the purpose of entitlement to any premium. For example, a widow's pension is

HBR
sch 2 para 7
CTBR
sch 1 para 7

sometimes paid instead of incapacity benefit. The claimant is nonetheless treated as receiving incapacity benefit.

Special cases

POLYGAMOUS MARRIAGES

HBR 17
sch 2
CTBR 9
sch 1

12.46 The applicable amount for a claimant in a polygamous marriage (para. 6.10) is the sum of the following. If the following could combine to produce more than one result, the result which is most favourable to the claimant applies:

◆ a personal allowance of £81.95, unless (in HB only) all the members of the polygamous marriage are under 18, in which case £62.35;

◆ £29.75 for each spouse in excess of two;

◆ additions to the personal allowance for any child or young person as in any other case;

◆ the basic rate of the family premium if there is at least one child or young person in their family;

◆ the double rate of severe disability premium if all members of the marriage fulfil all three conditions in paragraph 12.38; the single rate if all members of the marriage fulfil the first two of those conditions but someone receives an invalid care allowance for caring for at least one of them; and the single rate if the claimant fulfils all three conditions and all the other members of the marriage are registered or certified blind or ceased to be within the past 28 weeks;

◆ up to two carer premiums (but not more) if the ordinary conditions are satisfied;

◆ the couple rate of any other premium if the ordinary conditions are satisfied (subject to the rules in para. 12.5).

CHILDREN AND YOUNG PERSONS WITH CAPITAL

HBR 16(b)
sch 2 para 14
CTBR 8(b)
sch 1 para 15

12.47 If in the claimant's family there is a child or young person with capital of his or her own amounting to over £3,000 (assessed under the rules described in chapters 13-15):

◆ no addition is made in the calculation of the claimant's personal allowance for that child or young person;

◆ no disabled child premium is awarded for that child or young person;

◆ but the claimant's entitlement to a family premium (whether the basic rate or protected lone parent rate applies) is not affected (i.e. this is awarded regardless of any child's or young person's capital).

Example: Child with capital of her own

A lone parent qualifies for the protected lone parent rate of the family premium and has a daughter of 13. Neither has any disability. The daughter has capital of over £3,000, so no addition is made for her in the personal allowances. Her capital does not affect the award of a family premium.

Personal allowance:	
lone parent aged over 18	£52.20
Premium:	
family premium (protected lone parent rate)	£22.20
Applicable amount	£74.40

PEOPLE ON TRAINING COURSES

12.48 Once a person qualifies for any of the premiums for disability or for carers (para. 12.13), if he or she goes on a government-run or approved training course (para. 13.41), the premium does not cease just because entitlement to a state benefit has ended or the person no longer fulfils the rule about being incapable of work. The objective of this rule is that otherwise there would be a disincentive to join such courses.

HBR sch 2
paras 7,12(5)
CTBR sch 1
paras 7,13(5)

PEOPLE IN HOSPITAL

12.49 The following rules apply only in the case of a stay in an NHS hospital (including an NHS trust hospital). They do not apply at all to those serving a custodial sentence, nor to private patients whose fees cover all their costs.

12.50 If a claimant or any member of the family goes into hospital, and disability living allowance or attendance allowance (including the equivalents in para. 12.24 and also including cases where it is paid within a war disablement pension) stops being paid as a result (which normally happens after four weeks in hospital), this by itself does not mean that the claimant loses entitlement to a disability premium, higher pensioner premium or disabled child premium. However, the claimant's entitlement to a severe disability premium does stop after four weeks for this reason (except as described at the end of para. 12.40). And a carer's entitlement to a carer premium stops after the disabled person he or she is caring for has been in hospital for four weeks.

HBR sch 2
paras 12(1),(4),1
CTBR sch 1
paras 13(1),(4),1

12.51 Applicable amounts are, however, normally reduced after the claimant or any partner has been in hospital for six weeks (table 12.2). There is no reduction under this rule if a child or young person goes into hospital. For the purposes of counting the six-week period, two stays in hospital are added together if the break between them is four weeks or less. However, the DSS advises (GM para. C4.54)

HBR 18
CTBR IO

Table 12.2 APPLICABLE AMOUNTS AFTER SIX WEEKS IN HOSPITAL

(a) Single claimant	Applicable amount reduces to £16.90 only.
(b) Lone parent	Applicable amount reduces to £16.90 plus: ◆ additions for children and young persons; ◆ family premium; ◆ any disabled child premium(s).
(c) Couple where one only has been in hospital for six weeks or more*	Applicable amount is the same as if neither were in hospital minus £13.50.
(d) Couple where both have been in hospital for six weeks or more**	Applicable amount reduces to £33.80 plus any of the following which apply: ◆ additions for children and young persons; ◆ family premium; ◆ any disabled child premium(s).
(e) Polygamous marriage where not all have been in hospital for six weeks or more*	Applicable amount is the same as if none were in hospital minus £13.50 for each one who has been in hospital for six weeks or more.
(f) Polygamous marriage where all have been in hospital for six weeks or more**	Applicable amount reduces to £16.90 for each member of the marriage plus any of the following which apply: ◆ additions for children and young persons; ◆ family premium; ◆ any disabled child premium(s).

*   *In these cases entitlement to a premium remains even if the person in hospital fulfils the condition for it.*

** *For couples, there may be two succeeding reductions in the applicable amount. Case (c) applies six weeks after the first partner goes into hospital. Case (d) applies six weeks after the second partner goes into hospital. A similar phased reduction may apply for polygamous marriages.*

that this 'linking rule' should not be applied (and so there is no reduction in the claimant's applicable amount) if 'a claimant [or presumably any partner] is regularly discharged from hospital during the week, for example, to accustom [him or her] to being at home'. An income support commissioner's decision (CIS/571/1997) is persuasive for HB/CTB. It held that the day someone goes into hospital does not count as a day in hospital, whereas the day someone comes out does count as a day in hospital.

12.52 If the claimant is in hospital for 52 weeks or more, HB and CTB may cease altogether (chapter 4). If any partner, child or young person is in hospital for 52 weeks or more, he or she may cease to count as part of the family (paras. 6.11, 6.17).

12.53 Whilst day-to-day living expenses may reduce after a period in hospital, liability for rent and council tax usually do not. The reduction in applicable amounts after six weeks in hospital can cause hardship. Authorities should consider making payments of additional HB/CTB when the claimant's circumstances are exceptional (para. 9.42).

13 Income and capital

13.1 This and the following two chapters describe how income and capital are dealt with in the assessment of HB and main CTB. Chapters 14 and 15 give additional information relating to employed earners and the self-employed. This chapter covers:

◆ general matters;

◆ benefits, pensions, and other state help;

◆ the home, property and possessions;

◆ savings and investments;

◆ other items of income and capital;

◆ notional income and capital; and

◆ aggregation of income and capital.

Income and capital are assessed in the same way for HB and for main CTB purposes. They are assessed differently for all purposes relevant to second adult rebate (para. 10.24) and to non-dependant deductions (paras. 9.29-30); this chapter does not apply in such cases.

HBR sch 4 para 4
CTBR sch 4 para 4 **13.2** If a claimant is entitled to income support or income-based jobseeker's allowance (or his or her partner is), this chapter does not apply. Such claimants have already had their income and capital assessed for the purposes of those benefits and their income and capital is not taken into account in the assessment of their HB/main CTB (paras. 9.4-6).

General matters

WHOSE INCOME AND CAPITAL COUNTS

HBR 19, 39
CTBR 11, 30 **13.3** In assessing entitlement to HB and main CTB, a claimant is treated as possessing any income and capital belonging to:

◆ the claimant himself or herself;

◆ any partner he or she has; and

◆ in certain cases, his or her children and young persons.

All references in this chapter to the income or capital of a claimant should be read as also referring to the income and capital of a partner. Paragraph 13.105 describes how a child's or young person's income and capital is taken into account.

WHEN A CLAIMANT IS TREATED AS HAVING A NON-DEPENDANT'S INCOME AND CAPITAL

13.4   A special rule applies if: HBR 20
                                                                                CTBR 12

◆ it appears to the authority that the claimant and non-dependant have entered into arrangements to take advantage of the HB or CTB scheme; and

◆ the non-dependant has both more income and more capital than the claimant; and

◆ the claimant is not on income support or income-based jobseeker's allowance.

13.5   The rule in such cases is that:

◆ the claimant is treated as having the income and capital of the non-dependant; and

◆ the claimant's own income and capital is completely disregarded.

For the purposes of considering the amount (if any) of the non-dependant deduction (para. 9.28), the non-dependant is treated as having his or her own income and capital (not the income and capital of the claimant).

DISTINGUISHING CAPITAL FROM INCOME

13.6   HB and CTB law does not give a general definition of 'income' and 'capital'; though the regulations do define how certain types of payment should be treated: those rules are given as they arise in this and the next two chapters. Examples are given in table 13.1. The DSS gives good general advice (GM para. C2.08):

'Capital can take a variety of forms. A payment of capital can normally be distinguished from income because it is:

   i.   made without being tied to a period; and

   ii. made without being tied to any past payment; and

   iii. not intended to form part of a series of payments.

As a general rule, capital includes all categories of holdings which have a clear monetary value...'

WHICH TYPES OF INCOME AND CAPITAL COUNT

13.7   As described in the later parts of this chapter, some types of income and capital are wholly disregarded; some are partly disregarded; and some are counted in full. Examples are given in table 13.1. Also, in some cases a claimant can be treated as having income or capital he or she does not in fact possess: this is known as 'notional' income or capital (para. 13.96).

Table 13.1 EXAMPLES OF CAPITAL AND INCOME

Capital which is (wholly or partly) taken into account for HB/main CTB purposes

◆ Savings in a bank, building society, etc.

◆ National Savings Certificates, stocks and shares

◆ Property (unless it falls within one of the numerous disregards)

◆ Redundancy pay

◆ Tax refunds

Capital which is disregarded for HB/main CTB purposes

◆ The home a claimant owns and lives in

◆ A self-employed claimant's business assets

◆ Arrears of certain state benefits

◆ Certain compensation payments

◆ A life insurance policy which has not been cashed in

Income which is (wholly or partly) taken into account for HB/main CTB purposes

◆ Earnings from a job or from self-employment

◆ Pensions

◆ Certain state benefits (e.g. contribution-based jobseeker's allowance, retirement pension)

◆ Rental received from a sub-tenant or boarder in the claimant's home

◆ Tariff income from capital

Income which is disregarded for HB/main CTB purposes

◆ Expenses wholly incurred in the course of a job

◆ Certain state benefits (e.g. disability living allowance, attendance allowance)

◆ Certain charitable or voluntary payments

◆ Payments (e.g. 'keep') received from a non-dependant

◆ Fostering payments

These examples are simplified. In many cases further disregards apply. The detailed rules are given later in this chapter.

WHY CAPITAL IS ASSESSED

13.8   If a claimant's capital, assessed under the rules described in this chapter, amounts to:

HBR 37, 45
CTBR 28, 37

◆ more than £16,000, he or she is not entitled to HB or main CTB at all;

◆ £3,000 or less, it is completely ignored in the assessment of his or her HB and main CTB;

◆ more than £3,000 (but not more than £16,000), he or she is treated as having a weekly income from it in the assessment of HB and main CTB. This is called 'tariff income'. The amount of tariff income is found by deducting £3,000 from the assessed capital, then dividing by 250, then rounding up (if necessary) to the next whole £1. A simpler method is to use table 13.2.

13.9   For claimants in some kinds of residential accommodation, the amount of capital which is completely ignored is £10,000 (not £3,000); and they are treated as having tariff income from capital of more than £10,000. The amount of tariff income is found by deducting £10,000 from the assessed capital, then dividing by 250, then rounding up (if necessary) to the next whole £1. But if they have capital over £16,000 they are nonetheless not entitled to HB or main CTB. The kinds of residential accommodation in which the above applies are:

HBR 45
CTBR 37

◆ a residential care home or nursing home where the claimant has pre-1993 preserved rights (para. 4.9);

◆ local authority Part III accommodation so long as board is not provided (para. 4.13);

◆ an unregistered Abbeyfield Home (para. 4.10);

◆ accommodation which is not treated as a nursing home, but is provided together with both board and personal care under an Act of Parliament or Royal Charter. This can apply, for example, to accommodation provided by the Salvation Army or the Royal British Legion (para. 4.11).

Example: Calculating tariff income

A claimant (who does not live in residential accommodation: para. 13.9) has capital, assessed under the rules in this chapter, of £5,085.93.

◆ The first £3,000 is disregarded. The remainder is £2,085.93.

◆ The remainder is divided by 250, and the answer is rounded up to the next whole £1. This give £9 of tariff income per week. (The same answer may be obtained using table 13.2.)

Table 13.2 TARIFF INCOME FROM ASSESSED CAPITAL

Capital held £	Tariff income £ per week	Capital held £	Tariff income £ per week
3,000.01-3,250.00	1	9,500.01- 9,750.00	27
3,250.01 3,500.00	2	9,750.01-10,000.00	28
3,500.01-3,750.00	3	10,000.01-10,250.00	29
3,750.01-4,000.00	4	10,250.01-10,500.00	30
4,000.01-4,250.00	5	10,500.01-10,750.00	31
4,250.01-4,500.00	6	10,750.01-11,000.00	32
4,500.01-4,750.00	7	11,000.01-11,250.00	33
4,750.01-5,000.00	8	11,250.01-11,500.00	34
5,000.01-5,250.00	9	11,500.01-11,750.00	35
5,250.01 5,500.00	10	11,750.01-12,000.00	36
5,500.01 5,750.00	11	12,000.01-12,250.00	37
5,750.01-6,000.00	12	12,250.01-12,500.00	38
6,000.01-6,250.00	13	12,500.01-12,750.00	39
6,250.01-6,500.00	14	12,750.01-13,000.00	40
6,500.01-6,750.00	15	13,000.01-13,250.00	41
6,750.01-7,000.00	16	13,250.01-13,500.00	42
7,000.01 7,250.00	17	13,500.01-13,750.00	43
7,250.01-7,500.00	18	13,750.01-14,000.00	44
7,500.01 7,750.00	19	14,000.01-14,250.00	45
7,750.01-8,000.00	20	14,250.01-14,500.00	46
8,000.01-8,250.00	21	14,500.01-14,750.00	47
8,250.01-8,500.00	22	14,750.01-15,000.00	48
8,500.01-8,750.00	23	15,000.01-15,250.00	49
8,750.01-9,000.00	24	15,250.01-15,500.00	50
9,000.01-9,250.00	25	15,500.01-15,750.00	51
9,250.01-9,500.00	26	15,750.01-16,000.00	52

HOW CAPITAL IS ASSESSED

13.10 The whole of a claimant's capital is taken into account, including certain types of income which are counted as capital, but excluding capital which is disregarded. The general rules about how capital is valued are given below. Other rules about this, about which types of income are counted as capital, and about which types of capital are disregarded, are mentioned in the relevant places in this chapter. **HBR 38 CTBR 29**

Authorities may seek the assistance of the Valuation Office Agency in valuing capital items such as dwellings or other property. The DSS issued forms authorities may use for this purpose in circular HB/CTB A55/98.

VALUING CAPITAL IN GENERAL

13.11 The following rule applies whenever a property, shares, or anything else (except for national savings certificates: para. 13.72) has to be valued for HB/main CTB purposes. Other parts of this chapter mention considerations that also have to be taken into account for specific items. The rule has three steps: **HBR 41(a) CTBR 32(a)**

◆ take the current market or surrender value of the capital item;

◆ then disregard 10 per cent if selling it would involve costs;

◆ then disregard any mortgage or other 'incumbrance' (e.g. a loan) secured on it.

13.12 In practice, a claimant's capital is usually valued at his or her date of claim and revalued only if there is a reasonably large change. But it should be revalued whenever there is a change which affects tariff income.

VALUING JOINTLY HELD CAPITAL

13.13 To assess a particular person's share of capital which is held jointly: **HBR 44 CTBR 36**

◆ first assume that all the joint owners own an equal share in the capital item – even if they actually own it (or regard themselves as owning it) in differing proportions;

◆ then value the person's resulting share using the rules in the previous paragraph.

An example is given below. (The above rules are taken into account by the Valuation Office Agency when authorities seek its assistance.)

WHY INCOME IS ASSESSED

13.14 A claimant's earned and unearned income, assessed under the rules described in this chapter and chapters 14 and 15, is compared with his or her applicable amount in calculating how much HB or main CTB he or she is entitled to (paras. 9.11-15).

Examples: Valuing capital

SHARES WHOLLY OWNED BY A CLAIMANT

A claimant owns 1,000 shares in a company. The sell price is currently £0.50 each.

For HB/main CTB purposes, from the current market value (1,000 x £0.50 = £500) deduct 10% (£50) giving £450. Assuming no loan or other incumbrance is secured on the shares, the value for HB/main CTB purposes is therefore £450.

A JOINTLY OWNED PROPERTY

A claimant and her sister inherit some land from their father. In his Will, he stipulated that the claimant is to have two-thirds of the value of the land and her sister is to have one-third. The land has recently been valued by the Valuation Office Agency, and the authority accepts their valuations, which are as follows:

◆ if the whole of the land was sold, it would fetch £10,000;

◆ if a half-share in the land was sold, the half-share would fetch only £4,000 (because of certain covenants which affect the use of the land).

The claimant has recently taken out a loan for £2,000 using the land as security (and none of the loan has yet been repaid).

For HB/main CTB purposes, the claimant's share of the capital in the land is valued as follows:

◆ first the claimant is treated as owning half of the land;

◆ then this half share is valued. Using the Valuation Office Agency's figure, the authority values the half share as being £4,000;

◆ then 10% is deducted towards sales costs: £4,000 minus £400 leaves £3,600;

◆ then the claimant's loan is deducted: £3,600 minus £2,000 leaves £1,600.

So for HB/main CTB purposes, the claimant has capital of £1,600 (plus any other capital she may have).

HOW INCOME IS ASSESSED

13.15 The whole of a claimant's income is taken into account, including tariff income from capital (para. 13.8) and certain types of capital which are counted as income, but excluding income which is disregarded. General points about income are given below. Other rules about this, about which types of capital are counted as income, and about which types of income are disregarded in whole or in part, are mentioned in the relevant places in this chapter. The income tax payable on any kind of income is disregarded in the assessment of that income. Otherwise, no income can be disregarded unless a specific rule requires this.

HBR 21, 24, 33,
sch 4 para 1
CTBR 13, 16, 24
sch 4 para 1

13.16 The HB and main CTB rules distinguish earned income (i.e. earnings received by employed earners or by the self-employed) from unearned income (e.g. pensions, benefits, rent received by the claimant, and so on). Chapter 14 deals with earnings from a job, chapter 15 with self-employed earnings. The rules about unearned income are in this chapter.

DECIDING WHICH WEEKS INCOME BELONGS TO

13.17 The general objective for HB/main CTB purposes is 'estimating the amount which is likely to be [the claimant's] average weekly income over [his or her] benefit period' (para. 7.81). However, there are many specific rules and these are given in this and the next two chapters as they arise. Where there is no specific rule, it is usually straightforward to decide according to the facts of the case which week or weeks a claimant's income belongs to for HB/main CTB purposes.

HBR 21(1)
CTBR 13(1)

ARREARS OF INCOME

13.18 In broad terms, it is usually the case that if a claimant receives arrears of income, then those arrears should be treated as being income belonging to the week or weeks to which they relate (except to the extent that they are income which is disregarded). Exceptions to this and further specific rules are given in this and the next chapter as they arise.

HBR 68
CTBR 59

CONVERTING INCOME TO A WEEKLY FIGURE

13.19 For HB/main CTB purposes, income must be converted (if necessary) to a weekly figure. The details are given in paragraph 9.59.

Benefits, pensions, and other state help

13.20 The following section of this chapter gives the rules about the assessment for HB/main CTB purposes of state benefits, state pensions, other pensions, and other payments from state, local authority and related sources.

STATE BENEFITS: GENERAL RULE FOR CURRENT PAYMENTS

HBR 33(1)
CTBR 24(1)

13.21   Except when indicated in the following paragraphs, state benefits and pensions are counted in full as unearned income. For example, all the following are counted in full (as are many others):

◆   child benefit;

◆   contribution-based jobseeker's allowance;

◆   incapacity benefit;

◆   severe disablement allowance

◆   industrial injuries benefit;

◆   maternity allowance;

◆   retirement pensions.

STATE BENEFITS: GENERAL RULE FOR ARREARS

HBR 68
CTBR 59

13.22   Except when indicated in the following paragraphs, arrears of state benefits and pensions are counted:

◆   as unearned income for the period they cover, if they are for periods on or after 6th March 1995; or

◆   as current capital (and never as income) if they relate to periods before that.

Example: Arrears of incapacity benefit

A claimant, who has been receiving HB and main CTB for many years, has been receiving incapacity benefit since January 1999. It has been taken into account as her income for HB/main CTB purposes from that date. In June 2000, following a successful appeal, she is paid arrears of incapacity benefit for the period from September 1998 to January 1999.

The arrears are her income for the period from September 1998 to January 1999. The authority may therefore reassess her entitlement to HB/main CTB for that period, which may result in an overpayment (chapter 18).

REDUCED STATE BENEFITS

HBR 33(3)
CTBR 24(3)

13.23   If the amount of a state benefit received by a claimant has been reduced due to a Child Support Agency 'reduced benefit direction', the net amount (i.e. after the reduction) is counted as unearned income. But it it has been reduced for any other reason (typically in order to recover a previous overpayment), the gross amount (i.e. before the reduction) is counted as unearned income.

INCREASES IN STATE BENEFITS FOR DEPENDANTS

13.24 With some state benefits, an amount may be awarded for a dependent adult or dependent child(ren). Count the increase as unearned income if the benefit it is paid with counts as unearned income – unless the dependant is not a member of the family (para. 6.5), in which case disregard it.

HBR sch 4 para
CTBR sch 4 para

RULES FOR PARTICULAR BENEFITS, PENSIONS, ETC.

13.25 The following paragraphs give the rules about particular benefits, pensions and other forms of state help – whether they are paid currently or in arrears.

DISABILITY LIVING ALLOWANCE, OTHER BENEFITS FOR ATTENDANCE AND MOBILITY, AND GUARDIAN'S ALLOWANCE

13.26 Current payments of the following are disregarded in full as unearned income:

HBR sch 4
paras 5-8, 50,
sch 5 para 8
CTBR sch 4
paras 5-8, 49,
sch 5 para 8

◆ disability living allowance;

◆ attendance allowance and constant attendance allowance;

◆ exceptionally severe disablement allowance;

◆ severe disablement occupational allowance;

◆ 'old cases' attendance payments;

◆ mobility supplement;

◆ payments compensating for non-receipt of the above;

◆ guardian's allowance.

Arrears of the above are disregarded in full as income. They are also disregarded as capital for 52 weeks from the date of payment.

Example: Arrears of disability living allowance

A claimant, who has been receiving HB and main CTB for many years, has been receiving disability living allowance since January 1999. It has been disregarded in the assessment of his income for HB/main CTB purposes from that date. In June 2000, following a successful appeal, he is paid arrears of disability living allowance for the period from September 1998 to January 1999.

Because disability living allowance is income which is disregarded, the arrears have no effect on his income for the period from September 1998 to January 1999. If he still has any money derived from those arrears as at June 2001 (52 weeks after the arrears were paid), they will from that point begin to count as part of his capital.

'PRE-1973' WAR WIDOW'S PENSIONS

HBR sch 4
paras 43, 53-55,
ch 5 paras 8, 38

CTBR sch 4
paras 42, 52-54,
ch 5 paras 8, 37

13.27 Current payments of the special pensions paid to 'pre-1973' war widows are disregarded in full as unearned income. From April 1999, the current amount is £57.07 per week. Arrears of such payments are disregarded in full as income. They are also disregarded as capital for 52 weeks from the date of payment, as are payments compensating for non-receipt of such pensions.

OTHER WAR WIDOW'S AND WAR DISABLEMENT PENSIONS

R sch 4 para 14
R sch 4 para 14

13.28 From current payments of any other war widow's or war disablement pensions, disregard £10.00 (subject to the rules on aggregation in para. 13.103). Also disregard any amount included within the pension for attendance or mobility or for dependants who are not a member of the family. The above rule applies to:

◆ war widow's and war disablement pensions;

◆ payments to compensate for non-payment of those;

◆ analogous payments from Governments outside the UK;

◆ Nazi persecution compensation payments.

Arrears of the payments described above fall within the general rule (para. 13.22) – except that the £10.00 disregard mentioned above applies when they are income.

However, many councils operate a 'local scheme' whereby the whole of the above payments are disregarded currently and/or in arrears (para. 9.39).

PENSIONERS' CHRISTMAS BONUS

BR sch 4 para 31
BR sch 4 para 32

13.29 This is disregarded in full as unearned income.

FAMILY CREDIT AND DISABILITY WORKING ALLOWANCE

R 2(1),(4A), sch 4
paras 57, 58, 60,
sch 5 para 8
BR 2(1),(4A), sch
paras 56, 57, 59,
sch 5 para 8

13.30 Current payments of working families' tax credit (WFTC) and disabled person's tax credit (DPTC) are counted in full as unearned income (even though they are often administered by employers). Certain recipients of WFTC/DPTC qualify for an earned income disregard of £11.25 per week (para. 14.17). However, in the uncommon case that the earned income disregard cannot be made because the person has insufficient earned income (as explained in para. 14.19), £11.25 is instead disregarded from the person's WFTC/DPTC (or £11.05 in the case of awards of WFTC/DPTC begun before 11th April 2000).

13.31 Arrears of WFTC and DPTC fall within the general rule (para. 13.22). In other words, arrears usually count as past income (making the disregard referred to above in appropriate cases). The same is true for arrears of family credit and disability working allowance – which WFTC and DPTC replaced (though the way the disregard worked was different before October 1999).

13.32 The capital value of arrears of family credit, disability working allowance and family income supplement (which family credit replaced), and of payments compensating for non-receipt of any of those, is disregarded for 52 weeks from the date of payment; but no equivalent rule applies to the capital value of arrears of WFTC or DPTC.

INCOME SUPPORT, INCOME-BASED JOBSEEKER'S ALLOWANCE, HB, CTB, ETC

13.33 Current payments of these benefits are disregarded in full as income, as are the transitional payments awarded with some payments of income support and income-based jobseeker's allowance. Arrears of all these (including arrears of HB/CTB paid under the special provisions relating to refugees who were formerly asylum seekers: para. 5.51) are disregarded in full as income; as are arrears of the following former benefits: community charge benefit, housing benefit supplement, supplementary benefit and HB transitional payments. Arrears of HB and CTB are also disregarded as capital without time limit. Arrears of all the other items mentioned are also disregarded as capital for 52 weeks from the date of payment, as are payments compensating for non-receipt of any of these.

HBR sch 4 paras 35, 36, 40, 48, 61, 62, sch 5 paras 8, 2 29, 35, 42, 45, 51
CTBR sch 4 para 4, 36, 37, 38, 4 50, 60, 61 sch 5 paras 8, 2 29, 34, 35, 41, 50, 51

COUNCIL TAX REDUCTIONS

13.34 Disregard in full (both as income and capital) disability reductions, discounts and transitional reductions (chapter 3). In other words, the fact that the claimant gets one of these does not mean that it counts as his or her income or capital.

HBR sch 4 para sch 5 para 36
CTBR sch 4 para 41, sch 5 para 3

SOCIAL FUND PAYMENTS AND LOANS

13.35 Disregard payments and loans from the social fund (chapter 2) in full (both as income and capital) – including Winter Fuel Payments.

HBR sch 4 para sch 5 para 19
CTBR sch 4 para 31, sch 5 para 1

SOCIAL SERVICES PAYMENTS

13.36 Disregard in full (both as income and capital) any social services payment made for the purposes of avoiding taking children into care and any such payment made to children leaving care. Also disregard in full as income any social services payment made in lieu of providing community care.

HBR sch 4 paras 26, 67, sch 5 para 18
CTBR sch 4 paras 37, 62, sch 5 para 18

FOSTERING, BOARDING OUT AND RESPITE CARE PAYMENTS

HBR sch 4
paras 24, 25
CTBR sch 4
paras 25, 26

13.37 Disregard these payments in full (as income) if they are received from a local authority or voluntary organisation. In the case of respite care payments, contributions required under the National Assistance Act 1948 from the person cared for are also disregarded as income.

ADOPTION AND CUSTODIANSHIP ALLOWANCES

HBR reg. 2(i),
sch 4 para 23
CTBR reg. 2(i),
sch 4 para 24

13.38 If these payments are received from a local authority (including an authority in Northern Ireland), disregard any amount in excess of the dependant's allowance and any disabled child premium for the child or young person concerned. Count any balance as unearned income. However, if the child or young person concerned has capital valued at over £3,000 disregard the whole amount.

OCCUPATIONAL AND PERSONAL PENSIONS

HBR 28(2), 34(4),
sch 5 para 30
CTBR 19(2), 25(4),
sch 5 para 30

13.39 These count in full as unearned income, except that any deduction for tax is disregarded. Also disregard the capital value of any amount held in a pension scheme and of the right to receive money from it.

THE MACFARLANE TRUSTS, THE FUND, THE EILEEN TRUST, THE INDEPENDENT LIVING FUNDS

BR sch 4 para 34,
ch 5 paras 23, 32
TBR sch 4 para 35,
h 5 paras. 23, 32

13.40 The Macfarlane Trust, the Macfarlane (Special Payments) Trust, the Macfarlane (Special Payments) (No. 2) Trust, 'the Fund', and the Eileen Trust were all set up to assist certain people with HIV. The Independent Living Fund, the Independent Living (Extension) Fund, and the Independent Living (1993) Fund were all set up to enable severely disabled people to live independently. Any payment from any of these is disregarded in full (both as capital and income). Payments in kind from any of these are also disregarded. If money from any of these is passed on to a third party, it is usually also disregarded in the assessment of the third party's income and capital.

THE 'NEW DEAL', 'WELFARE TO WORK', AND DFEE SCHEMES GENERALLY

HBR sch 4 paras
11, 49, 64, 65,
sch 5 paras 33,
43, 44, 53, 54
CTBR sch 4 paras
11, 48, 64, 65,
sch 5 paras 33,
42, 43, 53, 54
SI 1998 No. 217
SI 1998 No. 2825

13.41 The following describes how income and capital are assessed in the case of people on the 'New Deal' or on other (current and recent) schemes run by the Department for Employment and Education (DfEE). The various options available under the 'New Deal' are summarised in table 13.3. (Most people on the 'New Deal' – other than 'welfare to work beneficiaries' – remain entitled to income support or income-based jobseeker's allowance – so their income and capital is disregarded: the following points apply to them only if they do not qualify for either of those benefits.)

◆ *The New Deal: mandatory and discretionary 'top-up' payments.* The general rule is as follows:

- disregard these in full as unearned income; and

- disregard these in full as capital – but only for 52 weeks from the date of payment.

An exception applies to people on a 'qualifying course of study'. In their case, the above points apply – except that discretionary 'top-up' payments made to them for travel expenses are not disregarded if an amount is disregarded for travel under the normal student rules (table 20.3).

◆ *The New Deal: payments towards child care costs.* Disregard these as unearned income.

◆ *The New Deal: training allowances.* The general rule is as follows:

- disregard as unearned income any travel allowance or living away from home allowance;

- count any maintenance and/or meals allowance as unearned income; and

- disregard as capital the first £200 of any training bonus.

The exceptions are that the above points do not apply to the income of employees on the 'employed earner's route' of the Employment Option; to the trading receipts of people on the 'self-employed earner's route' of the Employment Option (see also below); or to people undertaking an 'intensive activity period' (if they are a non-dependant, see also para. 9.36).

◆ *The New Deal: people on the 'self-employed earner's route' of the Employment Option.* In addition to the above points, there are several further rules for such people: see paragraph 15.39.

◆ *The New Deal: people undertaking a 'qualifying course of study' or on a 'workskill pilot scheme'.* In addition to the above points, such people count as 'students': see paragraphs 20.7-8.

◆ *The New Deal: 'welfare to work beneficiaries'.* The special concessions for welfare to work beneficiaries (as defined in table 13.3) are described in this Guide as they arise (in chapters 11 and 12). Their earnings are assessed in the normal way (chapter 14).

◆ *The New Deal: note on notional income/capital.* Payments to a *provider* of a New Deal arrangement are not treated as the notional income or notional capital of the claimant (paras. 13.99-100). Also, the notional earnings rule (about people paid less than the going rate for a job: para. 13.102) does not apply to people on the New Deal.

◆ *Access to work.* Disregard (both as income and capital) all payments under this scheme, which is available to certain disabled people.

◆ *Work Based Training for Young People, Work Based Training for Adults and Community Action.* If the person is receiving payments from any of these as an employed earner, count these are earnings. In any other case:

- disregard as income any travel or living away from home allowance, and any training premium;
- count any maintenance and/or meals allowance as unearned income;
- disregard as capital the first £200 of any training bonus.

◆ *Jobfinder's grant.* Count this in full as capital.

◆ *Jobmatch payments.* Count these in full as unearned income.

◆ *Project work.* People on this scheme should be on income support or income-based jobseeker's allowance – so their income and capital is disregarded.

Table 13.3 THE 'NEW DEAL' AND 'WELFARE TO WORK'

SUMMARY OF OPTIONS AVAILABLE UNDER THE 'NEW DEAL'

The 'New Deal' is designed to help participants to find work or to improve their prospects of doing so. It offers participants several options: in each case, there are several other rules and conditions (about age and other matters), not given here. (Paragraph 13.41 describes how to assess the income and capital of people on the New Deal.) The current options are:

◆ the 'Full-time Education and Training Option';

◆ the 'Voluntary Sector Option';

◆ the 'Environment Task Force Option';

◆ the 'employed earner's route' of the 'Employment Option';

◆ the 'self-employed route' of the 'Employment Option';

◆ the option of joining a 'qualifying course of study';

◆ the option (described below) of becoming a 'welfare to work beneficiary'.

DEFINITION OF 'WELFARE TO WORK BENEFICIARY'

For all HB/CTB purposes a 'welfare to work beneficiary' is defined (by reference to reg. 13A of the Social Security (Incapacity for Work)(General) Regulations 1995 No. 311) as being a person who:

- ◆ has been incapable of work for at least 28 weeks (196 days); and

- ◆ has stopped (on or after 5th October 1998) receiving a benefit or advantage which was dependent on his or her being incapable of work (the relevant benefits and advantages for HB/CTB purposes are indicated as they arise in chapters 11 and 12 of this Guide); and

- ◆ has – within 7 days of ceasing to be incapable of work – started:

  - • remunerative work (in broad terms, 16 hours or more per week: para. 9.33), or

  - • Work Based Training for Adults (in England and Wales), or

  - • Training for Work (in Scotland); and

- ◆ has notified the benefits agency of the fact that he or she has started work, and has done so within one month of the date on which he or she ceased to claim that he or she is incapable of work (or, in certain cases, has won a social security appeal relating to this).

Such a person counts as a welfare to work beneficiary for 52 weeks only. The Benefits Agency should inform authorities if someone is a welfare to work beneficiary (circular HB/CTB A41/98).

CAREER DEVELOPMENT LOANS

13.42 Career development loans are paid under arrangements between the DfEE and national banks (circular HB/CTB A1/97). They are dealt with as follows:

HBR 34(4),
sch 4 para 63
CTBR 25(4),
sch 4 para 63

- ◆ any amount which (over the period of the education or training to which the loan applies) relates to the claimant's or a member of the family's food, ordinary clothing or footwear (excluding school uniform and sportswear), household fuel, eligible rent (apart from any non-dependant deduction), council tax, or water charges, is counted in full as income;

- ◆ any amount relating to any other purposes (such as for course fees and course-related expenses) is disregarded in full (as both income and capital).

HEALTH BENEFITS

13.43 The following are disregarded in full as unearned income. The last two items are also disregarded as capital for 52 weeks from the date of payment:

HBR sch 4 paras
37, 44, 45, sch 5
paras 39, 40
CTBR sch 4 paras
39, 44, 45, sch 5
paras 38, 39

- ◆ hospital resettlement benefit;

- ◆ payments for travel for hospital visits;

- ◆ health service supplies or payments in lieu of free milk and vitamins.

PRISON VISITS PAYMENTS

R sch 4 para 46,
sch 5 para 41
CTBR sch 4 para
5, sch 5 para 40

13.44 Disregard in full as unearned income any Home Office payment for travel for prison visits. Disregard it as capital for 52 weeks from the date of payment.

The home, property and possessions

13.45 The following section of this chapter is about how things the claimant owns affect his or her entitlement to HB and main CTB. It covers:

◆ when the value of the home and other property is ignored and when it is taken into account;

◆ how property which is rented out is dealt with;

◆ possessions and miscellaneous items.

WHEN THE VALUE OF THE HOME AND PROPERTY IS DISREGARDED

13.46 The claimant's current, former or future home can be disregarded and so can a home or other property (including non-domestic property) which the claimant has never occupied, if the conditions in the next few paragraphs apply. The disregards described below can apply one after another, so long as the relevant conditions are met (as illustrated in the example following para. 13.58).

THE CLAIMANT'S CURRENT HOME

HBR sch 5 para 1
TBR sch 5 para 1

13.47 Disregard the capital value of the dwelling normally occupied as the claimant's home, and any land or buildings which are part of it or are impracticable to sell separately. There is no time limit. This disregard is limited to one home per claim but see the other headings below.

THE HOME OF AN ELDERLY OR INCAPACITATED PERSON

HBR sch 5
para 4(a)
CTBR sch 5
para 4(a)

13.48 Disregard the capital value of the home of a partner or relative of anyone in the claimant's family, if that partner or relative is aged 60 or more or incapacitated. There is no time limit. The property may be occupied by others as well as the partner or relative. Any number of properties may be disregarded under this rule. 'Relative' is defined in paragraph 11.20. 'Incapacitated' is not defined for this purpose; in particular, it is not linked to premiums or state benefits.

THE CLAIMANT'S INTENDED HOME

HBR sch 5
paras 2, 26, 27
CTBR sch 5
paras 2, 25, 26

13.49 Disregard the capital value of a property which the claimant intends to occupy as a home as follows:

◆ in all cases, for 26 weeks from the date of acquisition or such longer period as is reasonable; and/or

♦ if the claimant is taking steps to obtain or regain possession (e.g. if there are squatters or tenants), for 26 weeks from the date the claimant first seeks legal advice or begins legal proceedings, or such longer period as is reasonable; and/or

♦ if the property requires essential repairs or alterations, for 26 weeks from the date the claimant first takes steps to render it fit for occupation or reoccupation as his or her home, or such longer period as is reasonable. This could apply to the normal home of a claimant in temporary accommodation.

THE CLAIMANT'S FORMER HOME

13.50 There is no disregard of the capital value of a claimant's former home as such. However, a former home may well fall within one of the following headings (which also apply to other property): if it does not, then it is taken into account as capital.

PROPERTY THE CLAIMANT INTENDS TO DISPOSE OF

13.51 Disregard the capital value of any property the claimant intends to dispose of, for 26 weeks from the date when the claimant first takes steps to dispose of it, or for such longer period as is reasonable. This can apply to a former or second home or any other property. It can apply to more than one property.

HBR sch 5
para 25
CTBR sch 5
para 25

DIVORCED OR ESTRANGED COUPLES AND POLYGAMOUS MARRIAGES

13.52 If a claimant has actually divorced or become estranged from a former partner, disregard the whole capital value of the claimant's former home (and any land or buildings which are part of it or are impracticable to sell separately) as follows:

HBR sch 5
para 24
CTBR sch 5
para 24

♦ for any period when it is occupied by the former partner if he or she is now a lone parent. This could begin straight after the divorce/estrangement, or later on, and there is no time limit in this case;

♦ in any other case, for 26 weeks from the date of divorce or estrangement (e.g. if the former partner is not a lone parent at the time, or the property is empty). The time limit in this case cannot be extended, but the property may fall within one of the other disregards afterwards.

Note that (unlike in the next heading) the claimant must have formerly lived there as his or her home for this disregard to apply.

SEPARATED OR SPLIT COUPLES AND POLYGAMOUS MARRIAGES

13.53 If a claimant has not actually divorced or become estranged from a former partner, but the HB/CTB rules treat him or her as no longer being in a couple or polygamous marriage (e.g. because of the rules about absence of a partner: para.

HBR sch 5
para 4(b)
CTBR sch 5
para 4(b)

6.11), disregard the whole capital value of any property currently occupied as a home by the former partner. There is no time limit. Note that it is irrelevant who used to live there.

DISPUTED ASSETS WHEN A RELATIONSHIP ENDS

13.54 When a relationship ends, ownership of a property may be in dispute. This can sometimes mean the current market value of the property is nil until ownership of the property is settled.

HOUSING ASSOCIATION DEPOSITS

HBR sch 5 para 10
TBR sch 5 para 10

13.55 Disregard in full as capital any amount deposited with a housing association in order to secure accommodation.

HOME SALE PROCEEDS, ETC.

HBR sch 5 para 3
CTBR sch 5 para 3

13.56 Disregard in full as capital:

◆ money from the sale of the claimant's former home; and

◆ money refunded by a housing association with whom it was deposited (para. 13.55),

but only if it is intended for purchasing another home within 26 weeks, or such longer period as is reasonable. (However, interest accrued on the money is counted as capital in the normal way: para. 13.71.)

VALUING PROPERTY GENERALLY

13.57 The general rules about valuing capital apply to a property which has to be taken into account as capital for HB/main CTB purposes (paras. 13.11-13). In such cases, an authority can get a free valuation of property from the Valuation Office Agency (DSS circular HB/CTB A55/98 – which also encloses standard forms for authorities to use for this purpose).

VALUING PROPERTY WHICH IS RENTED OUT

HBR sch 5 para 6
CTBR sch 5 para 6

13.58 Unless it forms part of the capital assets of a business (or in certain circumstances a former business: para. 15.5), property a claimant owns and has rented out is is valued as described earlier (paras. 13.11-13). However, the fact that it is rented out will affect its market value; for example, the presence of a sitting tenant can reduce it. For information about rental income see the following paragraphs.

Example: The capital value of a property following relationship breakdown

◆ A married couple jointly own the house they live in. They do not own any other property. They have one child at school. They claim CTB. The man is the claimant.

The value of the house is disregarded as capital: it is their normal home (para. 13.47). However, they turn out not to qualify for CTB because they have too much income.

◆ The man leaves and rents a room in a shared house. He does not intend to return (and so they no longer count as a couple: para. 6.11). He claims HB and CTB for the flat. The woman does not make a further CTB claim for the house.

In the man's claim, his share of the house is disregarded: it is the home of his former partner from whom he is separated (para. 13.53).

◆ They divorce. The terms of the divorce are that the man retains a one-third share in the house; but that the house cannot be sold until their child is 18. The man notifies the council of this.

In his claim, his share of the house is disregarded: it is his former home and is occupied by his former partner from whom he is divorced and who is a lone parent (para. 13.52).

◆ More than 26 weeks after their divorce, their child leaves school. The house is not put up for sale and the man does not seek his share of its value.

In his claim, his interest in the house must now be taken into account (para. 13.52). As a joint owner, he is treated as possessing one-half of its value (and the other points in para. 13.13 are taken into account in valuing it).

◆ The house is put up for sale.

In the man's claim, his interest in the house is now disregarded as capital for 26 weeks (or longer if reasonable: para. 13.51).

◆ The house is sold, and the man puts his share into a building society account and starts trying to raise a mortgage using the money. It seems likely that he will be able to buy somewhere within the next two or three months.

In his claim, this money is disregarded: it is the proceeds of the sale of his former home and he plans to use it to buy another property within 26 weeks (para. 13.56).

RENTAL INCOME RECEIVED BY THE CLAIMANT

HBR sch 4
aras 19, 20, 42,
sch 5 para 31
CTBR sch 4
aras 19, 20, 21,
sch 5 para 31

13.59   Table 13.4 shows how rental income received by the claimant from people living in his or her home is taken into account. Paragraphs 13.60-61 deal with rent from property other than the claimant's home. Also, the value of the right to receive rent (para. 13.68) is disregarded as capital.

RENT ON DISREGARDED PROPERTY WHICH IS NOT THE CLAIMANT'S HOME

HBR sch 4
para 15(2)
CTBR sch 4
para 15(2)

13.60   The following applies if the claimant receives rent (or some other payment) on a property which is not his or her home, but is one of the types of property whose capital value is disregarded under the above rules (paras. 13.48-54) or the rules about the assets of the self-employed (para. 5.5). In such cases:

♦ take the amount of the rental income for an appropriate period (e.g. a month, a year);

♦ disregard any payment towards mortgage repayments (both interest and capital repayments) or any council tax or water charges the claimant is liable to pay during that period on the property (note that other outgoings cannot be disregarded);

♦ count the balance (converted to a weekly figure) as the claimant's unearned income.

Table 13.4 RENTAL INCOME RECEIVED FROM PEOPLE IN THE CLAIMANT'S HOME

Rent, keep, etc. from household members

♦ Disregard the whole of any rent, 'keep', etc. received from a child or young person in the family (paras. 6.12-20) or from a non-dependant (para. 6.21).

Rent from boarders (as defined in para. 6.23)

♦ Disregard the first £20.00 of that rent;

♦ count only half the rest as unearned income;

♦ a separate £20.00 is disregarded for each individual boarder who is charged for – even if a child – regardless of whether they have separate agreements.

Rent from tenants/sub-tenants (as defined in para. 6.25)

◆ Always disregard the first £4.00 of that rent;

◆ disregard a further £9.25 if the rent covers heating;

◆ count the rest as unearned income;

◆ a separate £4.00 (and, if appropriate, £9.25) is disregarded for each (sub-) tenant liable to pay rent for living in the claimant's home.

Example: Letting out a room

A couple on HB/CTB have a spare room. First they let it out to a man for £30 per week inclusive of gas, electricity and water charges. He is their sub-tenant.

For the purposes of their HB/CTB, their income from this sub-tenant is £30 minus the standard £4 and the additional £9.25 because they provides heating; which is £16.75.

Later the same couple agree with the man that if he pays them £45 per week each, they will feed him. He is now their boarder.

So now, for the purposes of their HB/CTB, their income from this boarder is £45 minus the standard £20 – which is £25; the result being divided by two – which is £12.50.

RENT ON NON-DISREGARDED PROPERTY

13.61 The following applies if the claimant receives rent (or some other payment) on a property the value of which is taken into account as capital (even if the capital value is nil for HB/main CTB purposes, perhaps because of negative equity). In such cases:

HBR 40(4), sch 4 para 15(1)
CTBR 31(4), sch para 15(1)

◆ take the amount of the rental income for an appropriate period (e.g. a month, a year);

◆ deduct any outgoings incurred in respect of the letting (e.g. estate agents' fees, tax due on the income, repayments of loans, repairs, etc.);

◆ the balance (if any) is not income for HB/main CTB purposes: it is taken into account in deciding the amount of the claimant's capital. As with any other capital received by the claimant, he or she may use it all for living or other costs, in which case it does not affect his or her capital for HB/main CTB purposes (unless the deprivation rule applies: para. 13.97).

PAYMENTS FOR ESSENTIAL REPAIRS AND IMPROVEMENTS TO THE HOME

HBR sch 5 para 10
TBR sch 5 para 10

13.62 Loans or gifts for these purposes are disregarded as capital for 26 weeks from the date paid, or such longer period as is reasonable. This disregard applies, for example, to home improvement grants, loans from a friend or relative, etc.

PORTABLE DISCOUNTS

HBR sch 5 para 37
TBR sch 5 para 36

13.63 Grants from a local authority to purchase, alter or repair a property to be used as a home, are disregarded as capital for 26 weeks from the date of the grant, or such longer period as is reasonable. An example is when a council tenant gets a grant to buy another property.

TAX REFUNDS FOR MORTGAGE INTEREST

HBR sch 5 para 20
TBR sch 5 para 20

13.64 Tax refunds for interest on a mortgage taken out for purchasing or acquiring a share in the home, or for carrying out home repairs or improvements, are disregarded in full as capital.

INSURANCE PAYMENTS UNDER A MORTGAGE OR LOAN PROTECTION POLICY

HBR sch 4 para 28
TBR sch 4 para 29

13.65 The following applies if a claimant has taken out insurance against being unable (perhaps because of sickness) to pay his or her mortgage or some other loan (for example a car loan), and is now receiving payments under that insurance policy. In such cases, payments the claimant receives under that insurance policy are disregarded as unearned income – but only insofar as they cover the cost of:

◆ the repayments on the mortgage or other loan; and

◆ any premiums due on the policy in question; and

◆ (only in the case of a mortgage protection policy) any premiums on another insurance policy which was taken out to insure against loss or damage to the home and which was required as a condition of the mortgage.

COMPENSATION AND INSURANCE PAYMENTS FOR THE HOME OR POSSESSIONS

HBR sch 5 para 9
CTBR sch 5 para 9

13.66 Such payments are disregarded as capital if they are for repair or replacement following loss of, or damage to, the claimant's home or personal possessions. They are disregarded for 26 weeks from the date paid, or such longer period as is reasonable.

PERSONAL POSSESSIONS

HBR sch 5 para 11
TBR sch 5 para 11

13.67 Disregard in full as capital the value of the claimant's personal possessions – unless they were purchased for the purpose of obtaining or increasing entitlement to HB/CTB (in which case they should be valued as in paras. 13.11-13).

Savings and investments

SUMMARY AND DEFINITIONS

13.68 The following paragraphs deal with the assessment of the claimant's savings and investments. When these are taken into account, they are valued as described in paragraphs 13.11-13. (But for national savings certificates, see para. 13.72.) The following terms are used below:

◆ the 'surrender value' (of an insurance policy, for instance) means what the claimant would be paid (by the insurance company, for instance) if he or she cashed it in now (rather than waiting for it to mature, for instance);

◆ the 'value of the right to receive income' (from an annuity, for instance) means what the claimant would be paid in return for transferring the right to receive the income to someone else.

SAVINGS AND CASH

13.69 These count in full as capital. For example, money in a bank or building society account is counted as capital (but see the next paragraph).

HBR 38(1)
CTBR 29(1)

INCOME PAID REGULARLY INTO AN ACCOUNT

13.70 Regular payments of income (e.g. earnings, benefits, pensions) into a claimant's bank, building society or similar account should be disregarded as capital for the period they cover. For example, if earnings are paid in monthly, only what is left at the end of the month is capital. In practice, authorities rarely do this unless claimants specifically ask them to do so.

INTEREST AND OTHER INCOME DERIVED FROM CAPITAL

13.71 Interest or other income derived from capital is dealt with as follows:

HBG 40(4)
CTBR 31(4)

◆ if it is from non-disregarded capital, it is counted as capital from the date it is due to be credited to the claimant (examples include interest on a bank or building society account, and rent received on certain property: para. 13.61);

◆ if it is from the claimant's normal home (e.g. rent: table. 13.4), or from self-employed business assets (para. 15.5), or from trust funds for personal injury (para. 13.83), it is counted as capital (as described in those paras.) from the date it is due to be credited to the claimant;

◆ if it is from any other form of disregarded capital, it is classified as capital and is itself then disregarded (examples include interest on house sale proceeds for 26 weeks: para. 13.56, and rent received on certain property: para. 13.60).

NATIONAL SAVINGS CERTIFICATES

HBR 41(b)
CTBR 32(b) **13.72** These count as capital, but the following applies instead of the normal rules about valuing capital. From 1st July in any year to 30th June in the next year, the capital amount for HB/main CTB purposes is their value as at 1st July in the first of those years. For current issues, this means their purchase price. The DSS issues valuation tables each year. The table applying from 1st July 1999 onwards is in circular HB/CTB A20/99.

INVESTMENTS

13.73 These count as capital. They are valued as described in the general rules (paras. 13.11-13), with the effect that:

♦ *shares* are valued at their 'sell' price. Then disregard 10 per cent towards the cost of their sale;

♦ *unit trusts* are valued at their 'sell' price. Normally this already allows for notional sales costs. If it does not, disregard 10 per cent for this;

♦ *income bonds* count in full.

LIFE INSURANCE POLICIES

HBR sch 5 para 16
TBR sch 5 para 16 **13.74** Disregard as capital the surrender value of a life insurance policy, and also the value of the right to receive income from it (para. 13.68). But count as capital any money actually received from it (e.g. if the claimant actually cashes all or part of it in).

ANNUITIES

HBR 34(2), sch 5
para 12
CTBR 25(2), sch 5
para 12 **13.75** If the claimant has an annuity, it means he or she has invested an initial lump sum with an insurance company who, in return, pay the claimant a regular income. Count this income in full as unearned income. Disregard as capital the surrender value of the annuity, and also the value of the right to receive income from it (para. 13.68).

HOME INCOME PLANS

HBR 34(2), sch 4
para 16
CTBR 25(2), sch 4
para 16 **13.76** If the claimant has a home income plan, it means he or she raised a loan using his or her home as security, has invested the loan as an annuity and, in return, gets a regular income: part of this income is used to repay the loan, part may be used to repay the claimant's mortgage, and part may be left over for the claimant to use. Count the income received by the claimant as unearned income, but only after deducting (if they have not been deducted at source):

♦ any tax payable on that income;

♦ any repayments on the loan which was raised to obtain the annuity; and

♦ any mortgage repayments made using the income (using the figures for the repayments which apply after tax has been deducted from them).

Disregard as capital the surrender value of the annuity, and the value of the right to receive income from it (para. 13.68).

LIFE INTEREST OR LIFERENT

13.77 If a claimant has a life interest or (in Scotland) liferent, it means he or she has the right to enjoy an asset during his or her or someone else's lifetime, after which it will pass to someone else. The actual value to the claimant (if any) of the life interest or liferent is counted as capital; and any actual income the claimant receives from it is counted as earned or unearned income as appropriate. Disregard as capital the value of the right to receive income from it (para. 13.68).

HBR sch 5 para 14
CTBR sch 5
para 14

REVERSIONARY INTEREST

13.78 If a claimant has a reversionary interest, it means he or he has an interest in property but will not possess it until some future event (for example, the death of a relative). Disregard in full the capital value of a reversionary interest. For HB and main CTB purposes, however, a property the claimant has rented out is not disregarded as a reversionary interest: the rules for dealing with such property are explained in paragraphs 13.60-61.

HBR sch 5 para 6
CTBR sch 5 para 6

Other items of income and capital

MAINTENANCE RECEIVED

13.79 If there is at least one child or young person in the claimant's family, disregard £15 of any maintenance received or due to be received from:

HBR sch 4 para 47
CTBR sch 4
para 46

♦ the claimant's former partner; or

♦ the claimant's partner's former partner; or

♦ the parent of any child or young person in the claimant's family (so long as that parent is not in the claimant's family).

The definitions of 'partner', 'child', 'young person', 'family' are in chapter 6. The £15 disregard applies whether the maintenance is payable to the claimant or to a child or young person. But payments direct to a third party (e.g. to a school for school fees, to a building society for mortgage payments, etc.) are fully disregarded. If two or more maintenance payments are received in any week, the maximum disregard is £15 per week. (There is no disregard compensating for the payment out of maintenance.)

CHARITABLE AND/OR VOLUNTARY PAYMENTS

HBR 40(6), sch 4
paras 13, 21, sch
5 para 32
CTBR 31(6), sch 4
paras 13, 22, sch
5 para 32

13.80 The following rules apply if the claimant receives payments which are charitable and/or voluntary. A lump sum payment counts as capital, as does a payment which is neither made nor due to be made at regular intervals. The following apply to a payment which is made or due to be made at regular intervals:

♦ if it is intended and used for the claimant's (or a member of the family's) food, ordinary clothing or footwear (excluding school uniform and sportswear), household fuel, eligible rent (apart from any non-dependant deduction), council tax, or water charges; disregard £20.00 (subject to the rules on aggregation: para. 13.105). Count the rest as unearned income;

♦ if it is for any other item, disregard it in full.

However, the above rules do not apply to payments in kind (i.e. goods not money) from a charity, which are always disregarded in full; nor to maintenance received (para. 13.79), nor to payments from the Trusts and Funds described in paragraph 13.40.

PAYMENTS IN KIND; CASH IN LIEU OF CONCESSIONARY COAL

13.81 Payments in kind (apart from those in paras. 13.80 and 14.26) count in full as unearned income. Cash in lieu of concessionary coal which is paid to a current employee of the British Coal Board counts as part of his or her earnings. If it is paid to an ex-miner or a miner's widow, it counts in full as unearned income.

VICTORIA & GEORGE CROSS PAYMENTS, ETC.

HBR sch 4 para 9,
sch 5 para 48
CTBR sch 4 para 9,
sch 5 para 48

13.82 Disregard these gallantry payments in full (as capital and income). Also disregard the lump-sum payments of up to £6,000 for those who have agreed not to receive any further payments of income from these. Also disregard analogous awards for gallantry from this country or another country.

TRUST FUNDS FOR PERSONAL INJURY, ETC.

HBR sch 5
paras 13, 46, 47
CTBR sch 5
paras 13, 46, 47

13.83 Disregard in full as capital any amount held in such a trust – and also the value of the right to receive income from it (para. 13.68). There is no time limit. Any payment actually received is counted as unearned income or capital as appropriate.

Compensation to children and young persons for personal injury or the death of a parent, if paid into a court on their behalf, is disregarded as capital.

OTHER TRUST FUNDS

13.84 Normally any amount in a trust fund is available and is therefore counted in full as capital. However, with a discretionary trust there may be no absolute entitlement to the money. In this case, only actual payments should be counted – as income or capital as appropriate.

PARENTAL CONTRIBUTIONS TO STUDENTS

13.85 If a claimant makes a contribution to his or her student son or daughter's maintenance (including assessed contributions towards a grant or student loan), disregard an equal amount from the claimant's income. (Technically, it is disregarded as far as possible from unearned income; then if necessary any balance is disregarded from earned income.) In the case of a student on a discretionary grant, or no grant, the maximum disregard is £41.35. Chapter 20 describes who counts as a student.

HBR sch 4
paras 17, 18
CTBR sch 4
paras 17, 18

EDUCATION MAINTENANCE AWARDS; ASSISTED PLACES ALLOWANCES

13.86 Disregard these in full. Examples of these include bursaries paid to 16-to-18-year-olds in non-advanced education, and payments towards a child's travel to school.

HBR sch 4 para 1
CTBR sch 4
para 10

SPORTS AWARDS

13.87 Sports Council sports awards are dealt with as follows:

HBR 2(1),
sch 4 para 71,
sch 5 para 59
CTBR 2(1),
sch 4 para 70,
sch 5 para 59

◆ any amount awarded in respect of the claimant's or a member of the family's food (excluding vitamins, minerals or other special performance-enhancing dietary supplements), ordinary clothing or footwear (excluding school uniform and sportswear), household fuel, rent, council tax, or water charges, is counted in full as income or capital as appropriate;

◆ any amount awarded for any other purpose is disregarded in full as unearned income, and as capital for 26 weeks from the date of payment.

COURT OF PROTECTION

13.88 If money is held on the claimant's behalf by the Court of Protection, count it in full as capital.

JURORS' ALLOWANCES

13.89 Disregard these in full except in so far as they compensate for loss of earnings or loss of a social security benefit.

HBR sch 4 para 38
CTBR sch 4
para 40

LOANS

13.90 The general principle is that if a claimant receives a genuine loan it increases his or her capital (until and to the extent that he or she spends it, perhaps on the thing it was lent for): the loan is not income. A pretended loan (for instance, a payment which is described as a loan but which will not be repaid) is not a loan: it is treated as capital or unearned income as appropriate (para. 13.6). Whether a payment is a genuine loan or a pretended loan can itself be a difficult question of fact. Completely different rules apply to student loans (chapter 20) and career development loans (para. 13.42).

OUTSTANDING INSTALMENTS OF CAPITAL

HBR 19(2), 34(1),
sch 5 para 17
TBR 11(2), 25(1),
sch 5 para 17
13.91 If, at the claimant's date of claim for HB/CTB (or at the date of any subsequent review of the claim), he or she is entitled to outstanding instalments of capital (i.e. instalments due after that date), the authority must consider whether the sum of the outstanding instalments and the claimant's other capital exceeds £16,000:

◆ if it does, the outstanding instalments are ignored as capital but are counted as income. The law does not lay down any particular way of doing this;

◆ if it does not, the outstanding instalments are counted in full as capital from the date of claim (or review).

13.92 When the above rule is applied to outstanding instalments of capital to which a child or young person is entitled (para. 13.106), the only difference is that £3,000 is substituted for £16,000.

OVERSEAS CAPITAL

HBR 42, sch 5
para 22
CTBR 33, sch 5
para 22
13.93 The following rules apply if a claimant possesses capital in a country outside the UK:

◆ if there is no prohibition in that country against bringing the money to the UK, value it at its market or surrender value in that country; then disregard 10 per cent if selling it would incur costs; then disregard any mortgage or other incumbrance secured on it; then disregard any charge which would be incurred in converting it into sterling; and count the remainder as capital;

◆ if there is such a prohibition, value it at what a willing buyer in the UK would give for it; then disregard 10 per cent if selling it would incur costs; then disregard any mortgage or other incumbrance secured on it; and count the remainder as capital.

OVERSEAS INCOME

HBR sch 4
paras 22, 32,
sch 5 para 15
CTBR sch 4
paras 23, 33,
sch 5 para 15
13.94 The following rules apply if a claimant is entitled to income payable in a country outside the UK:

◆ if there is no prohibition in that country against bringing the money to the UK, treat it as income in the normal way, allowing any disregard which may apply (including any earnings disregard in the case of earned income); also disregard any charge for converting it into sterling;

◆ if there is such a prohibition, disregard it in full; also disregard as capital the value of the right to receive income from it (para. 13.68).

OUTGOINGS

13.95   The only outgoings which can affect a claimant's income for HB/CTB purposes are payments for child care costs (para. 14.12) and payments by parents and spouses towards a student's maintenance (para. 13.85 and chapter 20). No allowance is made in the case of a person who pays maintenance or makes any other kind of payment to someone else (though see para. 13.24 in the case of certain additions within state benefits and para. 9.42 for additions to HB/CTB in the case of exceptional circumstances).

Notional income and capital

13.96   In the situations described below a claimant is treated, for HB/main CTB purposes, as possessing income and/or capital he or she does not in fact possess – known as 'notional' income and/or capital. The notional income or capital is assessed as if it was actual income or capital and any relevant disregards must be applied.

HBR 35(6),(7), 43(6)
CTBR 26(6),(7), 34(6)

DEPRIVATION

13.97   If a claimant deliberately deprives himself or herself of capital or income in order to qualify for HB (or for more HB), he or she is treated as still having it for HB purposes. The same applies independently for CTB. It is the claimant's intention which must be taken into account (not the item he or she spent the money on).

HBR 35(1), 43(1)
CTBR 26(1), 34(1

DIMINUTION OF NOTIONAL CAPITAL

13.98   If a claimant is treated as having notional capital for the above reason, the amount of notional capital taken into account is reduced each week, broadly speaking, by the amount of any HB, CTB, income support, income-related job-seeker's allowance, working families' tax credit and disabled person's tax credit lost as a result of the claimant being treated as having notional capital. For further details, please see GM paras. C2.79-102.

HBR 43A
CTBR 35

AVAILABLE ON APPLICATION

13.99   Any income or capital which a claimant could have on application (in other words, simply by applying for it) is treated as possessed by him or her from the date it could be obtained. This rule does not apply to income which could be obtained in the form of a DfEE rehabilitation allowance; nor does it apply to any payments (of income or capital) made to a provider of a New Deal arrangement (para 13.41); nor does it apply to income or capital which could be obtained from a discretionary trust (para. 13.84), a trust for personal injury (para. 13.83), or a personal pension scheme or retirement annuity contract; nor does it apply to any

HBR 35(2), 43(2)
CTBR 26(2), 34(2

kind of disregarded capital. Also, the DSS advises that this rule should not be applied in the case of income from any social security benefit unless the authority is sure about the amount the person could receive (GM para. C3.118). This rule is commonly used in the case of unclaimed child benefit.

PAYMENTS TO OR FOR THIRD PARTIES

HBR 35(3),(8),
43(3),(7)
CTBR 26(3),(8),
34(3),(7)

13.100 If income or capital is paid in A's name but used by B for food, household fuel, clothing or footwear (other than school uniform and sportswear), eligible rent (apart from any non-dependant deduction), council tax, or water charges, it is treated as belonging to B. This rule does not apply to concessionary coal (para. 13.81) or to payments to employers under the New Deal (para. 13.41); it does, however, apply to payments to a third party of occupational or personal pensions, except that when the intended beneficiary is bankrupt or subject to sequestration, payment is made to the trustee (or similar) and the beneficiary and any family have no other income.

UPRATINGS

HBR 35(4),(4A),
sch 4 para 59
CTBR 26(4),(4A),
sch 4 para 58

13.101 If the April uprating date for social security benefits is slightly different from that for HB/CTB, they are treated as uprated on the same date as HB/CTB.

WORK PAID AT LESS THAN THE GOING RATE

HBR 35(5)
CTBR 26(5)

13.102 If a claimant is paid less than the going rate for a job, he or she can be treated as having whatever additional pay is reasonable in the circumstances. The means of the employer must be taken into account; and this rule does not apply to voluntary work or to claimants provided with a New Deal arrangement (para. 13.41). When this rule is used, disregard notional tax and national insurance contributions (Appendix 4) and apply the earnings disregards (chapter 14).

RELATIONSHIP TO A COMPANY

HBR 43(4),(5)
CTBR 34(4),(5)

13.103 This applies to a claimant who is not the sole owner of, or a partner in, a company, but whose relationship to that company is analogous to someone who is. In such cases, the claimant's share of the capital of that company may be assessed as though he or she was the sole owner or partner and, if this is done, any actual share of the company he or she possesses is disregarded.

PENSION SCHEMES

HBR 35(2A)-(2C)
CTBR 26(2A)-(2C)

13.104 If a claimant aged 60 or more could get income from his or her pension scheme, but has failed to do so or chosen not to do so, then he or she is treated as having that income. Further details are given in the 1996-97 edition of this Guide (and in circular HB/CTB A25/95).

Aggregation of income and capital

13.105 As described at the beginning of this chapter, in assessing HB and main CTB, a claimant is treated as possessing any income and capital which belongs to himself or herself, any partner and, in certain cases, children and young persons. The details for children and young persons are dealt with below. (Paragraph 13.4 explains the rules which apply when a non-dependant's income and capital is treated as belonging to a claimant. Paragraph 13.109 explains a final rule about aggregation.)

CHILDREN'S AND YOUNG PERSONS' CAPITAL

13.106 Except as described in paragraph 13.92 (about outstanding instalments of capital), a child's or young person's capital is calculated in the same way – and with the same disregards – as for the claimant. But a child's or young person's capital is never counted as part of the claimant's capital.

HBR 19, 39
CTBR 11, 30

13.107 Instead, for any child or young person who has capital of over £3,000, the claimant is not awarded a dependant's allowance nor any disabled child premium (chapter 12). However, even if all the children/young persons in the family have capital over £3,000, the claimant keeps his or her family premium – whether this is payable at the basic rate or the protected lone parent rate.

CHILDREN'S AND YOUNG PERSONS' INCOME

13.108 A child's or young person's income is calculated in the same way – and with the same disregards – as for the claimant. But the following variations apply:

HBR 19, 36
CTBR 11, 30

◆ Payments of maintenance made to a child or young person are treated as if they were paid to the claimant (and dealt with as in para. 13.79).

◆ If a child or young person has capital over £3,000, his or her income is completely disregarded (apart from maintenance as just described).

◆ If a child or young person has left school and is in remunerative work (work averaging 16 hours per week or more), count any unearned income and earnings he or she has. Note that the earnings disregard is £15.00 if the claimant gets a disabled child premium for the child or young person in question; otherwise it is £5.00.

◆ For any other child or young person, count unearned income only.

◆ The child's or young person's income, calculated as above, is counted as part of the claimant's income – but only up to the amount of the dependant's allowance and any disabled child premium for the child or young person in question. Anything beyond that is disregarded.

Details of the allowances and premiums referred to above are in chapter 12.

THE OVER-RIDING £20 DISREGARD FROM CERTAIN INCOME OF THE FAMILY

HBR sch 4 para 33
CTB sch 4 para 34

13.109 In any particular claim for HB/main CTB, the maximum weekly disregard per claim is £20 from any or all of the following:

◆ certain charitable and voluntary payments (para. 13.80);

◆ student loans and covenants (chapter 20);

◆ certain war widow's and war disablement pensions (para. 13.28).

If two (or more) members of the family get any of these types of payment, the maximum weekly disregard is £20 for the whole family. In such cases, the disregard is used in whatever way is most favourable to the claimant. For example, if possible it should be used for a child or young person whose income does not exceed his or her personal allowance and (if applicable) disabled child premium.

14 Employed earners

14.1 This chapter describes the rules for assessing income (and capital) received by employed earners in connection with their employment. The rules apply to both HB and main CTB. The distinction between an employed earner and a person who is self-employed is described in paragraphs 15.3-4. The following matters are explained in this chapter:

◆ the assessment of earnings;

◆ earned income disregards generally;

◆ the child care disregard;

◆ the 30 hours per week disregard;

◆ particular kinds of earnings and expenses;

◆ starting work;

◆ absences from work and ending work.

HBR 28
CTBR 19 **14.2** This chapter applies equally to the employed earnings of the claimant, a partner or a child or young person in a claimant's family. *References to 'a claimant' should be read accordingly.* It does not apply to the employed earnings of a non-dependant or a second adult: the law does not lay down any particular way of assessing employed earnings in such cases (although it must be gross income, not net).

The assessment of earnings

HBR 21, 22, 28
CTBR 13, 14, 19 **14.3** The key steps for assessing employed earnings for HB/main CTB purposes are:

◆ averaging or estimating the gross earnings;

◆ deducting tax and national insurance contributions;

◆ deducting half of any approved pension contribution;

◆ converting the result, if necessary, to a weekly figure;

◆ deducting a fixed 'earned income disregard' and, if appropriate, amounts for child care costs and for certain people working 30 hours or more per week.

AVERAGING OR ESTIMATING GROSS EARNINGS

HBR 22
CTBR 14 **14.4** The general rule is that earnings are averaged over the five weeks immediately preceding the date of claim if the claimant is paid weekly; or the two months immediately preceding the date of claim if the claimant is paid monthly.

But if averaging the earnings over some other period would produce a more accurate estimate of what will be the claimant's earnings during his or her benefit period, they should be averaged over that period. (See also para. 13.102 in the case of work paid at less than the going rate.)

14.5   If the claimant has not been employed for long enough to assess earnings on the above basis, earnings should be estimated. This might be done by asking the claimant to provide an estimate from his or her employer: most authorities have standard forms which can be used for this.

14.6   If the claimant's earnings change during the course of the benefit period, an estimate should then be made of what they will be during the remainder of the benefit period.

DEDUCTING INCOME TAX AND NATIONAL INSURANCE CONTRIBUTIONS

14.7   If the claimant's actual earnings were averaged as described above, any income tax or class 1 national insurance contributions actually paid (or made from them) must be deducted from those earnings.   HBR 29
CTBR 20

14.8   If the claimant's earnings were estimated as described above, a notional amount for income tax and class 1 national insurance contributions must be deducted from those estimated earnings (appendix 4).

DEDUCTING HALF OF PENSION CONTRIBUTIONS

14.9   Whether the claimant's earnings were averaged or estimated, half of any contributions he or she makes to an occupational or personal pension scheme must be deducted from his or her earnings.   HBR 29
CTBR 20

CONVERSION TO A WEEKLY FIGURE

14.10   If a claimant's earnings are paid other than weekly, they must be converted to a weekly figure as described in paragraph 9.59.

Earned income disregards generally

14.11   A fixed earned income disregard must be deducted from each claimant's earnings. The amount depends on the type of case: the figures are given in table 14.1 (which also applies to self-employed earners). As shown in that table, only one of the amounts shown there is deducted from the combined earnings of a couple or polygamous marriage. (In certain cases, there are further disregards: paras. 14.12 and 14.17.)   HBR 29, sch 3
CTBR 20, sch 3

Table 14.1 WEEKLY EARNED INCOME DISREGARDS

For the details of the premiums referred to below, see chapter 12.

LONE PARENTS

The weekly disregard is £25 for all lone parents.

CERTAIN PEOPLE WHO ARE DISABLED OR LONG-TERM SICK

The weekly disregard is £15 in all the following cases. The maximum disregard in the following cases is £15 per single claimant or per couple.

◆ Single claimants and couples who are awarded a disability premium or severe disability premium.

◆ Couples who are awarded a higher pensioner premium – if they satisfy the condition for a disability premium (because one partner is aged under 60), but they are awarded a higher pensioner premium (because the other partner is aged 60 or more).

◆ Single claimants and couples who are awarded an enhanced pensioner premium or higher pensioner premium – if they qualified for the £15 disregard at any time in the 8 weeks up to and including the claimant's (or partner's) 60th birthday and if they have continued in employment since then. This applies regardless of breaks of any length in entitlement to HB or CTB. Also, it applies regardless of breaks in employment of up to 8 weeks.

CERTAIN CARERS, AND CERTAIN PEOPLE IN THE EMERGENCY SERVICES

The weekly disregard is £15 in the following cases. The maximum disregard in the following cases is £15 per single claimant or couple. If the earnings described below are less than £15, then up to £10 (for couples) or £5 (for single claimants) of the balance is applied to any other earnings they may have.

◆ From the earnings (from any source) of single claimants and couples who are awarded a carer premium – but in the case of a couple, only from the earnings of the partner(s) for whom the carer premium is awarded.

◆ From the earnings (of a single claimant or either partner in a couple) from employment in certain emergency services (as listed in para. 14.24).

COUPLES IN OTHER CASES

The weekly disregard is £10 for any couple not mentioned above. The maximum disregard is £10 per couple.

SINGLE CLAIMANTS IN OTHER CASES

The weekly disregard is £5 for any single claimant not mentioned above.

CHILDREN AND YOUNG PERSONS

The weekly disregard is £15 for each child/young person who qualifies for a disabled child premium. For each other child/young person, it is £5 (para. 13.106).

OTHER DISREGARDS

See paragraphs 14.12 and 14.17.

The child care disregard

14.12 In addition to the disregards in table 14.1, up to £70 or £105 per week per HB/main CTB claim is disregarded for child care costs in the circumstances described below. For the details of the premiums referred to below, see chapter 12. 'Remunerative work' is described in paragraphs 9.33 onwards.   HBR 21, 21A CTBR 13, 13A

WHO CAN QUALIFY?

14.13 The following groups qualify for the child care disregard in the circumstances described in the next two paragraphs:

◆ lone parents who are in remunerative work;

◆ couples if both are in remunerative work;

◆ couples if one of them (claimant or partner) is in remunerative work and the other one:

• satisfies the conditions for a disability premium, or

• is under 80 and satisfies the conditions for a higher pensioner premium, or

• would meet either of the above conditions apart from the fact that he or she has been in hospital etc. (para. 12.49) for more than six weeks, or

• would meet any of the above conditions apart from the fact that he or she is disqualified from incapacity benefit;

♦ couples if the partner is in remunerative work and the claimant:

  • is incapable of work, AND

  • has been incapable of work for a waiting period of 28 weeks. The waiting period may be made up of any number of periods of incapacity for work, so long as the gaps between them are no greater than 8 weeks long. 'Incapable of work' means satisfying the conditions for any rate of incapacity benefit (or its Northern Ireland equivalent).

IN WHAT CIRCUMSTANCES DO THEY QUALIFY?

14.14 The above groups qualify for the disregard if the claimant or partner pays one or more of the following to care for at least one child in his or her family, so long as that child satisfies the age condition:

♦ a registered child-minder; or

♦ a child-minding scheme for which registration is not required (e.g. run by a school or local authority); or

♦ any other out-of-school-hours scheme provided by a school on school premises or by a local authority but, in this case only, the child must be aged 8 or more.

The disregard does not, however, apply to payments in respect of compulsory education, nor to payments made by a claimant to his or her partner (or *vice versa*) if the child is the responsibility of at least one of them (para. 6.16).

THE AGE CONDITION

14.15 A child satisfies the age condition until the first Monday in September after his or her 15th birthday or, in the case of a child who meets the conditions for a disabled premium (para. 12.14), the first Monday in September after his or her 16th birthday.

AMOUNTS, ETC.

14.16 The amount of the disregard equals what the claimant or partner pays, up to a maximum of:

♦ £70 per week per HB/main CTB claim for claimants with one child who meets the above criteria (paras. 14.14-15); or

♦ £105 per week per HB/main CTB claim for claimants with two or more children who meet those criteria.

It is disregarded from the earnings (from employment or self-employment) of a claimant and/or partner who satisfies the conditions in paragraph 14.13. It cannot be disregarded from unearned income.

The amount the claimant or partner pays is averaged over whichever period, up to a year, gives the most accurate estimate of the charges during the benefit period, taking account of information provided by the person providing the care.

The 30 hours per week disregard

14.17 In addition to the earned income disregards mentioned above, a disregard of £11.25 per week is made if at least one of the following conditions is met (but see the following paragraph for the exception to this rule): HBR sch 3 para.
CTBR sch 3 para

◆ the claimant (or his or her partner) receives working families' tax credit (WFTC) or disabled person's tax credit (DPTC) which includes the addition for working 30 hours or more per week on average (although the amount of the addition to WFTC/DPTC is £11.05 for certain older awards, the earned income disregard is always £11.25);

◆ the claimant's applicable amount includes a family premium (para. 12.6) – but only if the claimant (or his or her partner) works 30 hours or more per week on average;

◆ the claimant's HB/CTB applicable amount includes a disability premium or higher pensioner premium (paras. 12.15-16) – but only if the claimant (or his or her partner) works 30 hours or more per week on average – and only if (in the case of a couple/polygamous marriage) at least one of them personally meets the conditions for the premium in question and works 16 hours or more per week on average.

14.18 For the above purposes, the question of whether anyone works 16 hours or more per week on average is decided as in paragraphs 9.33 onwards; and the question of whether anyone works 30 hours or more per week on average is decided in the same way (apart from the different number of hours).

14.19 The above £11.25 earned income disregard is not made if it (along with the other earned income disregard(s) which apply in any particular case) would result in a negative earned income figure. In such a case, a similar disregard is instead made from earned income (para. 13.30).

Particular kinds of earnings and expenses

BONUSES, TIPS AND COMMISSION

14.20 All forms of bonuses, tips and commission are included in the assessment of earnings. HBR 28(1)
CTBR 19(1)

ARREARS OF EARNINGS

HBR 68
CTBR 59

14.21 Pay arrears count as earnings for the period they cover if they relate to periods on or after 6th March 1995. They count as capital if they relate to periods before then.

TAX REFUNDS

HBR 40(2)
CTBR 31(2)

14.22 Tax refunds on earnings count as capital (not earnings).

EARNINGS PAID IN A LUMP SUM

HBR 34(3)
CTBR 25(3)

14.23 If earnings are paid in a lump sum (or in any other form which could in broad terms be characterised as capital), they are nonetheless counted as earnings. They are averaged over the period they cover.

EMERGENCY SERVICES ANNUAL BOUNTY

HBR 40(1)
CTBR 31(1)

14.24 Annual bounty paid by the emergency services counts as capital (not earnings) if it is paid annually or at longer intervals. For these purposes the 'emergency services' means part-time fire-fighters, auxiliary coast guards, part-time life-boat workers, and members of the Territorial Army or similar reserve forces.

NON-CASH VOUCHERS

HBR 28
CTBR 19
SI 1999 No. 1509

14.25 If an employee receives non-cash vouchers which are taken into account for the purposes of calculating his or her National Insurance contributions, their value is counted as employed earnings. The value of such vouchers should appear on pay slips (circular HB/CTB A17/99). In the case of a claimant on HB/CTB on 30th June 1999, this rule applies only from his or her first benefit period beginning on or after 1st July 1999: until then, such non-cash vouchers are wholly disregarded in the assessment of income.

PAYMENTS IN KIND

HBR 28
CTBR 19

14.26 With the exception of certain non-cash vouchers (para. 14.25) and concessionary coal (para. 13.81), payments in kind (i.e. payments of goods rather than money) are completely disregarded in the assessment of earnings. The DSS advises (circular HB/CTB A6/98) that credits received via Local Exchange Trading Schemes ('LETS') do not count as payments in kind, but should be given a cash value as earnings.

COUNCILLORS' ALLOWANCES

14.27 Councillors' allowances, apart from expenses payments, count as employed earnings. (For general advice on these, see GM para. C3.10).

WORK EXPENSES MET BY AN EMPLOYEE

14.28   Work expenses met by an employee may not be disregarded against the employee's earnings (but see paragraph 14.12 as regards child care expenses).

WORK EXPENSES MET BY AN EMPLOYER

14.29   The treatment of work expenses met by an employer is as follows:

♦   if they are for travel to work, or for the cost of caring for a child or other dependant, these must be added in as part of the employee's earnings;

♦   if they are for other items necessary for performance of the job, these are disregarded in full.

HBR 28, sch 4
para 3
CTBR 19, sch 4
para 3

EXPENSES IN UNPAID WORK

14.30   Expenses received by a person doing unpaid work are disregarded in full if they are paid by a non-profit-making voluntary or charitable organisation.

HBR sch 4 para
CTBR sch 4 para

Starting work

14.31   Although in HB and main CTB there are no specific rules about the period to which earned income should be attributed, the general principle is that, when a claimant starts work, his or her earnings should be taken into account from the beginning of his or her job – not (if different) the first pay day. (However, for Access to Work and similar schemes, see para. 13.41; for 'extended payments', see para. 17.54; and for the general rules about when changes of circumstances are taken into account, see chapter 17.)

ADVANCES OR LOANS FROM AN EMPLOYER

14.32   Advances and loans from an employer do not count as earnings. They count as capital if (and for as long as) the person has the money.

HBR 40(5)
CTBR 31(5)

Absences from work and ending work

14.33   The general rules are described below. More details are in tables 14.2 and 14.3. These rules may appear complicated. This is because (for example) during a holiday a person may get sick pay, or while on sick leave a person may get holiday pay. (For the general rules about when changes of circumstances are taken into account, see chapter 17.)

HBR 28
CTBR 19

HOLIDAY PAY

14.34   Holiday pay counts as earnings (but see tables 14.2 and 14.3). The exception is that it counts as capital (for as long as the person has the money) if

HBR 40(3)
CTBR 31(3)

it is payable more than four weeks after:

◆ the beginning of an absence or break from work (table 14.2), or

◆ ending work (table 14.3).

SICK PAY AND MATERNITY PAY

HBR 28(1)
CTBR 19(1)

14.35 Statutory sick and maternity pay and employer's sick and maternity pay count as earnings (but see tables 14.2 and 14.3).

RETAINERS

HBR 28(1)
CTBR 19(1)

14.36 Retainers (e.g. payments made in the holidays to employees of school meals services) count as earnings (but see tables 14.2 and 14.3).

STRIKE PAY

14.37 Strike pay does not count as earnings. It counts as unearned income (but see tables 14.2 and 14.3).

REDUNDANCY PAYMENTS

14.38 Redundancy payments (including those paid periodically rather than in a lump sum) do not count as earnings. They count as capital if (and for as long as) the person actually has the money (but see table 14.3 for the treatment of other payments which may be made on redundancy – such as payments in lieu of notice and compensation payments).

Table 14.2 ABSENCES FROM WORK

SHORT ABSENCES

◆ Because of the ordinary rules about changes of circumstances (para. 17.13), do not reassess earnings in any of the cases mentioned below unless the absence or break spans at least one Sunday/Monday midnight.

PERIODS WHILST SOMEONE RECEIVES A RETAINER

◆ Reassess earnings if they change (for example, if the person is paid less during the summer holidays).

HOLIDAYS, ABSENCES WITHOUT GOOD CAUSE, AND STRIKES

◆ Reassess earnings if they change (for example, if the person is paid less during holidays, or nothing during a strike). (See also the general rule about holiday pay: para. 14.34.)

SICK LEAVE, MATERNITY LEAVE, LAY OFF, SUSPENSION AND OTHER ABSENCES WITH GOOD CAUSE

The following rules apply so long as the employment has not terminated.

◆ *If the absence for any of these reasons began before the person's 'date of claim' (para. 7.54)*. Count only the following as earnings (and only if they are received during the absence):

  • retainers;

  • statutory or employer's sick or maternity pay;

  • holiday pay – but only if it is an absence from remunerative work (paras. 9.33 onwards). (See also the general rule about holiday pay: para. 14.34.)

◆ *If the absence for any of these reasons begins on or after the person's 'date of claim' (para. 7.54)*. Reassess earnings if they change (for example if the person receives a lower rate of pay for any of these reasons). (See also the general rule about holiday pay: para. 14.34.)

Table 14.3 ENDING WORK

'Remunerative work' is described in paragraphs 9.33 onwards.

RETIRING FROM REMUNERATIVE WORK AT OR AFTER THE AGE OF 60/65

◆ If the person retires and is entitled to a state pension immediately afterwards (including someone who has deferred entitlement to a state pension for up to five years), or is not entitled only because the necessary national insurance contributions have not been paid, all his or her earnings are disregarded during any period following the date of retirement.

ENDING REMUNERATIVE WORK IN OTHER CASES

◆ *If the termination occurred before the person's 'date of claim' (para. 7.54).* During any period following the date of termination, disregard all earnings except:

• retainers;

• payments in lieu of remuneration (but periodic redundancy payments count as capital: para. 14.38);

• payments in lieu of notice or compensating for loss of income;

• holiday pay (see also the general rule about holiday pay: para. 13.34);

• compensation awards made by industrial tribunals for unfair dismissal. Other compensation payments count as capital (not earnings).

◆ *If the termination occurs on or after the person's 'date of claim' (para 7.54).* Reassess to take changes and ending of earnings into account. There are no special rules.

ENDING WORK WHICH IS NOT REMUNERATIVE WORK

◆ *If the termination occurred before the person's 'date of claim' (para. 7.54).* Disregard all earnings apart from retainers.

◆ *If the termination occurs on or after the person's 'date of claim' (para. 7.54).* Reassess to take changes and ending of earnings into account. There are no special rules.

15 The self-employed

15.1 This chapter describes the rules for assessing income (and capital) received by the self-employed. The rules apply to both HB and main CTB. It describes the key steps for assessing income from self-employment, which are:

◆ deciding who is self-employed;

◆ deciding what assessment period to use;

◆ assessing the total income during that period;

◆ assessing allowable expenses during that period;

◆ calculating pre-tax profit (chargeable income) for that period;

◆ allowing for tax and national insurance;

◆ allowing for half of any pension contributions;

◆ calculating net profit.

HBR 19
CTBR 11 **15.2** This chapter applies equally to the self-employed income of the claimant, a partner or a child or young person in a claimant's family. *References to a 'claimant' should be read accordingly.* It does not apply to the self-employed income of a non-dependant or second adult: the law does not lay down any particular way of assessing income from self-employment in such cases (although it must be gross income, not net).

The special rules for self-employed people on the New Deal are given at the end of this chapter (paras. 15.39-41).

Who is self-employed?

CBA s.2(1)(b)
HBR 2(1), 30(2)
CTBR 2(1), 21(2)
HBR sch 5 para 7
TBR sch 5 para 7 **15.3** A 'self-employed earner' means someone who is gainfully employed in Great Britain except anyone employed under a contract of service (i.e. an employee) or employed in an office (e.g. a company director). A person may be a sole trader or in a business partnership (para. 15.27), and therefore be a self-employed earner. But someone who has set up a company, and is a director of it, counts as an employed earner (chapter 14). The DSS advises that the claimant's word should generally be accepted as to whether he or she is self-employed unless there are grounds for uncertainty (GM para. C3.37).

15.4 The following are not self-employed income: fostering payments and 'respite care payments' (para. 13.37); receipt of a Sports Council award (para. 13.87); rent received from someone living in the claimant's home (table 13.3);

and rent received on other property (paras. 13.60-61); unless, in the last case, the renting of property constitutes gainful self-employment.

A NOTE ON CAPITAL

15.5   Assets of a business wholly or partly owned by a claimant are disregarded in the assessment of capital if he or she:

HBR sch 5 para
CTBR sch 5 para

◆ is self-employed; or

◆ has ceased to be self-employed. In this case the assets are disregarded for as long as reasonably needed to dispose of them; or

◆ is not self-employed because of sickness or disability, but intends to be afterwards. In this case the assets are disregarded for 26 weeks from the date of any claim, including a renewal claim; or for such longer period as is reasonable to enable him or her to return to self-employment.

15.6   It is sometimes necessary to decide whether capital is personal or part of the business. The DSS advises that the test depends on whether the capital is (part of) 'a fund employed and risked in the business' (HB/CTB(93)16).

The assessment period

15.7   The income and expenses of a self-employed person are estimated by reference to an 'assessment period'. This is whatever period is appropriate to enable an accurate estimation of average weekly earnings in the benefit period. It must not be longer than one year. The general principle is that income and expenses in the past (in the assessment period) are used to calculate HB and CTB in the future (in the benefit period).

HBR 21(1), 23
CTBR 13(1), 15

PEOPLE WHO HAVE BEEN SELF-EMPLOYED FOR SOME TIME

15.8   For people who have been self-employed for some time, the assessment period is almost always in the past. For example, the DSS advises that the assessment period should normally be that of the last year's trading accounts, but that a shorter or different period may be used if appropriate (GM para. C3.40).

15.9   If claimants have not kept accounts, it is necessary for them to provide whatever evidence is reasonable in order to establish what their income and expenses were in the assessment period. In some cases their drawings from their business (what they have paid themselves) may provide some evidence. Drawings must not be used, however, where there is evidence of their actual business income.

PEOPLE SETTING UP IN BUSINESS

15.10   For people claiming HB or CTB at the point of setting up in business, the assessment period cannot be in the past: it must be in the future. To avoid delays for claimants, the DSS recommends that authorities should estimate income and expenses based on information from the claimant, and that HB or CTB should be awarded for only a short period, perhaps 13 weeks (GM para. C3.40).

IF THE NATURE OF A BUSINESS CHANGES

15.11 If the nature of a claimant's business changes, the authority should deal with it as though it was a new business from the point of change (para. 15.10). One example would be if a claimant changes from full-time to part-time self-employment.

CAN THE FIGURES BE ALTERED LATER?

15.12 Once the various figures have been assessed as described (paras. 15.8, 15.10), they can be altered later if they were based on a mistake of fact or law or there was an accidental error, or if there has subsequently been a relevant change of circumstances (e.g. as in para. 15.11). It is incorrect in any other case to revise the figures.

A NOTE ON ACCOUNTING METHODS

15.13 Self-employed people commonly account for their income (and expenses) using one of the following methods:

◆ a 'cash' basis – counting income as being received on the day they receive the money (and counting expenses as being incurred on the day they pay the money out); or

◆ an 'on paper' basis – counting income as being received on the day they issue their bill or invoice for it (and counting expenses as being incurred on the day they receive a bill or invoice for them); or

◆ the basis required (roughly speaking) for income tax purposes – counting income as being received on the day they issue their bill or invoice or the day they receive the money, whichever happens first (and counting expenses as being incurred on the day they receive a bill or invoice or the day they pay the money out, whichever happens first).

15.14 On the one hand, there is a body of opinion that HB and CTB should reflect a claimant's cash flow – the first method above. On the other hand, there is evidence that the HB and CTB regulations were originally written on the assumption that claimants use (or should use) the second or third method above. (For example, the rules about debts referred to in items (k) and (l) of table 15.1 would not be needed for claimants operating accounts on a purely cash flow basis.) It is probably reasonable to say that the method chosen by the claimant does not matter for HB/CTB purposes – so long as he or she operates that method consistently over the years.

Assessing total income

15.15 The total income (or 'gross earnings') of the employment means all the income coming into the business during the assessment period. There are two general points to bear in mind.   HBR 30(1), 31(1),(3) CTBR 21(1), 22(1),(3)

◆ Only payments of income are taken into account. A payment of capital into a business is not a payment of income. It is disregarded under the general rule about disregarded capital (para. 15.5).

◆ Only income 'derived from' the employment is taken into account. Income from some other source (e.g. as described in para. 15.16) falls under whatever rules apply to that kind of income (chapter 13).

GRANTS, LOANS AND THE ACCESS TO WORK SCHEME

15.16 The following additional points apply:

◆ Grants are not 'derived from' self-employment. They should be regarded as a separate source of income or capital – typically voluntary or charitable (para. 13.80).

◆ Genuine loans are not income (para. 13.90). Money from a loan forms part of the claimant's capital. If it is a loan to the business it is therefore disregarded (para. 15.5).

◆ Disabled people setting up in self-employment can get payments under the government's Access to Work scheme: these are disregarded as income (para. 13.41).

BUSINESS START-UP ALLOWANCES

15.17 Any payments of a business start-up allowance received by the claimant during the assessment period (except for capital payments) must be counted as part of the total income of the employment. They must not be counted as a separate source of income. But they are not included as income if payments ceased before the date of claim for HB or CTB.   HBR 30(1) CTBR 21(1)

15.18 Business start-up allowances are still sometimes called enterprise allowance. They may in some cases be used up completely to pay for business expenses (with the effect that the self-employed person has no profit at all).

Example: Business start-up allowances

The authority decides that a claimant's assessment period is the last year for which she has accounts. In that year she received a total of 52 payments of a business start-up allowance of £20 per week (total

£1,040), plus other gross earnings of £4,000; and her allowable business expenses were £1,500.

If at her date of claim she is still receiving business start-up payments, then her total income is £5,040. After deducting her expenses, she has a pre-tax profit of £3,540.

But if she ceased receiving business start-up payments before her date of claim, then her total income is £4,000. After deducting her expenses, she has a pre-tax profit of £2,500.

Assessing allowable expenses

HBR 31(3),(7)
CTBR 22(3),(7)

15.19 Having worked out the total income in the assessment period, the next step is to allow for the expenses incurred in running the business during the assessment period. The two general principles are:

◆ expenses are allowed for so long as they are 'wholly and exclusively incurred' for the purpose of the business;

◆ but the authority cannot allow for an expense if it is not satisfied, given the nature and the amount, that it has been 'reasonably incurred'.

15.20 Subject to those points, typical examples of expenses which would be allowable are:

◆ staff costs;

◆ rent, rates and mortgage payments on business premises;

◆ the purchase of stocks and supplies;

◆ fuel costs (see also para. 15.22);

◆ cleaning and protective clothing;

◆ transport connected with the business;

◆ advertising, telephone, postage and stationery;

◆ carriage and delivery costs;

◆ hire and leasing charges;

◆ legal and accountancy fees;

◆ bank charges;

◆ insurance; and

◆ subscriptions to trade and professional organisations.

HBR 31(4)-(6),(8)
CTBR 22(4)-(6),(8)

15.21 The law contains rules about special kinds of expenses. These are summarised in table 15.1.

Table 15.1 SPECIAL TYPES OF EXPENSES

	Allowable?
(a) Interest payments on any business loan	yes
(b) Sums (other than interest payments) employed or intended to be employed in setting up or expanding the business	no
(c) Income spent on repairing an existing business asset (except to the extent that any sum is payable under an insurance policy for this)	yes
(d) Capital repayments on loans for repairing an existing business asset (except to the extent that any sum is payable under an insurance policy for this)	yes
(e) Capital repayments on loans for replacing business equipment or machinery	yes
(f) Capital repayments on any other business loans	no
(g) Any other capital expenditure	no
(h) Depreciation of any capital asset	no
(i) Losses incurred before the beginning of the assessment period	no
(j) Excess of VAT paid over VAT received in the assessment period	yes
(k) Proven bad debts	yes
(l) Other debts	no
(m)Expenses incurred in the recovery of any debt	yes
(n) Business entertainment	no
(o) Any sum for a domestic or private purpose	no

Example: Expenses

A self-employed technical writer's accounts include the following expenditure. Before the purchase of her word-processor and laser printer, she used to do all her writing by hand. The references (a), (b), etc, are to table 15.1.

A cash payment to buy her word processor.	Not allowable (g).
Repayments on the loan she took out to buy her laser printer.	The capital element of the repayments is not allowable (f). The interest element is allowable (a).
Repayments on a smaller loan covering half the cost of repairing her laser printer, which was not insured.	Capital and interest elements are both allowable (d), (a).
A cash payment covering the other half of the cost of the laser printer repair.	Allowable (c)
Repayments on a general purpose business loan to help with her cash-flow.	The interest element of the repayments is allowable (a). The capital element is not (f).
A figure for depreciation in the value of the word-processor and laser printer.	Not allowable (h).

WORKING FROM HOME

15.22 A rent-paying claimant who works from home may regard part of his or her rent as a business expense. Whether it is an allowable expense depends on the circumstances of the case. It is clear that if part of the home is exclusively used for the business (e.g. an annexe), then the rent on this is an allowable expense but is also disregarded in the assessment of the claimant's eligible rent (para. 11.102). In all cases, however, an allowance should be made for a reasonable proportion of heating the home and of similar overheads.

DRAWINGS TAKEN BY THE CLAIMANT FROM THE BUSINESS

15.23 Claimants may take 'drawings' from their business as a kind of wages or salary for themselves. These must not be allowed as a business expense.

EMPLOYING A HUSBAND, WIFE OR UNMARRIED PARTNER

15.24 If the claimant pays his or her husband, wife or unmarried partner to work for the business, this is allowable as a business expense. It will then count as the partner's earnings. The rules are different if the couple are in a business partnership (para. 15.27).

HBR 31(8)
CTBR 22(8)

SELF-EMPLOYED CHILDMINDERS

15.25 For claimants who are self-employed childminders, instead of working out what their actual expenses are, two-thirds of their total income is disregarded in lieu of expenses. No actual expenses can be allowed for.

HBR 31(9)
CTBR 22(9)

Example: A self-employed childminder

A claimant earns £120 per week from working as a self-employed childminder. She is a lone parent with no other form of earned income. She does not make pension contributions. She does not use a childminder for her own children. Her income from childminding is assessed as follows:

♦ From the gross amount, two-thirds (£80) is disregarded.
  The remaining amount is   £40.00

♦ £40 per week is too low for a deduction to be made for
  notional tax and national insurance (tables 15.2, 15.3).

♦ She qualifies for an earned income disregard.
  For a lone parent (table 14.1) this is   £25.00

♦ So her assessed weekly earned income for HB/main CTB   _____
  purposes is   £15.00

Pre-tax profit

15.26 The next step is to work out the claimant's 'pre-tax profit' (referred to in the regulations as 'chargeable income'):

HBR 31(1)(a),(3)
CTBR 22(1)(a),(3)

Total income (paras. 15.13-18)

MINUS

♦ allowable expenses (paras. 15.19-25)

= pre-tax profit.

BUSINESS PARTNERSHIPS

HBR 31(1)(b),(4)
CTBR 22(1)(b),(4)

15.27 If the claimant is self-employed in a partnership, the pre-tax profit (as defined above) should be assessed for the partnership and then split between the business partners. This split should reflect how the business partners actually split their income. Similar rules apply to 'share fishermen'. This split is required even if the business partners are a couple because it will ensure the correct calculation of notional tax and national insurance (para. 15.32). The rules are different if one partner in a couple employs the other (para. 15.24).

NIL INCOME FROM SELF-EMPLOYMENT

15.28 If the claimant's allowable expenses exceed his or her total income, then pre-tax profit is nil. So his or her income from the self-employment is nil.

MORE THAN ONE EMPLOYMENT

HBR 31(10)
CTBR 22(10)

15.29 If a self-employed claimant is engaged in any other employment or self-employment, the losses from one cannot be set against the income from the other.

IF THE PRE-TAX PROFIT APPEARS UNREPRESENTATIVE

HBR 23(1)
CTBR 13(1)

15.30 If the pre-tax profit appears unlikely to represent income during the benefit period, the authority should consider whether selecting a different assessment period would produce a more accurate estimate of this (para. 15.7).

Notional income tax and notional NICs

HBR 32
CTBR 23

15.31 Allowances are made for income tax and national insurance contributions ('NICs'). However, the authority must work these out itself, based on the claimant's pre-tax profit. The figures calculated by the authority are known as 'notional income tax' and 'notional NICs'. They usually differ from the actual income tax and NICs paid by the claimant. One reason for the difference is that an amount for depreciation and certain expenses which are allowed by the Inland Revenue cannot be allowed for HB/CTB purposes.

THE CALCULATIONS

HBR 26, 32
CTBR 18, 23

15.32 The calculations are given in tables 15.2 and 15.3. An example is given near the end of this chapter. The tables apply to annual amounts of pre-tax profit. If a claimant's assessment period was a different length (e.g. three months), convert pre-tax profit into an annual figure before doing the calculations. In the case of a couple, work through the calculations separately for each one who has self-employed income.

15.33   Tables 15.2 and 15.3 give the figures for the tax year from 6th April 1999 to 5th April 2000. (At the time this Guide was written, insufficient information was available to give the figures for 2000-01.) Authorities must use the figures applying at the date of claim for HB/CTB (para. 7.44). However they may disregard for up to 30 benefit weeks any change in tax and NICs caused by a change in the law (typically the Budget). So 1999-2000's tax and NI figures may continue to be used if the date of claim occurs on or before Sunday 5th November 2000.

Table 15.2 CALCULATING NOTIONAL INCOME TAX (1999-2000 TAX YEAR)

(a) Start with the annual pre-tax profit figure.

(b Subtract £4,335*.

(c) If there is a remainder:
   multiply the first £1,500 (or all, if it is under £1,500) by 10%;
   multiply the rest (if any) by 23%, and add to the result of the above.

(d) From the result, subtract £197** – but only if the person is:
   a lone parent; or
   the only or main self-employed partner† in:

   • a married couple (with or without children/young persons), or

   • an unmarried couple with at least one child/young person.

(e) The result is the amount of notional tax.

Notes

*   £4,335 is the single person's tax allowance.

** £197 is 10% of the additional allowance (£1,970) for the lone parents and couples described. Ignoring this at step (b) and deducting £197 at step (d) achieves the result of allowing this allowance at only 10%.

†   The 'only or main self-employed partner' at step (d) means the partner who in fact qualifies (for actual income tax purposes) for the allowance just described.

   The 40% tax rate is not used in assessing notional income tax, nor are any allowances taken into account other than as above.

Pension contributions

HBR 31(11),(12)
CTBR 22(11),(12) **15.34** An allowance is made for half of any pension contributions payable by self-employed claimants towards:

♦ a self-employed personal pension scheme if they are payable on a periodical basis (e.g. monthly). No allowance is made for the lump sum payments some self-employed people make (often for tax purposes); or

♦ an annuity for a retirement pension for the claimant or a dependent (including husbands, wives and unmarried partners) – if the scheme is approved by the Inland Revenue as eligible for tax relief. People can no longer enter such schemes, but those who entered them in the past may still be in them.

Table 15.3: CALCULATING NOTIONAL NI CONTRIBUTIONS (1999-2000 TAX YEAR)

CLASS 2 NICS

If the annual pre-tax profit figure is £3,770* or more, then the amount of notional class 2 NICs is £340.60**.

CLASS 4 NICS

(a) Start with the annual pre-tax profit figure (unless this is greater than £26,000†, in which case start with £26,000).

(b) Subtract £7,530†.

(c) If there is a remainder, multiply it by 6%. The result is the amount of notional class 4 NICs.

Notes

The person may have class 2 notional NICs alone, or may have both class 2 and class 4 notional NICs.

*   £3,770 is the lower threshold for class 2 NICs. If the person's pre-tax profit is lower, then the notional class 2 NICs figure is nil (regardless of whether he or she has in fact applied to the Contributions Agency for exemption).

** £340.60 is 52 times £6.55 (the weekly rate of class 2 NICs), there being 52 Sundays in the 1999-2000 tax year.

†   £7,530 is the lower threshold, and £26,000 the upper threshold, for class 4 NICs.

15.35   The allowance applies only whilst the claimant is making such payments. So if a claimant starts or ceases making such payments whilst he or she is on HB or CTB (or the amount of the payments changes), this is taken into account as a change of circumstances and HB and/or CTB must be reassessed.

15.36   To find the annual equivalent of pension contributions:

◆   for contributions payable calendar monthly, multiply the monthly contribution by 12;

◆   in any other case, divide the contribution by the number of days it covers (e.g. in the case of a weekly contribution, divide by 7) and multiply by 366.

Example: Pension contributions

When a claimant claims HB and CTB, he is paying pension contributions of £50 per month. The annual equivalent is 12 x £50 = £600. Half of this (£300) is allowable in calculating his annual net profit.

After making three monthly payments, he reduces his payments to £40 per month. The annual equivalent is 12 x £40 = £480. Half of this (£240) is allowable in calculating his annual net profit. His claim must be reassessed taking his new annual net profit into account from the Monday after the day on which the first payment of £40 was due.

Net profit

15.37   The final step is to work out the claimant's net profit. It is always advisable to work this out initially on an annual basis.

HBR 31(1)-(3)
CTBR 22(1)-(3)

Pre-tax profit (paras. 15.26-30)

MINUS

◆   notional income tax and notional NI contributions (paras. 15.31-33)

◆   half of pension contributions (paras. 15.34-36)

=   net profit.

CONVERSION TO A WEEKLY FIGURE

15.38   The result must be converted to a weekly figure. Divide the annual figure by 366 and then multiply the result by 7. This weekly figure is the one used in calculating entitlement to HB and main CTB (subject to the earned income disregards: chapter 14).

HBR 25(2)
CTBR 17(2)

Example: Notional tax and NI contributions and net profit: 1999-2000

A married woman's annual pre-tax profit is £9,000. She contributes £480 per year to a personal pension scheme. Her husband has no source of earned income.

NOTIONAL INCOME TAX (TABLE 15.2)

(a) Start with the annual pre-tax profit figure. This is £9,000.

(b) Subtract £4,335. This leaves £4,665.

(c) Of this,

multiply the first £1,500 by 10%

10% of £1,500 is:	£150.00
multiply the rest (£4,665 − £1,500 = £3,165) by 23%	
23% of £3,165 is	£727.95
Adding these together gives:	£877.95
(d) In her case, subtract:	£197.00
(e) So her notional tax is:	£680.95

NOTIONAL CLASS 2 NICS (TABLE 15.3)

The annual pre-tax profit figure (£9,000) is greater than £3,770, so the amount of her notional class 2 NICs is £340.60.

NOTIONAL CLASS 4 NICS (TABLE 15.3)

(a) Start with the annual pre-tax profit figure (which is not greater than £26,000). This is £9,000.

(b) Subtract £7,530.

(c) Multiply the remainder (which is £1,470) by 6%.
    This is £88.20 − which is the amount of her notional class 4 NICs.

NET PROFIT	
Annual pre-tax profit	£9,000.00
minus notional income tax	£680.95
minus notional class 2 NICs	£340.60
minus notional class 4 NICs	£88.20
minus half of annual contributions to pension scheme	£240.00
Equals annual net profit:	£7,650.25
On a weekly basis this is (£7,650.25 ÷ 366 x 7 =)	£146.32
She qualifies for an earned income disregard of	£10.00
So her weekly net profit (after the disregard) is	£136.32

People on the self-employed route of the New Deal

15.39 The following rules apply to people on the 'self-employed route' of the 'Employment Option' of the New Deal (para. 13.41 and table 13.3). Most such people should be entitled to income support or income-based jobseeker's allowance: in their case, all their income and capital is disregarded for HB and main CTB purposes. The following rules apply in the uncommon cases in which such people are not on either of those benefits: in their case, their income and capital is assessed, for HB and main CTB purposes, in a special way (which differs from the rules in the other parts of this chapter).

BACKGROUND

15.40 A person on the self-employed route gets assistance from the Jobcentre with his or her 'commercial activity'. The Jobcentre keeps a 'special account' for that commercial activity, the main features of which are as follows:

◆ any income he or she makes on the commercial activity is payable into the special account;

◆ payments may be taken from the special account to meet business expenses or the repayment of business loans relating to the commercial activity;

◆ the amounts in the special account are treated as capital for IS and JSA(IB) purposes;

◆ when he or she reaches the end of the self-employed route, the balance in the special account is assessed for IS and JSA(IB) purposes in a special way as income for the future.

ASSESSMENT FOR HB/MAIN CTB PURPOSES

HBR 40(7), sch 4
paras 64,66, sch 5
paras 7,53,55
CTBR 31(7), sch 4
paras 64,66, sch 5
paras 7,53,55

15.41 The following rules apply in the assessment of HB and main CTB for people on the self-employed route (for references to 'commercial activity' and 'special account', see above):

◆ the gross receipts of the commercial activity are treated as capital for HB and main CTB purposes – but only to the extent that they are payable into the special account;

◆ payments the person takes from the special account are disregarded as unearned income for HB and main CTB purposes – but only if they are to meet expenses wholly and necessarily incurred in the commercial activity; or are used or intended to be used to maintain repayments on a loan taken out to establish or carry on the commercial activity;

◆ any capital acquired by the person for the purposes of establishing or carrying on the commercial activity (from whatever source) is disregarded for HB and main CTB purposes for 52 weeks from the date on which it was acquired;

◆ any business assets acquired by the person for establishing or carrying on the commercial activity (from whatever source) are disregarded as capital for HB and main CTB purposes for as long as the person remains on the self-employed route and then for as long as is reasonable in the circumstances to allow for their disposal (or, if he or she remains self-employed, see para. 15.5).

16 Determination, notification and payment

16.1 This chapter considers the process of determination, notification and payment. It covers the following:

◆ how quickly claims and changes of circumstances should be dealt with;

◆ who must be notified of the authority's determination;

◆ information that must be provided to the claimant and others;

◆ how, and when, HB/CTB should be paid;

◆ when a payment on account should be made in a rent allowance case;

◆ how often a rent allowance should be paid;

◆ when a landlord is paid direct;

◆ when a payment of HB/CTB is withheld or suspended;

◆ who else may receive payment of a rent allowance/CTB.

How quickly should the claim be dealt with and benefit paid?

16.2 Once the authority has received a claim and all the information and evidence it reasonably requires from the claimant it must:

HBR 76(3)
CTBR 66(3)
◆ reach a decision on entitlement within 14 days or as soon as possible after that;

HBR 77(a)
CTBR 67(a)
◆ notify everybody affected as soon as the claim is decided; and

HBR 88(3)
◆ in the case of HB, make payment within 14 days of the receipt of the claim or as soon as possible after that.

Authorities are required to give priority to 'in-work' claims made by people who have claimed extended payments (para. 17.54). The aim is to ensure that any ongoing entitlement to benefit is available at the end of the four week extended payment period. This requirement to prioritise such claims is encouraged through a system of set time limits underpinned by subsidy rewards and penalties (table 21.2) known as 'fast tracking' (HB/CTB A6/96).

In all rent allowance cases if the authority is unable to meet the 14 day determination timetable it must normally make a payment on account (para. 16.16).

EXCEPTIONS TO THE REQUIREMENT TO DETERMINE

16.3   The authority does not have to meet the above time limits however where a claim: HBR 76(2)
CTBR 66(2)

◆ is not made in the proper time and manner (para. 7.33); or

◆ is not supported by reasonably required information or evidence from the claimant (para. 7.37); or

◆ has been withdrawn (para. 7.51); or

◆ is made more than 13 benefit weeks prior to the expiry of the claimant's current benefit period (para. 7.70).

TIME PERIOD IN WHICH OTHER DETERMINATIONS SHOULD BE MADE

16.4   From time to time authorities have to make other determinations on a claim, e.g. a reassessment of entitlement following a change of circumstance. Notification of such determinations must be made within 14 days or as soon as possible after that. Notification is not required, however, where a change in CTB entitlement relates solely to a reduction in the council tax where government 'tax-capping' or a delayed award of transitional relief, disability reduction or discount leads to an overpayment of CTB. HBR 77(1)(b)
CTBR 67(1)(b)

REMEDIES FOR DELAYS

16.5   Authorities are expected to meet the time limits in the majority of cases. Delays are normally only justifiable, for example, in periods of peak pressure such as the annual up-rating or while handling a high level of enquiries following a take-up campaign. Many authorities fail to meet the time limit and it may be necessary for outside agencies and individuals to place pressure upon such authorities via campaigns and legal and other remedies to ensure that they meet this obligation in the future. Such remedies include:

◆ complaints to the local government ombudsman;

◆ action in the High Court or Court of Session in Scotland for judicial review to require authorities to make a determination; and

◆ action in the County Court or Sheriff Court to require authorities to make a payment if they have agreed that the claimant is entitled.

16.6   *R v Liverpool City Council ex parte Pauline Linda Johnson and others,* QBD, 23rd June 1994 considered a sample of the many applications made for judicial review of the authority's failure to meet its statutory duties. The judge said that 'in their discretionary decisions as to allocation of resources, authorities must, in making their arrangements for carrying the housing benefit regulations into effect, have specific regard to the time limits'. In response to the authority's assertion that it should not be singled out because the Audit Commission had found that many authorities were in breach of the regulations, the judge said 'if the legal rights of disadvantaged people to expeditious determination of their claims for benefit are being denied across the country, the need for the court's intervention is all the greater'.

Who should be notified and how?

PERSONS AFFECTED

HBR 77, 2(1)
CTBR 67, 2(1)

16.7 The authority is required to notify all persons affected by a determination. A 'person affected' means any of the following where their rights, duties or obligations are affected by a determination:

◆ the claimant;

◆ where a claimant, or would-be claimant, is unable to act on his or her own behalf:

 • a receiver appointed by the Court of Protection;

 • an attorney with a general power or a power to claim or as the case may be receive benefit appointed under the Powers of Attorney Act 1971 or the Enduring Powers of Attorney Act 1985;

 • a person appointed by the Council to act on behalf of someone who is unable to act on his or her own behalf;

 • a person appointed by the Secretary of State (in practice a manager at the Benefit Agency office) to act on behalf of someone who is unable to act on his or her own behalf;

◆ the landlord – but only in relation to a determination (not) to make direct payments (where the payment is made to an agent acting for the landlord the agent is the person affected); or

◆ anyone – including the landlord – from whom the Council has determined that an overpayment is recoverable.

16.8 The 'person affected' label is not confined to natural persons; it also applies to legal entities such as housing associations and letting companies.

INFORMATION TO BE PROVIDED

HBR 77, sch 6
CTBR 67, sch 6

16.9 The authority must send a written notification to a person affected by a determination. Table 16.1 illustrates the minimum amount of information that an authority must make available automatically following its determination of a claim. In practice, it is a regrettable fact that many notification letters contain insufficient information and/or are very hard to understand. It is also regrettable that many authorities do not keep copies of their own notification letters, thereby placing their own staff in the impossible position of being unable to explain to claimants what they have said to them.

16.10 Notifications are also required, for instance, where rent allowances are paid direct to the landlord (para. 16.27); where, in the case of HB or main CTB the income of a non-dependant is treated as the claimant's (para. 13.4); and in any case where a recoverable overpayment exists. HBR 77, sch 6
CTBR 67, sch 6

16.11 All notifications must include statements explaining the right of the person affected to: HBR sch 6 part 1
CTBR sch 6 part

◆ obtain a written statement of the authority's reasons for the determination; and

◆ make written representations.

Table 16.1 INFORMATION TO BE NOTIFIED FOLLOWING DETERMINATION OF A CLAIM

(HB AND CTB NOTIFICATIONS SHOULD BE SEPARATE)

A. WHERE THE CLAIMANT IS ENTITLED TO HB/MAIN CTB

Claimant on income support (IS)/income-based JSA (JSA(IB))

◆ Weekly eligible rent/weekly amount of council tax.

◆ HB – amount and explanation of fuel deductions from eligible rent where they have been estimated using the standard figures in table 11.7, together with the fact that the amount may be varied if the claimant supplies reasonable evidence.

◆ Amount and category of any non-dependant deductions.

◆ Normal weekly amount of benefit.

◆ Rent allowances – date of payment and period for which payment is made.

◆ First day of entitlement.

◆ End of benefit period.

◆ The claimant's duty to notify the authority of changes of circumstance and examples of the kinds of change that should be reported.

◆ CTB – details of any 'rounding' of figures.

Claimant not on IS/JSA(IB)

◆ The information given where the claimant is on IS/JSA(IB).

◆ The applicable amount and how it is worked out.

◆ Weekly earnings.

◆ Weekly unearned income.

B. WHERE THE CLAIMANT IS NOT ENTITLED TO HB/MAIN CTB BECAUSE OF INCOME OR THE MINIMUM HB PAYMENT RULE

IS/JSA(IB) claimants

◆ Weekly eligible rent/weekly amount of council tax.

◆ HB – amount and explanation of fuel deductions from eligible rent where they have been estimated using the standard figures in table 11.7, together with the fact that the amount may be varied if the claimant supplies reasonable evidence.

◆ Amount and category of non-dependant deductions.

◆ HB – normal weekly amount of benefit and the fact that it is not payable because it is below the minimum.

Claimants not on IS/JSA(IB)

◆ The information given where the claimant is on IS/JSA(IB).

◆ The applicable amount and how it is worked out.

◆ Weekly earnings.

◆ Weekly unearned income.

C. WHERE THE CTB CLAIMANT IS BETTER OFF ON SECOND ADULT REBATE

◆ The fact that the claimant is better off on second adult rebate and the amount.

◆ The lesser amount of main CTB.

D. WHERE THE CTB CLAIMANT IS ENTITLED TO SECOND ADULT REBATE

◆ Normal weekly amount of council tax rounded to nearest penny.

◆ Normal weekly amount of second adult rebate rounded to nearest penny.

◆ Rates of second adult rebate and related gross income levels.

◆ First day of entitlement.

◆ End of benefit period.

◆ Gross income of any second adult or the fact that the second adult is on IS/JSA(IB).

◆ The claimant's duty to notify the authority of changes of circumstance and examples of the kinds of change that should be reported.

◆ Details of any 'rounding' of figures.

E. ITEMS TO BE NOTIFIED WHERE SECOND ADULT REBATE IS NOT PAYABLE

Where gross income of second adult(s) too high

◆ Normal weekly amount of council tax rounded to nearest penny.

◆ Rates of second adult rebate and related gross income levels.

◆ Gross income of any second adult or the fact that the second adult is on IS/JSA(IB).

Where claimant better off on main CTB

◆ The fact that the claimant is better off on main CTB.

◆ The lesser amount of second adult rebate.

F. CLAIMANT NOT ENTITLED FOR SOME OTHER REASON

◆ The reason why the claimant is not entitled.

G. ITEMS TO BE NOTIFIED IN ALL CASES

◆ The right, time and manner in which to request a written explanation of a determination.

◆ The right, time and manner in which to make written representations.

◆ Any other appropriate matters.

Time and manner of payment

PAYMENT OF HB

HBR 88 **16.12** Authorities may decide on the time and manner in which to make payments of HB on the basis of the circumstances of the individual case. They are expected to have regard to the reasonable needs and convenience of the person they are paying, as well as the time and frequency with which the liability to make payments arises.

16.13 The requirement that the authority must have regard to the reasonable needs and convenience of the person receiving payment means that they should not make unreasonable demands, such as collection from a place not easily accessible, or insistence upon crossed cheques or credit transfer arrangements when the payee does not have a bank account (GM para. A6.27).

16.14 In the case of rent rebates, payment is usually in the form of a rebate applied to the rent account. Where the claimant has already made payments for the benefit period, for example where rent has been paid four months in advance, benefit should normally be paid direct to the claimant unless he or she is in arrears or agrees to the amount being credited to his or her rent account (GM para. A6.30).

HBR 89 **16.15** Where the claimant is a private tenant, he or she is normally paid direct, though in certain circumstances a rent allowance may be paid to the landlord (paras. 16.27-33).

PAYMENTS ON ACCOUNT (INTERIM PAYMENTS)

HBR 91(1) **16.16** A payment on account, (sometimes known as an interim payment), must be paid within 14 days if the following circumstances are met:

◆ the authority is unable to determine the amount of benefit payable within 14 days of receipt of the claim; and

◆ that inability has not risen out of the claimant's failure to provide necessary information or evidence (which the authority has requested from the claimant in writing) without good cause.

The authority must pay an amount it considers reasonable on the basis of whatever information is available to it about the individual claimant's circumstances, such as sources of income, and any relevant determination made by a rent officer (para. 21.25).

16.17 Payments on account are not discretionary and must be paid if the circumstances set out in paragraph 16.16 apply. In the case of *R v London Borough of Haringey ex parte Azad Ayub*, (1992) 25 HLR 566 QBD, the judge confirmed that a rent allowance claimant 'who has done all that he should is to be paid something within 14 days of a claim being made'. The judge also confirmed that no separate claim or request need be made in respect of a payment on account. The DSS (GM A6.38) considers it important for authorities to note that the duty to make a payment on account rests entirely with the authority. 'It is not the responsibility of the claimant to ask for such a payment and authorities should not wait for him to do so.' It should also be emphasised that the rule applies to all rent allowance claims including those from housing association tenants.

16.18 Many authorities fail to make payments on account or only make such payments when the claimant's tenancy is at risk. Such authorities are acting illegally. The DSS (HB/CTB(93)37) expresses its 'concern about continuing reports of delays by some authorities in processing rent allowance claims, and their failure to make payments on account where appropriate'. A high proportion of complaints to the local government ombudsman also concern failure to make payments on account. The ombudsman is likely to find maladministration with injustice and make a recommendation that compensation be paid in such cases.

16.19 Good cause for the claimant failing to provide necessary information and evidence would include, for example, a landlord's unwillingness to provide evidence of rent payments. The DSS (GM A6.40) points out that a claimant cannot be held responsible for delays in receiving confirmation of IS entitlement from the local Benefits Agency office unless asked to provide evidence of entitlement independently and any delay in doing so is directly attributable to the claimant. The DSS also reminds authorities (HB/CTB(93)37) that a claimant cannot be held responsible for a failure to supply evidence and information which he or she has not been asked specifically to provide. The claimant must also be given a reasonable time to provide any information which has been asked for before he or she can be judged to have failed to have done so. For example, if the authority does not write to the claimant asking for verification of, say, his or her earnings until the 13th day after the date on which the claim was made and the verification is supplied a few days later, the authority cannot then reasonably argue that it was impractical to determine the claim within 14 days because of the claimant's failure to provide the necessary information. The DSS advises that, in such a case, the claimant would clearly have good cause for failing to provide the information within the 14-day period. The authority is obliged to make initial payment on account on the 14th day following receipt of the claim based on the information originally available to it. This is the case even when the new payment rules (para. 16.21) apply.

16.20 If the authority finds, when it makes its formal determination on the claim, HBR 91(2),(3) that HB entitlement is different from the amount it has paid on account, further rent allowance payments will be adjusted to allow for under- or overpayments.

The letter advising of a payment on account must include a statement informing the claimant that if the payment is in excess of actual entitlement it will be recoverable from the person to whom the payment is made.

FREQUENCY OF RENT ALLOWANCE PAYMENTS BEFORE AND FROM 7TH OCTOBER 1996

HBR 90(1),(2), 88(3)

16.21 Following any 'payment on account', or first payment, the authority may choose to pay a rent allowance at intervals of two or four weeks or one calendar month or, with the consent of the person entitled to payment, at intervals greater than one month.

Prior to 7th October 1996 authorities had a duty, as far as possible, to make payments two weeks before the end of the period covered. So a fortnightly rent liability should be paid in advance, while four-weekly or monthly liabilities should be met midway through the period. However, where rent is paid in arrears the authority has the discretion to make payments at the end of the period.

From 7th October 1996, for claimants who are not exempt from the new rules (para. 16.22), the authority must make payments to claimants at the end of the period to which they relate. Where payment is being made direct to the landlord, and the claimant is not exempt from the new rules (para. 16.22), it should be made every 4 weeks (or, at the authority's discretion, monthly where there is a monthly rent liability) at the end of the period to which it relates. If, however, the authority is paying benefit direct to a landlord for more than one claimant a first payment may be made at a shorter interval than four weeks if the authority thinks that it is in the best interest of the efficient administration of housing benefit.

SI 1996 No. 965

16.22 The 7th October 1996 payment rules do not apply to claimants who are (or who are treated as) entitled to and in receipt of housing benefit before 7th October 1996 so long as they remain continuously entitled to and in receipt housing benefit for the same dwelling. People who claim benefit as a result of a partner's death are also not affected by the new rules if the partner is in receipt of benefit up to the date of death, *and* benefit is paid under the pre-October 1996 rules (or, if the death occurred between 30th September and 6th October 1996, would have been). For this exemption to apply, however, the new claim must be made, or treated as made, within four weeks of the death.

THE CLAIMANT'S RIGHT TO FORTNIGHTLY PAYMENTS

HBR 90(3)

16.23 Subject to the rules described in paras 16.21 and 16.22 (but excluding cases where HB is paid direct to a landlord), anyone who has a weekly entitlement to a rent allowance of more than £2 can require the authority to pay fortnightly.

AUTHORITY'S DISCRETION TO PAY WEEKLY

16.24   Subject to the rules described in paras 16.21 and 16.22 (but excluding   HBR 90(4)
cases where HB is paid direct to a landlord), authorities have discretion to pay
HB weekly if they consider that:

♦ paying HB over a longer period would lead to an overpayment; or

♦ the claimant pays rent weekly and it is in his or her interest (or that of the
family) to receive weekly payments.

The former instance covers cases where there is only a short period of entitlement
to HB, or where a change of circumstance is anticipated in the near future. The
latter instance may be helpful in cases where claimants have difficulty in
budgeting over a longer period.

PAYMENT OF CTB

16.25   Normally authorities pay CTB by means of a rebate (credit) to the   CTBR 77
individual's council tax account and thus reduce the liability for the tax. Where
the rebate is greater than the tax liability the authority may reduce the liability for
the tax in subsequent years. However, where the tax has been paid for the
financial year, and the claimant requires it, or the claimant is jointly and severally
liable for the tax and the authority considers it appropriate, the balance of any
CTB must be paid direct to the claimant. Also where a person has met the tax
liability in full and the tax account has been closed, e.g. because he or she has left
the area or is no longer liable, the authority must pay the outstanding amount of
CTB direct to the claimant. In all cases where the payment is direct to the
claimant rather than to the claimant's council tax account, payment should
normally be made within 14 days or as soon as reasonably practicable after that.

To whom should the payment be made?

16.26   The normal requirement of the schemes is that the benefit is paid to the   HBR 92 CTBR 7
claimant though with HB for council tenants and CTB for council tax payers this
is normally by way of a rebate to their account. However, in particular
circumstances:

♦ a rent allowance is paid to the claimant's landlord, or someone else to
whom rent is payable, e.g. a lettings agent, or a nominee; and

♦ a rent allowance or CTB is paid to an appointee or, in the case of a claimant
who has died, a personal representative or next of kin aged 16 or over.

When an amount of rent allowance is paid to a landlord or lettings agent this
discharges the claimant's liability to pay that amount of rent, unless and to the
extent that the authority recovers any such amount as a recoverable overpayment
from that landlord or lettings agent (para. 18.37).

RENT ALLOWANCE PAYMENTS DIRECT TO A LANDLORD OR LETTINGS AGENT

HBR 94(1A) **16.27** The authority has the discretion to make the first payment of a new or renewed rent allowance claim by sending the claimant a cheque or other instrument of payment payable to the landlord for part or all of the amount due. The DSS suggests that 'this will help remove the temptation for some claimants to abscond with the first payment of housing benefit without paying the landlord' (DSS Press Release *Housing Benefit Regulations Laid Before Parliament,* 2nd April 1996). The authority is, however, only able to make the first cheque, etc, payable to the landlord where:

◆ the authority is of the opinion that the claimant has not already paid the landlord for the period in respect of which any payment is to be made; and

◆ it is in the interests of the efficient administration of housing benefit.

The DSS has advised authorities (HB/CTB A9/96 para. 24) to consider using this power where:

◆ the amount due is £100 or more; or

◆ it has reason to think that the claimant might default; or

◆ there is a rent debt but the case is not appropriate for longer term direct payment arrangements.

MANDATORY DIRECT PAYMENTS

HBR 93 **16.28** If the authority is not withholding benefit (para. 16.35-16.44) it must make direct payments of a rent allowance to a landlord where:

◆ an amount of income support or either kind of JSA payable to the claimant, or partner, is being paid direct to the landlord to meet arrears; or

◆ the claimant has rent arrears equivalent to eight weeks or more, except where the authority considers it to be in the overriding interest of the claimant not to make direct payments when the authority must withhold payment (para. 16.39).

R 93(3), 94(1B), 95(1A) The exception to the above rules requiring direct payment is where the authority is not satisfied that the landlord is a 'fit and proper person' to receive direct payments. The authority may withhold payment whilst it considers this matter. The DSS advises (HB/CTB A48/97) that a landlord should be assumed to be a 'fit and proper person' in the absence of evidence to the contrary. The test enables the authority to refuse direct payments in cases where the landlord is involved in fraudulent acts related to HB. The DSS suggest that the authority might also consider whether the landlord has habitually failed to:

◆ report changes in tenants circumstances which he or she might reasonably be expected to know might affect entitlement; or

◆ repay an overpayment which the authority has decided is recoverable – despite the fact that a proper notification was issued and that the rights of review had been exercised or made available.

The authority should not base its judgment on:

◆ the landlord's undesirable activity in non-HB matters; or

◆ the fact that the landlord makes use of the right to review and further review before repaying any recoverable overpayment; or

◆ the fact that the landlord has made complaints of maladministration to the local government ombudsman.

Where the authority is satisfied that the landlord is not a 'fit and proper person' but it appears to be in the overriding interest of the claimant to pay the landlord direct – then direct payments may still be considered under the discretionary direct payment rules (para. 16.32).

16.29 In the case of *R v London Borough of Haringey ex parte Azad Ayub*, (1992) 25 HLR 566 QBD the judge found that the duty to pay a landlord direct once the claimant is eight weeks or more in rent arrears only arises if the landlord or someone else informs the authority that there are eight weeks or more arrears. It is not up to the authority to find this out for itself. If the tenant disputes that there are eight weeks arrears the authority must consider the available evidence and come to a finding of fact on the balance of probability. Either party (the claimant or landlord) can appeal about the authority's determination (para. 19.8).

16.30 If the claimant dies but the authority has already determined to make payment direct to the landlord, any amount of benefit outstanding at the time of the claimant's death must be paid to the landlord if a written application has been made for it.

Where deductions are being made from income support/JSA to meet rent arrears, direct payments of HB to the landlord should continue until such time as the Benefits Agency ceases to make the relevant deductions. Benefits Agency local offices should advise authorities of appropriate cases (GM para. A6.47).

16.31 Where the authority is making direct payments because the claimant is eight or more weeks in rent arrears, the direct payment should cease once the arrears fall below the eight-week level unless one of the circumstances in paras. 16.29 or 16.30 apply.

DISCRETIONARY DIRECT PAYMENTS

16.32 An authority may implement direct payment arrangements where: HBR 94

◆ the claimant requests, or consents to, such an arrangement; or

◆ the authority considers it to be in the interest of the claimant and family; or

◆   benefit is owing to a claimant who has left a dwelling with rent arrears.

In the last circumstance direct payment is limited to an amount equivalent to the rent owing.

As with mandatory direct payments, the authority may decide not to make direct payments where the landlord is not a 'fit and proper person' to receive such payments. However, where it appears to be in the overriding interest of the claimant for the landlord to be paid direct, and there are no practicable alternatives, the authority may make direct payments. This would apply, for example, where the risk to the claimant of not paying the landlord outweighs any risk associated with direct payment.

16.33   Authorities might use their power to pay direct in the interest of the claimant and family where, for example, the claimant has a history of rent arrears at a previous address or where social or medical problems (such as mental illness or drug addiction) indicate that help with budgeting is needed.

INFORMATION TO BE PROVIDED TO CLAIMANTS AND LANDLORDS OR LETTINGS AGENTS

HBR 77, sch 6
part IV

16.34   When a determination has been made that HB is to be paid direct to the landlord both the claimant and landlord should be notified of that fact within 14 days (para. 16.2). The notification must include the date from which the arrangement will commence and their right to obtain a written statement of reasons and make written representations. The notification must also inform both the landlord and claimant that where:

◆   an overpayment is recoverable from the landlord; and

◆   is recovered from direct payments made on behalf of a tenant to whom the overpayment does not relate,

that tenant's rent must be treated as paid to the value of the amount recovered.

The landlord must also be informed of his or her duty to report any change of circumstances which might affect the claimant's amount of, or right to, HB and the kind of change which should be notified.

Withholding HB/CTB

TO AVOID POSSIBLE OVERPAYMENTS

HBR 95
CTBR 80

16.35   Once it has determined entitlement, an authority may withhold all or part of the claimant's HB/CTB where it appears that:

◆   the claimant, or the person to whom HB/CTB is to be paid, may not be entitled; or

♦ a recoverable overpayment of HB or CTB has occurred.

As soon as these matters are resolved and a determination made, HB/CTB should be paid to the person from whom it has been withheld except to the extent that there is no entitlement or a recoverable overpayment.

WHERE A DOUBT ARISES ABOUT INCOME SUPPORT/INCOME-BASED JSA

16.36 While it is for the Benefits Agency to determine the claimant's capital and income for income support/income-based JSA purposes, the authority, once it has determined HB/CTB entitlement, is able to withhold benefit when it has evidence which raises a reasonable doubt as to the amount of the claimant's income or capital for income support/income-based JSA purposes if this would affect HB/CTB entitlement.

HBR 95
CTBR 80

16.37 The DSS advises (GM A6.52) that the authority is required to check with the Benefits Agency that the evidence has not already been considered by them. If the evidence has not been considered, the authority may withhold HB/CTB in full, or in part, from that date. The circular emphasises the discretionary nature of the authority's power, i.e. that all relevant factors should be taken into account and that there should be no automatic withholding of benefit. The circular also suggests that the authority should decide not to withhold benefit if the claimant is likely to have a continuing entitlement on low income grounds.

16.38 The DSS also advises (HB/CTB A4/95, part 1) authorities that if they do decide to withhold benefit where the claimant is in receipt of income support/income-based JSA, they must:

♦ refer cases immediately to the Benefits Agency requesting an urgent decision;

♦ inform the claimant (and the landlord if benefit is paid direct); and

♦ check with the Benefits Agency if no reply is received after seven days.

WHERE THERE ARE 8 WEEKS' RENT ARREARS

16.39 An authority must withhold a rent allowance where the claimant has rent arrears of eight weeks or more but the authority considers it in the overriding interest of the claimant not to make direct payments to the landlord (para. 16.28).

HBR 95

16.40 This rule might be useful, for example, in the event of a dispute between landlord and tenant over repairs where direct payments would undermine the claimant's position.

WHERE THE RENT OFFICER IS DENIED ACCESS

HBR 95   **16.41**   The authority has the discretion to withhold payment of a rent allowance where the rent officer has notified it that the claimant has denied him or her access to the dwelling for the purpose of making relevant determinations (chapter 8). Where it is the landlord who has denied access payment may only be withheld under this rule if a direct payment would have been made to the landlord. The authority's discretion to withhold payment also only applies if the rent officer:

◆ has given 7 days notice to the claimant or the landlord of the need to obtain entry; and

◆ there is no good reason why entry cannot be given.

The authority must notify the claimant (and landlord where benefit would have been paid direct to the landlord) within 14 days (paras. 16.10-11) of its determination to withhold payment. Benefit should only be withheld while the rent officer reports that he or she is unable to gain access and the above conditions are met.

WHERE CLAIMANT IS NOT PAYING RENT REGULARLY

HBR 95(2)   **16.42**   An authority may withhold a rent allowance where it is satisfied upon reasonable grounds that the claimant is not making regular rent payments. But it should be emphasised the HB payments do not have to be used to meet a rent liability. Indeed the claimant may be entitled to HB for a period in which the rent has already been paid or where the landlord has waived the liability (para. 4.26). In *Director of Public Prosecutions v Huskinson*, (1988) 20 HLR 562 QBD it was confirmed that there is no obligation to use HB to pay the rent.

GENERAL RULES

HBR 95(3)   **16.43**   HB withheld for any of the above reasons should be paid at a later date to the landlord or claimant as appropriate once the authority is satisfied that:

◆ it is no longer in the overriding interest of the claimant not to make payment;

◆ the claimant has discharged his or her liability to the landlord;

◆ the claimant will discharge the liability if payment is made; or

◆ the rent officer is no longer denied entry.

16.44   Before withholding a rent allowance an authority should give the claimant the opportunity to comment. Where the claimant has good grounds for withholding rent (for example the landlord has failed to carry out repairs) and the arrears do not amount to eight weeks or more, the authority is under no obligation to withhold HB payments.

WHERE THE LANDLORD MIGHT NOT BE A 'FIT AND PROPER PERSON'

16.45 The authority may withhold payment of a rent allowance that it would   HBR 95(1A), (6A)
otherwise make to a landlord if it has evidence that raises a reasonable doubt as
to whether the landlord is a 'fit and proper person'. The authority has 14 days
from the day the doubt arose, or such longer period as may be appropriate, to
satisfy itself on this matter. Once satisfied, if the conditions for direct payments
remain, the withheld payments should be made to the landlord. If the authority is
not satisfied that the landlord is a 'fit and proper person', or the conditions for
direct payment no longer exist, payment should be made to the claimant,
appointee or nominee (para. 16.52-16.53).

WHERE THE CONDITIONS FOR DIRECT PAYMENT MIGHT EXIST

16.46 The authority may withhold payment of a rent allowance that it would   HBR 95(1B), (6B)
otherwise make to a claimant whilst it consider whether or not direct payments
should be made to the landlord. The authority has 14 days from the day it
withheld benefit, or such longer period as may be appropriate, to consider this
matter. If it determines that payment should be made to the landlord, the withheld
payments should be paid to the landlord. Alternatively where it determines that
payments should not be made to the landlord, it should make payment to the
claimant, appointee or nominee (para. 16.52-53).

Suspending HB/CTB

16.47 Once the authority has determined and started paying benefit it may   HBR 96A, CTB 81
suspend payment if it considers that the claimant's entitlement is in doubt. The
authority must notify the claimant of the suspension within 7 days of making it
or as soon as reasonably practicable after that. It must also tell the claimant what
information, evidence, certificates and documents it requires. The requested
information, etc., must be reasonably required.

16.48 The claimant should supply the requested information, etc, within 4
weeks. The authority can, however, extend the period it allows for the supply of
information if it thinks it reasonable to do so. After considering the requested
information, etc, the authority can require the claimant to provide further
information. Again the request must be reasonable and again the information, etc,
should normally be supplied within 4 weeks of the request being made.

16.49 Where the authority has the information, etc, that it requires it must either:

◆ review the award of benefit; or

◆ restore payment to the claimant and include any payment which accrued
during the suspension period.

This should normally be done within 14 days of the receipt of the requested information or as soon as reasonably practicable thereafter.

16.50 Where the requested information, etc, has not been supplied within 4 weeks, or such longer period (not exceeding 13 weeks) as the authority considers appropriate, it must review the award of benefit.

16.51 Where payment of benefit is suspended, and the claimant's benefit period comes to an end whilst the suspension is in force, the following applies. If no further claim for benefit has been received by the authority before the end of the benefit period, it must invite the claimant to make a further claim for benefit. If the claim is made within four weeks of the end of the benefit period, it takes effect immediately after the end of that benefit period.

Other people who may receive a rent allowance or CTB

APPOINTEE

HBR 92(2)
CTBR 78(2)

16.52 Where an appointee acts on behalf of a claimant who is incapable of managing his or her own affairs (para. 7.6) then payment may be made to that person. In most cases, however, CTB will be paid by rebating the claimant's tax liability.

NOMINEE

HBR 92(3)

16.53 In the case of HB if the claimant requests in writing that the authority makes payment to another person (who must be 18 or more), the authority may make payments to that person. The DSS incorrectly refers to this person as an agent and advises that the claimant must be unable to collect the money himself or herself (GM para. A6.40). This is not the case.

A DEAD CLAIMANT'S PERSONAL REPRESENTATIVE OR NEXT OF KIN

HBR 96(1)-(3)
CTBR 81(1)-(3)

16.54 Following a claimant's death, the authority must, if a written application is received within 12 months (or such longer period as the authority may allow), pay a rent allowance – or any CTB above the dead claimant's residual council tax liability – to his or her personal representative or, if there is none, the next of kin. The next of kin take priority in the following order: spouse, issue (children, grandchildren), other relatives (parents, brothers, sisters or their children); and must be aged 16 or over.

17 Changes to entitlement

17.1   This chapter explains how a claimant's entitlement to HB and CTB may change, or be brought to an early end. It covers:

◆ the claimant's duty to notify a change of circumstances;

◆ the different ways of dealing with a change;

◆ the different types of change;

◆ other ways of revising HB/CTB;

◆ retrospective changes; and

◆ the rules about 'extended payments'.

Duty to notify a change of circumstances

HBR 75(1), (1A),
sch A1
CTBR 65(1), (1A),
sch A1
17.2   With one exception, the claimant has a duty to notify the authority's 'designated office' (para. 7.31), in writing, of any relevant change of circumstances. The exception is that if the claimant sent or delivered his or her HB/CTB claim to a 'gateway office' (para. 7.11), he or she may alternatively notify changes of circumstances to that office or to any other 'gateway office' mentioned on or with the claim form.

The duty to notify begins on the date the claim is made and continues for as long as the person is in receipt of HB or CTB (except in relation to 'extended payments': para. 17.54). In the special case of refugees who were formerly asylum seekers (para. 5.51), the claimant has a duty to notify relevant changes of circumstances which occurred in any previous period for which they have become entitled to HB/CTB. If HB/CTB is payable to someone other than the claimant (e.g. a landlord or an appointee), that person is also required to notify relevant changes. These duties apply to all HB and CTB claims including both main CTB and second adult rebate.

HBR 75(1)
CTBR 65(1)
17.3   For these purposes a relevant change is one which the claimant (or other person) could reasonably be expected to know might affect:

◆ entitlement to HB/CTB; or

◆ amount of HB/CTB; or

◆ method of payment.

Examples are given below. Whether a claimant (or other person) could reasonably be expected to know a change might affect HB or CTB, is of importance if failure to notify a change results in an overpayment, and the question of recovering the overpayment arises (chapter 18).

WHICH CHANGES MUST BE NOTIFIED?

17.4   The claimant need not inform the authority of:

HBR 75(2)
CTBR 65(2)

◆ changes in rent if he or she is a council tenant;

◆ changes in council tax liability;

◆ changes in the age of any member of the family or non-dependant;

◆ changes in the HB or CTB regulations;

◆ changes which affect his or her entitlement to income support or income-based jobseeker's allowance but do not affect his or her HB/CTB.

In the first two cases, the authority has made the changes, and so should not need to be informed of them. In the third case, the authority should be able to implement the change automatically.

17.5   The claimant must inform the authority of:

HBR 75(2)(e),(3)
CTBR 65(2)(e),(3)

◆ the end of his or her (or any partner's) entitlement to income support or income-based jobseeker's allowance;

◆ changes where a child or young person ceases to be a member of the family: for example, where a young person reaches 19 or leaves the household.

17.6   Claimants who have been awarded second adult rebate must also notify the authority of:

CTBR 65(4)

◆ changes in the number of adults in their home;

◆ changes in the total gross incomes of the adults in their home;

◆ the date any adult in their home ceases to receive income support or income-based jobseeker's allowance.

In the first two cases, the duty arises only if the change might reasonably be expected to alter the claimant's entitlement to second adult rebate. In the third case, the duty arises whenever such a change occurs – regardless of whether it could affect entitlement. The word 'adult' is not defined for these purposes, but may be presumed to mean anyone aged 18 or more.

17.7   Examples of other matters which must be notified to the authority include:

◆ changes of address;

◆ changes in rent if the claimant is not a council tenant;

◆ changes in the status of non-dependants/second adults;

◆ changes in family circumstances affecting the applicable amount;

◆ changes in capital and/or income;

◆ changes relating to payment of HB direct to a landlord.

The different ways of dealing with a change

17.8 When there is a change of circumstances affecting HB/CTB during the course of a claimant's benefit period (i.e. whilst the claimant is on HB/CTB), the authority has to decide whether to:

◆ end the benefit period early; or

◆ revise the determination.

The effect of each alternative is described below. Paragraphs 17.13-37 explain which alternative is available for each type of change, and the date it applies from.

ENDING A BENEFIT PERIOD EARLY

HBR 67
CTBR 58
17.9 In the case of some changes of circumstances, the authority must end the benefit period early (in other words, stop awarding the claimant HB/CTB). In the case of other changes of circumstances, the authority may choose to end the benefit period early.

17.10 In such cases, authorities should invite claimants to make a renewal claim or, when this is clearly inappropriate (e.g. if a claimant has capital valued for HB/CTB purposes at over £16,000 and has no second adults), remind claimants that they may make a further claim if their circumstances change again.

REVISING HB/CTB

HBR 79(1)(a)
CTBR 69(1)(a)
17.11 Except in cases when the benefit period must be ended early, an authority may revise any determination it has made if there is a relevant change of circumstances during the course of a benefit period (in other words, continue awarding the claimant HB/CTB but on the basis of the new circumstances). It may also revise a review board decision in such cases.

BR 77(1)(b), 79(6)
CTBR 67(1)(b),
69(7)
17.12 The claimant, and any person affected by the revised determination (paras. 16.7-8), must be notified in writing of the change, within 14 days or as soon as reasonably practicable. The ordinary appeal procedures apply to the revised determination (chapter 19).

The different types of change

THE GENERAL RULE

17.13 The following general rule applies for all changes other than those mentioned in the rest of this chapter. Typical examples are changes in income, capital, age or household composition – including cases where a claimant who has been awarded main CTB becomes entitled to second adult rebate instead, or *vice versa;* and including cases where a claimant becomes entitled to income support or income-based jobseeker's allowance.

17.14 If the result of a change is that the claimant's entitlement reduces to nil, the authority must end the benefit period early. If the result of a change is that entitlement continues, the most common practice is to revise HB/CTB; but the authority may end the period early in appropriate cases – e.g. if a change is very complicated.

HBR 26, 68(1), 79(3)(a)
CTBR 18, 59(1), 69(3)(a)

17.15 It is up to the authority to determine the date on which such a change actually occurs. This can be straightforward (e.g. in the case of a claimant's birthday) or can present difficulties (e.g. in the case of varying capital). In three cases there are specific rules:

♦ If entitlement to any social security benefit ends, the date the change actually occurs is defined as being the day after the last day of entitlement to that benefit.

♦ If there is a change in tax or national insurance caused by a change in the law (e.g. the Budget) it may be disregarded (i.e. treated as not occurring) until up to 30 benefit weeks later. This applies to the income of a claimant, partner, non-dependant or second adult whether earned (in employment or self-employment) or unearned.

♦ There are special rules about arrears of income (para. 13.18).

17.16 When the authority revises HB/CTB in general cases, the new amount of HB/CTB is awarded from the Monday after the date the change occurs, even if the change occurs on a Monday. (So for the benefit week including the change, benefit is calculated as if the change had not occurred.)

HBR 68(1), 79(3)
CTBR 59(1), 69(3)(a)

17.17 When the authority ends the benefit period early in general cases:

HBR 67(c), 79(3)
CTBR 58(c), 69(3)(a)

♦ the last week of HB/CTB entitlement is the benefit week (para. 7.53) in which the claimant's circumstances change; and

♦ in the last week, the claimant is entitled to a full week's HB/CTB (i.e. calculated as if the change had not occurred).

Example: A claimant's birthday

A claimant receiving HB and CTB (but not income support or JSA(IB)) reaches the age of 75 on Wednesday 12th July. The effect is that her HB and CTB increase.

Normally, it would be inappropriate to end the benefit period early in such a case. instead, the authority should revise HB and CTB.

The new amounts of HB and CTB are awarded from the benefit week after the change, i.e. benefit week commencing Monday 17th July.

WHEN INCOME SUPPORT OR JSA(IB) ENTITLEMENT ENDS

17.18 Entitlement to income support (IS) or income-based jobseeker's allowance – JSA(IB) – may end for a variety of reasons. As described in paragraphs 17.19-24, there are three rules about how this affects the person's HB/CTB.

END OF INCOME SUPPORT OR JSA(IB): GENERAL RULE

R 67(1)(a), 68(1)
R 58(1)(a), 59(1)

17.19 If the claimant's (or any partner's) entitlement to IS or JSA(IB) ends for any reason other than those described in paragraphs 17.20-24 (for example, if the claimant takes up work), the authority must end the benefit period early and must invite a renewal claim.

In such cases, the change actually occurs on the day after the last day of entitlement to IS or JSA(IB) (para. 17.15). The HB/CTB benefit period ends at the end of the benefit week containing the day the change actually occurs.

TRANSFERRING BETWEEN INCOME SUPPORT AND JSA(IB)

HBR 67(2), 68(1)
TBR 58(2), 59(1)

17.20 If the claimant's (or any partner's) entitlement to IS ceases but the claimant (or partner) immediately becomes entitled to JSA(IB) – or the reverse occurs – there is no change in the claimant's entitlement to HB or main CTB (unless some other change occurs at the same time). This is because receipt of either of those benefits entitles the claimant to maximum HB/CTB (para. 9.9). The claimant is nonetheless required to notify the authority of such a change (para. 17.5).

In such cases, the authority should usually simply continue awarding HB/CTB (and notify the claimant of the new reason why he or she qualifies for maximum HB/CTB). It may alternatively bring the benefit period to an early end, but this would normally be appropriate only in exceptional cases. If the authority does end the benefit period, it should do so according to the rule described in paragraph 17.19 and must invite a renewal claim.

TRANSFERRING FROM INCOME SUPPORT OR JSA(IB) TO ANOTHER SOCIAL SECURITY BENEFIT

17.21 If the claimant's (or any partner's) entitlement to IS or JSA(IB) ceases because any other social security benefit (e.g. contribution-based jobseeker's allowance, incapacity benefit, etc.) is awarded instead, the authority must end the benefit period early and must invite a renewal claim. HBR 67(1)(b), 6 CTBR 58(1)(b), §

In such cases, the HB/CTB benefit period ends at the end of the benefit week which contains the last day on which IS or JSA(IB) is *paid* (regardless of the date on which *entitlement* to IS or JSA(IB) ends or ended).

17.22 This rule often applies in cases where claimants were awarded IS or JSA(IB) while they were waiting to find out whether they qualify for some other social security benefit. As illustrated in the following example, the point of the rule is to ensure that they are able to satisfy the four weeks time limit for renewal claims (para. 7.80). Authorities sometimes have difficulty administering this rule since, when the Benefits Agency notifies them of a change of this kind on form NHB(IS) or NHB(JSA), it can be difficult to distinguish the date IS or JSA(IB) entitlement ended from the last date on which IS or JSA(IB) was paid.

17.23 The rule is only about when the claimant's benefit period ends – not about the amount of his or her HB/CTB. Therefore authorities may revise entitlement to HB/CTB retrospectively to take account of the social security benefit from the date entitlement to it began. This may result in an overpayment for that period. Except in certain cases where there has been an official error or delay, such overpayments are recoverable.

17.24 The following applies only in cases referred to the rent officer (chapter 8). In such cases, if the rent officer makes a determination following a 'relevant change of circumstances' (as listed in table 8.2), the authority extends the claimant's benefit period by a period of at least one benefit week and no more than 60 benefit weeks. Within those limits, it is for the authority to choose how long to extend it by. At the time of writing, authorities must make such an extension: it seems likely that the law will shortly be amended to give authorities a discretion whether or not to do this. HBR 66(3),(5)

WHEN RENT LIABILITY CHANGES OR ENDS

17.25 If a claimant's rent increases (or decreases), the authority may either revise his or her HB or (less commonly) bring the HB benefit period to an early end. If the claimant is a private tenant, the authority may in some cases need to refer the rent to the rent officer (chapter 8).

17.26   If a claimant moves within an authority's area, it is possible for his or her HB to be revised, though authorities may alternatively end the benefit period early in such a case (in which case the rules about renewal claims apply: chapter 7). If a claimant moves out of the authority's area, the authority must end the benefit period early (unless a relevant agency arrangement exists: para. 1.9).

Examples: When income support entitlement ends

GENERAL CASE

In (a) and (b) the claimants income support entitlement has stopped – but not because he or she has been awarded another social security benefit. The authority must end the HB/CTB benefit period early in such cases (and invite a renewal claim).

(a) Last day of income support entitlement: Thursday 8th June. Change occurs: Friday 9th June. HB/CTB benefit period ends: Sunday 11th June.

(b) Last day of income support entitlement: Sunday 11th June. Change occurs: Monday 12th June. HB/CTB benefit period ends: Sunday 18th June.

WHEN ANOTHER SOCIAL SECURITY BENEFIT IS AWARDED

On Thursday 1st June a single man claims incapacity benefit, but this is delayed. So he claims income support too, which is awarded from Thursday 1st June. He also claims HB and CTB, which are awarded from Monday 5th June.

In August his incapacity benefit is assessed. From 1st June, he has qualified for more incapacity benefit than he has been receiving in income support. Income support payments cease, the last one being made on Thursday 3rd August.

The authority must end the benefit period early in such cases (and invite a renewal claim).

The HB/CTB benefit period ends on Sunday 6th August – the end of the benefit week in which his last payment of income support was made. If the claimant makes a repeat claim by Sunday 3rd September (four weeks later) his new HB/CTB benefit period begins on Monday 7th August.

The authority may, however, revise entitlement to HB/CTB retrospectively for the period from 5th June to 6th August, to take account of the incapacity benefit. If it does this, the result will probably be that the claimant has been overpaid HB/CTB for that period (para. 17.24).

17.27 When HB is revised as a result of a change in liability for rent, this is done from the benefit week in which the date of the change falls: HBR 68(2), 69(4),(5)

◆ if rent is expressed on a weekly basis (or in multiples of weeks), a whole week's new entitlement is awarded in that benefit week;

◆ if rent is expressed on a non-weekly basis (e.g. daily or calendar-monthly), entitlement for that benefit week is assessed on a daily basis for both the old and new entitlements.

17.28 When the HB benefit period is brought to an early end as a result of rent liability ending: HBR 67(c), 69(4),(5)

◆ if rent is expressed on a weekly basis (or in multiples of weeks), no HB is awarded in the last benefit week; unless the claimant is liable for rent up to and including the Sunday, in which case a whole week's HB is awarded for that benefit week;

◆ if rent is expressed on a non-weekly basis (e.g. daily or calendar-monthly), entitlement in the last benefit week is calculated on a daily basis.

Example: Rent increase

A claimant receiving HB pays rent weekly on Saturdays. It increases on Saturday 15th July. In her case, the effect is that her HB increases.

It would be inappropriate to end the HB benefit early in such a case. Instead, the authority should revise HB entitlement.

The new amount of HB is awarded from the benefit week in which the change occurs, i.e. from benefit week commencing Monday 10th July.

WHEN COUNCIL TAX LIABILITY CHANGES OR ENDS

17.29 If a claimant's liability for council tax increases or decreases, the authority should revise his or her CTB from the benefit week in which the date of the change falls (on a daily basis in all cases: para. 17.33). It may alternatively bring the benefit period to an early end, but this would normally be appropriate only in exceptional cases. CTBR 59(2)

17.30 If the change is in the amount of entitlement to a council tax transitional reduction (para. 3.30), the change must be taken into account from the date on which it takes effect (usually 1st April). If the change is due to the authority setting revised council taxes due to council tax 'capping', the change must be taken into account from the beginning of the financial year (1st April). CTBR 59(3)

CTBR 59(3)   **17.31**   If the change is in entitlement to, or the amount of, a council tax discount (para. 3.35) or a reduction for disabilities (para. 3.32), the change must be taken into account from the date on which it actually occurs.

17.32   If a claimant moves within an authority's area, it is possible for his or her CTB to be revised, though authorities may alternatively end the benefit period early in such a case. If a claimant moves out of an authority's area, the authority must end the benefit period early.

TBR 57(2), 58(c), 59(2),(3)   **17.33**   In all the above cases:

◆ when CTB is revised: in the benefit week including the date of the change, CTB is calculated on a daily basis for both old and new entitlements;

◆ when the CTB benefit period is brought to an early end: entitlement for the last benefit week is calculated on a daily basis.

CHANGES RELATING TO COUPLES

TBR 57(2), 58(c), 59(5),(6)   **17.34**   In CTB only, a specific rule deals with cases in which:

◆ a claimant acquires a partner; or

◆ a claimant's partner dies; or

◆ a claimant and partner separate.

In all these cases the change is taken into account on the day on which that event occurs. The authority may revise the claimant's entitlement to CTB in such cases, or may bring the benefit period to an early end. In either case this is done on a daily basis following the rules in paragraph 17.33.

17.35   There is no specific rule in HB, where such changes fall within the general rule (para. 17.13), and are therefore taken into account from the Monday following the event in question. The reason for the discrepancy between the CTB and HB rules is that in CTB these types of change are often associated with a change in liability for council tax whereas in HB they are unlikely to be associated with a change in liability for rent.

CHANGES IN THE REGULATIONS; AND LOCAL GOVERNMENT REORGANISATION

HBR 68(3),(5) CTBR 59(4)   **17.36**   When the regulations are amended, the authority revises HB/CTB from the date on which the amendment takes effect. In the case of the annual April HB/CTB up-rating, this means 1st April. The one exception applies in HB only, and only for claimants whose rent is due weekly or in multiples of weeks: in their HB claims, the up-rating instead takes effect from the first Monday in April (in 2000, this is 3rd April); and furthermore any other change of circumstances occurring in the week beginning with that Monday also takes effect from the same day.

Following local government reorganisation, a newly-constituted authority may, within six months of reorganisation (or, in Scotland, twelve months), end the benefit period of any claimant whose claim was formerly administered by a different authority. A determination to do this is not appealable.

SI 1995 No. 531
SI 1996 No. 548
SI 1996 No. 549

WHEN THERE IS MORE THAN ONE CHANGE

17.37 Apart from the cases described in paragraph 17.36, if two or more changes occur in relation to the same claim, they are dealt with in turn, following the above rules. The exception to this is when changes which actually occur in the same benefit week would have an effect (under those rules) in different benefit weeks. In these cases:

HBR 68(4)
CTBR 59(6)

◆ for HB if one of the changes is in the amount of rent liability, the other changes in entitlement instead apply when that applies;

◆ for HB in any other case, work out the various days on which the changes have an effect (under the above rules): all the changes instead apply from the earliest of these;

◆ for CTB in all cases, work out the various days on which the changes have an effect (under the above rules): all the changes instead apply from the earliest of these.

Example: More than one change

The circumstances in two earlier examples (claimant's birthday and rent increase) apply to the same claimant.

The authority decides to revise HB and CTB (rather than bring the HB and CTB benefit periods to an early end).

Both the changes affect HB. They actually occur in the same benefit week, but would have an effect in different benefit weeks. So HB is revised to take into account both the claimant's birthday and the rent increase from benefit week commencing Monday 10th July.

Only the first change affects CTB, so CTB is revised to take into account the claimant's birthday from benefit week commencing Monday 17th July.

Other ways of revising HB/CTB

17.38 The following paragraphs describe the other powers which the authority itself has for changing entitlement to HB and CTB (i.e. apart from the appeal procedures described in chapter 19). These usually result in a retrospective change (paras. 17.48-53).

MISTAKES

HBR 79(1)
CTBR 69(1)

17.39 An authority may revise any determination it has made (without the claimant requesting this), even after entitlement to HB/CTB has ended, if:

◆ the determination was made in ignorance of a material fact, or based on a mistake as to a material fact; or

◆ the determination was based on a mistake as to the law.

For example, new facts may come to light, or a change of circumstances may be reported or discovered later than it actually occurred, or the authority may realise it has incorrectly interpreted the HB/CTB regulations.

HBR 79(1)
CTBR 69(1)

17.40 An authority may also revise a decision made by a review board, but only if there is fresh evidence that the decision was made in ignorance of a material fact, or fresh evidence that it was based on a mistake as to a material fact. The authority has no power to revise a review board decision on the grounds that the review board has made a mistake in law (though it may ask the review board to set the decision aside: para. 19.57).

HBR 79(3)
CTBR 69(3)

17.41 The revised determination applies from the date of the original determination or (if appropriate) from the date when a change of circumstances should have taken effect. If the claimant failed to report a number of successive changes, a separate revised determination must be made for each one.

HBR 77(1)(b), 79(6)
CTBR 67(1)(b),
69(7)

17.42 The claimant and any person affected (paras. 16.7-8) must be notified in writing of the change, within 14 days or as soon as reasonably practicable. The appeal procedures apply in relation to the revised determination (chapter 19).

ACCIDENTAL ERRORS

HBR 85, 87
CTBR 74, 76

17.43 The authority may correct any accidental errors which occur in a determination (e.g. arithmetical mistakes or mistakes in entering data on a computer). The correction becomes part of the original determination, and the change must be notified as soon as practicable. The discretion to correct an accidental error is not open to the appeal procedures.

17.44 The distinction between an accidental error and a mistake (para. 17.39) is crucial if the claimant was awarded too little HB or CTB (or community charge benefit) more than a year ago (paras. 17.52-53). The DSS advises that part of the distinction 'is between giving true effect to first thoughts or intentions' (correcting an accidental error) and 'having second thoughts or intentions' (GM para. A6.81). The latter may reveal that there has been an actual mistake of fact or law (in which case HB or CTB may be revised), or merely that the facts may be seen in different lights (in which case HB or CTB must not be revised).

SETTING ASIDE A DETERMINATION

17.45 The claimant or any person affected (paras. 16.7-8) may request an authority to set aside any determination it has made – even if entitlement to HB or CTB has expired. It is advisable to make it clear that the request is for setting aside, rather than, say, for an internal review. An authority cannot set a determination aside unless requested to do so, and determinations may be set aside only if:

HBR 86(1),(5)
CTBR 75(1),(5)

◆ a relevant document was not received by the claimant, representative or any person affected. The usual assumptions of the law about what counts as 'service' or 'delivery' do not apply; or

◆ the interests of justice require it.

17.46 The request must be considered if it is made in writing within 13 weeks of notification of the determination (no matter how late the notification is issued). In HB, the request must also be signed by the person affected (paras. 19.8, 19.10). The time limit does not include any period before the correction of an accidental error, or the setting aside of some other determination or review board decision, or a refusal to do either of these things. However there is no power for the time limit to be extended apart from this. The outcome must be notified as soon as practicable and include a statement of reasons. The discretion to set aside a determination is not open to the appeal procedures.

HBR 86(2),(2A),
(4), 87
CTBR 75(2),(4), 7

17.47 If an authority sets aside a determination, it must make a fresh determination to replace it. The fresh determination is open to the appeal procedures (chapter 19).

Retrospective changes

17.48 Each of the cases described in paragraphs 17.39-47 may entitle the claimant to some HB/CTB or to more HB/CTB for a past period – in which case the balance due should be awarded straight away, though there are time limits in some of these cases, described below (and see also para. 13.18 on the treatment of arrears of income). Alternatively, a balance of HB may be used to reduce an outstanding recoverable overpayment of HB; a balance of CTB may be used to reduce an outstanding recoverable overpayment of CTB or community charge benefit.

HBR 79(5)
CTBR 69(5), 79

17.49 In the case of CTB (where retrospective increases are sometimes referred to as 'shortfalls'), any balance due is normally credited to the claimant's council tax account. But if this is not possible, or if the claimant so requests, it must be paid to the claimant within 14 days, or as soon as practicable.

17.50 A retrospective increase is not a case of 'backdating' and so the authority does not lose subsidy on it. And if a claimant is entitled to a retrospective increase, there is no requirement that he or she must ask for it (or have a good reason for not having asked for it in the past) in order to be awarded it.

17.51 The cases mentioned may also entitle the claimant to no HB/CTB or to less HB/CTB for a past period in which case there has been an overpayment which may or may not be recoverable (chapter 18).

RETROSPECTIVE INCREASES WHERE THERE IS NO TIME LIMIT

HBR 85, 86
CTBR 74, 75

17.52 In the case of setting aside a determination, and in the case of correcting an accidental error in a determination, there is no time limit on how far back HB or CTB may be retrospectively increased. (This is also true when review boards set aside their own decisions or correct accidental errors in them: paras. 19.57, 19.55.) The lack of a time limit in relation to setting aside is not, however, particularly beneficial unless there is a long delay in notifying the original determination (since a determination may only be set aside if the claimant requests this within 13 weeks after it is notified: para. 17.46).

RETROSPECTIVE INCREASES WHERE THERE IS A TIME LIMIT

HBR 79(5)
CTBR 69(5)

17.53 In the case of revising a determination (or review board decision) following a mistake of fact or law (paras. 17.39-40), there is a time limit on how far back HB or CTB may be retrospectively increased. The time limit is 52 weeks before the date on which the revision is made. (Similar limits apply in relation to the appeal procedures: paras. 19.28, 19.53.) This does not prevent a claimant from seeking compensation from the authority for earlier periods if the authority itself was at fault.

Extended payments

HBR 2(1), 62A,
69(8), 76(4),
sch 5A
CTBR 2(1),
51(6), 53A,
66(4), sch 5A
SI 1988 No. 662

17.54 The rest of this chapter describes the rules designed to help long-term unemployed people who are returning to work. (The DSS's guidance on these rules is in GM paras. A2.35 onwards.) This section describes how they can get an 'extended payment' of two or four weeks extra HB/CTB.

ENTITLEMENT TO EXTENDED PAYMENTS

17.55 A claimant is entitled to an extended payment ('EP'), if all the conditions in table 17.1 are met. In the following (and in the table), 'claimant' means the EP-claimant.

In the case of a couple, the last point is important since:

◆ the EP-claimant must be the member of the couple who has been the IS/JSA(IB)-claimant (condition (b) of the table); but

◆ it is usually regarded as irrelevant which member of the couple has been the HB/CTB-claimant (condition (f) of the table).

However, some authorities disagree with the second of the above points. In their opinion, the EP-claimant must be the member of the couple who has been the HB/CTB-claimant (as well as being the member of the couple who has been the IS/JSA(IB)-claimant). This would mean that a couple, one of whom was the HB/CTB-claimant but the other of whom was the IS/JSA(IB)-claimant, could never qualify for extended payments: at least one Benefits Agency office is reported to make *ex gratia* payments to EP-claimants compensating for the effect of this interpretation.

METHOD OF CLAIM AND TIME LIMITS: GENERAL CASES

17.56   Except for many cases of lone parent claimants (para. 17.60), the claimant must 'properly' complete, and sign, a form approved by the authority. Most, if not all, authorities are using 'form NHB 1EP' for this, published by the DSS. It contains sections for the claimant and the Benefits Agency (BA) to complete. Claimants may obtain these forms from their Jobcentre or BA office (or, in some areas, from their local authority). The EP claim must be made at the Jobcentre, BA or authority 'within 8 days of' the claimant's last day of entitlement to income support (IS) or income-based jobseeker's allowance – JSA(IB). If the claim is made at the Jobcentre or direct to the authority, the form must be sent to the BA. In all cases, the BA will forward the claim to the authority certifying (or not) the matters it is required to deal with.

17.57   The DSS advises that the 8-day time limit includes the last day of entitlement to IS or JSA(IB). But there is a strong alternative argument that it excludes that day. For example, if the last day of entitlement to IS or JSA(IB) is a Sunday, the DSS's advice is that the claim must be made no later than the Sunday 7 days later; the alternative view is that it must be made no later than the Monday 8 days later.

17.58   If an EP claim is outside the time limit, the claimant does not qualify for an EP. EP claims cannot be backdated. However, the usual rules about what constitutes the 'date of claim' (chapter 7) do not apply: questions can arise about whether a claim was made but subsequently lost or mislaid (by the Jobcentre, BA or authority), and novel questions can arise about what constitutes the date an EP claim is made. The DSS has issued advice about when compensation may be paid to EP claimants who do not qualify because of wrong advice from BA offices and Jobcentres (circular HB/CTB A4/97).

17.59   The usual rules about defective claims (e.g. if the authority wishes further information from the claimant: para. 7.37) do not apply to EP claims. If an EP claim is 'properly completed', it must be determined. If an EP claim is not 'properly completed', it would be good practice for an authority to invite a claimant to rectify it, but the 8-day time limit still applies.

Table 17.1: CONDITIONS FOR EXTENDED PAYMENTS

CONDITION	HOW IT IS DECIDED
(a) The claimant or any partner starts employment or self-employment, or increases his or her hours or earnings.	The claimant certifies this.
(b) The claimant has been entitled to IS or JSA(IB) which has ceased as a result.	Both the BA and the claimant certify this. The BA also certifies the last day of IS or JSA(IB) entitlement.
(c) The new job, hours or earnings are expected to last for at least 5 weeks.	The claimant certifies this.
(d) The claimant satisfies the '26-week condition': i.e. for a continuous period of 26 weeks ending with the last day of IS or JSA(IB) entitlement, he or she was: • 'available for and actively seeking employment' (the claimant must also have been entitled to IS or JSA(IB) at the end of the 26 weeks, but need not have been during any earlier periods); or • in receipt of IS or JSA(IB) as a lone parent, or IS because of incapacity for work; or • in receipt of IS or JSA(IB) which included a carer premium or a disability premium; or • in receipt of IS or JSA(IB) whilst on a Government training scheme; or • a combination of the above.	The BA certifies this.
(e) The claimant or partner remains liable (or treated as liable) for rent/council tax during the EP period (para. 17.65), which may include liability on a new address (para. 17.71).	The claimant certifies this. The claimant also certifies (if appropriate) the date of the move and the new address.
(f) The claimant or partner was on HB/CTB which ceases because of the end of entitlement to IS or JSA(IB) (or as a result of the move, if appropriate).	The authority determines this.
(g) In the case of a claimant who was on IS, he or she is aged under 60 on the first day of non-entitlement to IS.	The authority determines this.
(h) The claimant • makes a claim for an EP in the method and time prescribed (para. 17.56); or	The authority determines this.
• is a lone parent who satisfies the conditions for a 'lone parent run-on' in his or her IS (para. 17.60)	The BA certifies this, and also certifies the dates the authority needs (para. 17.60).

METHOD OF CLAIM: 'LONE PARENT RUN-ON' CASES

17.60 In broad terms, 'lone parent run-on' is available for certain lone parents who have been on income support and who start work after being out of work for 26 weeks or more. It means they get two weeks extra income support after they start the job. During these two weeks they continue to qualify for HB/CTB in the ordinary way.

17.61 The above claimants:

♦ get an EP for only two weeks; but

♦ do not have to make any kind of claim to qualify for it: instead the BA informs the authority of their entitlement and it is awarded automatically.

Though no claim is required, the term 'claimant' is still used in the obvious sense.

DETERMINATIONS, NOTIFICATIONS AND APPEALS

17.62 The authority has a duty to determine EP claims and notify the outcome – even if a claimant does not qualify for an EP – and even if the only reason is that the BA has said that the claimant does not satisfy the '26-week condition' (table 17.1).

17.63 Table 17.1 shows how the various conditions are decided. A few matters are determined by the authority (in particular, whether the claim was made in time). But many matters rely on the claimant or the BA 'certifying' them. The DSS's advice is that the authority should accept what the claimant has 'certified', unless there are particular grounds for doubting this. For example, an authority might doubt a claimant who certified, in late December, that his new job impersonating Father Christmas would last at least five weeks.

17.64 The authority must accept what the the BA has certified. If the claimant appeals about this using the HB/CTB appeal procedure (chapter 19), the authority (and Review Board) can consider only whether the BA has 'certified' the matter, not whether it ought to have done. The DSS advises that if the BA has said that a claimant does not satisfy the '26-week condition', and the claimant disagrees with this, the claimant should be advised to raise this with the BA. The matters the BA is required to certify are 'Secretary of State decisions' and so not appealable to a Social Security Appeal Tribunal: the claimant could, however, challenge them by judicial review.

PERIODS AND AMOUNTS OF EXTENDED PAYMENTS: GENERAL CASES

17.65 Except for many cases of lone parent claimants (para. 17.60), an EP is awarded for the four weeks following the Sunday on which the authority ends the HB/CTB benefit period as a result of the claimant ceasing to be entitled to IS or JSA(IB) (para. 17.19), or (if appropriate) as a result of the claimant moving home

Examples: Extended payments

GENERAL CASE

A claimant – who satisfies all the conditions for an EP – gets a new job on Monday 10th April. The Benefits Agency decides that her last day of entitlement to income support is Sunday 9th April.

(a) The end of her HB/CTB entitlement under the usual rules (para. 17.19) is Sunday 16th April.

(b) Her EP period runs from Monday 17th April to Sunday 14th May (four weeks).

'LONE PARENT RUN-ON' CASE

A claimant – who satisfies all the conditions for an EP – gets a new job on Monday 10th April. Because she turns out to qualify for a 'lone parent run-on', the Benefits Agency decides that her last day of entitlement to income support is Sunday 23rd April.

(a) The end of her HB/CTB entitlement under the usual rules (para. 17.19) is Sunday 30th April.

(b) Her EP period runs from Monday 1st May to Sunday 14th May (two weeks).

(para. 17.26). Technically, an extended payment is not an extension to the old benefit period. It is a special period not forming part of any benefit period (though it may be replaced, later, by a new ongoing HB/CTB benefit period: para 17.65).

17.66 In each of those four weeks, the amount of the HB/CTB EP equals the amount awarded in the last benefit week of the (recently ended) HB/CTB benefit period – ignoring any part-week of entitlement and ignoring any rent-free period. This is the case regardless of the amount of HB/CTB awarded in that benefit week. All changes of circumstances are ignored for these purposes (though for movers see para. 17.67), and claimants are under no duty to notify changes: for example, if a non-dependant moves in or out, this is ignored. If an addition was awarded for exceptional hardship or exceptional circumstances in that week, it must be awarded throughout the EP period. This is the only way that such an addition can be awarded in the EP period.

PERIODS AND AMOUNTS: 'LONE PARENT RUN-ON' CASES

17.67 In the case of a claimant who is granted an EP because of qualifying for an income support 'lone parent run-on' (para. 17.60), the amount awarded is the same as in other EP cases (para. 17.66 – and the other general points in that para. apply); and the EP runs:

◆ from the day after the last day of entitlement to IS (i.e. the day after the last day of the IS 'lone parent run-on');

◆ to the end of the HB/CTB benefit week which contains the day four weeks after the day on which the claimant started remunerative work (unless the person's liability for rent or council tax ceases earlier, in which case entitlement to the EP also ceases at the same time).

17.68   In most cases, this is a two-week period (para. 17.60). The BA notifies the authority of both the last day of entitlement to IS and the date on which the claimant started remunerative work, in order that the authority can calculate the above period.

EXTENDED PAYMENTS AND RENEWAL CLAIMS

17.69   Claimants may remain entitled to HB/CTB despite their (or their partner's) new job or increase in hours or earnings. A renewal claim (by the claimant or partner) for ongoing HB/CTB runs consecutively from the end of the old HB/CTB benefit period if it is made during the EP period or during the four weeks after it.

◆ If the claimant is entitled to less ongoing HB/CTB than the amount of the EP (or exactly the same amount), the new amount is awarded from the benefit week immediately following the end of the EP period.

◆ If the claimant is entitled to more ongoing HB/CTB than the amount of the EP, the balance is awarded for the EP period, and the whole amount is awarded thereafter. (This could arise, for example, if a non-dependant left the household and the increase in entitlement due to this was greater than the decrease in entitlement due to the new income of the claimant or partner.)

If the authority fails to end the old HB/CTB benefit period for any reason, the amount awarded to the claimant is offset against the amount of the EP, i.e. the amount awarded during the EP period is treated as though it was the EP.

MISCELLANEOUS MATTERS

17.70   The following are the main further matters relating to EPs.

◆ A separate determination should be made (and notified) about whether to pay HB to a landlord during an EP period.

◆ A separate determination should be made (and notified) about whether to recover recoverable overpayments of HB by deduction from an EP for HB.

◆ A claimant who is entitled to an EP is entitled to it even if this means awarding an EP for HB in a rent-free week, and even if it means awarding an EP for CTB of a different amount from the amount of his or her current council tax liability.

◆ The question of whether an EP has been overpaid depends on who has to certify and/or determine what. For example, if a claimant certified that his new job would last at least 5 weeks and then the employer (unforeseeably) closed down, the extended payment was correctly paid: there has been no overpayment.

◆ A claimant who is entitled to an EP and who has been entitled to HB on two homes (para. 4.67) appears to qualify for an EP on both homes.

EXTENDED PAYMENTS FOR MOVERS

17.71 Claimants who are entitled to an EP are entitled to it even if they move home during the week before, or the week in which, they or a partner take up employment or self-employment – but not in cases of increasing hours or earnings. In practice, in nearly all cases, the claimant will be at the new address for the whole of the EP period.

17.72 The amount of the EP for HB at the new address (during the EP period) depends on whether the claimant's entitlements at the old and new addresses are to a rent allowance or a rent rebate, as shown in table 17.2, which also shows the amount of the EP for CTB at the new address.

17.73 In any case when the claimant moves to a new authority area, the law allows authorities to exchange information relevant to extended payments. The DSS advises that the old authority should keep all the documentation and write to the new authority confirming the details.

FAST-TRACKING

HBR 76(4), (5)
CTBR 66(4), (5)

17.74 An authority must 'give priority… over other claims' to a claim made by any claimant who:

◆ makes a claim for an EP within the time limit (para. 17.56) – regardless of whether he or she actually qualifies for it; and makes a claim for ongoing HB/CTB (on the basis of his or her new circumstances) no later than seven days after that – regardless of whether he or she actually qualifies for it; or

◆ is entitled to an EP because of qualifying for a 'lone parent run-on' (para. 17.67); and makes a claim for on-going HB/CTB no later than seven days after the date he or she started the work in question; and the BA certifies that the person qualifies no later than 14 days after that date.

17.75 This is known as 'fast-tracking'. In addition to the above requirement, there are subsidy incentives and penalties for authorities related to 'fast-tracking' as described in chapter 21.

Table 17.2: EXTENDED PAYMENTS FOR MOVERS

HB: A MOVE FROM RENT ALLOWANCE TO RENT ALLOWANCE

The amount of HB at the new address is exactly equal to the amount of HB at the old address.

If the move is to a new authority area, the old authority makes this payment.

HB: A MOVE FROM RENT ALLOWANCE TO RENT REBATE

The amount of HB at the new address is calculated using:

◆ the eligible rent at the new address, but

◆ the non-dependant deduction(s) (if any) at the old address.

If the move is to a new authority area, the new authority makes this payment.

HB: A MOVE FROM RENT REBATE TO RENT REBATE

The amount of HB at the new address is calculated using:

◆ the eligible rent at the new address, but

◆ the non-dependant deduction(s) (if any) at the old address.

If the move is to a new authority area, the new authority makes this payment.

HB: A MOVE FROM RENT REBATE TO RENT ALLOWANCE

The amount of HB at the new address is exactly equal to the amount of HB at the old address.

If the move is to a new authority area, the new authority makes this payment.

CTB: ALL CASES

The amount of CTB at the new address is calculated using:

◆ the eligible council tax liability at the new address, but

◆ the non-dependant deduction(s) (if any) at the old address.

If the move is to a new authority area, the new authority makes this payment.

18 Overpayments

18.1   This chapter explains:

◆ what an overpayment is;

◆ why the cause of an overpayment is important;

◆ when an overpayment is recoverable;

◆ how the amount of the overpayment is worked out;

◆ when, from whom, how, and at what rate an overpayment should be recovered;

◆ the information that should be provided to the claimant and any other person affected;

◆ how far recovery of an overpayment may be pursued; and

◆ when an administrative penalty may be added to a fraudulent overpayment.

HBR 98 AA
s.134(2)
CTBR 83 **18.2**   Where more HB is paid than a claimant is entitled to, this is referred to as an 'overpayment'. The term includes not only overpayments made by way of instruments of payment such as cheques but also any overpayment by way of a rebate to a rent account. Where more CTB is allowed (by way of a rebate to a council tax account or otherwise) than a claimant is entitled to, this is referred to as 'excess benefit'. As most of the rules relating to 'overpayments' and 'excess benefit' are the same, the term overpayment is used in this chapter to refer to both.

18.3   The overpayment and recovery of benefit has created major difficulties for claimants, landlords and authorities. Claimants and landlords have had their rights denied and unnecessary debts created. Many authorities have failed to follow the correct process of determination, notify claimants, keep adequate records, or account for overpayments properly. As a consequence they have made inaccurate subsidy claims and created rent and council tax arrears for themselves and debts for landlords.

What is an overpayment?

HBR 98
CTBR 83 **18.4**   Overpayments are established through a formal review of benefit entitlement or, in rare instances, the correction of an accidental error or the setting aside of the original determination (chapter 17). They are amounts of benefit which have been paid but to which there is no entitlement under the regulations. They include any overpayment of:

♦ a rent allowance paid on account;

♦ CTB due to a backdated award of a council tax discount (para. 3.35), council tax disability reduction (para. 3.32) or council tax transitional relief (para. 3.30).

Example: An overpayment

The claimant receives HB and CTB from 13th April 1998. On 14th May 1998 her adult son comes to live with her. the claimant has a duty to inform the authority of this change of circumstances but does not do so until 6th August 1998. The authority determines that a non-dependant deduction should have been made for the son from the benefit week commencing Monday 18th May 1998 (the date from which the change of circumstances should have taken effect). The claimant has received benefit up to and including the benefit week commencing 17th August 1998. An overpayment of benefit has occurred for 19 weeks.

18.5   Having identified that an overpayment has occurred the authority must:

♦ establish the cause of each overpayment;

♦ determine whether or not the overpayment is recoverable;

♦ identify the period and calculate the amount of the overpayment;

♦ consider whether or not recovery should be sought;

♦ determine from whom the recovery should be sought.

and, within 14 days (para. 18.42), notify the claimant and other persons affected, for example the landlord where recovery is sought from him or her, accordingly.

18.6   In the case of HB overpayments of rebates to an authority's rent account or overpaid CTB allowed to its council tax accounts, the regulations must not be circumvented by the automatic creation of debits applied retrospectively with the resulting creation of arrears for the claimant. The authority must perform the duties imposed by the regulations and make each determination required.

Establishing the cause of the overpayment

18.7   The authority must establish the cause of an overpayment in order to:

♦ determine whether or not it is recoverable;

♦ correctly notify the claimant, the person the authority is seeking to recover from (if not the claimant), and any other person affected;

♦ claim the correct amount of subsidy.

18.8   An overpayment might arise due to:

◆ local authority error, e.g. the authority fails to act on notification of a change of circumstances provided by the claimant;

◆ Benefits Agency or employment service error, e.g. the Benefits Agency makes a mistaken award of income support or income-based JSA;

◆ claimant error or claimant fraud, e.g. the claimant fails to inform the authority of a change in circumstance which he or she has a duty to report, such as the end of entitlement to income support or income-based JSA; or

◆ other reasons, e.g. the claimant obtains a retrospective award of a council tax discount and this reduces the council tax liability for that period.

Technical and advance overpayments are amounts of CTB or rent rebates (but not rent allowances) that are paid in advance by way of a rebate to an account.

18.9   Consecutive overpayments may result from different causes. For example, the claimant may fail to notify the authority that his or her earnings have increased. The authority may then delay acting on that information once it is informed. In such a case the cause and amount of each overpayment must be separately identified.

Recoverable overpayments

HBR 91(3),
99(1),(2)
CTBR 84(1),(2),(3)   **18.10**   An overpayment of a rent allowance payment on account may, where there is ongoing benefit once entitlement has been determined, be recovered whatever the cause of the overpayment. An overpayment of CTB may be due to a retrospective reduction in the claimant's council tax as a result of a delayed award of transitional relief, a discount or a disability reduction. Such overpayments are recoverable in all cases. All other amounts that have been overpaid are recoverable except where they are due to official error. Even an official error overpayment is recoverable if:

◆ the claimant, someone acting on his or her behalf, or the person to whom the payment was made, could reasonably have been expected to realise that an overpayment was taking place at the time of payment or upon receipt of any notification relating to the payment; or

◆ it is an amount of rent rebate or CTB that has been overpaid in respect of a period following the date of the review that identified overpayment.

HBR 99(3)
CTBR 84(3)   **18.11**   An official error is a mistake, whether in the form of an act or omission made by the authority, an external contractor acting for the authority, the Benefits Agency or the employment service. The definition of an official error does not include circumstances where the claimant, or someone acting on the claimant's behalf, or the person to whom payment has been made, caused or materially

contributed to that error. Such overpayments are categorised as claimant or third party error and are recoverable. An official error occurs, for example, where there is a mistaken award of IS or income-based JSA by the Benefits Agency or where the authority put the wrong information into its computer or delayed acting upon information it had received.

18.12   Where the claimant, a person acting on his or her behalf, or the person to whom the payment has been made, could reasonably have been expected to realise that it was an overpayment at the time of payment, or of any notice relating to that payment, an official error overpayment is recoverable. In *R v Liverpool City Council ex parte Griffiths,* (1990) 22 HLR 312 QBD, it was held that this rule requires the reasonable expectation, not that a payment might be an overpayment, but that it was an overpayment. The DSS is incorrect in its simple statement that an 'example of a recoverable overpayment, made as a result of an official error, would be where the claimant is notified that his weekly entitlement to rent allowance was £25 but he was actually paid £50 per week' (GM para. A7.24). Determination of recoverability would require examination of all the relevant facts. If, for example, the claimant had learning difficulties it may be that he or she could not reasonably have been expected to realise that it was an overpayment.

18.13   If the claimant, etc, did not have the information necessary to know that benefit was being overpaid at the time of payment or notification relating to the payment, then an official error overpayment is not recoverable. The DSS (HB/CCB(90)23) advises that when in rent rebate cases credits are made to the landlord's rent accounts before the claimant receives a written notification of the award, the claimant cannot know if he is being overpaid unless or until he receives written notification of the rebate. This will also be the case, for example, where HB is paid direct to a landlord (unless the landlord could reasonably have been expected to realise it was an overpayment) or CTB is paid into a council tax account. The claimant and/or any other person affected may seek an internal review, and ultimately a review board hearing, of the authority's determination that an overpayment is recoverable (chapter 19).

18.14   The rules regarding HB/CTB overpayments differ from those applicable to the other major welfare benefits. With the latter the power to recover rests on the adjudicating authority being satisfied that a material misrepresentation or non-disclosure has been proved.

Working out the amount of a recoverable overpayment

HBR 104
CTBR 90

18.15 The amount of recoverable overpayment is worked out as follows:

◆ the amount paid during the period in question;

MINUS

HBR 104(a)
CTBR 90(a)

◆ any smaller amount that was payable over that period including, in the case of CTB, any second adult rebate or main CTB if that would have been a 'better buy' (para. 9.18);

HBR 103(1)
CTBR 89(1)

◆ the difference between the amount of the overpayment and the amount of the recalculated overpayment if the diminishing capital rule applies (paras. 18.17).

HBR 104(b)
CTBR 90(b)

18.16 During the period of the overpayment the claimant may have paid money into a local authority rent or council tax account above his or her erroneous liability. If this is the case such payments may be deducted for the purpose of working out the amount of the recoverable overpayment.

Example: Claimant has continued to pay rent

A council tenant's eligible rent is £45. From week 1, he is unemployed, claiming JSA(IB) and in receipt of maximum HB of £45. The claimant starts work in week 5 and is no longer entitled to any HB from week 6. The claimant fails to inform the authority of the change of circumstance but starts to pay full rent from week 6. However, HB continues to be paid at £45 per week until week 10.

For the purpose of working out the amount of the recoverable overpayment (from weeks 6 to 10) the authority may deduct the amount of the additional rent paid (£45 per week) over the erroneous liability (nil per week) from the overpaid HB.

DIMINISHING CAPITAL RULE

HBR 103(1)
CTBR 89(1)

18.17 Where the overpayment arose as:

◆ a result of a misrepresentation or failure to disclose relevant information relating to the claimant's capital, or that of a child or young person; or

◆ an error relating to capital (other than a non-recoverable official error, paras. 18.10-11); and in either case

◆ the overpayment is in respect of more than 13 weeks;

Example: Diminishing capital rule

The claimant has been in receipt of a £5.73 rent allowance each week since 25th May 1998. She visits the authority's housing benefit office on 15th October 1998, to query the amount of benefit she is receiving.

During the course of her interview it emerges that she had accidentally forgotten to include on her original application form £250 which she has retained throughout the period in a building society account. When this amount is added to her previously declared and still existing capital of £15,783 it brings the amount that counts for HB purposes to £16,033. With capital above the maximum limit there has been no entitlement to benefit from the start of the claim.

The overpayment arose due to the claimant's failure to disclose a material fact relating to capital and is recoverable. The overpayment has taken place over 21 benefit weeks so the diminishing capital rule applies. There is only one complete 13-week period.

The amount of HB overpaid by the end of 13 benefit weeks is: £5.73 x 13 = £74.49

With the application of the diminishing capital rule for the rest of the period of payment – and for the sole purpose of calculating the overpayment – the claimant's capital is assumed to be £15,958.51, i.e.

Claimant's capital	£16,033.00
MINUS amount of overpaid HB during 13-week period	£74.49
Claimant's assumed capital for purpose of calculating overpaid HB =	£15,958.51

The original calculation of HB had taken into account the declared capital of £15,783. The tariff income from the actual and 'diminished' capital amount is the same. Therefore, under the diminishing capital rule, no overpayment has occurred between the 14th and last week in which the benefit has been paid. The total amount of recoverable overpayment is £74.49.

The claimant still actually has capital of £16.033. She is not entitled to HB until such time as the amount of her capital falls below £16,000.01 (as would be the case if, for example, she repaid the overpayment).

the authority must treat the amount of the capital as having been reduced by the amount overpaid during the first and each subsequent period of 13 benefit weeks for the purpose of working out the overpayment.

18.18 The reasoning behind this rule is that if the capital had been taken into account, so that the benefit was reduced or not awarded, the claimant's capital would in all probability have been reduced to meet his or her housing costs, council tax liability, or day-to-day living expenses.

HBR 103(2)
CTBR 89(2)

18.19 This notional reduction of capital does not count for any other purpose, e.g. calculating entitlement.

When should a recoverable overpayment be recovered?

HBR 99, 100
CTBR 84, 85

18.20 A recoverable overpayment may be recovered at the authority's discretion. The regulations say that such overpayments are recoverable and not that they must be recovered. Authorities 'should note that a determination that an overpayment is recoverable must be quite separate from a decision to recover it. Due regard should be given to the circumstances relating to individual cases when deciding whether or not recovery is appropriate.'

HBR 100,
83(2), 2(1)
CTBR 85, 72(2),
2(1)

18.21 There is no obligation upon the authority to attempt recovery of all recoverable overpayments. The determination to recover is a discretionary one which must be exercised judicially (paras. 1.42-43). Subsidy arrangements penalise those authorities that do not recover most recoverable overpayments. Authorities should not allow this fact to fetter their discretion but in accordance with the decision in *R v Brent London Borough Council ex parte Connery*, (1989) 22 HLR 40 QBD, reproduced in GM ch. 4, annex A, the authority may take the implications for its own financial position into account (para. 11.73). Repayment should not be sought where it would be unreasonable to do so.

18.22 The DSS has changed its position a number of times over the years with regard to the authority's choice as to whether or not recovery should take place and any 'appeal' rights that may attach to the exercise of this choice.

18.23 Its original position (HB/CCB(92)20 para 13.2) was that the exercise of this choice was a discretion and that the appropriate remedy for the claimant, or other person affected, where the authority had exercised its discretion unreasonably was an application for judicial review rather than an application for review and further review (Chapter 19). In more recent years the DSS has asserted (GM A7.51) the idea that the decision to seek recovery is a private law matter rather than one that is susceptible to the review process or judicial review. The alternative view is that the authority's choice regarding recovery is a prime example of the exercise of a discretionary power and that the resulting decision is one that can be 'appealed' through the process of review and further review. A third view is that as the exercise of a discretion it is not something which in itself can be the trigger for a review and further review. However, once the question of the recoverability of an overpayment has reached the review board it can decide the matter. This is because in reaching its decision the Review Board must apply the provisions of the regulations as though any discretion conferred on the authority were conferred upon the Review Board.

18.24 Court decisions certainly seem to support the idea that the review board has a discretion that can be exercised here. In *R v Ellesmere Port and Neston BC HBRB, ex p Williams* (1996) unreported 15 November, CA, Waller LJ stated that he was prepared to assume that the review board could exercise the discretion as to whether there should be recovery. In *R v South Hams District Council, ex p. Ash* (Times Law Report 27th May 1999) Moses, J., accepted the Review Board's discretion in this matter (though without the benefit of legal argument on the point at issue). It was held that in the exercise of its discretion to recover overpayments the review board had a duty to take into account the nature and purpose of an award of a war disability pension to relieve suffering and recognise service to the state, where the late award of that pension had led to the overpayment.

From whom may recovery be sought?

18.25 A recoverable HB/CTB overpayment may always be recovered from the claimant or the person to whom it has been paid. It may, for example, be recovered from a landlord to whom HB has been paid direct. The Court of Appeal, in *Warwick District Council v Freeman,* 31st October 1994 (27 HLR 616), confirmed that a recoverable overpayment may be recovered from a landlord where the overpayment was paid directly to the landlord, even where the landlord did not contribute to, or have any knowledge of, the overpayment. Nonetheless, in exercising its choice whether to recover the overpayment from either the claimant or the landlord, the authority must act reasonably and take into account all relevant factors (paras. 1.42-43). Here, and in the following paragraphs, references to a landlord include a landlord's agent.

HBR 101(1)(b) CTBR 86(1), 87

18.26 Where an overpayment of HB has arisen due to a misrepresentation or failure to disclose a relevant fact by:

HBR 101(1)(a)

◆ the claimant; or

◆ someone on his or her behalf such as an appointee or agent; or

◆ the person to whom a payment may be made such as a landlord;

then it may also be recovered from that person. This does not apply in the case of overpaid CTB.

HBR 101(2)
CTBR 86(2) **18.27**   Where an HB overpayment has been made to a claimant who has a partner it may be deducted from HB payable or, in the case of a CTB overpayment, CTB allowed to the partner. This may only occur if the claimant and partner are members of the same household (para. 6.11) both at the date of the overpayment and the date it is recovered.

18.28   If a recoverable overpayment has been made to a deceased person recovery may be sought from the estate.

Method of recovery

18.29   Authorities may recover a recoverable overpayment via any lawful method but an overpayment of HB cannot be recovered from a payment of CTB or *vice versa*. The following are the main methods adopted by authorities:

(a) by deduction from on-going benefit;

(b) from arrears of HB or CTB which become payable while there is an outstanding overpayment;

(c) by deduction from certain social security benefits;

(d) by setting up a sundry debtors' account and billing for the overpayment;

(e) in the cases of CTB only, by adding the overpaid CTB on to the claimant's council tax account as an amount of council tax owing.

Only method (a) is available where the authority has chosen to recover the overpayment from the claimant's partner (para. 18.27).

RECOVERY FROM THE CLAIMANT BY DEDUCTIONS FROM BENEFIT PAID DIRECT TO A LANDLORD OR TO A COUNCIL TENANT'S RENT ACCOUNT

18.30   Where the authority has determined to recover an overpayment from the claimant and is recovering it by deduction from his or her on-going benefit paid direct to a landlord or, in the case of a council tenant, in the form of a reduction to the rebate to the rent account, this counts not as recovery from the landlord but from the claimant. The landlord is not a 'person affected' and does not have any formal review rights in relation to the overpayment. The claimant must make up the subsequent shortfall in HB to avoid rent arrears accruing (GM para. A7.39 Example 1). Any such arrears are arrears of rent and the landlord should pursue recovery as such.

18.31   Authorities should not recover overpaid rent rebates by debiting the rent account of the claimant so that he or she is placed in rent arrears. Such arrears cannot, for example, be recovered by possession proceedings as they are not amounts of rent lawfully due and the tenant-claimant would have a defence against any such action. Authorities may, however, use their rent accounting systems to control recovery of overpayments. The DSS advises that authorities should be able to distinguish 'recovered' overpaid HB from arrears of rent. Authorities should also make it clear to claimants that the payments being sought represent overpaid HB (GM paras. A7.40-43) and should be able to distinguish payments the claimant makes to cover the overpayment and payments of rent.

RECOVERY FROM THE LANDLORD BY DEDUCTIONS FROM BENEFIT PAID DIRECT TO THE LANDLORD

18.32 In a rent allowance case the authority may, in appropriate circumstances, decide to recover the overpayment from the landlord. In such a case two of the methods of recovery available are: AA s. 75(5)

◆ deduction from HB paid to the landlord on behalf of other tenants/claimants to whom the overpayment does not relate; and.

◆ deduction from HB paid to the land lord on behalf of the claimant to whom the overpayment relates.

RECOVERY FROM THE HB OF TENANT(S) UNRELATED TO THE OVERPAYMENT

18.33 Where the authority recovers an overpayment by making deductions from the HB paid to the landlord for a tenant to whom the overpayment does not relate, that tenant is always deemed to have paid rent to the value of the recovered sum. In these circumstances the landlord is a 'person affected' but the tenant/claimant from whose benefit the deductions are being made is not. Consequently such tenant/claimants should not receive an overpayment notifications on this matter. Nor do they have the right to seek a review or further review of the authority's determinations. The authority should, however, have notified all claimants and landlords at the time direct payments commenced that:

◆ it had the power to make deductions from the amount paid to the landlord in order to recover an overpayment of benefit relating to another tenant; and

◆ that in such a case the claimant's rent liability will have been discharged to the full value of his or her HB entitlement.

RECOVERY FROM THE LANDLORD BY DEDUCTIONS FROM THE HB OF THE CLAIMANT TO WHOM THE OVERPAYMENT RELATES

18.34 Where the authority has decided to recover an overpayment from the landlord, but has chosen to do this by deduction from HB paid to the landlord on behalf of the claimant to whom the overpayment relates, then both the landlord and claimant are persons affected. In other words, in such a case the landlord and claimant have formal review rights in relation to the overpayment. Again,   AA S. 75(6) normally the claimant must make up the subsequent shortfall in HB to avoid rent arrears. It is unlikely that an authority would adopt this method in these circumstances except in cases of landlord fraud. Where the landlord:

◆ has agreed to pay a 30 per cent penalty (para 18.57) as an alternative to prosecution; or

◆ has been prosecuted in relation to that overpayment,

the claimant to whom the overpayment relates is deemed to have paid the rent to the value of the recovered sum.

SI 1997 No. 2435 **18.35** In the above circumstances the authority must write to the claimant and landlord:

◆ explaining the process; and

◆ stating that the landlord has no right to that sum from the tenant and that the tenant's obligation to the landlord is deemed to have been met by the amount recovered.

18.36 The DSS points out (HB/CTB A1/98, para. 16) that the legislation imposes no penalty upon landlords who attempt to recover such overpayment or evict a tenant due to non-closure of the tenant's liability but that the Courts have been advised that landlords would be in breach of the relevant legislation if they attempted this action.

METHODS BY WHICH THE LANDLORD MAY RECOVER THE REPAID OVERPAYMENT FROM THE CLAIMANT

HBR 93(2) **18.37** The landlord may seek to recover the sum repaid to the authority from the claimant to whom the overpayment relates. The exception to this rule is where the claimant's obligation to the landlord is deemed to have been discharged (paras. 18.33-36). Where the claimant is a current tenant the non-local authority landlord is able to treat the sum it has repaid to the authority as rent arrears and has the ultimate sanction of eviction to secure payment. Where the claimant to whom the overpayment relates is no longer the landlord's tenant the landlord may invoice the former tenant and then pursue the debt through normal civil debt recovery procedures.

RECOVERY FROM OTHER SOCIAL SECURITY BENEFITS

HBR 105
CTBR 91 **18.38** Where methods (a), (b) or (e) in para 18.29 are not possible, the authority may request the Benefits Agency to recover any overpayment from most social security benefits payable to any person identified in para. 18.26. It may not be recovered from guardians allowance, child benefit, retirement pensions or war pensions or tax credits. The Benefits Agency will recover overpayments from social security benefits where it is:

♦ requested by the authority to do so; and

♦ satisfied that the overpayment arose as a result of a misrepresentation or failure to disclose a material fact by, or on behalf of, the claimant; or by some other person to whom a payment of HB/CTB has been made; and

♦ that person is receiving sufficient amounts of one or more benefits to enable deductions to be made.

Rate of recovery

18.39 The regulations do not prescribe a specific rate of recovery. The question is one for the authority to decide. The possibilities range from recovery via one lump sum to a number of instalments over time. There are two situations to consider:

♦ recovery from claimants, private landlords and other individuals; and

♦ recovery from organisations and businesses, such as housing associations and lettings agencies.

18.40 In cases involving individuals, the DSS advises (HB/CTB A51/99 para. 21) that in cases where income support/income-based JSA is in payment, the authority should bear in mind that the Benefits Agency may be deducting up to £7.95 per week from those benefits or £10.40 where the claimant has been convicted of fraud. The authority should consider whether the proposed rate of recovery would cause the claimant hardship and, if it would, consideration should be given to recovery at a lower rate. In particular authorities should be careful not to cause undue hardship by simply stopping all benefit payment until the overpayment is recovered unless the amount of weekly benefit involved represents a reasonable level of repayment given the claimant's circumstances.

18.41 In deciding the rate of recovery from organisations the authority has the power to effect large recoveries in a single lump sum but it will often not be appropriate to do so. The authority should act reasonably in deciding a rate of recovery. In particular, as a matter of good practice, the authority should discuss the rate of recovery with the organisation concerned to ensure the rate of recovery does not undermine that organisation's financial stability or essential activities.

Information to be provided to claimants, landlords, etc

18.42 When the authority determines that a recoverable HB/CTB overpayment has occurred, and exercises its discretion to recover it, a letter should be sent to the person from whom recovery is sought and any other person affected by the determination. So, for example, if the authority decides to recover from the

HBR 77(1)(b)
CTBR 67(1)(b)

landlord, it must send letters to both the claimant and the landlord. This should happen within 14 days of the determination being made or as soon as reasonably practicable thereafter.

HBR sch 6 part VII
CBR sch 6 part VII

18.43 Overpayment letters to claimants, landlords and other persons affected must state:

◆ the fact that there is a recoverable overpayment;

◆ the reason why there is a recoverable overpayment;

◆ the amount of the recoverable overpayment;

◆ how the amount was calculated;

◆ the benefit weeks to which the recoverable overpayment relates;

◆ where recovery of HB is to be made by deduction from future HB, the amount of that deduction;

◆ in the case of overpaid CTB, the method of recovery to be adopted;

◆ the person's right to request a written statement setting out the authority's reasons for its determination of any matter set out in the letter and the manner and time in which to do so; and

◆ the person's right to make written representations (request a review) regarding the determinations made and the manner and time in which to do so; and

◆ any other appropriate matter, e.g. the opportunity to make representations with regard to hardship.

HBR 77(1)
sch 6 para 14(2)

18.44 Where the authority is seeking to recovery an overpayment from another claimant's direct payments to the landlord, the notice of determination to that landlord must also identify both:

◆ the original claimant on whose behalf the recoverable amount was paid to that landlord; and

◆ the other claimant from whose benefit recovery is going to be made.

SI 1997 No. 2435

18.45 Where the authority has decided to recover a recoverable overpayment from a rent allowance paid direct to the landlord in respect of any tenant; and the landlord in that case has either:

◆ been convicted of fraud; or

◆ agreed to pay a penalty as an alternative to prosecution in relation to the overpayment in question,

the authority must also notify both the landlord and the tenant that:

◆ the overpayment which it has recovered, or determined to recover, is one for which the landlord has been convicted of fraud or has agreed to pay a penalty; and

♦ any tenant from whose benefit the recovery is made must be deemed to have paid his or her rent to the value of the amount recovered.

18.46   The DSS advises (GM para. A7.51) that overpayment notifications should include an invitation to the person in question to either make a full repayment or negotiate some other arrangement within 28 days. A more appropriate period in fact is the six weeks normally allowed for a request for an internal review to be made.

DEFECTIVE NOTIFICATION

18.47   Failure by authorities to notify persons affected clearly and correctly of determinations about overpayments has caused problems for claimants, landlords and authorities. Experience has shown that overpayment notification letters, particularly those to landlords, are often defective in a number of ways. A significant number, for example, fail to give an adequate and intelligible reason why there is a recoverable overpayment or advise landlords of their appeal rights. The failure to provide the required information constitutes maladministration. Additionally authorities that have deficient notifications should be aware that they are undermining the legal basis of their debt recovery action (*Warwick District Council v Freeman* (1994) CA 27 HLR 616). There is no legally recoverable debt until such time as the authority makes the appropriate determinations and issues the required notification.

18.48   A more recent Court of Appeal decision (*Haringey London Borough Council v Awaritefe,* CA, [1999] All ER (D) 540), while agreeing with the approach taken in Warwick and Freeman, ruled that where the failure to provide a valid notification was only trivial, and no substantial harm was caused as a result, the authority was still entitled to pursue recovery of the overpaid amount.

18.49   *Jones v Waveney District Council* (1999) CA 1/12/99 concerned a case where the authority failed to follow the statutory procedures provided and had recovered an alleged overpayment from the landlord by making deductions from benefit due to him on other properties. The Court, applying Warwick and Freeman, held that the landlord was entitled to bring a county court action to recover from the authority the amount that the authority had recovered illegally.

The pursuit of recovery

18.50   The DSS advises (GM para. A7.28) that 'it is for authorities to decide how far to pursue recovery...' In the past many authorities have failed to pursue recovery actively if legal proceedings were required. Where an authority has determined an overpayment to be recoverable, exercised its discretion and decided to recover, the DSS expects it to make a serious attempt at recovery. The GM (para. A7.28) advises that at least two letters requesting payment should be   AA s. 76(6) issued, that an interview will often be appropriate and that a home visit might be cost-effective. As a matter of good practice authorities should include, in their recovery work, procedures that ensure that the claimant is receiving all the HB/CTB and other benefits to which he or she may be entitled, with the aim of reducing the overpayment and increasing resources to meet the debt.

18.51 The authority may take civil proceedings for debt in an appropriate court. The DSS advises that authorities should consider civil proceedings 'where attempts to achieve recovery by other means have failed and there is good reason to believe that the debtor can afford to make repayments' (GM para. A7.39iv).

SIMPLIFIED DEBT RECOVERY PROCEDURE

AA s.75 (7) **18.52** The authority has the power to recover HB overpayments by execution in the County Court in England and Wales as if under a court order; and in Scotland as if it were an extract registered decree arbitral.

18.53 In England and Wales this procedure allows an HB overpayment determination to be registered directly as an Order of the Court without the need to bring a separate action. This procedure remains intact under the Civil Procedure Rules 1998 introduced in April 1999. The authority applies to the Court on a standard County Court form (N 322A), attaching a copy of the overpayment determination notice and accompanied by the relevant fee. The DSS advise (DSS A 59/98, para 8) that the overpayment notification can only be used as proof of debt where it complies fully with the requirements for such notifications under Schedule 6 of the benefit regulations (para. 18.43). An Officer of the Court then makes an Order and a copy is sent to the authority and the debtor. Once an Order has been made the normal methods of enforcement are available to the authority, i.e. attachment of earnings, a garnishee order allowing the authority to obtain money owed to the debtor by a third party, a warrant of execution against goods executed by the County Court bailiff or a charging order normally against land.

18.54 There is no provision for any appeal against an Order made by the 'proper officer' of the Court. Consequently where the claimant or landlord disputes the determination that there is a recoverable overpayment or form whom it should be recovered this is a matter which can only be taken up by requesting an internal review and if necessary a review board hearing (Chapter 19). However, where, for example overpayment notification is defective or appeal rights ignored by the authority an application for the setting aside of the Order can be made to the Court.

18.55 In Scotland the HB determination is immediately enforceable as if it were an extract registered decree arbitral. There is no requirement to register the overpayment determination with the Sheriff Court. The usual methods of enforcement are available, i.e.: arrestment of earnings; poinding and warrant sale; arrestment of moveable property and inhibition of heritable property.

Overpayments and fraud

18.56 The subject of HB/CTB fraud and the authority's response goes beyond the remit of this chapter. The interested general reader is referred to the Audit Commission's *Countering housing benefit fraud: a management handbook* (1997) whilst officers working for an authority should also refer to the DSS's *Local authority fraud investigators manual* and the DSS Fraud Circulars. Overpayments are, however, often related to charges of fraud. The effective recovery of overpayments is one tool in the authority's anti-fraud strategy and as anti-fraud work increases, in the short term at least, the number and amount of overpayments that are identified by the authority increases. Additionally the authority's discretion to levy an administrative penalty (a fine), as an alternative to bringing a prosecution for fraud, is directly related to the question of overpayments.

THE ADMINISTRATIVE PENALTY

18.57 The penalty is equivalent to 30 per cent of the recoverable overpayment due from the person concerned and is recoverable by the same methods available to the authority as when seeking recovery of the overpayment.   AA s. 115A

WHEN WILL A PENALTY APPLY?

18.58 The authority has the discretion to levy the penalty as an alternative to bringing a prosecution for fraud. Prosecutions for HB/CTB offences are in fact extremely rare. In 1995/96 over 50 per cent of authorities failed to secure one successful prosecution for fraud.

18.59 The question of a penalty cannot arise until an overpayment has been properly determined to be recoverable under the regulations and the person from whom recovery is sought has been properly notified. The authority then has the discretion to invite a person to pay a penalty where it is satisfied that: AA s. 115A (1)

◆ the overpayment was caused by an 'act or omission' on the part of that person; and

◆ there are grounds for bringing a prosecution against that person for fraud relating to that overpayment under the Social Security Administration Act or any other enactment.

18.60 Where the conditions for a penalty apply it can only be levied with the agreement of the person concerned. However, if that person refuses to agree to pay a penalty they could be liable to have fraud proceedings brought against them instead.   AA s.115A(2)(a)

CALCULATION OF THE PENALTY

AA s.115A(3) **18.61** The penalty is equivalent to 30 per cent of the recoverable overpayment due from the person concerned. Where an ongoing overpayment started before the penalty provision came into force, a penalty can only be calculated on the amount of recoverable overpayment that accrued after 18 December 1997. (See also section 25(7) of the Social Security Administration (Fraud) Act 1997.)

AGREEING TO PAY A PENALTY

18.62 It is up to the authority to decide how any agreement to pay a penalty will be made. However, where the authority considers that a penalty may be appropriate in any particular case it must give a written penalty notice to the person liable for prosecution.

18.63 This notice advises them:

◆ that they may be invited to agree to pay a penalty; and

◆ that if they make the agreement to do this in the manner specified by the authority (e.g. by signing a standard written undertaking) no fraud proceedings will be brought against them for the overpayment in question.

18.64 The penalty notice must, by law, contain the following points of information about the penalty system:

◆ the manner specified by the authority by which the person may agree to pay a penalty;

◆ that the penalty only applies to an overpayment which is recoverable under section 75 or 76 of the Social Security Administration Act 1992;

◆ that the penalty only applies where it appears to the authority that the overpayment was caused by an act or omission by the person and that there are grounds for commencing criminal proceedings for an offence relating to the overpayment;

◆ the penalty is 30 per cent of the overpayment, is payable in addition to repayment of the overpayment and is recoverable by the same methods as those by which the overpayment is recoverable;

◆ a person who agrees to pay a penalty may withdraw the agreement within 28 days (including the date of the agreement) by notifying the authority in the manner specified by the authority (i.e. in writing or by using a notice provided by the authority for this specific purpose, etc);

◆ where the person withdraws their agreement, any amount of the penalty which has already been recovered will be repaid and the person will no longer be immune from proceedings for an offence;

◆ where it is decided on review or appeal (or in accordance with regulations) that the overpayment is not recoverable or due, any amount of the penalty which has already been recovered will be repaid;

♦ where the amount of the overpayment is revised on review or appeal, except as covered by a new agreement to pay the revised penalty, any amount of the penalty which has already been recovered will be repaid and the person will no longer be immune from proceedings for an offence; and

♦ the payment of a penalty does not give the person immunity from prosecution in relation to any other overpayment or any offence not relating to an overpayment.

19 Appeal procedures

19.1   This chapter describes what can be done if a claimant (or in certain cases, a partner, a landlord or a landlord's agent) disagrees with the authority's determination about HB or CTB, or simply does not understand it. The chapter includes:

◆ who may appeal?

◆ obtaining a written statement of reasons;

◆ which matters can be appealed?

◆ requesting the authority to hold an internal review;

◆ requesting a review board hearing;

◆ review board procedures and decisions;

◆ setting aside a review board's decision; and

◆ the courts and the ombudsman.

19.2   'It is important to recognise' that there is 'a right under the law [to appeal] and the authority should not filter or obstruct the process in any way.' (DSS, *Good Practice Guide:* see para. 19.6 below.)

Overview and terminology

19.3   In HB and CTB, appeals are also sometimes known as 'reviews'. The appeal procedures for HB and CTB are identical. They are illustrated in table 19.1. An appeal may be about almost any aspect of HB or CTB, and may be requested by the claimant or by any other 'person affected' (paras. 16.7-8) by the matter in question.

19.4   There are two stages to dealing with appeals:

◆ The first stage is known as an 'internal review' (sometimes referred to as an 'officer review') and is dealt with by staff of the authority.

◆ The second stage is known as a 'further review' and is dealt with by a body known as a 'review board' at a hearing.

Independent of these two stages it is also possible to obtain a written statement of reasons about any aspect of a claim.

Table 19.1 HB AND CTB APPEAL PROCEDURES AND TIMETABLE

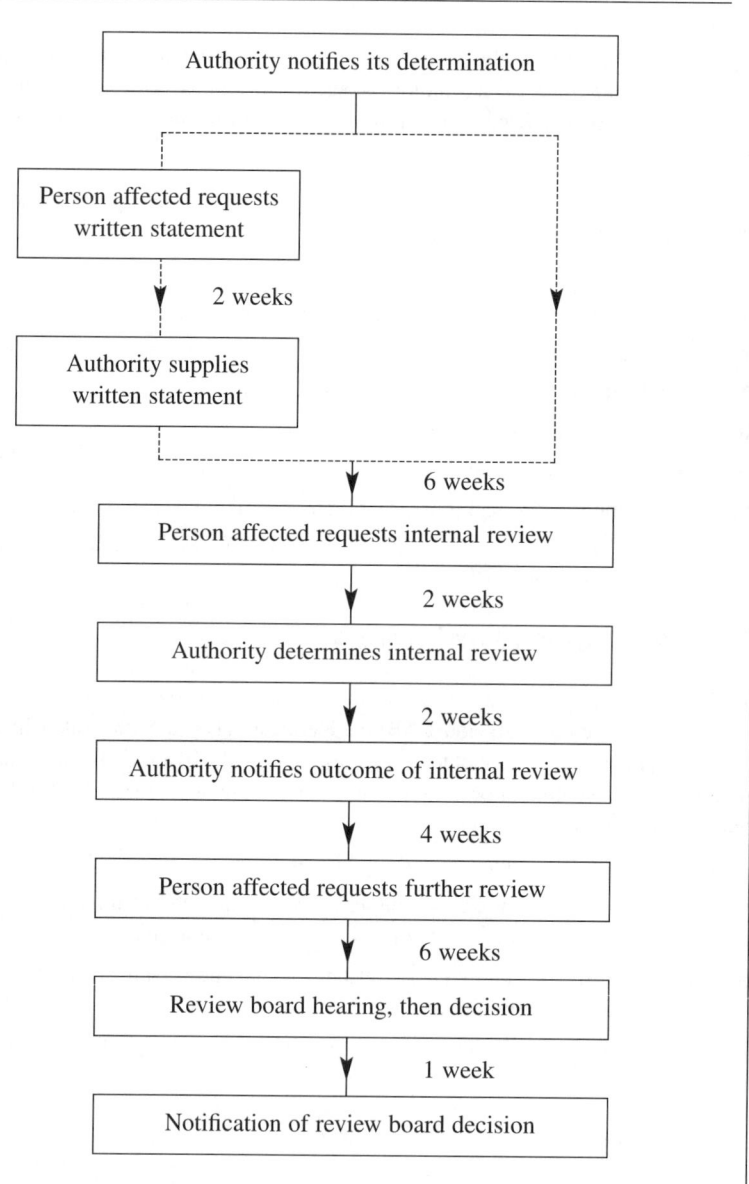

19.5   Both authority staff and review boards have a duty to decide various matters under the HB and CTB regulations. The law uses two terms for this. Review boards are said to make a 'decision' – when an appeal goes to them. Authority staff are said to make a 'determination' when the claim is first assessed, or when it is revised following a change of circumstances or a mistake (paras. 17.11, 17.39), or after a request for an internal review.

19.6   There has been criticism of the structure and operation of the appeal procedures, in particular in *Housing benefit reviews: an evaluation of the effectiveness of the review system in responding to claimants dissatisfied with housing benefits decisions;* DSS research report series no. 3 by R Sainsbury and T Eardley (HMSO, 1991). Partly in response to this, the DSS produced a *Good Practice Guide* (in circular HB/CCB(92)20) dealing with internal reviews; and *Review Boards: A Good Practice Guide* (DSS, 1994). The government has announced its intention (DSS A5/2000) to change the HB/CTB review procedures by bringing them into line with the arrangements for decision-making and appeals in child support and Social Security. These changes are expected to take place from April 2001. As now, people will be able to ask the authority to look again at any disputed decision, but if the differences cannot be resolved they will have a right of appeal to a tribunal administered by the Appeals Service.

PUBLICISING APPEAL RIGHTS

19.7   The number of appeals about HB/CTB has rapidly increased in recent years. Publicising the right to appeal and encouraging the use of it, are in the interests of authorities: a positive approach to appeals is an excellent way of ensuring that rules and policies are properly implemented. The DSS encourages 'all authorities to produce leaflets or information sheets both to publicise the [appeal] procedure and to explain what happens at each step' and suggests what such leaflets should contain (HB/CCB(92)20).

Who may appeal?

HBR 2(1), 77(1)
79(2)
CTBR 2(1), 67(1),
69(2)

19.8   The authority has a duty to notify any 'person affected' by a determination it has made (paras. 16.7-8); and every such person has a right to use the appeal procedures described in this chapter. Each of the following is a 'person affected' and thus entitled to use the appeal procedures:

◆ the claimant;

◆ an appointee dealing with a claim on behalf of someone who is unable to manage his or her affairs (para. 7.6);

◆ a landlord or landlord's agent in the circumstances described below;

◆ any other person from whom the authority intends to recover an overpayment.

Any such 'person affected' may ask a representative to act on his or her behalf. However (as mentioned later) HB appeals must always be signed by the person affected, not (only) by the representative.

LANDLORDS AND LANDLORDS' AGENTS

19.9   A landlord (see also para. 19.10) is defined as being a 'person affected'   HBR 2(1) for HB purposes (and so entitled to use the appeal procedures) as regards:

◆ any question arising in connection with whether HB should be paid direct to the landlord, including both the mandatory cases and the discretionary cases in which this may be done (paras. 16.27-33);

◆ any question arising in connection with the recovery of an overpayment which is sought to be recovered from the landlord (para. 18.21).

In these two cases landlords have the right to appeal in their own capacity as a landlord. When a signature is required (as detailed in later parts of this chapter), it must be the signature of:

◆ the landlord personally, if he or she is an individual;

◆ a person aged 18 or more authorised to act for the landlord, if the landlord is a company, etc.

19.10   However, if the landlord employs an agent (e.g. an estate agent) to collect the rent, then the agent (not the landlord) is a 'person affected' as regards:

◆ any matter in connection with the payment of HB direct to the agent (as in para. 19.9);

◆ the recovery of any overpayment which is sought to be recovered from the agent (para. 18.21).

In such cases, agents have the right of appeal in their own capacity as landlords' agents. When a signature is required, it must be that of the agent personally if he or she is an individual; or a person aged 18 or more authorised to act for the agent if the agent is a company.

But if the landlord employs an agent for purposes which exclude the collection of rent, the landlord is a person affected for the above purposes (as in para. 19.9) and the agent is not.

19.11   Overpayments may be recovered direct from a landlord/agent when HB has been paid direct to him or her (or it) or where the landlord/agent has caused the overpayment. The details are in chapter 18. In such cases, a landlord/agent is directly affected by each of the following matters, and so has a right to appeal about them:

◆ whether there is an overpayment;

◆ whether the overpayment is a recoverable overpayment;

◆ whether a recoverable overpayment should be recovered from the landlord/agent (as opposed to recovering it in some other way – for example, from the claimant);

◆ whether the authority should exercise its discretion not to recover a recoverable overpayment.

However, a landlord/agent to whom HB is being paid direct is not entitled to appeal about whether a recoverable overpayment should be recovered by making deductions from the HB entitlement of the tenant whose HB was overpaid: this constitutes recovery from the tenant, not the landlord/agent.

19.12 In cases in which a landlord/agent is entitled to appeal, the DSS has advised that 'the deliberations on [appeal] must be confined to those which affect the [landlord/agent]' (HB/CCB(92)20). It can be difficult to draw such a dividing line. For example, if the authority has determined that an official error overpayment is recoverable because the claimant could reasonably have been expected to realise he or she was being overpaid (and has also determined that the overpayment will be recovered from a landlord/agent), then in order to argue a case the landlord/agent must be able to raise matters relating to whether the claimant did so realise.

LANDLORDS ACTING ON BEHALF OF THEIR TENANTS

19.13 There is in principle no reason why a landlord cannot act as a representative for a tenant as regards any HB or CTB matter, so long as the tenant is competent to authorise the landlord to do so. When, in HB, a signature is required (as detailed in later parts of this chapter), it must be the signature of the tenant, not the landlord. This should normally be sufficient to satisfy the authority that the landlord is genuinely acting for the tenant. In certain cases, though (e.g. if the signature does not match those held on file), it would be reasonable for the authority to take steps to confirm this separately. When landlords act for tenants, authorities and review boards sometimes have difficulties with the evidence provided by landlords. Whether the landlord's motives for acting as representative may be partly or wholly personal is not relevant. The true question is whether the evidence tendered relates to the facts that need to be established.

Written statement of reasons

BR 77(4), (4A), (5)
CTBR 67(2), (3) **19.14** Any person affected by a determination may ask the authority for a written statement of the reasons for it. If a person affected makes this request in writing (and, in HB, signs it as described earlier), the authority must send the written statement within two weeks, or as soon as reasonably practicable. The right to a written statement extends to all determinations, including revised determinations (paras. 17.11, 17.39), and determinations relating to discretionary matters (such as whether or not to award additional benefit in exceptional circumstances).

19.15 A person affected may request a written statement at any time, once the authority has notified him or her of the determination. However, it is advisable to request a written statement well within six weeks of notification of the determination if the intention is to ask for an internal review after receiving it (para. 19.23). The request may be in general terms; for example, how the authority calculated entitlement. Or it may relate to a particular matter; for example, why the authority assessed income in a particular way. A request may even be made after entitlement to HB or CTB has expired.

19.16 Whilst this is sometimes a useful first step preparatory to requesting an internal review, it is not an obligatory one. It is advisable to balance the advantages of asking for a written statement first (having the authority's reasons may make it easier to challenge them at internal review) against the disadvantages (the person affected may not be able to afford the delay). If the person affected chooses not to ask for a written statement first, the DSS emphasises that it is not appropriate for the authority to treat a request for an internal review as though it were a request for a written statement (HB/CCB(92)20).

19.17 Apart from their duty to provide a written statement of reasons as described above, the DSS advises that authorities should provide the following information to a claimant on request (GM para. C8.07):

♦ general factual information about his or her claim;

♦ details of HB/CTB payments and the periods they covered;

♦ copies of statements made and forms completed by the claimant; and

♦ copies of letters or documents he or she has sent to the authority.

Which matters can be appealed?

19.18 Any determination made by the authority about HB or CTB is open to appeal, both at the internal review stage and, at the further review stage, before a review board. The exceptions are that the following matters are not open to appeal (other than by judicial review: para. 19.62). The general regulations specifically exclude (a) to (d) from the appeal procedure; other regulations exclude (e); (f) and (g) are not determinations made by the authority; and (h) is not a 'determination': HBR 79(1),(1A),(2) 81(1) CTBR 69(1),(1A), (2), 70(1) SI 1995 No. 531 SI 1996 No. 548 SI 1996 No. 549

(a) the discretion whether to grant a time extension for requesting an internal review (para. 19.24) or a further review (para. 19.33);

(b) the discretion whether to set aside a determination or decision (paras. 17.45, 19.57);

(c) the discretion whether to correct an accidental error (paras. 17.43, 19.55);

(d) whether the Secretary of State went beyond the powers exercisable by him or her in the making of statutory instruments (para. 1.28);

(e) determinations to end a benefit period early following local government reorganisation (para. 17.36);

(f) determinations made by the rent officer (though see paras. 8.34-38);

(g) determinations by the Secretary of State – for example, those relating to the amount of an authority's 'permitted totals' (paras. 9.54 and 11.23), and certain matters relating to 'extended payments' of HB/CTB (though see para. 17.62);

(h) whether the authority should run a local scheme (para. 9.39).

19.19 Nearly everything else done in relation to HB and CTB (including both main CTB and second adult rebate) is a determination and is open to appeal. Appeals may be about issues of fact or law (paras. 1.22-26). Issues of judgment (para. 1.40) are clearly determinations, and so open to appeal.

19.20 In the past it was sometimes argued that issues of discretion (para. 1.41) are not determinations, and so not open to appeal. However, it is notable that the general regulations themselves specifically exclude three discretionary powers from the appeal procedures (the first three matters listed in para. 19.18). The existence of such an exclusion clearly implies that all other discretions, since they are not specifically excluded, are open to appeal; and the general regulations specifically give review boards the same discretionary powers as the authority itself (para. 19.50). Indeed, it is now almost universally accepted that discretionary matters (e.g. whether to award an addition for exceptional circumstances – para. 9.42, or for exceptional hardship – para. 11.21) are open to appeal.

Request for internal review

HBR 79(2), (2A)
CTBR 69(2)

19.21 Any person affected who is dissatisfied with the authority's determination may ask the authority to hold an internal review. The authority must do this if the request is in writing (and, in HB, is signed as described earlier) and is received within six weeks of the date of notification of the determination.

19.22 There is no requirement for the person affected to state the grounds for requesting an internal review; simply that he or she must 'make representations'. The right to internal review extends to all determinations including revised determinations (paras. 17.11, 17.39). However, certain determinations are not open to internal review (para. 19.18).

HBR 79(4), 87(2)
CTBR 69(4), 76(2)

19.23 The six weeks time limit does not include:

◆ any delay (no matter how long) before the authority sends a correct letter of notification (para. 16.2);

- any time taken by the authority to provide a written statement (para. 19.14) if the person affected asked for one;

- any period before the correction of an accidental error (para. 17.43), or the setting aside of a determination or decision (paras. 17.45, 19.57), or a refusal to do either of these things.

19.24 The authority may extend the time limit for 'special reasons', even if the six weeks have already run out. It may choose to do this itself, or the person affected may request it in writing. If the authority refuses an extension, it may be able to revise the determination anyway (para. 17.39), but a refusal is not open to appeal.   HBR 78(3)-(5) CTBR 68(3)-(5)

Procedure on internal review

19.25 The authority must decide whether or not to change the determination, taking into account what the person affected says in the letter requesting the internal review. The DSS advises (HB/CCB(92)20) that in appropriate cases the authority should also invite any further information from the person affected needed to perform the internal review. The authority is required to complete the internal review within 14 days, or as soon as reasonably practicable. In certain circumstances (para. 8.34) the details must be referred to the rent officer. In such cases this time limit does not start until the authority receives the re-determination from the rent officer. The internal review is normally done by staff in the authority's HB/CTB section. The DSS advises (HB/CCB(92)20) that as a matter of good practice it should be done by different or more senior staff – not by the person who made the original determination.   HBR 79(2), (4A) CTBR 69(2)

19.26 Any revised determination applies from the date of the original determination. If there has been a relevant change of circumstances, the authority may revise the determination from the date of the change (para. 17.8).   HBR 79(3)(b) CTBR 69(3)(b)

19.27 On completing the internal review, the authority must notify the outcome to each person affected by it in writing within 14 days, or as soon as reasonably practicable. The rules in chapter 16 apply to the notification of determinations on internal review. Each person affected should be told of the right to request a   HBR 77, 79(6) CTBR 67, 69(7)

Example: Backdating

A claimant applies for HB on 1st May 1999 and at the same time writes requesting the authority to backdate the claim for 12 months. The authority refuses. The claimant applies on 1st July 1999 for an internal review, and the authority agrees to accept this late request. On 15th July 1999, the authority determines the internal review in the claimant's favour. HB may be backdated to 12 months prior to 1st May 1999.

further review by the review board (para. 19.31), and of the right to request a written statement of reasons (para. 19.14) relating to the new determination.

HBR 79(5)
CTBR 69(5), 79

19.28   If the new determination entitles the claimant to more HB or CTB, the balance should be awarded straight away (paras. 17.48-49). However, an increase in HB or CTB cannot be awarded more than 52 weeks before the date of the written request for the internal review. The only exception is where the authority determines on internal review to reverse an earlier refusal to backdate a claim.

After the internal review

HBR 79(6)
CTBR 69(7)

19.29   Any person affected who is dissatisfied with the outcome of an internal review has two options: to request a review board hearing (para. 19.31 onwards), or to request another internal review.

19.30   The latter alternative may be appropriate if there are new grounds for arguing the case. Authorities should pay careful attention to distinguishing the two kinds of requests. It should always be assumed that a person affected is requesting a review board hearing, unless he or she expressly states the contrary (or unless the authority agrees to alter its determination in the manner he or she has requested).

Request for further review by a review board

HBR 81(1),(1A),(2)
CTBR 70(1),(2)

19.31   Any person affected who is still dissatisfied may request a further review to be heard by a review board appointed by the authority. The review board must hear the case if the request:

◆   is in writing (and, in HB, is signed as described earlier);

◆   gives the grounds for the further review; and

◆   is received within four weeks of the date of notification of the result of the internal review.

19.32   Though the person affected must give his or her grounds, it is not necessary for these to be detailed or for them to refer to the Acts, regulations, etc. The review board provides a second level of review of any determination. It is not possible to 'skip' the internal review stage. However certain determinations are not open to further review (para. 19.18).

HBR 78(3)-(5),
87(2)
CTBR 68(3)-(5)

19.33   The four weeks time limit does not include any period before:

◆   the correction of an accidental error (paras. 17.43, 19.55);

◆   the setting aside of a determination or decision (paras. 17.43, 19.57); or

◆   a refusal to do either of these things.

The review board may extend the time limit for 'special reasons', even if the four weeks have already run out. It may choose to do this itself, or the person affected may request it in writing. A refusal is not open to appeal. This is a discretion held by the review board itself, not by authority staff.

THE PARTIES TO THE HEARING

19.34 Each of the following has equal rights (as described below) as a party to a review board hearing:

HBR 82(2)
CTBR 71(2)

◆ the person affected who requested the hearing; and

◆ any other person affected by the matter in question, including the authority.

DATE OF HEARING AND NOTICE

19.35 The review board hearing should take place within six weeks of the request or as soon as possible thereafter. For claimants on low incomes the delays involved in the review procedure are very long, especially if it transpires that the authority is wrongly awarding too little HB or CTB. It is therefore important for review board hearings to be held as soon as possible.

HBR 82(1),(1A),(
CTBR 70(5),
71(1),(3)

Each party should be given at least ten days' notice of the date, time and place. If such notice is not given, the hearing should not go ahead, unless each party consents.

Constitution and status of the review board

19.36 Review boards are composed of councillors of the administering authority, at least three members being appointed at any one time. In the case of new town corporations and Scottish Homes, members are drawn from the appropriate board or council of management. The members of the review board appoint one member to act as chairman or chairwoman. At least three members of the review board should be present at each hearing. But a hearing may go ahead (or continue) with only two members present if each party consents. When the review board sits, its role is that of an impartial, semi-judicial tribunal. It is not a committee of the authority but an independent legal entity (*R v Birmingham City Council Review Board ex parte Birmingham City Council,* QBD, 1991). Its members are expected to act independently, and not be influenced by their other role as councillors. Further guidance for review board members, their legal advisers, and those attending a review board hearing may be found in *Review Boards: a guide for members, officers and appellants,* John Zebedee (Institute of Revenues, Rating and Valuation, 1999).

HBR 81(3),82(7),
sch 7
CTBR 70(3),71(7
sch 7

19.37 The HB review board and the CTB review board are two separate boards. In practice, they are almost always composed of the same members. If a person affected requests a further review about both HB and CTB, the same review board can deal with both benefits, so long as all the parties agree. If one of the parties does not agree, two review board hearings must be held – one for each benefit.

HBR 81(4)
CTBR 70(4)

The review board hearing

HBR 82(2)
CTBR 71(2)

19.38 The regulations provide some general rules about how the review board should conduct its hearing and about the rights of the parties to the hearing. It must consider written representations made by each party, and may also request or accept evidence from anyone present. However, it cannot compel anyone to appear.

HBR 82(2)
CTBR 71(2)

19.39 Each party (para. 19.34) has the right to:

◆ be heard;

◆ be accompanied (the claimant could bring a friend, for example);

◆ be represented by a solicitor, an adviser or anyone else. In such a circumstance, that representative has the rights of the person he or she is representing;

◆ call witnesses; and

◆ question each other's witnesses.

HBR 82(9)
CTBR 71(9)

19.40 The Legal Aid scheme does not provide financial assistance towards the cost of representation before a review board, though it may do so for the cost of preparatory advice, assistance and written submissions. If a person affected who is not the claimant (e.g. a landlord) requests a review board hearing, the claimant retains the right to be a full party to the proceedings. The authority may pay the travelling expenses of each party and of one other person accompanying each. All other questions about procedure are for the chairman or chairwoman to determine, subject to the rules of natural justice.

19.41 The courts have emphasised that the review board must afford fair and equal opportunity to all interests appearing before it, with the principles of natural justice applying. For example, in an early case, it was decided that the exclusion of one party (but not the other) during the board's deliberations created a breach of the rules: justice was not seen to be done (*McDonnell v Cumbernauld Development Corporation Review Board,* Court of Session, 10th September 1986).

19.42 Comparison may be drawn with the law that has developed around other similar tribunals. For example, a review board is generally expected to be inquisitorial: the members of the board have a duty to consider (and if necessary tease out) any point which may be made on behalf of each party.

19.43 The following issues are not governed by the regulations, and so need consideration.

◆ Should members of the review board be drawn from the council committees responsible for administering HB/CTB, or from committees with no such connection?

◆ What training should review board members have?

◆ Who should be responsible for advising the review board?

◆ What documents should be available in advance, and at the hearing?

◆ How formal or informal should the hearing be? Should it be in private? Should witnesses be present throughout?

◆ Should a person affected be invited to put his or her case first, or should the authority go first? To what extent should review board members intervene by asking questions?

Table 19.2 REVIEW BOARD HEARINGS: A TYPICAL ORDER OF PROCEEDINGS

◆ The chairman or chairwoman introduces the members of the review board and parties, and outlines the order of the hearing.

◆ The authority puts its case and calls any witnesses.

◆ The appellant and then the members of the review board ask questions.

◆ The appellant puts his or her case and calls any witnesses.

◆ The authority and then the members of the review board ask questions.

◆ The authority sums up its case.

◆ The appellant sums up his or her case.

◆ The parties withdraw, and the review board makes its decision. If the clerk or legal adviser remains with the board, it should be made clear that he or she will not take part in the making of the decision.

◆ The review board may be able to give an oral decision (if the parties have been invited to wait for one) – but must nonetheless notify its decision formally in writing (para. 19.52).

Notes

◆ The above order of proceedings is not laid down in the law: it is based on the DSS's *Good Practice Guide* (para. 19.44). As a matter of law, it is for the chairman or chairwoman of the review board to decide the order of proceedings.

◆ In the above, the authority puts its case before the appellant puts his or hers. This may help the appellant to become familiar with the form of the hearing, and to be more prepared and at ease. This order should be reversed if the appellant so requests (though the appellant should nonetheless sum up after the authority).

19.44 Advice on many of these points is contained in *Review Boards: A Good Practice Guide* (para. 19.6). Interested parties may be able to obtain copies from their local authority. Table 19.2 summarises the most common order of proceedings.

Postponement, withdrawal and adjournment

HBR 82(5)
CTBR 71(5)

19.45 Any party (other than the authority) may write requesting withdrawal of the appeal at any time. Any party (including the authority) may request postponement. The chairman or chairwoman has discretion whether to consent or not. It is possible for an appeal to be withdrawn in writing during the course of the hearing, or even after it has finished – so long as the review board has not yet given its decision. (A claimant might choose to request this if it seemed likely that the review board were about to reduce his or her award of HB/CTB.)

HBR 82(2),(4),(6)
TBR 71(2),(4),(6)

19.46 If any party fails to appear, the review board may proceed or not as it considers appropriate. The review board may adjourn during the hearing at any time, whether or not at the request of one of the parties. If the hearing is part way through, the reconvened hearing must begin afresh unless the same members are present or (if there were three at the original hearing) one is absent and the parties consent.

The review board's decision

R 82(8),83(1),(4)
CTBR 71(8),
72(1),(4)

19.47 The review board must decide whether to confirm or revise the authority's determination. Majority decisions are allowed. The chairman or chairwoman has a casting vote if necessary and must, in every case, record the decision in writing, giving:

◆ the findings of fact;

◆ the interpretation of the law applying to those facts;

◆ the review board's reasoning; and

◆ the decisions which flow from this.

In the *Solihull* case (para. 4.39), it was emphasised that the making of the decision by the review board requires the chairman or chairwoman to ensure that the review board members focus their minds on exactly what has to be decided, within what legal framework and according to what relevant material. It is not enough for the secretary or clerk to notify the decision without at least stating that the chairman or chairwoman has approved it. (In fact it is standard practice nowadays for him or her to sign it.)

19.48 It is also important that the record of the decision is carefully made. It may be tempting, in cases where conflicting evidence makes it difficult to reach a decision, to fail to reach a finding particularly as regards the facts of a case. This, however, is not a choice the review board may make. Failure to record the decision properly is an error of law (*MacLeod v HB Review Board of Banff and Buchan,* (1987) [1988] SLT 753).

19.49   The courts have also emphasised the review board's duty to make specific findings of fact, to give its reasons and to base its decision on the relevant evidence before it. In *R v Sefton Metropolitan Borough Council ex parte Cunningham,* (1991) 23 HLR 534 QBD (which was about unreasonable rent issues), the judge said, 'In a context such as this it is plain on authority that the reasons need not be elaborate; they need not be the sort of reasons that one would expect to find, for example, in a judgment of the court, but they should be sufficient to enable the parties to appreciate that the relevant matters have been taken into consideration and to understand why it is that they have succeeded or failed as the case may be.'

19.50   In reaching its decision, the review board is not bound by its own decisions, nor by those of other review boards. It is bound by:

HBR 83(2)
CTBR 72(2)

◆   the same duties, powers and discretions as are imposed or conferred on the authority – that is, primarily under the HB and CTB (General) Regulations (para. 1.28); and

◆   precedents from the courts on HB/CTB law (para. 1.38).

19.51   For example, the review board is bound by the 'permitted total' of additional benefit which a local authority may grant in exceptional circumstances (para. 9.54) or for 'exceptional hardship' (paras. 11.23). However, the question of whether the authority has reached its 'permitted total' is open to consideration by the board.

After the review board hearing

19.52   The review board must send a copy of its decision to each party (para. 19.34) within seven days or as soon as possible thereafter.

HBR 83(5)
CTBR 72(5)

19.53   The review board's decision is binding on the authority for the case to which it applies. Any change in entitlement is implemented from the original date of the determination or (if appropriate) from the date of revision at internal review. If the review board's decision entitles a claimant to more HB or CTB, the balance should be awarded straight away (para. 17.49). However a review board cannot award an increase in HB or CTB more than 52 weeks before the date the authority determined the internal review. The only exception is where the review board decides to reverse a refusal by the authority to backdate a claim.

HBR 79(5),83(3),
CTBR 69(5),
72(3),73

19.54   The above appears to be the intention of the regulations, which are somewhat unclear. They also appear unfair, since the 52 weeks limit takes no account of delays caused by the authority in determining the internal review. Claimants who lose out as a result of the limit, may be able to obtain compensation from the authority outside the HB/CTB schemes, perhaps following a referral to the ombudsman (para. 19.63).

ACCIDENTAL ERRORS

HBR 85, 87
CTBR 74, 76

19.55 The review board may also correct any accidental errors which appear in a decision (e.g. slips of the pen, etc. as discussed in para. 17.43). The board may be of different composition where it would be inexpedient for the original members to be reconvened. The correction is deemed to become part of the original decision, and the change must be notified as soon as practicable. The discretion to correct an accidental error is not open to appeal.

FURTHER CHANGES

19.56 It should be noted that entitlement to HB or CTB may change again if:

◆ the benefit period ends (para. 7.83);

◆ there is a change of circumstances (para. 17.11);

◆ the authority itself revises the decision (para. 17.39);

◆ the decision is set aside (para. 19.57);

◆ the decision is overturned by a court (para. 19.60).

Setting aside a review board decision

HBR 86(1),(5)
CTBR 75(1),(5)

19.57 Any person affected (including the authority) may request a review board to set aside a decision it has made – even if the entitlement to HB or CTB has expired. The review board may do this only if:

◆ a relevant document was not received by any person affected or representative. The usual assumptions of the law about what counts as service or delivery of a document do not apply;

◆ any person affected or representative was absent from a review board hearing; or

◆ the interests of justice require it.

BR 86(2),(2A),(3)
CTBR 75(2),(3)

19.58 The request must be considered if it is made in writing within 13 weeks of the notification (and, in HB, it must be signed as described earlier). A copy of the request must be sent to each person affected (including the authority). Any such party must be given a reasonable opportunity to make representations before the review board considers the matter. The review board doing this may be of different composition if it would be inexpedient for the original members to be reconvened.

19.59   The 13 weeks time limit does not include any period before the correction of an accidental error (para. 19.55), or the setting aside of some other determination or decision, or a refusal to do either of these things. However there is no power for the 13 weeks time limit to be extended apart from this. The outcome must be notified as soon as practicable and include a statement of reasons. The discretion to set aside a decision is not open to appeal (other than by judicial review: see below).   HBR 86(4),87(2)
CTBR 75(4),76(2

The courts and the ombudsman

19.60   A review board decision may be the subject of judicial review in the High Court or, in Scotland, the Court of Session. Applications for judicial review should be made as quickly as possible, and in any case within three months of the review board decision (or of a refusal to set it aside) unless there are special reasons for delay.

19.61   Illustrative examples of when such an application is likely to be successful (and these may overlap) are if the review board:

◆   wrongly interpreted the law; or

◆   took into account irrelevant considerations, or ignored relevant considerations; or

◆   reached a decision which no reasonable review board could have reached; or

◆   acted *'ultra vires'* (outside its powers); or

◆   adopted blanket rules rather than looking at each case independently; or

◆   acted in bad faith or dishonestly; or

◆   did not follow the principles of natural justice; or

◆   did not properly record its decision (e.g. did not include relevant findings of fact, or did not give adequate reasons: paras. 19.48-49).

Where the reasons given in a review board's record of its decision are grossly flawed, the Court will not allow supplementary affidavit evidence from the board *(R v Lambeth London Borough Council Housing Benefit Review Board ex p. Harrington,* (1996), *The Times,* 10.12.96).

19.62   Not only the claimant, but also others with a sufficient interest in a matter may apply for judicial review, including the authority *(R v HB Review Board ex parte Birmingham City Council,* (1991) 24 HLR 279 QBD) and in some circumstances landlords (paras. 16.6-8). In certain cases, the DSS can require to be joined as an interested party *(R v Liverpool City Council ex parte Muldoon, The Times,* 18 April 1995; and circular HB/CTB A11/95).

19.63 If an authority fails to administer the HB or CTB scheme properly (e.g. in the case of recurrent delays in payment), it may also be possible to obtain a court order requiring the authority to fulfil its legal obligations (para. 16.5).

19.64 Another possibility, in the case of injustice as a result of maladministration, is for the case to be investigated by the local government ombudsman. The procedure is slow, and in rare cases the authority may choose not to implement an ombudsman's findings. However, there have recently been more findings (and awards of compensation) by the ombudsman in favour of claimants and landlords. A free booklet, *How to Complain to the Local Government Ombudsman,* explains the procedure and includes a complaint form. It is available in several languages from many local authorities, libraries, Citizens Advice Bureaux and other advice agencies.

Improving local policy

19.65 Authorities are not obliged to revise similar cases in line with review board decisions, though they may be willing to do so where it is clear that the circumstances are similar. If a review board member identifies a problem with local policy, or identifies errors in the administrative system, he or she may submit a report to the appropriate committee of the authority. Individuals and their advisers can use successful review board cases to improve authority policies by:

◆ bringing anomalies to the attention of sufficiently senior officers (including, for example, the authority's Monitoring Officer), or councillors;

◆ encouraging a wide level of support from groups representing the interests of claimants; and

◆ where appropriate, involving local newspapers and radio stations.

20 Students

20.1   The general rules in the rest of this guide apply to students, but with a number of variations. This chapter explains all these variations. It covers:

◆ the terminology used in student cases;

◆ which students can get HB and CTB;

◆ how HB and CTB are assessed for students; and

◆ the rules for assessing students' income and rent.

As described in this chapter, the student rules vary between HB and CTB, and also between main CTB and second adult rebate. Also, there have been several changes in the rules since the last edition of this Guide – and not all of the new legislation is well drafted. These factors make assessing student claims very complicated. All students are advised to check carefully that their claims have been dealt with correctly – perhaps by requesting a written statement from the authority (para. 19.14).

Terminology

20.2   Several terms used in this chapter have particular meanings in HB and CTB. The main definitions are given below. Paragraph 20.15 compares these with the definitions used in council tax law – which are different.

WHO IS A 'STUDENT'?

BR 2(1),46,47,52
CTBR 2(1),38,39
SI 1997 No. 791

20.3   For HB and CTB purposes, a student is defined as any person 'who is attending a course of study at an educational establishment'. This includes:

◆ study at any level (from school onwards);

◆ both full-time and part-time students;

◆ students with or without grants;

◆ both state-funded and private establishments; and

◆ both term-times and vacations.

Some special cases are mentioned below (paras. 20.6-9).

20.4   Once a course has started, a person carries on counting as a student until his or her course finishes or he or she abandons it or is dismissed from it. So someone does count as a student during the Christmas and Easter vacations and any summer vacation(s) occurring within the course, even if he or she takes up full-time work then.

But someone does not count as a student during the summer vacation after the end of a course or between two different courses. (A slightly different rule applies to people on 'qualifying courses' under the New Deal: para. 20.7.)

20.5 However, to count as a student, the person must be 'attending' the course. In this connection, a person counts as attending a course even during 'intercalated periods' (periods when he or she temporarily suspends attendance, for example because of sickness or for personal reasons – or to re-take exams: *O'Connor v Chief Adjudication Officer,* CA, *The Times,* 11.3.99).

HEALTH CARE STUDENTS

20.6 The following count as students if (which is almost always the case) they fit the definition given above (para. 20.3):

◆ students undertaking nursing and midwifery diploma courses, formerly known as the Project 2000 training scheme. These students receive a non-means-tested bursary but are not eligible for a student loan. They get a £55 allowance in their first year for 'initial course costs': the DSS no longer advises that this should be disregarded (circular HB/CTB A54/99);

◆ NHS-funded students undertaking degree programmes. These students receive a means-tested bursary and are eligible for a student loan.

QUALIFYING COURSES UNDER THE NEW DEAL

20.7 Studying on a 'qualifying course' is one of the options under the New Deal (para. 13.41 and table 13.3) for certain people. Such people count as students. All the student rules apply to them, apart from following variations:

HBR 35(3), (3A) 43(3), (3A), 46, sch 4 para 68, sch 5 para 56

◆ they carry on counting as a student until either the last day of their course or the date of their last examination, whichever comes later (and the points in para. 20.4 do not apply);

CTBR 26(3), (3A) 34(3), (3A), 38, sch 4 para 67, sch 5 para 56

◆ discretionary payments made to them under the New Deal (para. 13.41) are disregarded:

• as income: the one exception is that no discretionary payment for travel is disregarded if the normal student disregard for travel applies to them (para. 20.39 and table 20.4);

• as capital in all cases – but only for 52 weeks from the date of payment;

• as notional income and as notional capital in all cases.

20.8 However, most people on a 'qualifying course' continue to receive income-based jobseeker's allowance: in their case, all their income and capital is disregarded for HB and main CTB purposes (and they are eligible for HB and CTB: table 20.1).

TRAINING SCHEMES

HBR 46, CTBR 38   **20.9**   The following additional rules apply in considering who counts as a 'student':

◆ people on government training schemes (para. 13.41) do not count as students;

◆ people on any other training course do not count as students if their course does not take place at an educational establishment.

STUDENTS WITH PARTNERS

HBR 47,52
CTBR 39   **20.10**   In the case of a couple, the HB and CTB rules vary depending on whether one or both are students and which partner makes the claim. Details are given as each rule is described.

FULL-TIME AND PART-TIME STUDENTS

HBR 46
CTBR 38   **20.11**   Some of the HB and CTB rules apply to both full-time and part-time students; some apply only to full-time students. Details are given as each rule is described. There is a definition of 'full-time' in the case of further education courses (para. 20.12); also all sandwich courses count as full-time courses. But there is no definition of 'full-time' (or 'part-time') in any other cases. In those cases, the DSS suggests (GM para. C5.03) that, if doubt arises, the educational establishment should be consulted about whether a course is full-time, and that the nature of the student's grant (if any) may also be a useful indication. Note that a student who transfers from full-time to part-time study counts (thereafter) as part-time (*Chief Adjudication Officer v. Webber*, 1997, CA). However, a student who takes leave of absence from a full-time course may in some circumstances continue to count as a full-time student (*O'Connor v. Chief Adjudication Officer and Another*, 1999, CA).

FURTHER EDUCATION: DEFINITION OF 'FULL-TIME'

HBR 46
CTBR 38   **20.12**   A student studying at a further education college (i.e. one funded by the Further Education Funding Council) counts as a full-time student if (and only if) his or her course involves:

◆ in England, more than 16 hours per week of 'guided learning', as set out in the 'learning agreement' obtainable from his or her college;

◆ in Wales, more than 16 hours per week of 'guided learning', as set out in a college document;

◆ in Scotland:

• more than 16 hours of classroom-based or workshop-based 'guided learning', or

- more than 21 hours per week of a combination of that and additional hours using structured learning packages,

as set out (in either case) in a college document.

HIGHER EDUCATION

20.13 Whether a student is in higher education or not, is one of the main descriptions used in HB and CTB to distinguish different levels of education. Higher education is defined as meaning: HBR 46, 48A CTBR 38, 40

- first degree, postgraduate and higher degree courses;
- courses for the further training of teachers and youth and community workers;
- courses for the Diploma of Higher Education, the BTEC/SVEC Higher National Diploma (HND) or Higher National Certificate (HNC), the Diploma in Management Studies, or the Certificate in Education;
- any other courses at a level higher than GCE A level or BTEC/SVEC Ordinary National Diploma (OND) or Ordinary National Certificate (ONC), whether or not leading to a qualification.

PERIOD OF STUDY AND SUMMER VACATION

20.14 Some of the HB and CTB rules apply only in a student's period of study, others only in the summer vacation (if he or she has a summer vacation), others in both: HBR 46 CTBR 38

- the period of study for any course requiring more than 45 weeks study in a year (e.g. for many postgraduate courses) runs from the first day of the academic year to the day before the first day of the next academic year. The course is treated as not having a summer vacation;
- for courses of less than one year, the period of study is the whole of the course;
- in all other cases, the period of study runs from the first day of the academic year to the last day before the summer vacation (or in the final year of a course of more than one year, to the last day of the course). This usually means three terms plus the Christmas and Easter vacations;
- subject to the above points, for students on sandwich courses, periods of work experience are included in the period of study.

HB AND CTB DEFINITIONS vs COUNCIL TAX DEFINITIONS

20.15 For council tax purposes, four groups of people – including certain foreign language assistants and student nurses – are defined in the law as being 'students' (categories 5 to 8 in appendix 7). These council tax definitions are relevant for considering whether a dwelling is completely exempt from council tax (para. 3.12) and whether a council taxpayer can get a discount (para. 3.35).

The council tax definitions rather than the HB and CTB definitions are also used for certain purposes to do with second adult rebate (paras. 10.6, 10.17-18).

20.16 But for all the HB and CTB rules described in this chapter, the council tax definitions are irrelevant: only the definitions in paragraphs 20.3-14 are relevant.

20.17 There is some overlap between the council tax definitions and the HB and CTB definitions. For example, a person who counts as a 'student' in council tax law (apart from a foreign language assistant) is usually a 'student' (but not necessarily a 'full-time student': category 10 in appendix 7) in HB and CTB law. Every other matter depends on the individual circumstances of the case. As indicated above, appendix 7 gives fuller information about the relevant categories of people.

Which students can get HB and CTB?

20.18 To be eligible for HB a student must satisfy all of the following rules. To be eligible for main CTB a student need satisfy only the first rule. None of the rules affects eligibility for second adult rebate:

◆ the primary rule – which prevents full-time students from getting HB or main CTB (but not second adult rebate) unless they fall within certain groups (paras. 20.19-21);

◆ the rule preventing full-time and part-time students from getting HB on halls of residence, etc, but which is irrelevant in CTB (paras. 20.22-24);

◆ the rule preventing full-time students from getting HB (but not main CTB or second adult rebate) on their term-time accommodation if they are absent during their summer vacation (paras. 20.25-27).

THE PRIMARY RULE: SUMMARY

HBR 6(2)(e), 48A
CTBR 40

20.19 This primary rule prevents full-time students from getting HB or main CTB unless they fall within certain groups. This rule does not apply to second adult rebate. The rule works as follows:

◆ Students who are single claimants are eligible for HB and main CTB only if they are in one (or more) of the groups in table 20.1.

◆ Students who are lone parents are in all cases eligible for HB and main CTB.

◆ Couples are eligible for HB and main CTB in all cases unless both are students and neither of them is in any of the groups in table 20.1.
(Information about which partner should claim is given in paragraph 20.20.)

Table 20.1 HB AND MAIN CTB ELIGIBLE GROUPS: THE PRIMARY RULE

◆ All students who are currently receiving income support or income-based jobseeker's allowance (but student eligibility for IS and JSA(IB) is also restricted).

◆ All part-time students.

◆ Students under 19 not in higher education.

◆ Students (men or women) aged 60 or more.

◆ Students (couples or lone parents) who are responsible for a child or young person.

◆ Students who are responsible for a foster child.

◆ Students who qualify for a disability premium (para. 12.15).

◆ Students who are disqualified from incapacity benefit.

◆ Students who have been incapable of work for 28 weeks or more.*

◆ Students whose grant assessment (if made by an English, Welsh, Scottish or Northern Ireland grant-awarding body) includes a disabled student's allowance for deafness – even if they get a grant for fees only.

Note

* 'Incapable of work' means what it does for incapacity benefit purposes. The student is not eligible during the first 28 weeks of incapacity for work – referred to here as a 'waiting period'.

In calculating the 'waiting period', periods of incapacity for work are added together if they are separated by gaps of eight weeks or less.

Once the waiting period is completed, the student is eligible. After a gap (i.e. a period in which the student is capable of work or is disqualified from incapacity benefit) of eight weeks or less, the student does not have to start a new waiting period: he or she becomes eligible again straightaway. But after a gap of more than eight weeks, the student is not eligible until he or she has completed a fresh waiting period.

THE PRIMARY RULE: WHICH PARTNER IN A COUPLE SHOULD CLAIM?

HBR 6(2)(e), 48A
CTBR 40

20.20   Table 20.2 explains which partner in a couple is eligible to claim HB and main CTB on behalf of both. In all cases where a claim may be made, it takes into account the income, capital and applicable amount relating to them both. Authorities who receive claims from the 'wrong partner' (i.e. in the cases in the second and fifth rows of table 20.2) should return the application form with an explanation and a suggestion that the other partner should be the claimant.

Table 20.2 SUMMARY: STUDENT COUPLES: HB AND MAIN CTB

Partner A	Partner B	Who can claim HB and main CTB?	HB on two homes?
◆ Student in the eligible groups	Student in the eligible groups	Either	Yes on both, if reasonable, and if maintaining two is unavoidable
◆ Student in the eligible groups	Student not in the eligible groups	Partner A only	Only on the home occupied by partner A
◆ Student in the eligible groups	Non-student	Either	Yes on both, if reasonable, and if maintaining two is unavoidable
◆ Student not in the eligible groups	Student not in the eligible groups	Neither	Not on either
◆ Student not in the eligible groups	Non-student	Partner B only	Only on the home occupied by partner B
◆ Non-student	Non-student	Either	Student rules do not apply

The 'eligible groups' referred to in this table are those listed in table 20.1

THE PRIMARY RULE: STUDENTS WHO MAINTAIN TWO HOMES

20.21 Some students have to maintain two homes – one near their educational   HBR 5(3),5(b)
establishment, and one elsewhere. There are special rules for students in these
circumstances which apply for HB purposes only:

◆   students without partners (i.e. single claimants and lone parents) can, if they
     are in one of the eligible groups in table 20.1, get HB on only one home
     (paras. 4.59-60);

◆   for couples, the rules are given in table 20.2.

There are other rules about HB on two homes (para. 4.65) which apply in addition
to these. For CTB there are no special rules for students maintaining two homes.

HALLS OF RESIDENCE, ETC.

20.22 In addition to the previous rules, students (whether full-time or part-time,   HBR 46, 50
and including couples whether one or both are students) are not eligible for HB
on halls of residence or any other accommodation where the rent is payable to the
educational establishment they attend. This rule only applies in the period of
study, so such students are eligible for HB during their summer vacation (if they
have one).

20.23 This rule applies to any accommodation which the establishment owns,
leases under a lease granted for more than 21 years, or rents from another
educational establishment or an education authority. It does not apply (i.e. the
students are eligible for HB) if the establishment itself rents accommodation on
a temporary basis from a council, housing association or private landlord and then
sublets it to its students – unless it has arranged this in order to take advantage of
the HB scheme.

20.24 There is no equivalent rule in CTB. This is because halls of residence are
exempt from council tax (para. 3.12).

ABSENCE DURING THE SUMMER VACATION

20.25 Finally, full-time students are not eligible for HB on their term-time   HBR 48
accommodation if they are absent from it during the summer vacation. The rule
does not apply unless the student is absent for at least one Sunday/Monday
midnight. Once the rule applies, it continues to apply (but only during the
summer vacation) until the end of the benefit week in which the student returns
to the accommodation. (This is because of the ordinary rules about start of
entitlement to HB: chapter 7.) This rule never applies to part-time students, and
for couples it applies only if both are full-time students.

20.26 Furthermore the rule applies only if the student's main purpose in
occupying the accommodation during his or her period of study is to facilitate

attendance on the course. The DSS advises that the rule would not therefore apply (GM para. C5.26) if the student:

◆   has a child or young person living with him or her; or

◆   is aged 25 or over and has no other accommodation; or

◆   is under 25 and has no parent or guardian and no other accommodation.

Authorities should also take into account any other relevant factor in reaching a decision. For example, if the student lived in the accommodation before starting the course, or moved to the area to be near relatives, or is a council or housing association tenant, it is unlikely that the main purpose of occupying the home is to attend the course.

20.27   There is no equivalent rule in CTB. There may therefore be cases in which a student is eligible only for CTB during a period of absence from his or her term-time accommodation.

Assessing HB and main CTB for students

20.28   For students who are eligible, the calculation of their HB and main CTB follows the same rules as for anyone else. But for students not on income support or income-based jobseeker's allowance there are two main variations:

◆   in HB only, part of a full-time student's rent and income is not counted; and

◆   in HB and main CTB, there are special rules for assessing students' income.

Examples of calculations for students are given at the end of this chapter. There are no special rules about calculating second adult rebate for students. The ordinary rules in chapter 10 apply.

20.29   The student figures given in the remainder of this chapter apply from 1st September 1999 to 31st August 2000 (subject to the rule described in para. 20.44). These and other relevant figures for the 1999-2000 academic year are summarised in DSS circular HB/CTB A54/99.

BACKGROUND: 'NEW ENTRANT STUDENTS' v. 'EXISTING STUDENTS'

20.30   Entitlement to student loans and grants varies depending on whether a student is a 'new entrant student' or an 'existing student':

◆   a 'new entrant student' means any student who began his or her course in
    Autumn 1998 or later (apart from one who was offered a place which would
    have begun in Autumn 1997 but who then took a year out);

◆   an 'existing student' means any student who began his or her course in
    Autumn 1997 or earlier (and also one who was offered a place which would
    have begun in Autumn 1997 but who then took a year out, and so did not in
    fact begin it until Autumn 1998).

In the 1999-2000 academic year, most new entrant students are eligible for a student loan but not a grant (unless they have certain additional needs); whereas most existing students continue to qualify for at least some grant as well as a student loan. The main loan and grant figures are in table 20.3.

Table 20.3 STUDENT LOANS AND GRANTS

1999-2000 academic year English, Welsh and Scottish grants		'New entrant students': Loan	'Existing students': Loan	'Existing students': Grant
Courses in London:	final year	£3885	£1605	£2280
	other years	£4480	£2200	£2280
	per extra week	£84	–	£84*
Courses outside London:	final year	£3150	£1295	£1855
	other years	£3635	£1780	£1855
	per extra week	£63	–	£63**

*   £78.50 in Scottish grants only.   **   £57.40 in Scottish grants only.

Notes:

Paragraph 20.30 describes the difference between 'New entrant students' and 'Existing students'.

The student loan figures are the maximum a student could obtain.

The grant figures are for the basic maintenance element only. 'New entrant students' cannot get this.

The figures for health care students are lower. See DSS circular A54/99, from which all the above figures are taken.

THE RENT DEDUCTION AND INCOME DISREGARD FOR FULL-TIME STUDENTS CLAIMING HB

20.31   The effect of this rule is that the student receives less HB. The rule does not apply in main CTB. However, in HB it applies regardless of whether the student has a loan or a grant or indeed any form of income at all. If the student's circumstances are exceptional, the authority can award additional HB (para. 9.42). The details of the rule follow.

HBR 51(1), 58(2)   **20.32**   With the exceptions mentioned below (para. 20.34), a full-time student's eligible rent is reduced by the following amount in every week during his or her period of study. In those weeks, the same amount is disregarded from his or her income, whether from a grant or any other source, in the assessment of HB.

◆ £27.10 in London (the City of London and the Metropolitan Police District); or

◆ £18.75 outside London

For a student who attends an educational establishment in London but lives outside London, the London figure applies – and *vice versa*.

20.33   The rule applies for couples (with the exceptions mentioned below), whether one or both are full-time students, and regardless of which partner claims. Even if both are full-time students, there is only one rent deduction and only one income disregard. Technically, the income disregard is applied as follows:

◆ if only one partner is a full-time student: first to the full-time student's income, then (if that does not use up the disregard) to the other partner's income;

◆ if both partners are full-time students: first to the claimant's income, then (if that does not use up the disregard) to the other partner's income.

EXCEPTIONS

HBR 46, 51(2)   **20.34**   There is no rent deduction or income disregard in any of the following cases:

◆ if the student or any partner is on income support or income-based jobseeker's allowance; or

◆ if the student or any partner receives an allowance (covering the needs of any member of the family) for attendance on a government training scheme; or

◆ during any period of work experience for a student on a sandwich course (para. 20.11); or

◆ if making the student income disregard would mean that the student had income below his or her applicable amount, and

• the student is a lone parent, or

• the disability premium applies (para. 12.15), or the student is disqualified from incapacity benefit, or the student has been incapable of work for 28 weeks or more (as described in the note to table 20.1), or

• the student has a partner who is not also a full-time student.

TERMLY PAYMENT OF HB

20.35   The authority may pay a student's HB once a term. However, if the student is entitled to more than £2.00 HB per week, he or she can insist on being paid under the normal rules about frequency of payment (chapter 16). This rule applies to full-time and part-time students, and to couples where either or both are students.

ASSESSING STUDENT LOANS

20.36   With the exceptions mentioned in the following paragraph, all full-time students in higher education are eligible to apply for a student loan. In the 1999-2000 academic year, for students living away from home, the maximum student loan is shown in table 20.3. Parents, spouses and students themselves may, depending on the circumstances, be assessed as having to make a contribution to a student loan.

20.37   The following are not eligible for a student loan:

◆   students aged 50 or more;

◆   students undertaking nursing and midwifery diploma courses (para. 20.6);

◆   postgraduates - except that students studying for a Postgraduate Certificate of Education (PGCE) are eligible for a student loan.

TREATING STUDENT LOANS AS INCOME

20.38   In calculating HB and main CTB, all students who are eligible to apply for a student loan are treated as receiving one at the maximum level applicable to them (as shown in table 20.3) if they 'will be able to acquire [a student loan] by taking reasonable steps to do so'. This is done regardless of whether they actually apply for a student lone and/or actually receive one. In the case of a couple this means taking up to two student loans into account as appropriate.   HBR 57A CTBR 47

20.39   A student loan (actual or treated as received) is then assessed as follows: HBR 46, 53, 57A CTBR 38, 43, 47

(a) Take the whole amount into account as income (even though it is in fact a loan).

(b) Treat any parental or spouse's (or student's own) assumed contribution to it as being received (even if not actually paid).

(c) Disregard £303 for books and equipment in all cases – unless the student receives a grant which includes a specified amount for books and equipment (table 20.4), in which case disregard nothing for books and equipment from the student loan.

(d) Disregard a further £250 for travel in all cases.

(e) Average the resulting amount 'equally between the weeks in the academic year in respect of which the loan is payable' (for more information see paras. 20.40-47).

(f) Then disregard £10 from the weekly figure (in the case of a couple, disregard £10 from their combined weekly figure), subject to the over-riding £20.00 limit on certain disregards (para. 13.109).

WHEN DOES STUDENT LOAN INCOME COUNT?

HBR 57A
CTBR 47

20.40 The requirement in step (e) above to average a student loan (after disregards) 'equally between the weeks in the academic year in respect of which the loan is payable', has led to several difficulties of interpretation caused by poor drafting of the law. The DSS (circular HB/CTB A54/99) advises that this means the amount is averaged over the following period(s):

◆ in England and Wales, the period 1st September to 30th June;

◆ in Scotland, the period 1st August to 30th June;

◆ in either case, any amounts for extra weeks being attributed to the actual weeks in question. This is the case even if it would result in this coinciding with a week to which student loan income has already been attributed.

The above seems to be the DSS's advice for final years as well as other years (even though the student loan for a final year is lower because it was historically intended to cover a shorter period).

20.41 It is also possible to interpret the law as meaning that (as in all previous years) student loans should be averaged over the full academic year (except in final years, when they should be averaged over the period of study only). The examples in this Guide apply the DSS's advice: this does reduce many students' entitlement to HB/CTB; it does create certain absurdities (the last two sentences in the previous paragraph contain two); it does mean that many 'existing student' cases have to be re-assessed four times or more a year rather than twice or more; but many authorities are likely to follow it.

A final surprising effect of the DSS's advice results from the fact that a person does not count as a student before he or she starts the course in question. So, from 1st September in his or her first year to the first day of the course, the student rules on assessing a student loan do not apply; so the loan, being a loan, is capital not income. But once the course begins, the student rules do apply, therefore it is still averaged over the 304 days in question (303 days in a non-leap year) as income.

3R 33(3A), 79(5A)
CTBR 24(4), 69(6)

20.42 For students who have left a course part way through a year, only the amount of the student loan actually received is taken into account (over the period described above), but there is no £10.00 disregard. In all cases, when in future years former students begin repaying student loans, they will not be able to offset them against earnings or other income for HB or main CTB purposes; and the repayment will not count as a change of circumstances for HB/CTB purposes.

HBR 58(1), 58A
CTBR 48, 48A

20.43 To avoid counting the same money twice, if a student loan is assessed on the assumption that the student, or his or her partner, will make a contribution, the amount of that contribution is disregarded from the student's or partner's other income. (Similarly, a parent who makes a contribution has that amount disregarded in the assessment of his or her own HB and main CTB: para. 13.85.)

Example: A student loan

In the 1999-2000 academic year, a 'new entrant student' in his second year of a degree course in Wales could get a student loan of £3635. (He is not in receipt of a grant of any kind.) His wife is not a student and has claimed HB and CTB for them both. His student loan is assessed as follows in the assessment of his wife's HB/CTB claim.

Whether or not he applies for or receives it, he is treated as receiving it and it is assessed as follows:

◆ Treat the whole £3635 as income (even though it is in fact a loan).

◆ Disregard £303 for books and equipment and £250 for travel, leaving £3082.

◆ Average this (paras. 20.40-41) over the period 1st September 1999 to 30th June 2000. Because of the leap year, this period contains 304 days. So this gives (£3082 ÷ 304 x 7) = £70.97 per week.

◆ Disregard £10. So he has income from the student loan of (£70.97 − £10.00) = £60.97 per week.

Because of the rules on when changes of circumstances are taken into account (chapter 17), this income is taken into account from 6th September 1999 (the first Monday after 1st September) to Sunday 2nd July 2000 (the Sunday at the end of the benefit week containing 1st July 2000).

Note that if this was a student in his or her first year, the loan income would be taken into account at £60.97 per week only from the Monday after the first day of his or her course (to Sunday 2nd July) for the reasons in paragraph 20.41.

ASSESSING GRANT INCOME

20.44 In calculating HB and main CTB, grant income is assessed according to the following rules. These apply to full-time and part-time students. For couples, they apply to each partner who is a student. Table 20.3 gives the main grant figures. The DSS provides authorities with a summary of relevant grant and bursary levels (currently in circular HB/CTB A54/99).

20.45 The whole amount of any grant income is counted (minus the disregards described below). This includes any kind of educational grant, award, scholarship, studentship, exhibition, allowance or bursary, whether paid by an education authority or from any other source. Some education authority grants

HBR 46, 53(1)
CTBR 38, 42(1)

are reduced by an amount which the education authority decides that a parent or partner – or the student himself or herself – should contribute to the grant. Such a contribution is counted as part of the grant income, and treated as received regardless of the actual facts of the case, e.g. even if a parent refuses to pay it.

HBR 58(1), 58A
CTBR 48, 48A

20.46 To avoid counting the same money twice, if a student's grant is assessed on the assumption that the student, or his or her partner, will make a contribution, the amount of that contribution is disregarded from the student's or partner's other income. (Similarly, a parent who makes a contribution has that amount disregarded in the assessment of his or her own HB and main CTB: para. 13.85.)

DISREGARDED GRANT INCOME

HBR 46,
3(1),(2),(2A),57A
CTBR 38,
42(1)-(3),47

20.47 Any grant income paid or intended to be used in connection with any of the items in table 20.4 is disregarded. It is usually possible to identify these from the grant notification sent to the student by the education authority (or other body making the grant).

Table 20.4 DISREGARDS FROM GRANT INCOME

◆ Tuition and/or examination fees.

◆ Awards because the student has a disability.

◆ Expenses for term-time residential study.

◆ 'Two homes grant' (awarded where the student has to maintain a home other than that at which he or she resides during the course).

◆ Additions for anyone residing outside the UK, where the student's applicable amount does not include an amount for him or her. (For example, a student from abroad may receive an addition for his or her family. If they remain abroad, this addition is disregarded.)

◆ Books and equipment as follows. If the student receives a grant which includes a specified amount for books and equipment, disregard that amount (however much it is). If that does not apply and the student neither receives nor is treated as receiving a student loan (paras. 20.38-39), disregard £303 for books and equipment. In any other case, disregard nothing for books and equipment (because £303 is instead disregarded from the student loan).

◆ Travel expenses as follows. If the student neither receives nor is treated as receiving a student loan (paras. 20.38-39), disregard £250 for travel expenses. In any other case, disregard nothing for travel (because £250 is instead disregarded from the student loan). There is no longer any disregard for travel expenses included in grants or loans for extra weeks' attendance. (For people on 'qualifying courses' under the New Deal, see also para. 20.7.)

WHEN DOES GRANT INCOME COUNT?

20.48 Grant income which is not disregarded is normally averaged over the number of weeks in the student's period of study – excluding, for sandwich students, any period of work experience. However, any part of a grant which is intended to cover some other period is averaged over that period. Most commonly, this applies to grant additions which are awarded for the whole academic year and are averaged separately over that year. So to assess an education authority grant: HBR 53(3),(4)
CTBR 42(4),(5)

◆ Add the following together and average over the period of study:

- the basic amount of the grant (see table 20.3) after making the relevant disregards (table 20.4) and

- additions for extra attendance (after disregarding any travel element).

◆ Average the following separately over the whole academic year:

- additions for older students, and

- additions for dependants (whether for an adult or a child).

20.49 Once grant income has been assessed, any change in the standard maintenance grant occurring during the summer vacation is ignored until the end of the summer vacation. The standard maintenance grant is uprated with effect from 1st September each year. So for a student whose autumn term begins on (say) 2nd October, the change is ignored until that date. HBR 60
CTBR 50

Example: A student grant

In the 1999-2000 academic year, an 'existing student' in his third year of a degree course in London gets a basic maintenance grant of £2280. (He also qualifies for a student loan.) His period of study is 40 weeks.

His grant income is assessed as follows:

◆ The whole amount of the grant (£2280) is taken into account. No disregards are made for books and equipment or for travel (because amounts are disregarded for these in the assessment of his student loan.)

◆ It is averaged over his period of study (40 weeks) as £57.00 per week.

HARDSHIP FUND PAYMENTS

20.50 Three hardship funds (sometimes known as 'access funds') are administered by educational establishments, who may make payments to students who fall within the student loan scheme, to postgraduates, and to students aged 19 or more in further education. Hardship fund payments are counted as charitable or voluntary payments (para. 13.80).

COVENANT INCOME

20.51 In the past, many parents paid their student son or daughter income through a covenant (a legally enforceable promise to pay money). The tax advantages of creating a covenant ended on 15th March 1988, and so such covenants are now rare. There remain, however, special rules for assessing any covenant paid to a full-time student by his or her parent. The details are in the 1999-2000 edition of this Guide and in GM chapter C5.

OTHER INCOME

20.52 If a full-time or part-time student receives earned or unearned income other than (or as well as) grant or covenant income or a student loan, the ordinary earned and unearned income disregards apply to it (chapters 13-15).

THE EXTRA STUDENT INCOME DISREGARD

20.53 In addition to the above points, there is a disregard

◆ from other income the student has (para. 20.50);

◆ of any amounts intended for necessary expenditure of any of the items listed in table 20.3.

But if the student has a student loan or grant (or covenant) income, this disregard only applies so far as the student's necessary expenditure on such items exceeds that allowed for in the assessment of that loan, grant (or covenant) income. This important disregard is often overlooked: students are advised to check that it has been applied properly.

20.54 For example, a deduction of £303 is made for books and equipment in the assessment of a full-time student's loan or grant income. If the student is single, has part-time net earnings of £20 per week, and contributes a further £4 per week towards books and equipment from this, £4 per week is disregarded in the assessment of her part-time earnings, so long as the additional expenditure is necessary for the course. The ordinary £5 earned income disregard (table 14.1) also applies, so the student's net earnings for HB and main CTB purposes are £11 per week.

Example: Student assessment, 'new entrant student' (1999-2000 academic year)

INFORMATION

Student claimant	Single woman, student aged 20, lives alone.
Course	1999-2000, outside London (but not Scotland), first year of course, full-time, undergraduate.
Period of study	Tuesday 5th October 1999 to Thursday 29th June 2000 (38 weeks 3 days).
Summer vacation	Friday 30th June 2000 onwards.
Student loan	She receives £3,635 (the maximum amount available in her case).
Grant	She gets a disabled student's grant only.
Other income	Net earnings (after all appropriate disregards) of £50 per week at all material times; no capital.
Applicable amount	Personal allowance plus disability premium: £63.60 from April 2000.
Eligible rent	Would be £45.00 per week if she was not a student.
Council tax	Her home is exempt.
Note	This example follows DSS guidance on student loans (see paras. 20.40-41).

ELIGIBLE FOR HB?

Yes – because she qualifies for a disability premium (table 20.1).

(For the sake of simplicity, it is assumed that the student is not ineligible for any of the reasons in paras. 20.22-27).

INCOME FROM LOAN

She qualifies for a student loan, and is treated as receiving one at the maximum level available – which in her case is £3,635. (In fact she actually receives this amount.)

Disregard £303 for books and equipment and £250 for travel, leaving £3,082.

Average this (£3,082) over the 304 days from 1st September 1999 to 30th June 2000, giving £70.97 per week.

Disregard £10.00, giving £60.97.

This counts as her income from Monday 11th October 1999 (the Monday after the start of her course) to Sunday 2nd July 2000 (the Sunday at the end of the benefit week containing 1st July 2000). For the period before 11th October 1999, she is not treated as having income from the loan (para. 20.41).

INCOME FROM GRANT

Her disabled student's grant is disregarded completely.

HB: INCOME DISREGARD AND RENT DEDUCTION?

During her period of study, her total income is £110.97 (which is £60.97 from the student loan plus £50.00 from her net earnings). Making the income disregard (£18.75) leaves £92.22.

£92.22 is more than her applicable amount (£63.60) so the student income disregard and rent deduction must be applied in her case (even though she qualifies for a disability premium) during her period of study.

HB: ASSESSED INCOME AND ELIGIBLE RENT

Throughout her period of study, her assessed income is £92.22 per week and her eligible rent is £26.25 per week (£45.00 minus £18.75). These figures apply from Monday 11th October 1999 (the Monday after the first day of her course) to Sunday 2nd July 2000 (the Sunday at the end of the week containing the first day of her summer vacation.

During the first part of her summer vacation, her assessed income is £50.00 (from her net earnings only – and no income disregard) and her eligible rent is £45.00 per week (with no rent deduction). These figures apply from Monday 3rd July 2000 (the Monday after the first day of her summer vacation) to Sunday 3rd September 2000.

During the remainder of her summer vacation, her assessed income will again include student loan income (using whatever the figures for the 2000-01 academic year are), but there will still be no income disregard or rent deduction (because it is still her summer vacation).

21 Subsidy

21.1   This chapter examines how HB and CTB are paid for in 1999-2000. It considers:

◆ the different types of expenditure;

◆ government objectives in establishing who pays for what;

◆ the different types of central government subsidy;

◆ subsidy penalties and incentives for authorities to control certain types of HB and CTB expenditure;

◆ the HB element of the housing revenue account (HRA) subsidy that applies in England and Wales; and

◆ subsidy to meet HB and CTB administration costs.

The special subsidy arrangements that apply to new towns or Scottish Homes are not described in this chapter. The impact of local government reorganisation on subsidy arrangements is described in Annex B of DSS circular HB/CTB S3/98.

21.2   The importance of an appropriate level of central government subsidy has sometimes been overlooked by authorities and advisers. Yet not only do these payments form a significant proportion of most authorities' total income, they are also a vital factor in determining the quality, effectiveness and style of HB and CTB administration. Studies of HB and CCB administration have highlighted the tension between proper adjudication (para. 1.21) and some of the 'perverse' penalties and incentives built into the subsidy systems (see, for example, *Remote Control: The National Administration of Housing Benefit*, Audit Commission, HMSO 1993).

Legislation

21.3   Benefit subsidy, except the subsidy relating to HRA benefit expenditure in England and Wales, is governed by amendments to SI 1998 No. 562 the Income-Related Benefits (Subsidy to Authorities) Order. These are normally issued at the end of the year to which it applies. The rules covering subsidy relating to HRA benefit expenditure in England and Wales for 1999-2000 are contained in the Housing Revenue Account Subsidy Determination 1999-2000. Separate determinations are issued by the DETR and the Welsh Office. Details of the subsidy arrangements for 1999-2000 are summarised in HB/CTB S3/99.

Expenditure and government objectives

21.4   Money spent on the different aspects of the HB and CTB schemes consists of:

◆ benefit payment costs, i.e. the money paid out in the form of HB or CTB; and

◆ on-going administrative costs, which include salaries, accommodation, postage, computer running costs and giro charges.

21.5   Money to meet these costs comes from three different sources:

◆ central government subsidy;

◆ the authority's own general fund; and

◆ (in England and Wales in the case of HRA rent rebates) the authority's own housing revenue account.

The government's stated objective for the subsidy arrangements is to provide 'incentives for local authorities to monitor and control costs whilst providing a fair level of support for expenditure which they properly incur' (*Hansard,* 25th June 1986, col. 210).

Types of central government subsidies

21.6   The following central government subsidies are paid to meet the costs of the schemes: AA s.135

◆ rent allowance subsidy to meet the cost of rent allowances;

◆ rent rebate subsidy to meet the cost of non-HRA rent rebates, and in Scotland only, the cost of HRA rent rebates;

◆ CTB subsidy to meet the cost of CTB expenditure; and

◆ HRA subsidy – which may help meet the cost of HRA rent rebate expenditure in England and Wales (but not in Scotland).

HB and CTB subsidies are described in paras. 21.8-30. The rent rebate element of HRA subsidy is described in paras. 21.31-38. Subsidy arrangements are summarised in table 21.1.

Table 21.1 SUMMARY OF BENEFIT EXPENDITURE SUBSIDY ARRANGEMENTS 1999-2000

	Benefit expenditure (except HRA rent rebate expenditure in England and Wales)	HRA rent rebate (England and Wales)
Basic rate of subsidy	95% Central government has the power to restrict the amount of subsidy in relation to an authority's CTB expenditure where council tax is increased above guidelines	100% taken into account in subsidy calculation where an authority's rent increases have kept to government guidelines
Backdated benefit	50%	nil
Overpayments		
◆ authority error	nil	nil
◆ claimant/third party error	25%	nil
◆ claimant/third party fraud	80%	100% taken into account in subsidy calculation
◆ rebate credited in advance of entitlement	nil	nil
◆ DSS error	95%	100% taken into account in subsidy calculation
◆ CTB overpaid due to delayed award of council tax discounts, disability reductions, transitional relief or budget capping	nil	N/A
◆ other	25%	nil
Duplicate rent allowance payment where original lost/stolen/not received and later found to have been encashed	25%	N/A
HB attributable to disproportionate increase in authority's rent	nil on HB attributable to disproportionate increase (Scotland)	nil on HB attributable to disproportionate increase

Unreasonably high private rents not covered by the January 1996 rules	*Benefit expenditure (except HRA rent rebate expenditure in England and Wales)*	*HRA rent rebate (England and Wales)*
◆ regulated tenancies	25% of HB attributable to rent above the specified threshold, 95% of rest	N/A
◆ deregulated tenancies (where authority unable to restrict the claimant's eligible rent)	60% on HB attributable to rent above rent officer determination, 95% of rest	N/A
◆ deregulated tenancies	nil on HB attributable to rent above rent officer determination, 95% of rest	N/A
Homeless people in board and lodging accommodation	12.5% on HB attributable to rent above the specified threshold up to level of newly introduced cap, nil above, 95% of rest	N/A
Accommodation licensed by authority	12.5% on HB attributable to rent above the specified threshold up to level of newly introduced cap, nil above, 95% of rest	N/A
Short-term leased accommodation	12.5% on HB attributable to rent above the specified threshold up to level of newly introduced cap, nil above, 95% of rest	N/A
Short-term leased accommodation in Scottish authorities' HRA	nil on HB attributable to rent above the specified threshold, 95% of rest	N/A

Period overruns

Overrun weeks as a % of benefit weeks in year	*% of total qualifying expenditure to be deducted from net subsidy claimed*	*See formula in Subsidy Determination*
◆ 81 to 100%	5%	
◆ 61 to 80.99%	4%	
◆ 41 to 60.99%	3%	
◆ 21 to 40.99%	2%	
◆ 5 to 20.99%	1%	
◆ less than 5%	nil%	

HRA AND NON-HRA RENT REBATE EXPENDITURE

21.7 HRA rent rebate expenditure includes all rent rebates paid in respect of dwellings which are accounted for within the authority's HRA. They include mainstream council housing to council tenants. Non-HRA rent rebates include those paid for:

◆ homeless people housed by the authority in bed and breakfast accommodation;

◆ accommodation leased by the local authority from a private landlord, e.g. hotel annexes; and

◆ occupants of accommodation that has been leased to the authority for a period which does not exceed three years (short-term leased accommodation).

HB and CTB subsidies

QUALIFYING EXPENDITURE

21.8 Benefit expenditure that counts for subsidy purposes is known as qualifying expenditure. The following are the main items of benefit expenditure that do not count as qualifying expenditure and that therefore are not eligible for HB or CTB subsidy as appropriate:

◆ any additional benefit awarded to claimants because their circumstances are considered exceptional (para. 9.42);

◆ increased rent allowance above the maximum rent for exceptional hardship (para. 11.21);

◆ any old scheme (pre-April 1988) overpayments;

◆ any benefit expenditure attributable to a local scheme (para. 9.39).

PERMITTED TOTALS

SI 1996 No 677
SI 1996 No 678
SI 1998 No 566
SI 1999 No 642

21.9 An authority's discretionary expenditure i.e.

◆ increases in benefit for exceptional circumstances (para. 9.42);

◆ increased rent allowance above the maximum rent level for exceptional hardship (para. 11.21);

◆ modified schemes to enhance the mandatory disregards of Navy and Army war widows' pensions (para. 9.39)

should be contained within the relevant permitted total.

MODULAR IMPROVEMENT SCHEMES

21.10 In Scotland, for the purpose of rent rebate subsidy (and also in England and Wales, for the purpose of HRA subsidy), rent rebate expenditure attributable to modular or menu improvement schemes for council tenants are not eligible for subsidy. These are schemes where tenants choose to pay increased rents in return for additional rights, services or facilities such as a door entry system or improved heating. Authorities are exempt from the reduction, however, where the rights, services or facilities:

◆ were made available with the sole purpose either of improving the physical condition of the dwellings or of meeting the needs of tenants or both; and

◆ were available for tenants to choose regardless of whether the tenants were or were not in receipt of rebates; and

◆ were not an influence on the authorities' letting policies and practices in 1996-97, 1997-98 or 1998-99 in relation to tenants eligible to receive rebates; and

◆ were made available at reasonable cost.

21.11 In Scotland, for the purpose of rent rebate subsidy rent rebate expenditure attributable to rent-free weeks not taken account of in calculating the rent rebate does not count as qualifying expenditure. Qualifying rent rebate expenditure is also reduced by the amount of any cash payments or payments in kind made to a local authority tenant by the authority except:

◆ payments made that are unrelated to the fact that the claimant is a tenant of the local authority, e.g. educational bursaries;

◆ awards required by law;

◆ discretionary payments made under section 137 of the Local Government Act 1972;

◆ reasonable compensation for repairs or redecorating carried out by the tenant which would normally have been carried out by the landlord; and

◆ one-off compensation payments for the loss, damage or inconvenience caused because the tenant occupies a particular property. This provision catches, for example, certain rent payment incentive schemes.

SUBSIDY ON QUALIFYING HB/CTB BENEFIT EXPENDITURE

21.12 The normal subsidy rate on benefit expenditure, except HRA benefit in England and Wales, is 95 per cent. A lower rate is payable in specific circumstances (para. 21.13). Different rules apply to HRA rent rebate expenditure in England and Wales in the same circumstances (para. 21.31).

Penalised benefit expenditure

21.13 To provide authorities with a firm incentive to monitor and control costs, the following areas of benefit expenditure are penalised:

◆ the backdating of claims (para. 21.15);

◆ identified overpayments (para. 21.16);

◆ disproportionately high increases in rents for local authority tenants (para. 21.19);

◆ rent allowances paid in respect of unreasonably high rents on most pre-1988 Housing Act tenancies without a registered or reasonable rent (para. 21.21);

◆ rent allowances paid under the rules introduced on 2nd January 1996 (para. 21.22);

◆ rent allowances which do not fall to be calculated under the rules introduced on 2nd January 1996 (para. 21.26), paid in respect of most rents of, in Scotland, post-2nd January 1989 lettings, and in England and Wales, post-15th January 1989 lettings; which are above reasonable market rents determined by the rent officer or which the rent officer determines to be exceptionally high, or accommodation which the rent officer considers unreasonably large;

◆ non-HRA rent rebates paid for certain homeless families in bed and breakfast accommodation and occupants of certain short-term leased accommodation where the rent payment is above a certain level (para. 21.20);

◆ cases that have overrun the maximum benefit period without a review taking place (benefit period overruns) (see GM paras. C10.50-57).

The same areas of English and Welsh HRA benefit expenditure are penalised (paras. 21.31 onwards).

21.14 Authorities must apply the rules of the scheme fairly, objectively and impartially. They must not allow the subsidy penalties to interfere with this duty though, following the *Brent and Connery* case (para. 11.73), where the authority has a discretion, one factor it may take into account is its own financial position.

BACKDATING OF CLAIMS

21.15 A 50 per cent subsidy is payable on amounts of benefit, except HRA benefit in England and Wales, that have been backdated where the claimant has good cause for a late claim (para. 7.84). In general, where an overpayment was backdated and is subsequently found to be overpaid, it should be treated as a backdated payment. The exception is where a backdated amount is later identified as a fraudulent overpayment. In such a case the fraudulent overpayment category (para. 21.6) takes priority.

OVERPAYMENTS

21.16 The subsidy payable on benefit overpayments, except HRA benefit in England and Wales, varies with the cause shown in table 21.1.

21.17   In the case of overpayments the subsidy arrangement acts, at least in part, as an incentive to authorities. Subsidy is paid on the identified overpayments. Amounts recovered, except in the case of Benefits Agency error overpayments, are not deducted from the authority's subsidy entitlement. For example, if the authority recovers a fraudulent overpayment, it receives 80 per cent subsidy and keeps the money it has recovered.

21.18   The nil rate of subsidy on authority error overpayments, which are often non-recoverable, acts as a severe penalty on the authority and as an incentive to misclassification.

DISPROPORTIONATE INCREASE IN RENTS REBATED THROUGH HB

21.19   The objective of this rule is to stop authorities from maximising subsidy entitlement by disproportionately increasing the rents of tenants who receive rent rebates as opposed to those tenants who are not on rebates. In Scotland, if the authority falls foul of the rule, benefit attributable to the higher increase for tenants receiving rent rebates qualifies for nil rent rebate subsidy. In England and Wales, HRA benefit attributable to such a higher increase also does not qualify for subsidy at all. Authorities who consider that they have open and fair rent-setting arrangements which apply in exactly the same way to all tenants, whether or not they are in receipt of rent rebates, are able to seek exemption from the penalty. Authorities have to convince their external auditors that this is in fact the case. Exemptions may also apply to any authority which had no reduction under this rule in the immediately preceding year, and which increases the rents of all of its tenants in the subsidy year by the same percentage.

HOMELESS PEOPLE IN B & B, LICENSED AND SHORT-TERM LEASED ACCOMMODATION OUTSIDE THE HRA

21.20   Threshold figures cover rent rebates awarded to homeless people placed in bed and breakfast accommodation by the local authority under the Housing Act 1985 or Housing (Scotland) Act 1987 as well as other licensed accommodation, e.g. hotel annexes, and also for short-term leased accommodation. Subsidy of 12½ per cent is paid on any HB equal to or less than the amount by which the eligible rent exceeds the threshold figure up to the level of a cap with nil entitlement above the capped figure. Benefit attributable to that part of the eligible rent which does not exceed the threshold attracts direct subsidy at the usual rate of 95 per cent.

UNREASONABLY HIGH RENTS ON OLD STYLE TENANCIES

21.21   If the claimant occupies a regulated tenancy without a registered rent, or is a restricted contract holder without a reasonable rent determined by a rent tribunal, and his or her eligible rent exceeds the local threshold, the amount of any HB equal to or less than that excess figure only qualifies for a 25 per cent subsidy. The local threshold is a figure equivalent to a multiple of the average registered rent in the relevant registration area for each authority. This subsidy penalty does not apply where the claimant's rent (though above the threshold) is registered or (in the case of a restricted contract) is a reasonable rent determined by a rent tribunal.

Examples: Old style tenancies

The claimant's eligible rent (after any restriction) is £65. The rent is not registered. The weekly threshold figure notified to the authority by the DSS is £50. The claimant's eligible rent exceeds the threshold figure by £15.

If the claimant's rent allowance is £15 or less it only attracts a 25 per cent subsidy.

If the claimant's rent allowance is £30, £15 attracts a 25 per cent subsidy and £15 a 95 per cent subsidy,

i.e. subsidy = £3.75 + £14.25 = £18.00.

If the claimant's rent allowance is £65, £15 attracts 25 per cent subsidy and £50 attracts a 95 per cent subsidy,

i.e. subsidy = £3.75 + £47.50 = £51.25.

RENT ALLOWANCES PAID UNDER THE RULES THAT OPERATE FROM 2ND JANUARY 1996

21.22 From 2nd January 1996 new rules have applied to certain rent allowance claims. Under the arrangements that existed prior to that date and which continue for some claimants, the rent officer's determinations restrict the amount of subsidy paid by central government (paras. 21.26-21.30) but do not necessarily restrict the rent on which HB is assessed. Under the new arrangements, the rent officer's determinations are used directly to calculate the maximum rent on which HB can be assessed. 95 per cent subsidy is normally payable on the HB calculated under the new rules. This entitlement to maximum subsidy includes those cases where the authority cannot restrict the rent because there has been a bereavement in the household or where the rent could be afforded when the tenancy was taken up and the claimant has not been in receipt of HB for 52 weeks prior to the current claim.

21.23 The one exception to the full subsidy entitlement under the new rules is where the authority uses a lower value for ineligible services than the ineligible service figure provided by the rent officer. In such cases any additional HB attributable to the use of the lower ineligible service figure does not qualify for subsidy.

21.24 Discretionary payments made in exceptional hardship cases do not count as qualifying expenditure for HB subsidy purposes (para. 21.8) and must be contained within the permitted totals figure (para. 21.9).

INDICATIVE RENT LEVELS

21.25 From 2nd January 1996 rent officers have supplied authorities with indicative rent levels (IRLs) which replace the former interim determinations. These are supplied on the first working day of each month for eight types of property (table 8.5). As the authority is unable to determine rent allowance entitlement under the January 1996 rules until the rent officer has made a full determination, IRLs can be used by the authority in working out the amount of a payment on account (para. 16.16). Where the authority is unable to recover all or part of an overpaid payment on account caused by the difference between the final determination (and consequent maximum rent) and the IRL, full subsidy is payable on the unrecovered amount providing the IRL used was the correct one and provided the authority applies the final determination in the HB assessment by the Monday following the date it was received.

SUBSIDY ON HB PAID ON NEW STYLE TENANCIES NOT PAID UNDER THE JANUARY 1996 RULES

21.26 In most cases falling under the pre-January 1996 rules, no DSS subsidy is payable on any HB equal to or less than the amount by which the eligible rent exceeds the rent officer's significantly high rent figure or exceptionally high rent determination less the rent officer's valuation for certain services. The exception is where the authority is unable to treat a claimant's eligible rent as reduced (para. 21.27).

21.27 In certain cases falling under the pre-January 1996 rules, the authority is unable to restrict the claimant's eligible rent, or a rent increase. This applies, for example, where the claimant falls into a 'protected' category, e.g. the claimant is 60 or over and there is no suitable alternative accommodation available.

21.28 In such cases subsidy at the rate of 60 per cent is payable on any HB equal to or less than the amount by which the eligible rent exceeds the rent officer's significantly high rent determination or exceptionally high rent determination.

21.29 The aim of these subsidy penalties is to encourage authorities to use their powers to restrict eligible rents under the pre-January 1996 rules where they consider them unreasonable.

21.30 The subsidy threshold figure and the rent officer's significantly high rent and size-related rent determinations represent the point above which the DSS are not prepared to pay subsidy or only prepared to pay a reduced amount of subsidy. These two figures do not represent the level above which authorities should not meet rents. Authorities are required to consider the individual circumstances of each case before deciding whether or not to meet the rent in full.

HRA subsidy

21.31 A housing authority's housing revenue account (HRA) records its income and expenditure on local authority housing. In England and Wales, but not Scotland, HRA subsidy was introduced under part VI of the Local Government and Housing Act 1989.

21.32 The amount of HRA subsidy that an English or Welsh authority is entitled to is calculated under a formula laid down by the Secretary of State to make up the assumed deficit on the authority's HRA.

21.33 The formula takes account of seven items of debit and credit of which qualifying rent rebate expenditure is only one. An English or Welsh authority's HRA subsidy entitlement equals its government assumed expenditure minus its government assumed income. If the assumed income is greater than the assumed expenditure then an amount equivalent to the excess income must be debited to the authority's HRA and transferred to its general fund.

21.34 Items of expenditure consist of:

◆ government-set allowances for the management and maintenance of council property;

◆ charges for capital borrowing;

◆ 100 per cent of most qualifying rent rebate expenditure;

◆ other reckonable items.

21.35 Items of income consist of:

◆ its rental income assumed by government;

◆ interest on certain capital receipts invested by the authority.

21.36 Whilst most qualifying rent rebate expenditure scores 100 per cent for HRA subsidy purposes, rent rebate expenditure itself is only one element in a deficit subsidy equation and consequently the HRA subsidy received by an authority may be significantly less th an its qualifying rent rebate expenditure.

QUALIFYING HRA BENEFIT EXPENDITURE

21.37 The categories of expenditure which are deducted from the total of HRA rent rebates granted in calculating qualifying HRA benefit expenditure are those described in paras. 21.8-10, and 100 per cent of the spending in the appropriate penalised areas described in para. 21.13. Benefits Agency error overpayments, however, less recovered amounts, score 100 per cent for HRA subsidy. A fixed allowance of 1.2 per cent of rent rebate expenditure is also allowed in each authority's HRA subsidy entitlement to cover the cost of overpayments and backdating.

LIMITING HRA SUBSIDY ON RENT REBATES TO GUIDELINE RENT INCREASES

21.38 For 1996-97 onwards HRA subsidy is not paid on any additional rent rebate expenditure which results from an authority increasing its average actual rents by more than its central government guideline rent increase. An authority may, however, apply for special determinations to disapply the new rule where it can show that it faces exceptional circumstances outside its control. The details of the new rules are described in the Department of the Environment and Department of Social Security paper: *Limiting Subsidy on Rent Rebates to Guideline Rent Increases,* 22nd December 1995.

SHORT-TERM LEASED ACCOMMODATION IN THE HRA

21.39 From April 1995 there is no longer any short-term leased accommodation within English authorities' HRAs (HB/CTB S2/95 para. 5.1).

Subsidy on administrative costs

21.40 Authorities are reimbursed for their administrative costs via a cash-limited specific grant. 50 per cent of this grant is added to their HB and CTB subsidy entitlement. The remaining 50 per cent is reflected in the revenue support grant (RSG) for English and Welsh authorities and the grant aided expenditure (GAE) arrangements in Scotland. In the case of English and Welsh authorities no addition is made to their HRA subsidy entitlement, as the costs of rent rebate administration are met outside the HRA and subsidised via the specific administration grant.

21.41 The non-RSG/GAE element of administration subsidy is allocated amongst authorities on the basis of assumed workload rather than actual expenditure. The assumed workload is determined by a formula that takes into account type of case, caseload, turnover data and tenure.

21.42 This unit cost subsidy fails to take account of 'quality of service' objectives such as the percentage of claims processed within the 14-day time period and error rates. As well as penalising inefficient authorities, a unit cost subsidy penalises those authorities that have sought to administer HB in a positive manner, for example by providing home visits to maximise take-up or by making their offices more accessible.

FRAUD SUBSIDY INCENTIVES; AND WEEKLY BENEFITS SAVINGS

21.43 Identified fraudulent overpayments qualify for 80 per cent benefit subsidy, and in England and Wales score 100 per cent for HRA subsidy purposes, as part of the government's incentive package for tackling fraud. In addition the DSS operates a Weekly Benefits Savings incentive scheme related to the savings of fraudulent HB, CTB and associated income support designated fraud staff achieve in relation to a threshold figure set for each authority. The 1999-2000 anti-fraud incentive scheme is banded so that Weekly Benefit Savings achieved:

◆ up to 75 per cent of threshold incur a pound for pound reduction in subsidy;

◆ above 75 per cent and up to 100 per cent of threshold do not incur a reduction nor do they receive additional subsidy;

◆ above 100 per cent and up to 200 per cent of threshold receive 25p in the pound additional subsidy;

◆ above 200 per cent and up to 300 per cent of threshold receive 30p in the pound additional subsidy; and

◆ above 300 per cent of threshold receive 40p in the pound additional subsidy.

Details of the anti-fraud incentive package including the consequences of the Verification Framework funding are contained in circular HB/CTB F20/98 and F9/99.

'Fast-tracking' subsidy arrangements for 'in-work' HB/CTB claims

21.44 Authorities are required to give priority to 'in-work' claims made by people who have claimed extended payments (para. 16.2). This requirement is reinforced through a system of time limits and subsidy rewards and penalties known as 'fast-tracking' (HB/CTB A6/96).

WHAT ARE THE TIME LIMITS FOR THE AUTHORITY?

21.45 Where a claim for an extended payment and for 'in-work' HB/CTB have both been made within the specified time limits the authority must then determine the in-work claim by a set date. This date is:

◆ 14 days starting from the date the in-work claim is made (as determined by the normal rules for establishing the date of claim); or

◆ 14 days starting from the date the claim for the extended payment is made (as determined by the first day of receipt at either the Benefits Agency, Jobcentre or the authority's benefit office); or

◆ 7 days starting with the date all the relevant information is received (i.e. from all sources including the claimant, rent officer, employer etc);

whichever happens to occur last in the particular circumstances of the claim.

21.46   To gain extra subsidy the authority must, in addition to meeting the above time limit, also correctly determine the in-work claim within the 4 week extended payment period (or – where the claim for an extended payment does not succeed – the 4 week extended payment period that would have applied in that case).

HOW DO THE 'FAST-TRACKING' SUBSIDY RULES WORK?

21.47   The subsidy rules are summarised in table 21.2.

Table 21.2 'FAST-TRACKING' SUBSIDY

Claim correctly determined within the specified 7/14 day time limit?	*Claim correctly determined within the extended payment period?*	*Subsidy gained or lost*
YES	YES	Authority gains £10 extra subsidy
YES	NO	Authority incurs no subsidy gain/loss
NO	YES	Authority incurs no subsidy gain/loss
NO	NO	Authority loses £10 subsidy

21.48   The rules above apply for each claim. This means that for combined HB and CTB cases any subsidy gain or loss will be £20. In the case of rent allowances, any subsidy gain or loss is decided by the date the claim is correctly determined and not by the date a payment on account is made.

Appendix 1:
Chronological list of statutory instruments

HOUSING BENEFIT AND COUNCIL TAX BENEFIT

◆ **SI 1987 No. 1971** **The Housing Benefit (General) Regulations**

◆ SI 1987 No. 1972 The Housing Benefit (Transitional) Regulations

◆ SI 1988 No. 458 The Housing Benefit (Transitional) Amendment Regulations

◆ SI 1988 No. 661 The Housing Benefit (General) Amendment Regulations

◆ SI 1988 No. 662 The Housing Benefit (Supply of Information) Regulations

◆ SI 1988 No. 909 The Housing Benefit (General) Amendment No. 2 Regulations

◆ SI 1988 No. 1444 The Housing Benefit (General) Amendment No. 3 Regulations

◆ SI 1988 No. 1971 The Housing Benefit (General) Amendment No. 4 Regulations

◆ SI 1989 No. 416 The Housing Benefit (General) Amendment Regulations

◆ SI 1989 No. 566 The Housing Benefit (General) Amendment No. 2 Regulations

◆ SI 1989 No. 1017 The Housing Benefit (General) Amendment No. 3 Regulations

◆ SI 1990 No. 127 The Income-Related Benefits Schemes Amendment Regulations

◆ SI 1990 No. 396 The Rent Officers (Additional Functions) (Scotland) Order

◆ SI 1990 No. 428 The Rent Officers (Additional Functions) Order

◆ SI 1990 No. 534 The Housing Benefit (Permitted Totals) Order

◆ SI 1990 No. 546 The Housing Benefit (General) Amendment Regulations

◆ SI 1990 No. 671 The Income-Related Benefits (Miscellaneous Amendments) Regulations

◆ SI 1990 No. 1549 The Social Security Benefits (Student Loans and Miscellaneous Amendments) Regulations

◆ SI 1990 No. 1657 The Income-Related Benefits Amendment Regulations

◆ SI 1990 No. 1775 The Housing Benefit (General) Amendment No. 2 Regulations

◆ SI 1990 No. 2208 The Social Security (Miscellaneous Provisions) Amendment Regulations

◆ SI 1990 No. 2564 The Housing Benefit (General) Amendment No. 3 Regulations

◆ SI 1991 No. 235 The Housing Benefit (General) Amendment Regulations

◆ SI 1991 No. 426 The Rent Officers (Additional Functions) (Amendment) Order

◆ SI 1991 No. 441   The Housing Benefit and Community Charge Benefit (Subsidy) Regulations

◆ SI 1991 No. 533   The Rent Officers (Additional Functions) (Scotland) Amendment Order

◆ SI 1991 No. 1175   The Income-Related Benefits Schemes and Social Security (Recoupment) Amendment Regulations

◆ SI 1991 No. 1599   The Housing Benefit and Community Charge Benefits (Miscellaneous) Amendment Regulations

◆ SI 1991 No. 2695   The Income-Related Benefits Schemes (Miscellaneous Provisions) Amendment Regulations

◆ SI 1991 No. 2742   The Disability Living Allowance and Disability Working Allowance (Consequential Provisions) Regulations

◆ SI 1992 No. 50   The Income-Related Benefits Schemes (Miscellaneous Amendments) Regulations

◆ SI 1992 No. 201   The Housing Benefit (General) Amendment Regulations

◆ SI 1992 No. 432   The Housing Benefit and Community Charge Benefits (Miscellaneous Amendments) Regulations

◆ SI 1992 No. 701   The Housing Benefit and Community Charge Benefit (Subsidy) Amendment Regulations

◆ SI 1992 No. 1101   The Income-Related Benefits Schemes and Social Security (Recoupment) Amendment Regulations

◆ SI 1992 No. 1326   The Income-Related Benefits Amendment Regulations

◆ SI 1992 No. 1585   The Income-Related Benefits Schemes (Miscellaneous Amendments) No.2 Regulations

◆ **SI 1992 No. 1814**   **The Council Tax Benefit (General) Regulations**

◆ SI 1992 No. 1909   The Council Tax Benefit (Transitional) Order

◆ SI 1992 No. 2148   The Housing Benefit and Community Charge Benefits (Miscellaneous Amendments) No. 2 Regulations

◆ SI 1992 No. 3147   The Social Security Benefits (Amendments Consequential upon the Introduction of Community Care) Regulations

◆ SI 1993 No. 317   The Housing Benefit (General) Amendment Regulations

◆ SI 1993 No. 349   The Social Security Benefits Up-rating Order

◆ SI 1993 No. 518   The Social Security Benefits (Miscellaneous Amendments) Regulations

◆ SI 1993 No. 646   The Rent Officers (Additional Functions) (Scotland) Amendment Order

◆ SI 1993 No. 652   The Rent Officers (Additional Functions) (Amendment) Order

- SI 1993 No. 688   The Council Tax Benefit (General) Amendment Regulations
- SI 1993 No. 689   The Council Tax Benefit (Permitted Total) Order
- SI 1993 No. 935   The Housing Benefit and Community Charge Benefit (Subsidy) No. 2 Order
- SI 1993 No. 945   The Housing Benefit and Community Charge Benefit (Subsidy) Amendment No. 2 Regulations
- SI 1993 No. 963   The Social Security Benefits (Miscellaneous Amendments) No. 2 Regulations
- SI 1993 No. 1150   The Income-Related Benefits Schemes (Miscellaneous Amendments) No. 2 Regulations
- SI 1993 No. 1249   The Income-Related Benefits Schemes and Social Security (Recoupment) Amendment Regulations
- SI 1993 No. 1540   The Income-Related Benefits Schemes (Miscellaneous Amendments) No. 3 Regulations
- SI 1993 No. 2118   The Housing Benefit and Council Tax Benefit (Miscellaneous Amendments) Regulations
- SI 1994 No. 470   The Housing Benefit and Council Tax Benefit (Amendment) Regulations
- SI 1994 No. 523   The Housing Benefit and Council Tax Benefit (Subsidy) Order
- SI 1994 No. 542   The Social Security Benefits Up-rating Order
- SI 1994 No. 568   The Rent Officers (Additional Functions) (Amendment) Order
- SI 1994 No. 578   The Housing Benefit and Council Tax Benefit (Miscellaneous Amendments) Regulations
- SI 1994 No. 579   The Housing Benefit (Permitted Totals) Order
- SI 1994 No. 582   The Rent Officers (Additional Functions) (Scotland) (Amendment) Order
- SI 1994 No. 781   The Housing Benefit and Council Tax Benefit (Subsidy) Regulations
- SI 1994 No. 1003   The Housing Benefit (General) Amendment Regulations
- SI 1994 No. 1608   The Income-Related Benefits Schemes (Miscellaneous Amendments) No. 2 Regulations
- SI 1994 No. 1807   The Income-Related Benefits Schemes (Miscellaneous Amendments) No. 3 Regulations
- SI 1994 No. 1924   The Income-Related Benefits Schemes (Miscellaneous Amendments) No. 4 Regulations
- SI 1994 No. 1925   The Housing Benefit (Supply of Information) and Council Tax Benefit (General) Amendment Regulations

- ◆ SI 1994 No. 2137   The Housing Benefit and Council Tax Benefit (Miscellaneous Amendments) No. 2 Regulations
- ◆ SI 1994 No. 2138   The Council Tax Benefit (Permitted Total) Order
- ◆ SI 1994 No. 3040   The Rent Officers (Additional Functions) (Amendment No. 2) Order
- ◆ SI 1994 No. 3061   The Income-Related Benefits Schemes (Miscellaneous Amendments) No. 6 Regulations
- ◆ SI 1994 No. 3108   The Rent Officers (Additional Functions) (Scotland) (Amendment No. 2) Order
- ◆ SI 1995 No. 511   The Housing Benefit and Council Tax Benefit (Amendment) Regulations
- ◆ SI 1995 No. 531   The Local Government Changes for England (Housing Benefit and Council Tax Benefit) Regulations
- ◆ SI 1995 No. 559   The Social Security Benefits Up-rating Order
- ◆ SI 1995 No. 560   The Housing Benefit and Council Tax Benefit (Miscellaneous Amendments) Regulations
- ◆ SI 1995 No. 625   The Housing Benefit, Council Tax Benefit and Income Support (Amendments) Regulations
- ◆ SI 1995 No. 626   The Housing Benefit and Council Tax Benefit (Miscellaneous Amendments) No. 2 Regulations
- ◆ SI 1995 No. 872   The Housing Benefit and Council Tax Benefit (Subsidy) Order
- ◆ SI 1995 No. 874   The Housing Benefit and Council Tax Benefit (Subsidy) (Amendment) Regulations
- ◆ SI 1995 No. 1339   The Income-Related Benefits Schemes (Miscellaneous Amendments) No. 2 Regulations
- ◆ SI 1995 No. 1642   The Rent Officers (Additional Functions) Order
- ◆ SI 1995 No. 1643   The Rent Officer (Additional Functions) (Scotland) Order
- ◆ SI 1995 No. 1644   The Housing Benefit (General) Amendment Regulations
- ◆ SI 1995 No. 1742   The Social Security Benefits (Miscellaneous Amendments) Regulations
- ◆ SI 1995 No. 1954   The Housing Benefit (Permitted Totals) Order
- ◆ SI 1995 No. 2303   The Income-Related Benefits Schemes and Social Security (Claims and Payments) (Miscellaneous Amendments) Regulations
- ◆ SI 1995 No. 2361   The Rent Officers (Additional Functions) (Scotland) Amendment Order
- ◆ SI 1995 No. 2365   The Rent Officers (Additional Functions) (Amendment) Order

- SI 1995 No. 2792   The Income Related Benefits Schemes Amendment (No. 2) Regulations
- SI 1995 No. 2793   The Housing Benefit (Permitted Totals) and Council Tax Benefit (Permitted Total) (Pensions for War Widows) Amendment Order
- SI 1995 No. 2868   The Housing Benefit (General) Amendment (No. 2) Regulations
- SI 1995 No. 3148   The Rent Officers (Additional Functions) (Amendment No. 2) Order
- SI 1995 No. 3151   The Housing Benefit (Permitted Totals) Amendment Order
- SI 1995 No. 3185   The Rent Officers (Additional Functions) (Scotland) Amendment (No. 2) Order
- SI 1995 No. 3282   The Income-Related Benefits Schemes (Widows' etc Pensions Disregards) Amendment Regulations
- SI 1996 No. 30   The Social Security (Persons from Abroad) Miscellaneous Amendments Regulations
- SI 1996 No. 194   The Housing Benefit, Supply of Information and Council Tax Benefit (Amendment) Regulations
- SI 1996 No. 462   The Income-Related Benefits Schemes (Miscellaneous Amendments) Regulations
- SI 1996 No. 547   The Local Government Changes for England (Housing Benefit and Council Tax Benefit) Amendment Regulations
- SI 1996 No. 548   The Local Government Changes for Scotland (Housing Benefit and Council Tax Benefit) Order
- SI 1996 No. 549   The Local Government Reorganisation (Wales) (Housing Benefit and Council Tax Benefit) Order
- SI 1996 No. 599   The Social Security Benefits Up-rating Order
- SI 1996 No. 677   The Housing Benefit (Permitted Totals) Order
- SI 1996 No. 678   The Council Tax Benefit (Permitted Totals) Order
- SI 1996 No. 959   The Rent Officers (Additional Functions) (Amendment) Order
- SI 1996 No. 965   The Housing Benefit (General) Amendment Regulations
- SI 1996 No. 975   The Rent Officers (Additional Functions) (Scotland) (Amendment) Order
- SI 1996 No. 1217   The Housing Benefit and Council Tax Benefit (Subsidy) Order
- SI 1996 No. 1314   The Housing Benefit and Council Tax Benefit (Subsidy) Amendment Regulations
- SI 1996 No. 1510   The Housing Benefit, Council Tax Benefit and Supply of Information (Jobseeker's Allowance) (Consequential Amendments) Regulations

◆ SI 1996 No. 1759   The Income-related Benefits Schemes (Miscellaneous Amendments) (No. 2) Regulations

◆ SI 1996 No. 1803   The Child Benefit, Child Support and Social Security (Miscellaneous Amendments) Regulations

◆ SI 1996 No. 1944   The Income-related Benefits Schemes and Social Fund (Miscellaneous Amendments) Regulations

◆ SI 1996 No. 2006   The Income-related Benefits (Montserrat) Regulations

◆ SI 1996 No. 2326   The Housing Benefit (Permitted Totals) (Amendment) Order

◆ SI 1996 No. 2432   The Council Tax Benefit and Housing Benefit (Miscellaneous Amendments) Regulations

◆ SI 1996 No. 2545   The Income-related Benefits and Jobseeker's Allowance (Personal Allowances for Children and Young Persons) (Amendment) Regulations

◆ SI 1997 No. 65   The Income-related Benefits and Jobseeker's Allowance (Miscellaneous Amendments) Regulations

◆ SI 1997 No. 543   The Social Security Benefits Up-rating Order

◆ SI 1997 No. 576   The Social Security Benefits Up-rating Regulations

◆ SI 1997 No. 584   The Housing Benefit (General) Amendment Regulations

◆ SI 1997 No. 791   The Jobseeker's Allowance (Workskill Courses) Pilot Regulations

◆ SI 1997 No. 852   The Housing Benefit and Council Tax Benefit (General) Amendment Regulations

◆ SI 1997 No. 1000   The Rent Officers (Additional Functions)(Amendment) Order

◆ SI 1997 No. 1003   The Rent Officers (Additional Functions)(Scotland) Amendment Order

◆ SI 1997 No. 1004   The Housing Benefit and Council Tax Benefit (Subsidy) Order

◆ SI 1997 No. 1671   The Social Security (Miscellaneous Amendments) (No. 3) Regulations

◆ SI 1997 No. 1790   The Social Security (Lone Parents)(Amendment) Regulations

◆ SI 1997 No. 1841   The Council Tax Benefit (General) Amendment Regulations

◆ SI 1997 No. 1909   The Jobseeker's Allowance (Workskill Courses) Pilot (No. 2) Regulations

◆ SI 1997 No. 1974   The Housing Benefit (General) Amendment (No. 2) Regulations

◆ SI 1997 No. 1975   The Housing Benefit (General) Amendment (No. 3) Regulations

◆ SI 1997 No. 1984   The Rent Officers (Housing Benefit Functions) Order

◆ SI 1997 No. 1995   The Rent Officers (Housing Benefit Functions) (Scotland) Order

◆ SI 1997 No. 2197   The Income-related Benefits and Jobseeker's Allowance (Amendment) (No. 2) Regulations

◆ SI 1997 No. 2434   The Housing Benefit and Council Tax Benefit (General) Amendment (No. 2) Regulations

◆ SI 1997 No. 2435   The Housing Benefit (Recovery of Overpayments) Regulations

◆ SI 1997 No. 2436   The Housing Benefit (Information from Landlords and Agents) Regulations

◆ SI 1997 No. 2619   The Housing Benefit (Recovery of Overpayments) (No. 2) Regulations

◆ SI 1997 No. 2676   The Social Security (National Insurance Number Information: Exemption) Regulations

◆ SI 1997 No. 2793   The Income-related Benefits (Miscellaneous Amendments) Regulations

◆ SI 1997 No. 2813   The Social Security (Penalty Notice) Regulations

◆ SI 1997 No. 2863   The Social Security Amendment (New Deal) Regulations

◆ SI 1998 No. 217   The New Deal (Miscellaneous Provisions) Order

◆ SI 1998 No. 470   The Social Security Benefits Up-rating Order

◆ SI 1998 No. 562   The Income-related Benefits (Subsidy to Authorities) Order

◆ SI 1998 No. 563   The Social Security (Miscellaneous Amendments) Regulations

◆ SI 1998 No. 566   The Housing Benefit (Permitted Totals) (Amendment) Order

◆ SI 1998 No. 766   The Social Security (Lone Parents) Regulations

◆ SI 1998 No. 865   The Social Security (Miscellaneous Amendments) (No. 2) Regulations

◆ SI 1998 No. 911   The Council Tax Benefit (General) Amendment Regulations

◆ SI 1998 No. 1173   Social Security (Miscellaneous Amendments) (No.3) Regulations

◆ SI 1998 No. 1174   Social Security (Miscellaneous Amendments) (No.4) Regulations

◆ SI 1998 No. 1274   Social Security Amendment (New Deal) Regulations

◆ SI 1998 No. 1379   Social Security (Student Amounts Amendment) Regulations

◆ SI 1998 No. 1425   The New Deal (Miscellaneous Provisions) Amendment Order

◆ SI 1998 No. 1541   Social Security Amendment (Personal Allowances for Children) Regulations

◆ SI 1998 No. 1732   Housing Benefit (General) Amendment Regulations

◆ SI 1998 No. 2164   Housing Benefit and Council Tax Benefit Amendment (New Deal) Regulations

◆ SI 1998 No. 2231   The Social Security (Welfare to Work) Regulations

◆ SI 1998 No. 2250   The Social Security Amendment (Capital) Regulations

◆ SI 1998 No. 2454   The Housing Benefit (Recovery of Overpayments) Amendment Regulations

◆ SI 1998 No. 2825   The Social Security (New Deal Pilot) Regulations

◆ SI 1998 No. 2865   The Income-related Benefits (Subsidy to Authorities) Amendment Order

◆ SI 1998 No. 3257   The Housing Benefit (General) Amendment (No. 2) Regulations

◆ SI 1999 No. 264   Social Security Benefits Up-rating Order

◆ SI 1999 No. 550   The Income-Related Benefits (Subsidy to Authorities) Amendment Order

◆ SI 1999 No. 642   The Housing Benefit (Permitted Totals)(Amendment) Order

◆ SI 1999 No. 920   The Housing Benefit and Council Tax Benefit (General) Amendment Regulations

◆ SI 1999 No. 976   Social Security (New Deal Pilot) Amendment Regulations

◆ SI 1999 No. 1539   Housing Benefit and Council Tax Benefit (General) Amendment (No.2) Regulations

◆ SI 1999 No. 1509   Social Security Amendment (Non-cash Vouchers) Regulations

◆ SI 1999 No. 1677   Social Security Amendment (Educational Maintenance Allowance) Regulations

◆ SI 1999 No. 1935   Social Security Amendment (Students) Regulations

◆ SI 1999 No. 2165   Social Security Amendment (Sports Awards) Regulations

◆ SI 1999 No. 2401   Housing Benefit (General) Amendment (No.2) Regulations

◆ SI 1999 No. 2555   Social Security Amendment (Personal Allowances for Children and Young Persons) Regulations

◆ SI 1999 No. 2556   Social Security (Miscellaneous Amendments) (No.2) Regulations

◆ SI 1999 No. 2566   Social Security and Child Support (Tax Credits) Consequential Amendments Regulations

◆ SI 1999 No. 2640   Social Security Amendment (Notional Income and Capital) Regulations

◆ SI 1999 No. 2734   Housing Benefit (General) Amendment (No.3) Regulations

◆ SI 1999 No. 3108   Social Security (Claims and Information) Regulations

◆ SI 1999 No. 3156   Social Security (New Deal Pilot) Regulations

◆ SI 2000 No. 1   Rent Officers (Housing Benefit Functions) (Amendment) Order

◆ SI 2000 No. 3   Rent Officers (Housing Benefit Functions) (Scotland) Amendment Order

◆ SI 2000 No. 4   Housing Benefit and Council Tax Benefit (General) Amendment Regulations

◆ SI 2000 No. 55   Social Security Amendment (Education Maintenance Allowance) Regulations

Appendix 2:
Table of selected cases

NAME	REPORT	SUBJECT
Andrew v Glasgow City Council, 20th January 1995	1996 SLT 814	Eligibility for higher pensioner premium
Chief Adjudication Officer and another v Clarke; Same v Faul, CA, 14th February 1995	The Times 22nd February 1995	Income support case Claimant not a 'student' during year of course HB/CTB regulations subsequently amended
Chief Adjudication Officer and another v. Palfrey; Same v Dowell; Same v McDonnell: Same v Pelter; Same v McNamara, CA, 8th February 1995	The Times 17th February 1995	Income support case Valuation method to be used where claimant has beneficial joint tenancy Reversionary interest Regulations amended (S.I. 1995 No. 2303) with effect from 2nd October 1995
Director of Public Prosecutions v. Huskinson, QBD, 9th May 1988	20 HLR 562 The Times 24th May 1988	No duty to use HB to pay rent
Fallwood v Chesterfield Borough Council, CA, 9th June 1993	The Times 15 June 1993	Non-dependants Normally resides with the claimant
Haringey LBC v Cotter, CA, 21st November 1996	29 HLR 682 The Times 9th December 1996	An alleged underpayment of rent allowance could not be set off against a claim for overpayment of HB because in this case there was no private law right of action in relation to payment of HB
Haringey LBC v Awaritefe, CA, 26th May 1999	The Times 3rd June 1999	Recovery of overpayment: degree to which authority must comply with HB Regs. Sch. 6 requirements
Keanan v. South Hams DC, CA, 26th June 1997	Unreported	Delay Possession of land
MacLeod v. Banff and Buchan HB Review Board, Court of Session, Outer House, 3rd December 1987	[1988] SLT 753	Unreasonably high rent Failure of review board to give adequate reasons Review board's failure to have regard to statutory tests imposed upon it
Malcolm v. Tweeddale DC HB Review Board, Court of Session, Outer House, 6th August 1991	[1984] SLT 1212	Unreasonably high rent

Mehanne v Westminster City Council HB Review Board, CA, 21st December 1998	[2000] 1 WLR 16	Review Board had a residual discretion under HB reg.11(2) to decide the amount of any reduction in benefit to be applied
Nessa v Chief Adjudication Officer, CA, 5th February 1998	*The Times,* 11th February 1998	In order to qualify for income support, an applicant had to show that she was in the United Kingdom voluntarily and for settled purposes for an appreciable period of time before she could claim to be habitually resident.
Osinuga v Director of Public Prosecutions, QBD, 21 October 1997	30 HLR 853 *The Times* 26th November 1997	A HB claim form was a document used for accounting purposes; therefore false information in such a form could constitute the offence of false accounting under section 17 of the Theft Act 1968.
Plymouth CC v. Gigg, CA, 16th May 1997	30 HLR 284	Meaning of 'unavoidable' liability to pay rent on two homes, overpayments
Re: James McDonnell Court of Session, Outer House, 10th September 1986 (Cumbernauld Development Corporation HB Review Board)	[1987] SLT 486	Exclusion of one party at review board hearing a breach of natural justice
R v Arun DC ex p. Bayley and another, QBD, 15th May 1995	Unreported	Withholding benefit where claimant has not paid rent but has expended sums in excess of disputed rent in the discharge of the landlord's obligations Review Board's inconsistent facts/reasons
R v Aylesbury Vale DC HB Review Board and Secretary of State for Social Security ex p. John Boot England, QBD, 18th July 1995	28 HLR 783	Regulation 72(15) limits the power to backdate HB to a period of 12 months before the date on which the request for backdating was made. Regulations amended 1.4.96 by SI 1996 No 462
R. v. Aylesbury Vale DC HB Review Board, CA, reversing, 22nd July 1996	29 HLR 303	
R v. Birmingham CC HB Review Board ex p. Ellery and Weir, QBD, 4th April 1989	21 HLR. 398 [1989] RVR 70 *The Independent* 7th April 1989 *The Times* 11th April 1989 *Guardian* 11th April 1989	Co-ownership tenant is not entitled to claim HB

R v Birmingham CC HB Review Board and Fitzpatrick ex p. Birmingham CC, QBD, 31st October 1991	24 HLR 279	Exceptional circumstance additions Authority's right to seek judicial review of review board's decision
R v Birmingham CC ex p. Connolly and Millard, QBD, 15th March 1994	26 HLR 551	Landlord's right to appeal to review board. Claimant's right to appoint a representative. Regulations amended (SI 1994, No. 2137)
R v Brent LB HB Review Board and others ex p. Connery, QBD, 20th October 1989 R v Caerphilly County Council, ex p Jones, QBD, 1st February 1999	[1990] 2 ALL ER 353 [1990] RVR 96 22 HLR 40 The Times 25th October 1989 Unreported	Unreasonably high rents Implications of subsidy loss for authority's determinations Review Board's decision quashed – failure to consider relevant evidence and delay in producing reasons for a decision
R v Brent L B Council ex p. Kalibala, QBD, 19th April 1991	Unreported	Requirement to exhaust normal appeal mechanism prior to seeking judicial review
R v Bristol City Council ex p. Jacobs, QBD, 3rd November 1999	The Times 16th November 1999	Water charges paid directly to a water authority do not form part of the 'eligible rent'
R v Caerphilly CBC ex p. Jones, QBD, 1st February 1999	Unreported	Review board's decision quashed – failure to consider relevant evidence and delay in producing reasons for decision
R v Cambridge CC ex p. Thomas, QBD, 10th February 1995	Unreported	Residing with a close relative Liability contrived to take advantage of the scheme Liable to make payments in respect of a dwelling
R v Camden LBC HB Review Board ex p. W, CA, 26th November 1999	Unreported	HB Reg. 61(3) (the 'exceptional hardship provision') did not apply to cases determined under HB Reg. 11 in its unamended form
R v Canterbury CC ex p. Woodhouse and another, QBD, 2nd August 1994	Unreported	Unreasonably high rent Meaning of 'suitable alternative accommodation' and 'reasonable to expect the claimant to move'
R v Canterbury CC ex p. Goodman, QBD, 11th July 1995	Unreported	Good cause backdating reliance on advice from an accountant Information and evidence reasonably required and time to supply it

R v Cardiff CC HB Review Board ex p. Thomas, QBD, 8th February 1991	25 HLR 1	Review board's failure to give intelligible reasons and failure to refer to regulations
R v Chesterfield BC ex p. Fullwood; R v. Derbyshire Dales DC ex p. Cooper, QBD, 29th July 1992	24 HLR 706 *The Independent* 9th September 1992	Meaning of 'jointly occupies' for non-dependant definition
R v Chorley BC ex p. Bound, QBD, 20th October 1995	28 HLR 791	Review Board Chairman's responsibility in relation to the production of the Review Board's decision note Occupancy as a home Authority's power to review review board decisions where it is satisfied by fresh evidence that the decision was made in ignorance of or was based on a mistake as to a material fact
R v Coventry CC ex p. Waite and Others, QBD, 7th July 1995	Unreported	Unreasonably high rents Meaning of 'suitable alternative accommodation' Need for suitable alternative accommodation to be available
R v Doncaster BC HB Review Board ex p. Boulton, QBD, 11th December 1992	25 HLR 195	Meaning of 'unreasonably high' Meaning of 'voluntary payments'
R v Doncaster MBC ex p. Nortrop, 9th February 1996	28 HLR 862	The Review Board has inquisitorial function. It should consider all relevant information whether submitted by the parties or not. The Board should have provided reasons for accepting the authority's valuation of a capital asset
R v Ealing LB HB Review Board ex p. Saville, QBD, 2nd May 1986	18 HLR 349 84 LGR 842	Assessment of income (Pre-1988 regulations)
R v East Devon DC HB Review Board ex p. Gibson and Gibson, QBD, 29th November 1991	24 HLR 411	Unreasonably high rent – alternative cheaper accommodation
R v East Devon DC HB Review Board ex p. Gibson and Gibson, CA, reversing earlier hearing, 10th March 1993	25 HLR 487	Unreasonably high rent – alternative cheaper accommodation Adequacy of review board's decision note

R v East Devon DC HB Review Board ex p. P., QBD, 2nd November 2, 1998	31 HLR 936	In deciding what constituted 'suitable alternative accommodation' the review board had come to an irrational conclusion. It had ignored evidence that the claimant was particularly vulnerable and required particular services
R v East Yorkshire Borough of Beverley HB Review Board ex p. Hare, QBD, 21st February 1995	27 HLR 637 *The Times* 28th February 1995	Unreasonably high rent Review board's failure to give adequate reasons for decision
R. v. Ellesmere Port and Neston BC HB Review Board ex p. Williams, CA, 15th November 1996	Unreported	Overpayments Discretionary powers
R v Fenland DC ex p. Halfacree, QBD, 19th June 1997	Unreported	Title to land; liability for rent and HB entitlement
R. v. Gloucestershire CC ex p. Dadds, QBD, 3rd December 1996	29 HLR 700	Contrived tenancy
R v Greenwich LBC ex p. Moult, QBD, 19th June 1998	Unreported	Non-commercial/contrived agreement
R v Greenwich LB ex p. Dhadly, 6 July 1998	31 HLR 446	Requirement that HB Officer prove applicant not under true liability to pay rent
R v Hackney LBC, ex p. Adebiri. R v Merton LBC, ex p Inparaja. R v Same, ex p. Parupathpilli. R v Ealing LBC, ex p. Jehan, QBD. 31st July 1997	*The Times* 5th November 1997	An authority which brought proceedings to enforce payment of council tax by asylum seekers who had no means of paying was entitled to do so, and was not acting unreasonably
R v Haringey LB ex p. Azad Ayub, QBD, 13th April 1992	25 HLR 566	Payment on account Direct payments to landlord Recovered overpaid HB does not count as rent arrears Regulations amended to preserve rent liability [SI1997 No 65] Recovery of overpayments from a landlord
R v Ipswich BC ex p. Flowers, R v Same ex p. Copland, QBD, 1st March 1994	Unreported	Unreasonably high rent Meaning of suitable alternative accommodation No requirement that alternative accommodation must be available where the claimant does not fall into a protected group

R v Islington LB HB Review Board ex p. De Grey and Hornby, QBD, 11th February 1992	Unreported	'Official error' overpayments
R v Islington LB HB Review Board ex p. Sutton, QBD, 26th January 1995	Unreported	Right to assistance from lay persons in judicial review proceedings
R v Kensington and Chelsea RB HB Review Board ex p. Robertson, QBD, 10th February 1988	86 LGR 409 [1988] RVR 84 *The Times* 15th February 1988 *The Independent* 5th March 1988	Occupation as a home Temporary absence (Pre-1988 regulations) Status of DSS Guidance Manual
R v Kensington and Chelsea RB HB Review Board ex p. Raeuchle, QBD, 8th September 1994 R v Kensington and Chelsea RB ex p. Brandt, QBD, 15th December 1995	Unreported 28 HLR 538 *The Times* 21st December 1995 *The Independent* 11th January 1996	'Evidence reasonably required' in support of a claim and the discretion to receive evidence out of time An authority which has lawfully withheld payments of HB has no power to arrange for the withheld payments to be placed in an interest-bearing account pending payment
R. v. Kensington and Chelsea RB ex p. Carney, QBD, 15th August 1996	Unreported	Unreasonably high rent Factors to take into account in deciding whether it is reasonable to expect the claimant to move
R. v. Kensington and Chelsea RB HB Review Board ex p. Sheikh, QBD, 14th January 1997	Unreported	Review board's duty to give reasons Unreasonably high rent Meaning of suitable alternative accommodation Whether reasonable to expect the claimant to move
R v Kensington and Chelsea RB ex p. Pirie, QBD, 26th March 1997	Unreported	Administrative decisions; Rent
R v Lambeth LB ex p. Crookes and others, QBD, 4th July 1995	29 HLR 28	HB complaints that should be addressed to the local government ombudsman rather than be the subject of judicial review
R v Lambeth LB ex p. Crookes and others, QBD, 21st December 1995	Unreported	Authority's failure to determine HB claims Authority not entitled to lapse claims for HB if access denied to rent officer only to withhold Authority not entitled to demand HB applicants attend interviews, bring proof of identity or suspend claim if they do not turn up Authority not allowed to enter private property without claimant's or landlord's permission

R. v Lambeth LBC HB Review Board, ex p. Harrington, QBD, 22nd November 1996	*The Times* 10th December 1996	Review board's duty to give facts and reasons for its findings. Where reasons were grossly flawed it is not permissible for the court to refer to supplementary affidavit evidence.
R v Lambeth LBC, ex parte Ogunmuyiwa, 3rd March 1997	29 HLR 950 *The Times* 17th April 1997	An application for judicial review is not barred on the ground that other remedies had not been exhausted where an authority had raised an expectation of a review of the case but had not carried out that review
R v Lambeth LBC ex p. Crookes, QBD, 11th February 1998	31 HLR 59	Request for HB Review Board must be signed by applicant not solicitor as agent
R v Liverpool CC ex p. Griffiths, QBD, 14th March 1990	22 HLR 312 *The Times,* 27th April 1990	Recoverable overpayments
R v Liverpool CC, ex p. Johnson et al, QBD, 23rd June 1994	Unreported	Failure to meet statutory dates with regard to time of payment, etc.
R v Liverpool CC, ex p. Johnson QBD, 31st October 1994	Unreported	The authority's right to information and evidence does not enable it to insist that it be given at a personal interview
R v Liverpool CC, ex p. Muldoon R v Rent Officer Service and Another ex p. Kelly, QBD, 16th March 1995	28 HLR 208 *The Times* 18th April 1995	The Secretary of State is not entitled, as of right, to service of notice of every application for judicial review proceedings against the relevant authorities regarding HB
R v Liverpool City Council ex p. Connolly, QBD, 20th November 1995	Unreported	Determination of claim; duty to give reasons
R. v Liverpool CC, ex p Muldoon, and ex parte Kelly, Lords, affirming CA, 10th July 1996	[1996] IWLR 1103 *The Times* 11th July 1996	
R v Macclesfield BC HB Review Board, ex p. Temsamani, QBD, 24th February 1999	Unreported	In restricting the amount of rent eligible for the calculation of HB in accordance with regulation 10(6B) of the HB Regs the review board were not bound to accept a Rent Officer's pre-tenancy determination but had a wide discretion
R v Maidstone BC ex p. Bunce, QBD, 23rd June 1994	27 HLR 375 *The Times* 30th June 1994	Discretionary addition

R v Manchester CC ex p. Baragrove Properties Ltd. QBD, 15th March 1991	23 HLR 337 *The Times* 21st March 1991 *Telegraph* 28th March 1991	Unreasonably high rents Contrived tenancies Letting agent's right to seek judicial review
R v Manchester CC ex p. Harcup, QBD, 28th May 1993	26 HLR 402	Unreasonably high rent – alternative cheaper accommodation Adequacy of Review Board's decision note
R v Middlesbrough BC and another ex p. Granville, QBD, 26th March 1993	Unreported	Entitlement to higher pensioner premium
R v Middlesbrough BC ex p. Holmes, QBD, 15th February 1995	Unreported	Arrears of benefit income – date of change of circumstance Regulations amended (SI 1995 No. 511)
R v Milton Keynes BC HB Review Board ex p. Macklen, QBD, 30th April 1996	Unreported	Contrived arrangements – has to be improper conduct. Judicial review proceedings v request for a set aside; importance of a letter before action
R v Newham LBC ex p. Hassan, QBD, 17th July 1997	Unreported	The authority's power to review determinations
R v North Cornwall DC HB Review Board ex p. Singer and others, QBD, 9th December 1993	26 HLR 360 *The Times* 12th January 1994	Eligible service charges, counselling and support services Regulations amended (SI 1994 No. 1003)
R v North Norfolk DC HB Review Board and North Norfolk DC, ex p. Swift, QBD, 26th February 1993	Unreported	Non-allowable business expense for self employed claimant Meaning of 'expansion of business'
R v Oadby and Wigston BC ex p. Dickman, QBD, 13th November 1995	28 HLR 806	Unreasonably large accommodation Unreasonably high rent Meaning of 'suitable alternative accommodation elsewhere' Meaning of 'available suitable alternative accommodation' Factors to take into account when deciding whether it is 'reasonable to expect the claimant to move?'
R v. Oxford CC ex p. Jack, QBD, 21st November 1984	17 HLR 419	Meaning of 'income'
R v Penwith DC ex p. Burt, QBD, 26th February 1990	22 HLR 292 *The Times* 16th March 1990	Temporary absence

R v. Penwith DC HB Review Board ex p. Menear, QBD, 11th October 1991	24 HLR 120 [1991] RVR 221 *The Times* 21st October 1991	DSS determination of income support entitlement automatically means claimant meets capital and income requirement for HB/CTB Co-habitation
R v Poole BC ex p. Ross, QBD, 5th May 1995	28 HLR 351	Liable to make payments in respect of a dwelling Commercial basis Contrived agreements
Remelien v Secretary of State for Social Security and Another R v Same, ex p. Wolke, House of Lords, November 27, 1997	30 HLR 853 *The Times,* 1st December 1997	A letter from the Home Office to a European national saying that she must make arrangements to leave the country as she had become a charge on public funds did not constitute a requirement to leave so as to end her entitlement to income support.
R v Salisbury DC ex p. Markham-David, CA, 15th April 1997	Unreported	Local authorities powers and duties
R v Sandwell Metropolitan Borough Council, ex p. Wilkinson, QBD, 29th January 1998	31 HLR 22	Role of Rent Officer's decision at Review Board hearing (prior to Jan 96 maximum rent calculation rules)
R v. Secretary of State for Social Security ex p. AMA, QBD, 3rd July 1992	25 HLR 131 *The Times* 23rd August 1992	Secretary of State's duty to consult local authority associations on proposed rule changes
R v Secretary of State for Social Services ex p. Sarwar and others, QBD, 11th April 1995	*The Independent* 12th April 1995	Legality of habitual residence test
R. v Secretary of State for Social Security, ex p. Joint Council for the Welfare of Immigrants. R. v Secretary of State for Social Security, ex parte B, CA, June 21st, 1996)	*The Times* 27th June 1996	Regulations withdrawing benefit from asylum seekers unlawful Regulations restored by the Asylum and Immigration Act 1996 with effect from 24 July 1996
R v Secretary of State for Social Services ex p. AMA, QBD, 21st May 1985	[1986]1 ALL ER 164 [1986]1 WLR 1 17 HLR 487 83 LGR 796	Secretary of State's duty to consult local authority associations on proposed rule changes
R v Sefton MBC HB Review Board ex p. Cunningham, QBD, 22nd May 1991	23 HLR 534 *The Times* 8th July 1991	Unreasonably high rent – alternative cheaper accommodation Adequacy of Review Board's decision note

R v Sefton MBC ex p. Harrison, QBD, 5th December 1994	Unreported	Not appropriate to make an order as to costs against the authority as the claimant was aware that she could appeal against the Board's decision other than by judicial review proceedings.
R v Sefton MBC ex p. Jones and another, QBD, 5th December 1995	Unreported	Authority's duty to notify claimant when it withholds benefit Circumstances in which a declaration will be made even where the particular interest of the applicant have been accommodated following R v Liverpool ex p. Johnson and others
R. v. Sefton HB Review Board ex p. Brennan, QBD, 13th December 1996	29 HLR 735	Unreasonably high rent Meaning of suitable alternative accommodation Review Board's failure to establish relevant fact
R v Sefton MBC ex parte Read, QBD, 6th March 1998	Unreported	Circumstance when payment on account need not be made
R v Sheffield CC HB Board ex p. Smith and Others; R v Rugby BC HB Review Board ex p. Harrison and Others; R v Daventry DC HB Review Board ex p. Bodden and Others, QBD, 8th December 1994	93 LGR 139 *The Times* 28th December 1994	Non-commercial arrangements Review Board may look at all aspects of arrangement to see if on a commercial basis
R v Solihull MBC HB Review Board ex p. Simpson, QBD	26 HLR 370 *The Times* 4th January 1994 *The Times* 5th January 1994 and correction	Contrived tenancy Adequacy of Review Board's decision note
R. v. Solihull MBC HB Review Board ex p. Simpson, CA; affirming QBD	27 H.L.R. 41; [1995] 1 F.L.R. 140; [1995] 92 L.G.R. 719; [1995] Fam. Law 17; *The Times,* 19th July, 1994.	
R v South Hams DC ex p. Ash, QBD, 11th May 1999	*The Times,* 27th May 1999	A review board, in the exercise of its discretion to recover overpayments was under an obligation to consider the nature and purpose of a retrospectively awarded war disability pension

R v South Herefordshire DC HB Review Board ex p. Smith, QBD, 30th January 1987	19 HLR 217	Unreasonably high rent – alternative cheaper accommodation
R v South Tyneside MBC HB Review Board ex p. Tooley, QBD, 20th October 1995	[1996] COD 143	Contrived tenancy Deprivation of capital Review Board's failure to find facts or give reasons Quality of review board's reasoning
R v Spelthorne BC ex p. Khan, CA, 21st March 1997	Unreported	Housing Benefit Review Boards; Judicial review, Reapplication for judicial review refused
R v Stoke on Trent CC ex. p. Highgate Projects Ltd. QBD, 25th March 1994	26 HLR 551 *The Times* 14th April 1994	Adequacy of review board's decision note Landlord's right of appeal to review board. Claimant's right to appoint a representative. Regulations amended (S.I. 1994, No. 2137)
R v. Stratford-on-Avon DC HB Review Board and the Secretary of State for Social Security ex. p. White, QBD, 15th January 1997	30 HLR 178	Contrived tenancy
R v Stratford upon Avon HB Review Board ex p. White, CA, reversing, 18th March 1998	*The Times* 23rd April 1998	
R v Sutton LB HB Review Board ex p. Keegan, QBD, 15th May 1992	27 HLR 92	Contrived tenancy Review board's findings contrary to evidence Review Board's breach of natural justice
R v Sutton LB HB Review Board ex p. Partridge, QBD, 4th November 1994	28 HLR 315	Non-commercial arrangements Review Board's failure to find facts and give reasons
R v Sutton LBC ex p. Harrison. R v Swansea City and County Council, ex p. Littler. R v Welwyn Hatfield DC ex p. Nunan and Others. R v St Edmundsbury BC ex p. Sandys, QBD, 24th 1997	30 HLR 800 *The Times* 22nd August 1997	A general counselling or support service was eligible to be met by HB only where the service tended to preserve the condition of the accommodation's fabric as the landlord undertook to provide it
R v Swale BC HB Review Board ex p. Marchant 17th December 1998	[1995] 1 FLR 1087	Whether children spending equal amounts of time at father's home and that of mother could be treated as occupying father's home for purposes of size criteria

R v Swale BC ex p. Marchant, CA, affirming earlier decision, 9th November 1999	*The Times,* 17th November 1999 [2000] Fam. Law 87	
R v Swansea City and County Council HB Review Board for , ex p. Littler R v HB Review Board for St Edmundsbury, ex p. Sandys, CA, confirming, 15th July 1998	*The Times,* 9th September 1998 [1999] 48 BMLR 24	Eligible counselling and other support services relationship to the provision of adequate accommodation
R v Waltham Forest LB ex p. Holder and another, QBD, 9 February 1996	29 HLR 71 *The Independent* 28th February 1996	Unreasonably high rent Meaning of 'suitable alternative accommodation' No specific test of availability where claimant does not fall into protected group.
R. v. Warrington BC ex p. Williams, QBD, 28 January 1997	29 HLR 827	Use of business tenancy as a home
R v Warrington BC ex p. Williams, CA, 18th July 1997	Unreported	Business tenancies; Housing benefit; Local authorities powers and duties
R v West Dorset DC ex p. Poupard, CA, 21st December 1987	20 HLR 295 *The Times* 5th January 1988	Meaning of 'income' A bank overdraft secured by capital and used for day-to-day living expenses constituted 'income' for HB purposes. (Pre 1988 regulations) No longer considered good law.
R. v Westminster City Council and others, ex p. A and others; CA, 17th February 1997	*The Independent* 26th February 1997	Asylum seekers who are excluded from social security benefits etc. are entitled to apply to local authorities for relief under section 21(1) of the National Assistance Act 1948
R v Westminster City Council ex p. Hamandi QBD	Unreported	Meaning of 'elsewhere' in HB Reg.11(2)(c) for purpose of comparing rent for accommodation in question with suitable alternative accommodation.
R v Westminster CC HB Review Board, ex parte Sier, QBD, 16th July 1999	Unreported	Review board chair has a duty not only to record the findings of fact and conclusions but also the reasons for those conclusions
R v Winston, CA, 7th July 1998	*The Times,* 24th July 1998	Claimant provided authority with forged document. The fact that the document asserted the true position was no defence
R. v. Woking BC ex p. Crawley, QBD, 19th June 1996	Unreported	Liability for housing costs as opposed to an arrangement to pay

R v Wyre BC ex p. Lord, 24th October 1997	Unreported	Overpayments, Review Board's discretion to recover
Saint v Barking and Dagenham LBC, CA, 21st August, 1998	31 HLR 620	Failure to supply HB renewal forms. Authority could not rely on own wrongdoing to obtain possession
Thamesdown BC v Goonery, CA, 13th February 1995	Unreported	Meaning of 'residing with' a close relative
Warwick DC v Freeman, CA, 31st October 1994	27 HLR 616	Landlord's right to be notified and rights of review Extent to which the county court can consider the authority's determinations regarding overpayments Recoverable overpayments and recovery of overpayments from landlords
Waveney DC v Jones, CA, 1st December 1999	*The Times,* 22nd December 1999	Landlord entitled to bring action in county court where authority hasn't followed HB overpayment rules
West Somerset DC v Sykes, CA, 14th March 1997	Unreported	Overpayments, meaning of 'official error' overpayments, authority's choice regarding who to recover the overpayment from

ABBREVIATIONS

All ER	All England Reports		FLR	Family Law Reports
AMA	Association of Metropolitan Authorities		HLR	Housing Law Reports
			LB	London Borough
BC	Borough Council		LGR	Local Government Reports
CA	Court of Appeal		MBC	Metropolitan Borough Council
CC	City Council		QBD	Queen's Bench Division
Crim LR	Criminal Law Review		RB	Royal Borough
DC	District Council		RVR	Rating and Valuation Reporter
DSS	Department of Social Security		SLT	Scots Law Times (Reports)
Fam Law	Family Law		WLR	Weekly Law Reports

Appendix 3:
Current HB and CTB circulars

The following list includes all DSS circulars issued since 1996, along with two earlier circulars which remain useful.

HB/CCB(92)17	Overpayments of HB/CCB: a good practice paper
HB/CCB(92)20	Good practice guide – HB and CCB reviews`

ADJUDICATION AND OPERATIONS CIRCULARS

HB/CTB A1/96	Asylum seekers and sponsored immigrants
HB/CTB A2/96	1. Findings of a Benefits Agency evaluation form NHB(IS) 2. Income Support reasons for exclusion
HB/CTB A3/96	1. Further advice on accounting and administrative procedures for payments made to Navy and Army war widows. 2. War Pension disregards
HB/CTB A4/96	Document image processing
HB/CTB A5/96	Amendment of the HB/CTB regulations (from 114196)
HB/CTB A6/96	Further guidance on four week extended payment of Housing and Council Tax Benefit and Fast Tracking of the in-work HB/CTB claim
HB/CTB A796	Consolidation of HB/CTB Circulars A23/95, A29/95 and A36/95 (the January 96 rent restriction rules)
HB/CTB A8/96	1. The Income-related Benefits Schemes (Miscellaneous Amendments) Regulations 1996. 2. The Social Security Benefits Up-rating Order 1996. 3. Permitted totals for discretionary expenditure 1996-97. 4. Disregard of the '30 hours' premium payable in Family Credit and Disability Working Allowance. 5. Increase in the childcare disregard. 6. Adelphi Enquiry Points. 7. War widows – circular HB/CTB A3/96
HB/CTB A9/96	Payment of Housing Benefit in arrears, including new direct payment arrangements
HB/CTB A10/96	1. HB/CTB – Shortened claim forms and claims made in advance. 2. HB/CTB – correction to Circular A6/96 extended payments/fast tracking
HB/CTB A11/96	1. Calculation of Housing benefit for single claimants who are under 25 years of age. 2. Minor amendments to Circular HB/CTB 9/96
HB/CTB A12/96	Deduction of Income Tax at source from payments made to overseas landlords.
HB/CTB A13/96	Problems with the distribution of claim form NHB1-EP (Claim form for HB/CTB Extended Payments)
HB/CTB A14/96	Amendment of the Model National Liaison Service Level Agreements between the Benefits Agency and the Local Authority Associations
HB/CTB A15/96	Amendment of the Model National Liaison Service Level Agreements between the Local Authority Associations and the Employment Service

HB/CTB A16/96	Housing Benefit claims from young people assisted by Social Services Departments
HB/CTB A17/96	Changes to the HB/CTB regulations from 7 October 1996 following the introduction of the Job Seeker's Allowance
HB/CTB A18/96	Changes to the way in which referrals are made to Rent Officers
HB/CTB A19/96	HB/CTB Extended Payments: specimen article for use in local publicity
HB/CTB A20/96	Operational instructions to implement Court of Appeal decision on 21 June 1996 which revises benefit rules for *Asylum Seekers*
HB/CTB A21/96	Operational instructions for asylum seekers following Royal Assent to the Asylum and Immigration Bill
HB/CTB A22/96	Changes to the HB/CTB regulations from April 1997 affecting the Family Premium, Lone Parent Premium, Child Benefit and One Parent Benefit.
HB/CTB A23/96	1. War Widows 2. Family Credit 3. National Savings Certificates 4. Greenwich Hospital Estate 4. Project Work Pilots
HB/CTB A24/96	Benefit for persons evacuated from Montserrat
HB/CTB A25/96	Income Support Computer System Remote Access Terminals in Local Authority Premises
HB/CTB A26/96	1. Amendments to the HB/CTB regulations from 7 October 1996 2. Student grant rates for the academic year 1996-97 – amendment to circular A27/96 3. Publicity for Housing Benefit changes for single people under 25
HB/CTB A26A/96	Pilot Earnings Top-up from October 1996 (treatment of new allowance in HB/CTB for LAs in pilot areas)
HB/CTB A27/96	I Increased disregards for books and equipment, and new student 'rent deduction' rates for 1996-97 II New student grant and loan rates for the academic year 1996-97 (NB: original page 5 contains an error – new page supplied via HB/CTB A26/96)
HB/CTB A28/96	Jobseeker's Allowance: Operational Issues
HB/CTB A29/96	I Court of Appeal judgment – Aylesbury Vale/John Boot England II Effect of judgment on claims for backdating (made before 1 April 1996) III Action by local authorities
HB/CTB A30/96	Assessment of capital: valuation of jointly owned property
HB/CTB A31/96	Good Practice Guide On Second Adult Rebate (NB – copy of *Council Tax Benefit: Second Adult Rebate – A Good Practice Guide* enclosed with this circular)
HB/CTB A32/96	Childcare Disregard: proposed amendments to regulations
HB/CTB A33/96	Retrospective award of Housing Benefit and Council Tax Benefit to asylum seekers who have been granted refugee status
HB/CTB A34/96	1. This part is now superseded by circular HB/CTB A2/97 2. Amendment to title page of Circular HB/CTB A28/96 (delete the word 'Draft')
HB/CTB A35/96	This circular contained an error and was superseded by HB/CTB A36/96
HB/CTB A36/96	Introduction of two new non-dependant deductions in HB/CTB
HB/CTB A37/96	I Proposed Pilot schemes for people receiving Jobseeker's Allowance ('Workskill' pilots). II Effect of the proposals on claimants in receipt of Housing Benefit and/or Council Tax Benefit. III Copy of the text of press release about the proposals and notes

	for editors *(Note: this section was missing from the original circular and was subsequently supplied via a separate addendum).*
HB/CTB A38/96	Changes to HB/CTB regulations from April 1997 affecting allowances for children and childcare disregards
HB/CTB A39/96	Housing Benefit/Council Tax Benefit Policy Contact Points (Adelphi)
HB/CTB A40/96	Uprating 1997 *(Note: this was corrected by circular HB/CTB A9/97.)*
HB/CTB A1/97	Amendments to HB/CTB regulations from April 1997
HB/CTB A2/97	Jobseeker's Allowance suspensions, disallowances and sanctions: replacement for circular A34/96
HB/CTB A3/97	Change of address on form L2 (request for property valuations contained in Circular HB/CTB A12/95)
HB/CTB A4/97	Further guidance on four week extended payment of Housing and Council Tax Benefit
HB/CTB A5/97	I Additional guidance on the October 1996 changes to Housing Benefit for claims from young people under age 25. II Redetermination by rent officers.
HB/CTB A6/97	Contracting out of Housing and Council Tax Benefit Administration.
HB/CTB A7/97	I Jobseeker's Allowance (Workskill Pilot) Regulations 1997. II Further information and guidance for benefit officers. III Local authorities affected by Workskill Pilots.
HB/CTB A8/97	Correction of earlier guidance – Benefit help for victims of violence.
HB/CTB A9/97	Correction to circular HB/CTB A40/96.
HB/CTB A10/97	Contracting Out of Housing and Council Tax Benefit Administration
HB/CTB A11/97	Jobseeker's Allowance: Income-based, Contribution-based Award Letters sent to Claimants
HB/CTB A12/97	Exemption from Council Tax liability for relatives in self-contained accommodation which forms part of a larger property.
HB/CTB A13/97	*Superseded by Circular A36/97*
HB/CTB A14/97	Jobseeker's Allowance: Income-based, Contribution-based Award Letters sent to Claimants
HB/CTB A15/97	Additional guidance on: 1. HB entitlement of certain members of the Jesus Fellowship Church 2. Regulation 7(1)(b)
HB/CTB A16/97	HB/CTB – Guidance on taking appointee action
HB/CTB A17/97	Part 1: Treatment of Nursery Education Vouchers Part II: Treatment of the ANCVO Grant Part III: Property Valuation Part IV: Treatment of Rented Properties Part V: Share Fisherman – NI contributions: 1997/98 rate
HB/CTB A18/97	Referrals to Rent Officers – who to include as occupiers in referrals and pre-tenancy determination applications.
HB/CTB A19/97	*Superseded by Circular A31/97*
HB/CTB A20/97	Changes to HB notifications (landlord direct cases)
HB/CTB A21/97	*Superseded by Circular A36/97*

HB/CTB A22/97	Housing Benefit claims from young people assisted by Local Authorities in Scotland
HB/CTB A23/97	Social Security Administration (Fraud) Act 1997
HB/CTB A24/97	National Savings Certificates: July 1997
HB/CTB A25/97	*Superseded by Circular A31/97*
HB/CTB A26/97	Rent determinations: electronic link between local authorities (LAs) and the rent officer service (ROS)
HB/CTB A27/97	Definition of close relative
HB/CTB A28/97	NHB notifications (where JSA claims are transferred to another BA office)
HB/CTB A29/97	I Increased disregards for books and equipment, and new student 'rent deduction' rates for 1997/98. II New student grant and loan rates for the academic year 1997/98 N.B. original pages 3, 4, 5, 11 and 12 contained errors – replacements were supplied through HB/CTB A35/97
HB/CTB A30/97	Restriction of the amount of Council Tax Benefit awarded for people living in council tax bands F, G and H
HB/CTB A31/97	The Upheaval List. Replacement of HB/CTB circulars A19/97 and A25/97, which should be destroyed.
HB/CTB A32/97	Housing Benefit & Council Tax Benefit Policy Contact Points (Adelphi) – *superseded by Circular A56/97*
HB/CTB A33/97	Family Premium (lone parent) – Changes to be implemented from 6 April 1998
HB/CTB A34/97	Amendment regulations 12 and 13 of the Income-Related Benefits and Jobseeker's Allowance (Miscellaneous Amendments) Regulations 1997 (which amended Regulations 93 and 94(2) of the Housing Benefit (General) Regulations 1987)
HB/CTB A35/97	Amendment to Circular A29/97 (replacement pages 3, 4, 5, 11 and 12 supplied). A correction to the student grant travel disregard for students living away from the parental home for the 1997/98 academic year. *(Note the amendments also contained an incorrect figure – see the correction made via Circular A43/97)*
HB/CTB A36/97	Single Room Rent and Local Reference Rent: New guidance on the changes to Housing Benefit regulations coming into force on 6 October 1997. *(This circular contained some errors – a new Glossary and page 3 were supplied by HB/CTB A44/97)*
HB/CTB A37/97	Service charges in supported accommodation.
HB/CTB A38/97	Jobseeker's Allowance: Amendment of the Model National Liaison Service Level Agreements between the Benefits Agency and the Local Authority Associations
HB/CTB A39/97	Jobseeker's Allowance: Amendment of the Model National Liaison Service Level Agreements between the Local Authority Associations and the Employment Service

HB/CTB A40/97	Changes to HB/CTB regulations from 6 October 1997 affecting:
	 Part 1: Personal injury compensation payments
	         Bursaries paid to 16 -18 year olds (Scotland only)
	         Concessionary coal
	
	 Part 2: Housing Benefit in respect of two dwellings

HB/CTB A41/97	Revised guidance on administration of claims for payment of Housing Benefit on two homes under Regulation 5(5)(d)

HB/CTB A42/97	Student rent deduction: exemption on low income grounds.
HB/CTB A43/97	An amendment to Circular A35/97. A correction to the supplement of the basic maintenance grant – extra attendance (per week) – for students living in parental home for the 1997-98 academic year.
HB/CTB A44/97	Amended guidance on the changes to Housing Benefit regulations coming into force on 6 October 1997
HB/CTB A45/97	Part 1: Notional Income third party provision Concessionary Coal Single school leaving date Part 2: Family Premium (lone parent)
HB/CTB A46/97	I The 'Webber' case and judgment II The Student Unions' Campaign III Action to be taken
HB/CTB A47/97	Part I Referrals to the Rent Officer Part II Pre-tenancy determinations. (Effects of the 6 October 1996 changes that you should be aware of)
HB/CTB A48/97	New measures to combat fraud
HB/CTB A49/97	HB overpaid to young people assisted by Service Providers: Children Act provisions.
HB/CTB A50/97	Montserrat evacuees
HB/CTB A51/97	I Exchange of information between DSS and authorities II Unauthorised disclosure of information
HB/CTB A52/97	Section 19 of the Social Security (Fraud) Administration Act
HB/CTB A53/97	Changes to the Childcare Disregard provisions effective from 1 June 1998
HB/CTB A54/97	Further Advice on the restriction of the amount of Council Tax Benefit awarded for people living in property in council tax bands F, G and H.
HB/CTB A55/97	Family Premium (lone parent) and Extended Payments.
HB/CTB A56/97	Housing Benefit & Council Tax Benefit Policy Contact Points (Adelphi)
HB/CTB A57/97	Uprating 1998
HB/CTB A58/97	Compensation Scheme – service charges for care in certain 'existing supported accommodation' *(Note that an amended page 27 of Annex C was supplied by HB/CTB A4/98)*
HB/CTB A1/98	New powers under section 16 of the Social Security Administration (Fraud) Act 1997 The Housing Benefit (Recovery of Overpayments) Regulations 1997 The Housing Benefit (Recovery of Overpayments) (No.2) Regulations 1997
HB/CTB A2/98	Introduction of new disregards affecting participants in the New Deal for 18 -24 year olds
HB/CTB A3/98	Consolidated and updated guidance on the rent restrictions which apply in the calculation of Housing Benefit
HB/CTB A4/98	Amendment to Annex C of Circular HB/CTB A58/97
HB/CTB A5/98	PFA rules for asylum seekers (and others) with 'temporary admission' to UK *(Note: updates advice on these cases in Circulars A1/96 and A21/96 which is incorrect)*

HB/CTB A6/98	Part 1: Childcare disregard in respect of children aged under 8 who are attending out of school clubs run by schools or local authorities Part 2: Local Exchange Trading Schemes (LETS)
HB/CTB A7/98	Amendments to HB/CTB regulations (from April 1998)
HB/CTB A8/98	Part I: Winter Fuel Payments Part II: Compensation Scheme
HB/CTB A9/98	Circular to invite LAs to receive HB/CTB Circulars by e-mail
HB/CTB A10/98	Family Premium (lone parent)
HB/CTB A11/98	The Social Security (Miscellaneous Amendments) Regulations 1998
HB/CTB A12/98	Service charges in supported accommodation
HB/CTB A13/98	Property valuations
HB/CTB A14/98	Advice on the introduction of transitional protection for the measure to restrict Council Tax Benefit awarded for people living in property in council tax bands F, G and H
HB/CTB A15/98	Asylum seekers – savings provision. Revised legal opinion as to which asylum seekers may benefit from the savings provision
HB/CTB A16/98	Decision of the Court of Appeal on the entitlement of Elders of the Jesus Fellowship Church to Housing Benefit
HB/CTB A17/98	Additional advice and copy of the amendment regulations on the introduction of transitional protection for the measure to restrict Council Tax Benefit awarded for people living in property in council tax bands F, G and H
HB/CTB A18/98	HB/CTB Circulars by E-Mail
HB/CTB A19/98	1. Backdating in HB/CTB – Update on the Social Security Bill 2. Change of personnel at the Adelphi
HB/CTB A20/98	Amalgamation of circulars A1/96, A21/96, A5/98 and A15/98 and provision of supplementary guidance on the handling of benefit claims from asylum seekers, refugees and persons from abroad
HB/CTB A21/98	Treatment of income from creditor insurance policies – including mortgage protection policies
HB/CTB A22/98	Introduction of disregards affecting self-employed participants in the New Deal for 18-24 year olds
HB/CTB A23/98	Part I: 1998/99 Income Tax Rates and Allowances Part II: Share Fisherman NI Contributions – 1998-99 rate
HB/CTB A24/98	Victims of Domestic Violence
HB/CTB A25/98	Remote Access Terminals (RATs)
HB/CTB A26/98	Housing Benefit Computing Strategy (HBCS)
HB/CTB A27/98	Abolition of the lone parent rate of Child Benefit
HB/CTB A28/98	Working Benefits Campaign
HB/CTB A29/98	I – Increased disregards for books and equipment, and student 'rent deduction' rates for 1998-99 II – New student grant and loan rates for existing students for academic year 1998-99. III – New student grant and loan rates for new entrant students for the academic year 1998-99

<table>
<tr><td></td><td>IV – Changes to the student support system; payment of contributions to tuition fees from the start of the 1998-99 academic year and the effect on student claims</td></tr>
<tr><td>HB/CTB A30/98</td><td>Valuation of jointly owned property</td></tr>
<tr><td>HB/CTB A31/98</td><td>Part I – Increase in the under 11 year rate of child's personal allowance (now replaced by A48/98)
Part II – National savings certificates – July 1998 rates</td></tr>
<tr><td>HB/CTB A32/98</td><td>Housing Benefit and Council Tax Benefit Policy Contact Points (Adelphi) (see correction in A43/98)</td></tr>
<tr><td>HB/CTB A33/98</td><td>Service charges in supported accommodation (supersedes Circular HB/CTB A12/98)</td></tr>
<tr><td>HB/CTB A34/98</td><td>Clarification of Part 1 of Circular HB/CTB A31/98 (now replaced by A48/98))</td></tr>
<tr><td>HB/CTB A35/98</td><td>New data protection legislation</td></tr>
<tr><td>HB/CTB A36/98</td><td>Service charges in 'existing supported accommodation'</td></tr>
<tr><td>HB/CTB A37/98</td><td>HB/CTB Circulars by E-Mail</td></tr>
<tr><td>HB/CTB A38/98</td><td>Revised Model National Service Level Agreement (MNSLA) between Local Authorities (LAs) and Chief Rent Officers (CROs)</td></tr>
<tr><td>HB/CTB A39/98</td><td>Good Practice guidance for authorities considering or undertaking preparations for market testing of HB and CTB administration (supplied with a copy of Guidance to Authorities – Competitive Tendering of Housing Benefit and Council Tax Benefit Administration, DSS, August 1998)</td></tr>
<tr><td>HB/CTB A40/98</td><td>Action to take upon receipt of NHB1 claim forms where JSA has not been adjudicated (because of problems with the new National Insurance Recording System [NIRS])</td></tr>
<tr><td>HB/CTB A41/98</td><td>New 52 week benefit protection period for certain people who move from incapacity into work (welfare to work beneficiaries).
Part 1: Deals with the effect on Disability Premium and Higher Pensioner Premium
Part 2: Deals with the effect on transitional protection for CTB bands F, G and H
Part 3: Deals with the effect on transitional protection for 'old' Scheme and Local Reference Rent Scheme cases</td></tr>
<tr><td>HB/CTB A42/98</td><td>Incapacity Benefit: Exchange of information with the Benefits Agency</td></tr>
<tr><td>HB/CTB A43/98</td><td>Part I – Discretionary payments from the Employment Service for those who are undertaking training or education under the New Deal provisions
Part II – Correction to Adelphi contact list circular A32/98</td></tr>
<tr><td>HB/CTB A44/98</td><td>Closer Working with BA – Edinburgh Local Authority & Benefits Agency Project</td></tr>
<tr><td>HB/CTB A45/98</td><td>Valuation of jointly owned property</td></tr>
<tr><td>HB/CTB A46/98</td><td>Action to take upon receipt of NHB1 claim forms where JSA has not been adjudicated</td></tr>
<tr><td>HB/CTB A47/98</td><td>Welfare reform</td></tr>
<tr><td>HB/CTB A48/98</td><td>Clarification of Circulars 31 and 34 (N.B. replaces A34/98 and Part 1 of A31/98)</td></tr>
<tr><td>HB/CTB A49/98</td><td>Housing Benefit Computing Strategy (HBCS)</td></tr>
<tr><td>HB/CTB A50/98</td><td>Uprating 1999 (see corrections issued in HB/CTB A54/98 and clarification made in HB/CTB A57/98)</td></tr>
<tr><td>HB/CTB A51/98</td><td>Winter Fuel Payments (for clarification)</td></tr>
<tr><td>HB/CTB A52/98</td><td>Revised Model National Liaison Service Level Agreement between the Benefits Agency and the Local Authority Associations</td></tr>
</table>

HB/CTB A53/98	Change of Immigration Service telephone and fax numbers from 7 December 1998
HB/CTB A54/98	Uprating. Correction to Uprating Circular HB/CTB A50/98
HB/CTB A55/98	Valuation of jointly owned properties.
HB/CTB A56/98	New Deal Pilot Schemes
HB/CTB A57/98	Supported Accommodation Part I – Publication of consultation paper: *Supporting People: A new policy and funding framework for support services* Part II – An addition to Rent Officer notifications in respect of service charges for general counselling and support Uprating Part III – Clarification of paragraph 13 of circular A50/98 (Uprating 1999)
HB/CTB A58/98	The classification of fraudulent overpayments
HB/CTB A59/98	Recovery of HB overpayments: Civil Proceedings
HB/CTB A60/98	Prison Service Home Detention Curfew Scheme
HB/CTB A1/99	Persons who are to be treated as not liable for their housing costs
HB/CTB A2/99	Change to qualifying conditions for Housing Benefit and Council Tax Benefit *(claimants to provide National Insurance Numbers)*
HB/CTB A3/99	Housing Benefit and Council Tax Benefit Subsidy Arrangements – Specific Grant for Local Authorities' Administration Costs in 1999-2000
HB/CTB A4/99	National Insurance Contribution Rates 1999-2000
HB/CTB A5/99	Closer Working with the Benefits Agency – Progress Report
HB/CTB A6/99	1999/2000 Income Tax Rates and Allowances
HB/CTB A7/99	I Childcare charges II Disregards for claimants working at least 30 hours a week.
HB/CTB A8/99	National Minimum Wage (and the notional earnings rule)
HB/CTB A9/99	Kosovar evacuees
HB/CTB A10/99	New Deal schemes and Employment Zones (Summary of options – see circulars A2/98, A22/98, A43/98 and A56/98 for details of specific options)
HB/CTB A11/99	Nursing Diploma Students – Formerly known as 'Project 2000' Nurses
HB/CTB A12/99	Application of Habitual Residence Test to returning former UK residents (the effect of the Swaddling case, ECJ: C-90/97)
HB/CTB A13/99	Judicial Review: *Regina v Macclesfield Borough Council Housing Benefit Review Board ex parte Temsamani* (regulation 10(6B))
HB/CTB A14/99	Welfare Reform ('One' the single work-focused gateway)
HB/CTB A15/99	Supported Accommodation: The Government announcement on 31 March 1999 to proceed with the proposals for long term funding arrangements for supported accommodation as laid out in the consultation paper *Supporting People: A new policy and funding framework for support services.*
HB/CTB A16/99	Section 19 – Progress Report 1 (Requirement to provide a national insurance number – pilot project)
HB/CTB A17/99	Treating Non-Cash Vouchers as earnings

HB/CTB A18/99	1. General Information about Working Families' Tax Credit (WFTC) and disabled Person's Tax Credit (DPTC) 2. WFTC/DPTC the "Better off" issue
HB/CTB A19/99	Educational Maintenance Allowance
HB/CTB A20/99	National Savings Certificates – July 1999 rates
HB/CTB A21/99	Valuation of Property and contact number for the Valuation Office Agency
HB/CTB A22/99	Closer Working with BA – Progress Report
HB/CTB A23/99	i) Department for Education and Employment arrangements for student support in respect of 'new' and 'existing' students; ii) Details of changes to the disregard provisions to take account of student loans; iii) Details of the new rates of disregards and rent deductions. (Note: the final page of this circular was replaced by a new annex supplied with circular A50/99)
HB/CTB A24/99	Verification Framework – Revised Guidance on Establishing Identity
HB/CTB A25/99	More information about Working Families' Tax Credit (WFTC) and Disabled Person's Tax Credit (DPTC)
HB/CTB A26/99	Notional HB assessments for Crown Tenants
HB/CTB A27/99	Increase in personal allowances of children under 11
HB/CTB A28/99	Housing Benefit & Council Tax Benefit Policy & Housing Benefit Management contact points
HB/CTB A29/99	Sports awards
HB/CTB A30/99	Electronic Transfer of Data (ETD)
HB/CTB A31/99	HB/CTB Guidance Manual (delay in publishing updated version in hard copy and electronic formats)
HB/CTB A32/99	Verification Framework: Management Information (MIS)
HB/CTB A33/99	Changes from 4th October to HB/CTB Extended Payments, consequential to the introduction of the Lone Parent's Benefit Run-On and the extension of the Extended Payments scheme to disabled people.
HB/CTB A34/99	Disapplication of section 19 (requirement to provide a national insurance number) to hostel dwellers
HB/CTB A35/99	Enhanced guidance on operating the Exceptional Hardship Scheme
HB/CTB A36/99	Definition of a hostel – Disapplication of section 19 (requirement to provide a national insurance number) to hostel dwellers
HB/CTB A37/99	Changes to the implementation of the Verification Framework and Section 19 requirement and funding
HB/CTB A38/99	Confirmation of the laying of Regulations in respect of: 1) Changes to personal allowances for children and young persons from 4 October 1999; 2) Changes to extended payments regulations from 4 October 1999
HB/CTB A39/99	HB/CTB Circular A23/99 notified authorities about the changes to regulations introduced by the Social Security Amendment (Students) Regulations 1999 (SI 1999/1935). This circular clarifies the period over which student loans should be taken into account.

HB/CTB A40/99	Closer Working with BA – Progress Report
HB/CTB A41/99	1. Working Families' Tax Credit (WFTC) and Disabled Person's Tax Credit (DPTC) 2. Changes to regulations consequential to the introduction of WFTC & DPTC 3. WFTC & DPTC Publicity Material
HB/CTB A42/99	General information about the New Deal 50 Plus and how it affects HB/CTB
HB/CTB A43/99	Effect of the fast tracking changes from 4 October to HB/CTB Extended Payments, consequential to the Lone Parent's Benefit Run-On.
HB/CTB A44/99	DfEE support for Further Education students, and to post 16 year old pupils in schools
HB/CTB A45/99	Occupational or Personal Pension paid to third parties.
HB/CTB A46/99	1. Occupiers of the home 2. Further guidance on ex-owners and definition of a company 3. Volunteers 4. Absent partner
HB/CTB A47/99	Service Charges in Supported Accommodation
HB/CTB A48/99	Verification Framework: further administrative simplifications, additional information and clarification.
HB/CTB A49/99	WFTC and DPTC: Exchange of information between Inland Revenue and local authorities
HB/CTB A50/99	i) Grant and loan rates for Health Care students (the information is provided in the form of a new annex to replace the final page of circular A23/99) ii) Clarification of the changes in the way loan and dependants grants are taken into account
HB/CTB A51/99	Uprating 2000
HB/CTB A52/99	What constitutes a new and a renewal claim for Housing Benefit and Council Tax Benefit – legislative and subsidy requirements.
HB/CTB A53/99	Remote Access Terminals (RATs): Programme for 1999/2000
HB/CTB A54/99	Amalgamation of circulars A23/99, A39/99 and A50/99 – treatment of student loans etc.
HB/CTB A1/2000	Section 19 – Progress report 2
	Information from Landlords and Agents – amendment to regulations
HB/CTB A2/2000	Closer Working with the Benefits Agency – Progress report
HB/CTB A3/2000	1. Summary 2. Introduction 3. Claim-related rent and ineligible service charges 4. Validity of determinations 5. Rent Officer redeterminations 6. Correcting errors in RO determinations 7. Transitional arrangements
HB/CTB A4/2000	Annual uprating of Social Security Benefit from April 2000 (Amendment to previous circular)
HB/CTB A5/2000	Reform of HB/CTB Reviews
HB/CTB A6/2000	Amendment to member countries of the EU and additions to ECSMA and CESC

FRAUD CIRCULARS

HB/CTB F1/96	Jobseeker's Allowance training for LA fraud investigators
HB/CTB F2/96	Challenge Funding
HB/CTB F3/96	Anti-fraud training for local authority benefit investigators
HB/CTB F4/96	1996-97 Anti-fraud financial incentive scheme thresholds
HB/CTB F5/96	The use of average HB/CTB figures by Benefits Agency Sector Fraud
HB/CTB F6/96	Launch of a national benefit fraud telephone hotline
HB/CTB F7/96	Secondments between local authority and Benefits Agency fraud investigation staff.
HB/CTB F1/97	Challenge Funding 1997-98
HB/CTB F2/97	1. Local authority anti-fraud training 2. Sharing weekly benefit savings
HB/CTB F3/97	1997-98 anti-fraud incentive scheme.
HB/CTB F4/97	Verification and Benefit Administration Framework
HB/CTB F5/97	1. Interviews under caution (IUC): – appointment letters; – explanation prior to the IUC.
HB/CTB F6/97	Additional guidance on the completion of STATS 124 – questions 29 & 30
HB/CTB F7/97	Cheque shops: national survey
HB/CTB F8/97	Housing Benefit Matching Service
HB/CTB F9/97	HB/CTB accuracy reviews 1997/98
HB/CTB F10/97	Local Authority inspectors' powers
HB/CTB F11/97	Social Security Administration (Fraud) Act 1997
HB/CTB F12/97	Social Security Administration (Fraud) Act 1997: new Social Security offences
HB/CTB F13/97	The second Income Support Benefit Review
HB/CTB F14/97	Family Credit Fraud investigations
HB/CTB F15/97	Housing Benefit Matching Service (HBMS) guidance
HB/CTB F16/97	Social Security Administration (Fraud) Act 1997 (provisions related to obtaining information from landlords and recovering overpayments of HB paid to a third party from prescribed benefits are now expected to come into force on 3 November 1997 and not on 6 October 1997 as originally indicated)
HB/CTB F17/97	New powers under section 11 of the Social Security Administration (Fraud) Act 1997. The Housing Benefit (Information from Landlords and Agents) Regulations 1997.
HB/CTB F18/97	Housing Benefit Matching Service (HBMS): • change of telephone number • HBMS service standards
HB/CTB F19/97	1998/99 Local Authority Weekly Benefit Savings Anti-Fraud Incentive Scheme
HB/CTB F20/97	Challenge Funding 1998/99 – Visiting Initiatives Fund
HB/CTB F21/97	Verification Framework
HB/CTB F1/98	Housing Benefit Matching Service (HBMS) rules.
HB/CTB F2/98	Recording JAS Weekly Benefit Savings (WBS)

HB/CTB F3/98	Impounding of Income Support Order Books
HB/CTB F4/98	Section 15 of Social Security Administration (Fraud) Act 1997: Administrative Penalties
HB/CTB F5/98	Post Office mail monitoring
HB/CTB F6/98	Verification Framework (N.B. issued with a copy of *The Verification Framework – Core Instructions* [11/3/98]')
HB/CTB F7/98	1) 1998/99 Final thresholds for the Local Authority Weekly Benefit Savings (WBS) Anti-Fraud Incentive scheme 2) Amendment to Form WBS2 (originally issued with circular F2/98 – Recording JSA WBS)
HB/CTB F8/98	Verification Framework
HB/CTB F9/98	Housing Benefit Matching Service
HB/CTB F10/98	Housing Benefit Matching Service (HBMS)
HB/CTB F11/98	Housing Benefit Matching Service (HBMS)
HB/CTB F12/98	Local authority weekly benefit savings (WBS)
HB/CTB F13/98	Department of Social Security Code of Practice for Data Matching
HB/CTB F14/98	Data Scans – Housing Benefit Matching Service (HBMS)
HB/CTB F15/98	Verification framework [N.B. Issued with a copy of *Verification Framework*: Core Instructions; 11.11.98]
HB/CTB F16/98	Prosecution pilot using DSS solicitors
HB/CTB F17/98	Guidance on local authority fraud weekly benefit savings (WBS)
HB/CTB F18/98	Housing Benefit Matching Service (HBMS) Data Take on and Processing Schedule and a New Rule
HB/CTB F19/98	Model National Fraud Service Level Agreement
HB/CTB F20/98	Verification Framework and financial incentive scheme arrangements for 1999/2000
HB/CTB F21/98	Fraud Investigator's Manual (England and Wales) [originally incorrectly numbered 'F20/98']
HB/CTB F1/99	HB/CTB Fraud Circular F20/98 [corrects the numbering of what is now F21/98]
HB/CTB F2/99	Royal Mail 'Do not Redirect' service
HB/CTB F3/99	Incorporating the collection of HB Accuracy data into IS/JSA Area Benefit Reviews
HB/CTB F4/99	Minister of State's speech to the Institute of Rating Revenues and Valuation and the accompanying press release
HB/CTB F5/99	Incorporating the collection of HB Accuracy Data into IS/JSA Area Benefit Reviews
HB/CTB F6/99	Housing Benefit Matching Service (HBMS) Data Take on and Processing Schedule
HB/CTB F7/99	Verification Framework – Continuing costs for 1999-2000
HB/CTB F8/99	Closer anti-fraud working with the Benefits Agency
HB/CTB F9/99	Local Authority anti-fraud incentive scheme thresholds for 1999-2000
HB/CTB F10/99	Social Security Administration (Fraud) Act 1997: Section 110A: Appointment of inspectors.
HB/CTB F11/99	Final local authority anti-fraud incentive scheme thresholds for 1999-2000

HB/CTB F12/99	Housing Benefit Matching Service (HBMS) Data Take on and Processing Schedule
HB/CTB F13/99	Royal Mail 'do not direct' service.
HB/CTB F14/99	Information from the Inland Revenue
HB/CTB F15/99	Monitoring of fraud service level agreements (SLAs)
HB/CTB F16/99	Housing Benefit Matching Service (HBMS): Review of matching rules on occupational pension
HB/CTB F17/99	*Not issued*
HB/CTB F18/99	Housing Benefit Matching Service (HBMS) Data Take on and Processing Schedule
HB/CTB F19/99	Housing Benefit Matching Service (HBMS) Data Take on and Processing Schedule
HB/CTB F1/2000	Closer anti-fraud working with the Benefits Agency
HB/CTB F2/2000	Important changes to the 1999-2000 local authority anti-fraud incentive scheme and arrangements for 2000-01.

SUBSIDY CIRCULARS

HB/CTB S1/96	HB/CTB Management Information System (MIS) data requirements for 1996-97 Introduction of new MIS guide
HB/CTB S2/96	Provisional 1995/96 HB/CTB subsidy arrangements (update of C10 of the HB/CTB Guidance Manual)
HB/CTB S3/96	Distribution of the £15.75m discretionary rent allowance for 1996-97 and the Permitted Total for discretionary HB increases above the maximum rent.
HB/CTB S4/96	Housing Benefit and Council Tax Benefit subsidy: Arrangements for 1996-97
HB/CTB S5/96	Identifying New Claims
HB/CTB S6/96	HB and CTB transitional arrangements for reorganised authorities
HB/CTB S7/96	1. Increase to the 1996-97 Permitted Total for discretionary spending above the maximum rent and associated subsidy addition 2. Mid-year subsidy estimates: additional information 3. Indicative rent level overpayments: recovered amounts
HB/CTB S8/96(2)	Housing Benefit and Council Tax Benefit subsidy: Guidance and amendment to claim form MPF720A/B *(NB: replaces circular HB/CTB S8/96 originally issued)*
HB/CTB S9/96	Changes to HB/CTB MIS data requirements for 1996-97 as a consequence of payment of rent allowance in arrears, changes of applicable to claims form single claimants under 25 and the introduction of Job Seeker's Allowance
HB/CTB S10/96 (2)	Distribution of the discretionary rent allowance subsidy addition 1997-98. Accuracy of 1994/95 subsidy returns *(Note: this circular replaces the original HB/CTB S10/96)*
HB/CTB S1/97	Issue of the new edition of the HB/CTB Management Information System Guide for 1997-98
HB/CTB S2/97	Housing Benefit and Council Tax Benefit subsidy arrangements for 1997-98 (includes details of the distribution of the £18.25m discretionary rent allowance for 1997-98)
HB/CTB S3/97	Provisional 1996/97 HB/CTB subsidy arrangements
HB/CTB S4/97	Amendments to the 1996-97 HB/CTB subsidy arrangements chapter (detailed in Circular HB/CTB S3/97)
HB/CTB S5/97	Issue of new edition of the HB/CTB Management Information System Guide for 1998-99

HB/CTB S1/98   Distribution of the discretionary rent allowance subsidy addition 1998-99. Accuracy of 1995-96 subsidy returns.

HB/CTB S2/98   Certification of 97-98 HB/CTB subsidy claims

HB/CTB S3/98   Housing Benefit and Council Tax Benefit subsidy: arrangements for 1998-99 (including details of the distribution of the £20m discretionary rent allowance subsidy contribution for 1998-99)

HB/CTB S4/98   Calculation of subsidy in Rent Officer referral cases where Housing Benefit has met charges for general counselling and support under the interim regulations

HB/CTB S5/98   Certification of 1997-98 HB/CTB subsidy claims – an amendment to the auditor's certificate.

HB/CTB S6/98   1997-98 HB/CTB subsidy arrangements

HB/CTB S7/98   Housing Benefit and Council Tax Benefit subsidy: amendment to 1997-98 final claim form; fast tracking of rent rebates

HB/CTB S8/98   The timetable for the return of the 1997-98 final subsidy claim form and the issue of Chapter 17 and associated Annexes to Circular HB/CTB S6/98 (1997-98 subsidy arrangements for Weekly Benefit Savings)

HB/CTB S1/99   Issue of new edition of the HB/CTB Management Information System Guide for 1999-2000

HB/CTB S2/99   Housing Benefit and Council Tax Benefit Subsidy Arrangements – Specific Grant for Local Authorities' Administration Costs in 1999-2000

HB/CTB S3/99   Housing Benefit and Council Tax Benefit subsidy: arrangements for 1999-2000 (includes details of the distribution of the £20m discretionary rent allowance contribution for 1999-2000)

HB/CTB S4/99   This circular concerns the final subsidy claim and was sent directly to finance directors by the DSS at Norcross, Blackpool.

HB/CTB S5/99   1998-99 HB/CTB subsidy arrangements *(NB the original Appendix A contained errors – a replacement Appendix A was supplied later)*

HB/CTB S6/99   Final Subsidy claim form: Amendment to Guidance Notes

HB/CTB S7/99   Issue of new edition of the HB/CTB Management Information System Guide for 2000-2001

HB/CTB S8/99   The Transitional Housing Benefit Scheme – Management Information and Subsidy arrangements

Appendix 4:
HB and CTB figures (from April 2000)

MAXIMUM BENEFIT AND TAPER PERCENTAGES (chapter 9)

	HB	Main CTB
Maximum benefit	100%	100%
Taper	65%	20%

NON-DEPENDANT DEDUCTIONS (chapter 9)

	HB	Main CTB
Non-dependants in remunerative work (16 or more hours per week) whose gross income is		
£259.00 pw or more	£47.75	£6.95
£207.00 to £258.99pw	£43.50	£5.80
£157.00 to £206.99pw	£38.20	£4.60
£120.00 to £156.99 pw	£23.35	£4.60
£81.00 to £119.99 pw	£17.00	£2.30
below £81.00	£7.40	£2.30
Non-dependants in other work – regardless of income	£7.40	£2.30

AMOUNT OF SECOND ADULT REBATE (chapter 10)

Second adult(s) on income support or JSA(IB)	25%
Second adult(s) whose gross income is below £120.00 pw	15%
£120.00 to £156.99 pw	7½%
£157 pw or more	nil

STANDARD DEDUCTIONS FROM ELIGIBLE RENT (HB ONLY)
(chapter 11)

FUEL

If claimant and any family occupy more than one room

for heating	£9.25
for hot water	£1.15
for lighting	£0.80
for cooking	£1.15

If claimant and any family occupy one room only

for heating alone, or heating with hot water or lighting or both	£5.60
for hot water when no heating supplied	£1.15
for lighting when no heating supplied	£0.80
for cooking	£1.15

MEALS

If at least three meals are provided every day

claimant; and each other person from the first Monday in September following his or her 16th birthday	£18.65
each other person	£9.40

If breakfast only is provided

claimant and each other person	£2.25

All other cases

claimant; and each other person from the first Monday in September following his or her 16th birthday	£12.40
each other person	£6.25

APPLICABLE AMOUNTS
(chapter 12)

PERSONAL ALLOWANCES

Single claimant	aged under 25	£41.35
	aged 25 or over	£52.20
Lone parent	aged under 18 (HB only)	£41.35
	aged 18 or over	£52.20
Couple	both aged under 18 (HB only)	£62.35
	at least one aged 18 or over	£81.95
Child/young person addition	lower rate	£26.60
	higher rate	£31.75
Polygamous partner addition		£29.75

PREMIUMS

Family premium	basic rate	£14.25
	protected lone parent rate	£22.20
Disabled child premium	each child/young person	£22.25
Severe disability premium	single rate	£40.20
	double rate	£80.40
Carer premium	claimant or partner or each	£14.15
Pensioner premium	single claimant/lone parent	£26.25
	couple	£40.00
Enhanced pensioner premium	single claimant/lone parent	£28.65
	couple	£43.40
Higher pensioner premium	single claimant/lone parent	£33.85
	couple	£49.10
Disability premium	single claimant/lone parent	£22.25
	couple	£31.75

CAPITAL
(chapter 13)

Capital limit	£16,000
Lower capital limit	£3,000 *
Tariff income between these	£1 per £250 or part thereof

* For certain cases this is £10,000: para. 13.9.

EARNED INCOME DISREGARDS
(chapters 13-15)

Earnings of claimant or partner	
lone parents	£25.00
certain disabled or elderly people, certain carers and certain occupations	£15.00
couples in other cases	£10.00
single claimants in other cases	£5.00
Earnings of certain children and young persons	
certain disabled children/young persons	£15.00
other cases	£5.00
Childcare earnings disregard for certain couples/lone parents	
care for one child	£70.00
care for two or more children	£105.00

STUDENT RENT DEDUCTION AND INCOME DISREGARD (HB ONLY)
(chapter 20)

	Sept 1999 to August 2000
Courses in London	£27.10
Courses elsewhere	£18.75

NOTIONAL TAX AND NI FIGURES (chapters 13-15)

These are used for claims for HB/CTB made in the 1999-2000 tax year, in calculating

◆ net estimated or notional earnings (tax and class 1 NI)

◆ net profit from self-employment (tax and classes 2 and 4 NI).

(Figures for 2000-01 were not available at the time of writing.)

TAX

Personal allowance

single person/each partner in a couple	£4,335
addition for lone parent/married couple/couple with children (allowed at 10% tax rate: see table 15.2)	£1,970

(other allowances are ignored)

Rate of tax

first £1,500 above personal allowance	10%
remainder	23%

(the 40% rate is not used)

NATIONAL INSURANCE

Class I contributions
for gross notional/estimated earnings of

first £66 per week	nil
balance to £500 per week	10% of this balance

Class 2 contributions
for chargeable income of

under £3,770 per year	nil
£3,770 or more per year	£340.60 per year

Class 4 contributions
for chargeable income

first £7,530 per year	nil
balance to £26,000 per year	6% of this balance

Appendix 5:
Other benefit rates (from April 2000)

INCOME SUPPORT AND INCOME-BASED JOBSEEKER'S ALLOWANCE

AMOUNT OF INCOME SUPPORT/JSA(IB)

100 per cent of the difference between net income and applicable amount.

INCOME AND CAPITAL

The capital limit is £8,000 (except for people in residential care and nursing homes, for whom it is £10,000).

Income and capital are assessed in approximately the same way as in HB and main CTB, except that the earned income disregard for lone parents is £15.00.

APPLICABLE AMOUNTS

Personal allowances and premiums are the same as in HB and main CTB, except:

◆ personal allowance for most single
  claimants and lone parents under 18   £31.45

◆ family premium (protected lone parent rate)   £15.90

Additions to the applicable amount are also made for certain housing costs (para. 2.14).

OTHER SELECTED BENEFITS (main figures only)

Child benefit

only or older/oldest child (general rate)	£15.00
only or older/oldest child (protected lone parent rate)	£17.10
each other child (couple or lone parent)	£10.00

Contribution-based jobseeker's allowance

claimant aged under 18	£31.45
claimant aged 18 to 24	£41.35
claimant aged 25 or more	£52.20

Incapacity benefit
Long-term rate

single person	£67.50
couple	£107.90

Short-term higher rate

single person	£60.20
couple	£91.70

Short-term lower rate

single person	£50.90
couple	£82.40

Retirement pension standard rate

single person	£67.50
couple	£107.90

Disability living allowance
Care component

highest rate	£53.55
middle rate	£35.80
lowest rate	£14.20

Mobility component

higher rate	£37.40
lower rate	£14.20

Special payment for pre-1973 war widows   £57.07

Appendix 6:
Categories of people for non-dependant deduction and second adult rebate purposes

There are many categories of people relevant for non-dependant deductions in HB, for non-dependant deductions in main CTB, and for second adult rebate. The categories are not always the same for these three purposes.

This appendix defines all the categories relevant for these purposes (as they apply from 1st April 2000), and answers the following questions for each category:

◆ Is there a non-dependant deduction for them in HB and main CTB (paras. 9.23, 9.26)?

◆ Are they 'disregarded persons' for second adult rebate purposes?

The second question is relevant because a 'disregarded person' cannot be a second adult (para. 10.6); and because the rules about whether couples and joint occupiers can qualify for second adult rebate refer to 'disregarded persons' (paras. 10.17-18). It is also relevant to the rules about council tax discounts (para. 3.35).

People may fall into more than one category. If a particular category (e.g. category 1) indicates that a non-dependant deduction applies (or that they are not 'disregarded persons'), this is over-ridden if they fall into another category (e.g. category 13) where no non-dependant deduction applies (or where they are 'disregarded persons').

The category numbers have no significance except to aid cross-referencing.

1. PEOPLE ON INCOME SUPPORT OR JSA(IB)

HB	No non-dependant deduction if aged under 25. Otherwise a non-dependant deduction applies.
Main CTB	No non-dependant deduction.
Second adult rebate	Not 'disregarded persons'.

This means anyone in receipt of income support or income-based jobseeker's allowance – JSA(IB) – including people receiving these benefits whilst on government training schemes. It also includes people who would get JSA(IB) except that they are currently subject to a sanction.

2. PEOPLE UNDER 18

HB and main CTB	No non-dependant deduction.
Second adult rebate	'Disregarded persons' (because they do not count as 'residents').

This means anyone under 18 whether a member of the claimant's family or not.

3. 18-YEAR-OLDS FOR WHOM CHILD BENEFIT IS PAYABLE

HB and main CTB	No non-dependant deduction.
Second adult rebate	'Disregarded persons'.

This means 18-year-olds for whom someone receives or could receive child benefit – e.g. at school and shortly after leaving school (see also category 4).

4. EDUCATION LEAVERS UNDER 20

HB	A non-dependant deduction applies unless they fall within categories 2 or 3.
Main CTB	No non-dependant deduction.
Second adult rebate	'Disregarded persons'.

This only applies from 1st May to 31st October inclusive each year. It means anyone who leaves the type of education described in category 5 or 6 within that period. It lasts until that person reaches 20 or until 31st October, whichever comes first.

5. STUDENTS UNDER 20 AT SCHOOL OR COLLEGE

HB and main CTB   Whether there is a non-dependant deduction depends on whether they fall within category 2, 3 or 10.

Second adult rebate   'Disregarded persons'.

The full definition is not given here. Its main elements are that the person:

◆ is under 20; and

◆ is studying up to (but not above) A level, ONC, OND or equivalent; and

◆ is on a course of at least 3 months' duration; and

◆ is normally required to study at least 12 hours per week in term times; and

◆ does not fall within categories 6 to 8.

6. FULL-TIME STUDENTS IN FURTHER OR HIGHER EDUCATION

HB and main CTB   Whether there is a non-dependant deduction depends on whether they fall within category 10.

Second adult rebate   'Disregarded persons'.

The full definition is not given here. Its main elements are that the person:

◆ is attending a course of further or higher education (e.g. university); and

◆ is on a course of at least one academic or calendar year's duration; and

◆ is normally required to study at least 21 hours per week for at least 24 weeks per year.

7. FOREIGN LANGUAGE ASSISTANTS

HB and main CTB   Whether there is a non-dependant deduction depends on whether they fall within category 10.

Second adult rebate   'Disregarded persons'.

They must be registered with the Central Bureau for Educational Visits and Exchanges.

8. STUDENTS ON NURSING AND RELATED COURSES

HB and main CTB	Whether there is a non-dependant deduction depends on whether they fall within category 10.
Second adult rebate	'Disregarded persons'.

Students undertaking nursing, midwifery or health visitors' courses (if they also fall within category 6) count as students in this category.

9. STUDENT NURSES STUDYING FOR THEIR FIRST NURSING REGISTRATION

HB and main CTB	Whether there is a non-dependant deduction depends on whether they fall within category 10.
Second adult rebate	'Disregarded persons'.

This means anyone studying for a first inclusion in Parts 1 to 6 or 8 of the nursing register.

10. FULL-TIME STUDENTS

HB	No non-dependant deduction except during any period they take up remunerative work (16 hours per week or more) in a summer vacation.
Main CTB	No non-dependant deduction.
Second adult rebate	'Disregarded persons'.

A student at a further education college counts as 'full-time' if he or she is normally expected to undertake more than 16 guided learning hours per week. All students on sandwich courses count as 'full-time'. Otherwise 'full-time' is not defined.

11. YOUTH TRAINING TRAINEES

HB and main CTB	No non-dependant deduction.
Second adult rebate	'Disregarded persons' only if under 25.

This means people on approved Youth Training or Youth Credit courses who are in receipt of an allowance as a trainee (not employees).

12. APPRENTICES ON NCVQ/SVEC COURSES

HB   A non-dependant deduction applies.

Main CTB   No non-dependant deduction.

Second adult rebate   'Disregarded persons'.

This means someone who:

◆ is in employment; and

◆ is studying for a qualification accredited by the National Council for
  Vocational Qualifications (England and Wales) or Scottish Vocational
  Education Council (Scotland); and

◆ receives a reduced rate of pay because of being an apprentice; and

◆ receives gross pay which does not exceed £160 per week.

13. PEOPLE WHO ARE 'SEVERELY MENTALLY IMPAIRED'

HB   A non-dependant deduction applies.

Main CTB   No non-dependant deduction.

Second adult rebate   'Disregarded persons'.

This means someone who has 'a severe impairment of intelligence and social
functioning (however caused) which appears to be permanent'; and has a medical
certificate confirming this; and is receiving one or more of the following (or
would do so apart from the fact that he or she has reached pension age):

◆ the highest or middle rate of the care component of disability living
  allowance (DLA), or

◆ attendance allowance, constant attendance allowance or certain equivalent
  additions to industrial injuries and war pensions, or

◆ incapacity benefit (IB), or severe disablement allowance (SDA), or

◆ disability working allowance (DWA) but *only if* he or she was receiving IB
  or SDA in the eight weeks before claiming DWA or was receiving income
  support or JSA(IB) which included a disability premium before claiming
  SDA, or

◆ income support or JSA(IB) (or his or her partner is) – but *only if* it includes
  a disability premium awarded because of the person's incapacity for work.

14. CARERS OF PEOPLE RECEIVING CERTAIN BENEFITS

HB	A non-dependant deduction applies unless they fall within category 17.
Main CTB	No non-dependant deduction.
Second adult rebate	'Disregarded persons'.

This applies to someone if:

◆ he or she is providing care or support for at least 35 hours a week; and

◆ he or she resides with the person receiving the care or support; and

◆ that person is not a child of his or hers under 18, nor his or her partner; and

◆ that person is entitled to the highest rate of the care component of disability living allowance, or a higher rate attendance allowance, or certain equivalent additions to industrial injuries and war pensions.

15. CARERS INTRODUCED BY AN OFFICIAL OR CHARITABLE BODY

HB	A non-dependant deduction applies unless they fall within category 17.
Main CTB	No non-dependant deduction.
Second adult rebate	'Disregarded persons'.

This means someone who:

◆ is engaged or employed to provide care or support for at least 24 hours a week for no more than £36 per week; and

◆ is resident (for the better performance of this work) in premises provided by or on behalf of the person receiving the care or support; and

◆ is employed by that person; and

◆ was introduced to that person by a local authority, government department or charitable body.

16. CARERS RESIDENT IN OFFICIAL OR CHARITABLE PREMISES

HB   A non-dependant deduction applies unless they fall
                            within category 17.

Main CTB   No non-dependant deduction.

Second adult rebate   'Disregarded persons'.

This means someone who:

◆   is engaged or employed to provide care or support for at least 24 hours a
    week for no more than £36 per week; and

◆   is resident (for the better performance of this work) in premises provided by
    or on behalf of a local authority, government department or charitable body,
    on whose behalf the care or support is provided.

17. CARERS FOR WHOM THE CLAIMANT OR PARTNER IS CHARGED

HB and main CTB   No non-dependant deduction.

Second adult rebate   'Disregarded persons' only if they fall within
                            categories 14 to 16.

This means carers caring for the claimant or partner, who are provided by a
charitable or voluntary body which charges the claimant or partner for this.

18. PEOPLE IN PRISON OR OTHER FORMS OF DETENTION

HB   No non-dependant deduction.

Main CTB   No non-dependant deduction unless detained only for
                            non-payment of a fine or (in England and Wales)
                            council tax.

Second adult rebate   'Disregarded persons' unless detained only for non-
                            payment of a fine or (in England and Wales) council
                            tax.

The full definition is not given here, but this includes people in almost any kind
of detention.

19. PEOPLE WHO HAVE BEEN IN AN NHS HOSPITAL FOR MORE THAN SIX WEEKS

HB and main CTB   No non-dependant deduction.

Second adult rebate   'Disregarded persons' only if they fall within category 20.

This means someone who is in hospital and has been for more than six weeks – but only in the case of NHS hospitals (including NHS Trust hospitals) and not for wholly private patients. Two or more stays in hospital are added together if the break between them is four weeks or less.

20. PEOPLE ACTUALLY RESIDENT ELSEWHERE

HB and main CTB   No non-dependant deduction.

Second adult rebate   'Disregarded persons' (because they are not 'residents').

A person is 'resident' in his or her 'sole or main residence'. It does not matter what type of accommodation this is: it could be an ordinary home, a hospital, a care home, a hostel, or any other type of accommodation. This category could apply to a visitor or to a student returning just for the holidays.

21. PEOPLE NORMALLY RESIDENT ELSEWHERE

HB and main CTB   No non-dependant deduction.

Second adult rebate   Not 'disregarded persons' unless they fall within category 20.

The concept is not defined. In practice, it is very difficult to distinguish it from category 20.

22. RESIDENTS IN HOSPITALS, CARE HOMES AND CERTAIN HOSTELS

'Disregarded persons'.

Although a claim for HB is possible in some of these types of accommodation (and in rare cases a claim for CTB might be possible), it is unlikely that any claimant would have a non-dependant/second adult. This category is included because it affects council tax discounts in such accommodation. It applies to any of the following:

◆ patients with sole or main residence in an NHS hospital, military hospital, residential care home, nursing home or mental nursing home;

◆ people with sole or main residence in non-self-contained accommodation which provides them with personal care for old age, disablement, or past or present alcohol or drug dependence or mental disorder;

◆ people with sole or main residence in non-self-contained accommodation which provides licences (not tenancies) for people of no fixed abode and no settled way of life;

◆ people with sole or main residence in a bail hostel or probation hostel.

23. MEMBERS OF RELIGIOUS COMMUNITIES

HB   A non-dependant deduction applies.

Main CTB   No non-dependant deduction.

Second adult rebate   'Disregarded persons'.

This means someone who:

◆ is a member of a religious community whose principal occupation is prayer, contemplation, education, the relief of suffering, or any combination of those; and

◆ has no income (other than an occupational pension) or capital; and

◆ is dependent on the community for his or her material needs.

24. (a) MEMBERS OF CERTAIN INTERNATIONAL BODIES OR OF VISITING FORCES, (b) THEIR NON-BRITISH SPOUSES, AND (c) CERTAIN NON-BRITISH SPOUSES OF STUDENTS

HB   A non-dependant deduction applies.

Main CTB   No non-dependant deduction.

Second adult rebate 'Disregarded persons'.

The full definitions are not given here. Group (a) includes members of certain international headquarters and defence organisations and certain visiting forces (and in some cases their dependents). For groups (b) and (c), in broad terms, the spouse must be prevented from working or claiming. For group (c), 'student' means someone in category 4, 5 or 6.

25. ANYONE ELSE

HB and main CTB   A non-dependant deduction applies.

Second adult rebate Not 'disregarded persons'.

This means anyone who does not fall into any of the previous categories.

Index